AF560807

Modern Political Economics

Modern Political Economics

Vikash Kumar

RANDOM PUBLICATIONS
NEW DELHI (INDIA)

Modern Political Economics

ISBN 978-93-5111-638-7

Published in 2015 in India by

RANDOM PUBLICATIONS

4376-A/4B, Gali Murari Lal, Ansari Road
New Delhi-110 002
Phone : +9111-43580356, 011-23289044, 011-43142548
e-mail: sales@randompublications.com,
info@randompublications.com, randomexports@gmail.com

Reprinted 2022

Type Setting by : Friends Media, Delhi-110089
Digitally Printed at : Replika Press Pvt. Ltd.

Preface

Modern economic analysis is used not just in the formal sense of a mathematical approach; it is also conceptual, viewing political phenomena in terms of optimization, incentives, constraints, et cetera. Hence, what really distinguishes the new political economy is not so much the volume, but the sort of research being done. Formal technique sometimes clouds, rather than enhances, our understanding of phenomena, and sometimes seems to be used as a substitute for insights into the phenomenon being studied. The relative newness of political economy in its current form may make this problem more acute. It has led some people to thc pcrccption, incorrect in my opinion, that the new political economy is simply a not very insightful formalization of the obvious. Recent research has also been criticized as being too broad, seen as trying to cover everything, with widely differing degrees of success.

This definition of positive political economy may be better understood by reference to some examples of the questions it addresses. Some phenomena are so clearly in the realm of political economy that little discussion is required as to what are the political influences on the economic outcomes. Political Economists are concerned with the allocation of scarce resources in a world of infinite wants and needs. In order to allocate these resources, politics are used within a state to provide for the people. Political economy is the study of the relationships between individuals and society, and more specifically, the relationships between citizens and states.

Political economy is a study of philosophy and ideology that studies the evolution of political and economic ideas. Political economy is a mixture of politics, economics, sociology, philosophy, and history, which all bring together evidence to the study of how humans exist within societies. Political economists study political ideology, economic structure, human interaction, human nature, and theories in philosophical thought. It is a study that studies not only the mechanics of a particular structure, but also the reasoning behind why a structure is regarded to be the best by various people with different beliefs.

This wide-ranging work is destined to become a landmark in the field of political economy. This book is a challenge to orthodox economic assumptions.

I would like to thank my team for standing beside me throughout my career and writing this book. My special thanks go to "Random Publications" who have published the book.

– *Vikash Kumar*

Contents

1

Political Economy

Political economy was the original term used for studying production and trade, and their relations with law, custom, and government, as well as with the distribution of national income and wealth. originated in moral philosophy. It was developed in the 18th century as the study of the economies of states, or *polities*, hence the term *political* economy.

In the late 19th century, the term *economics* came to replace *political economy*, coinciding with the publication of an influential textbook by Alfred Marshall in 1890. Earlier, William Stanley Jevons, a proponent of mathematical methods applied to the subject, advocated *economics* for brevity and with the hope of the term becoming "the recognised name of a science."

Today, *political economy*, where it is not used as a synonym for economics, may refer to very different things, including Marxiananalysis, applied public-choice approaches emanating from the Chicago school and the Virginia school, or simply the advice given by economists to the government or public on general economic policy or on specific proposals. A rapidly growing mainstream literature from the 1970s has expanded beyond the model of economic policy in which planners maximize utility of a representative individual toward examining how political forces affect the choice of economic policies, especially as to distributional conflicts and political institutions. It is available as an area of study in certain colleges and universities.

HISTORICAL DEVELOPMENT

Political economy is a very old subject of intellectual inquiry but a relatively young academic discipline. The analysis of political economy (in terms of the nature of state and market relations), both in practical terms and as moral philosophy, has been traced to Greek philosophers such as Plato and Aristotle as well as to the Scholastics and those who propounded a philosophy based on natural law. A critical development in the intellectual inquiry of political economy was the prominence in the 16th to the18th century of the mercantilist school, which called for a strong role for the state in economic regulation. The writings of the Scottish economist Sir James Steuart, 4th Baronet Denham, whose

Inquiry into the Principles of Political Economy (1767) is considered the first systematic work in English on economics, and the policies of Jean-Baptiste Colbert (1619–83), controller general to Louis XIV of France, epitomizemercantilism in theory and in practice, respectively.

Political economy emerged as a distinct field of study in the mid-18th century, largely as a reaction to mercantilism, when the Scottish philosophers Adam Smith (1723–90) and David Hume (1711–76) and the French economist François Quesnay (1694–1774) began to approach this study in systematic rather than piecemeal terms. They took a secular approach, refusing to explain the distribution of wealth and power in terms of God's will and instead appealing to political, economic, technological, natural, and social factors and the complex interactions between them. Indeed, Smith's landmark work—*An Inquiry into the Nature and Causes of the Wealth of Nations* (1776), which provided the first comprehensive system of political economy—conveys in its title the broad scope of early political economic analysis. Although the field itself was new, some of the ideas and approaches it drew upon were centuries old. It was influenced by the individualist orientation of the English political philosophers Thomas Hobbes (1588–1679) and John Locke (1632–1704), the Realpolitik of the Italian political theorist Niccolò Machiavelli (1469–1527), and the inductive method of scientific reasoning invented by the English philosopher Francis Bacon (1561–1626).

Many works by political economists in the 18th century emphasized the role of individuals over that of the state and generally attacked mercantilism. This is perhaps best illustrated by Smith's famous notion of the "invisible hand," in which he argued that state policies often were less effective in advancing social welfare than were the self-interested acts of individuals. Individuals intend to advance only their own welfare, Smith asserted, but in so doing they also advance the interests of society as if they were guided by an invisible hand. Arguments such as these gave credence to individual-centred analysis and policies to counter the state-centred theories of the mercantilists.

In the 19th century English political economist David Ricardo (1772–1823) further developed Smith's ideas. His work—in particular his concept of comparative advantage, which posited that states should produce and export only those goods that they can generate at a lower cost than other nations and import those goods that other countries can produce more efficiently—extolled the benefits of free trade and was pivotal in undermining British mercantilism. About the same time the utilitarianism of Jeremy Bentham (1748–1832), James Mill (1773–1836), and Mill's son John Stuart Mill (1806–73) fused together economic analysis with calls for the expansion of democracy.

Smith's notion of individual-centred analysis of political economy did not go unchallenged. The German American economist Friedrich List (1789–1846) developed a more-systematic analysis of mercantilism that contrasted his national system of political economy with what he termed Smith's "cosmopolitical" system, which treated issues as if national borders and interests did not exist. In the mid-19th century communist historian and economist Karl Marx (1818–83) proposed a class-based analysis of political economy that culminated in his massive treatise *Das Kapital*, the first volume of which was published in 1867.

The holistic study of political economy that characterizes the works of Smith, List, Marx, and others of their time was gradually eclipsed in the late 19th century by a group of more narrowly focused and methodologically conventional disciplines, each of which sought to throw light on particular elements of society, inevitably at the expense of a broader view of social interactions. By 1890, when English neoclassical economist Alfred Marshall (1842–1924) published his textbook on the *Principles of Economics*, political economy as a distinct academic field had been essentially replaced in universities by the separate disciplines of economics, sociology,political science, and international relations. Marshall explicitly separated his subject—economics or economic science—from political economy, implicitly privileging the former over the latter, an act that reflected the general academic trend toward specialization along methodological lines.

In the second half of the 20th century, as the social sciences (especially economics but also political science) became increasingly abstract, formal, and specialized in both focus and methodology, political economy was revived to provide a broader framework for understanding complex national and international problems and events. The field of political economy today encompasses several areas of study, including the politics of economic relations, domestic political and economic issues, the comparative study of political and economic systems, and international political economy. The emergence of international political economy, first within international relations and later as a distinct field of inquiry, marked the return of political economy to its roots as a holistic study of individuals, states, markets, and society.

As many analyses by political economists have revealed, in actual government decision making there is often a tension between economic and political objectives. Since the 1970s, for example, the relationship between the United States and China has been replete with difficulties for both countries. China consistently has sought integration into the world economy—an effort best illustrated by its successful campaign to join the World Trade Organization (WTO)—but has resisted domestic political liberalization. The United States often has supported China's economic reforms because they promised to increase trade between the two countries, but the U.S. government has been criticized by other countries and by some Americans for "rewarding" China with most-favoured-nation trading status despite that country's poor record of upholding the basic human rights of its citizens. Likewise, China's government has faced domestic criticism not only from supporters of democracy but also from conservative Chinese Communist Partymembers who oppose further economic reforms. This example reflects the complex calculus involved as governments attempt to balance both their political and their economic interests and to ensure their own survival.

ECONOMICS AND POLITICAL ECONOMY

The relationship between political economy and the contemporary discipline of economics is particularly interesting, in part because both disciplines claim to be the descendants of the ideas of Smith, Hume, and John Stuart Mill. Whereas political economy, which was rooted in moral philosophy, was from the beginning very much a normative field of study, economics sought to become objective and value-free. Indeed, under the influence of Marshall, economists endeavoured to make their discipline like the 17th-century physics of Sir Isaac Newton (1642–1727): formal, precise, and elegant and the foundation of a broader intellectual enterprise. With the publication in 1947 of *Foundations of Economic Analysis* by Paul Samuelson, who brought complex mathematical tools to the study of economics, the bifurcation of political economy and economics was complete. Mainstream political economy had evolved into economic science, leaving its broader concerns far behind.

The distinction between economics and political economy can be illustrated by their differing treatments of issues related to international trade. The economic analysis of tariff policies, for example, focuses on the impact of tariffs on the efficient use of scarce resources under a variety of different market environments, including perfect (or pure) competition (several small suppliers), monopoly (one supplier), monopsony (one buyer), and oligopoly (few suppliers). Different analytic frameworks examine the direct effects of tariffs as well as the effects on economic choices in related markets. Such a methodology is generally mathematical and is based on the assumption that an actor's economic behaviour is rational and is aimed at maximizing benefits for himself. Although ostensibly a value-free exercise, such economic analysis often implicitly assumes that policies that maximize the benefits accruing to economic actors are also preferable from a social point of view.

In contrast to the pure economic analysis of tariff policies, political economic analysis examines the social, political, and economic pressures and interests that affect tariff policies and how these pressures influence the political process, taking into account a range of social priorities, international negotiating environments, development strategies, and philosophical perspectives. In particular, political economic analysis might take into account how tariffs can be used as a strategy to influence the pattern of national economic growth (neo-mercantilism) or biases in the global system of international trade that may favour developed countries over developing ones (neo-Marxist analysis). Although political economy lacks a rigorous scientific method and an objective analytic framework, its broad perspective affords a deeper understanding of the many aspects of tariff policy that are not purely economic in nature.

NATIONAL AND COMPARATIVE POLITICAL ECONOMY

The study of domestic political economy is concerned primarily with the relative balance in a country's economy between state and market forces. Much of this debate can be traced to the thought of the English political economist John Maynard Keynes (1883–1946), who argued in*The General Theory of Employment, Interest, and Money* (1935–36) that there exists an inverse relationship between unemployment and inflation and that governments should manipulate fiscal policy to ensure a balance between the two.

The so-called Keynesian revolution, which occurred at a time when governments were attempting to ameliorate the effects of the worldwide Great Depression of the 1930s, contributed to the rise of the welfare state and to an increase in the size of government relative to the private sector. In some countries, particularly the United States, the development of Keynesianism brought about a gradual shift in the meaning of liberalism, from a doctrine calling for a relatively passive state and an economy guided by the "invisible hand" of the market to the view that the state should actively intervene in the economy in order to generate growth and sustain employment levels.

From the 1930s Keynesianism dominated not only domestic economic policy but also the development of the post-World War II Bretton Woods international economic system, which included the creation of the International Monetary Fund (IMF) and the World Bank. Indeed, Keynesianism was practiced by countries of all political complexions, including those embracingcapitalism (e.g., the United States and the United Kingdom), social democracy (e.g., Sweden), and even fascism (e.g., the Nazi Germany of Adolf Hitler). In the 1970s, however, many Western countries experienced "stagflation," or simultaneous high unemployment and inflation, a phenomenon that contradicted Keynes's view.

The result was a revival of classical liberalism, also known as "neoliberalism," which became the cornerstone of economic policy in the United States under President Ronald Reagan (1981–89) and in the United Kingdom under Prime Minister Margaret Thatcher (1979–90).

Led by the American economist Milton Friedman and other proponents of monetarism (the view that the chief determinant of economic growth is the supply of money rather than fiscal policy), neoliberals and others argued that the state should once again limit its role in the economy by selling off national industries and promoting free trade. Supporters of this approach, which influenced the policies of international financial institutions and governments throughout the world, maintained that free markets would generate continued prosperity.

Opponents of neoliberalism have argued that the theory overlooks too many of the negative social and political consequences of free markets, including the creation of large disparities of wealth and damage to the environment. In the 1990s one focal point of debate was the North American Free Trade Agreement (NAFTA), which created a free-trade zone between the United States, Canada, and Mexico. Since it went into effect in 1994, the agreement has generated a good deal of controversy about whether it has created or eliminated jobs in the United States and Canada and about whether it has helped or harmed the environment, labour conditions, and local cultures in Mexico.

Comparative political economy studies interactions between the state, markets, and society, both national and international. Both empirical and normative, it employs sophisticated analytic tools and methodologies in its investigations. Rational-choice theorists, for example, analyze individual behaviour and even the policies of states in terms of maximizing benefits and minimizing costs, and public-choice theorists focus on how policy choices are shaped or constrained by incentives built into the routines of public and private organizations. Modeling techniques adapted from econometrics are often applied to many different political economic questions.

Political economists attempting to understand domestic macroeconomic policy often study the influence of political institutions (e.g., legislatures, executives, and judiciaries) and the implementation of public policy by bureaucratic agencies. The influence of political and societal actors (e.g., interest groups, political parties, churches, elections, and the media) and ideologies (e.g., democracy, fascism, or communism) also is gauged. Comparative analysis also considers the extent to which international political and economic conditions increasingly blur the line between domestic and foreign policies in different countries. For example, in many countries trade policy no longer reflects strictly domestic objectives but also takes into account the trade policies of other governments and the directives of international financial institutions.

Many sociologists focus on the impact that policies have on the public and the extent of public support that particular policies enjoy. Likewise, sociologists and some political scientists also are interested in the extent to which policies are generated primarily from above by elites or from below by the public. One such study is so-called "critical political economy," which is rooted in interpretations of the writing of Marx. For many Marxists (and contemporary adherents of varying strands of Marxist thought), government efforts to manage different parts of the economy are presumed to favour the moral order of bourgeois values. As in the case of tax policy, for example, government policies are assumed to support the interests of the rich or elites over those of the masses.

Ultimately, comparative analysts may ask why countries in certain areas of the world play a particularly large role in the international economy. They also examine why "corporatist" partnerships between the state, industry, and labour formed in some states and not in others, why there are major differences in labour and management relations in the more-industrialized countries, what kinds of political and economic structures different countries employ to help their societies adjust to the effects of integration and globalization, and what kinds of institutions in developing countries advance or retard the development process. Comparative political economists also have investigated why some developing countries in Southeast Asia were relatively successful at generating economic growth whereas most African countries were not.

ETYMOLOGY

Originally, *political economy* meant the study of the conditions under which production or consumption within limited parameters was organized in nation-states. In that way, political economy expanded the emphasis of economics, which comes from the Greek *oikos* (meaning "home") and *nomos* (meaning "law" or "order"); thus political economy was meant to express the laws of production of wealth at the state level, just as economics was the ordering of the home. The phrase *économie politique* (translated in English as *political economy*) first appeared in France in 1615 with the well-known book by Antoine de Montchrétien, *Traité de l'economie politique*. The French physiocrats, Adam Smith, David Ricardo, Henry George, and German philosopher and social theorist Karl Marx were some of the exponents of political economy. The world's first professorship in political economy was established in 1754 at the University of Naples Federico II, Italy (then capital city of the Kingdom of Naples); the Neapolitan philosopher Antonio Genovesi was the first tenured professor; in 1763, Joseph von Sonnenfels was appointed a Political Economy chair at the University of Vienna, Austria. In 1805, Thomas Malthus became England's first professor of political economy, at the East India Company College, Haileybury, Hertfordshire. Glasgow University, where Smith was Professor of Logic and of Moral Philosophy, changed the name of its Department of Political Economy to the Department of Economics (ostensibly to avoid confusing prospective undergraduates) in the academic year 1997–98, leaving the class of 1998 as the last to be graduated with a Master of Arts in Political Economy.

In the United States, political economy first was taught at the College of William and Mary, where in 1784, Smith's *The Wealth of Nations* was a required textbook.

CURRENT APPROACHES

In its contemporary meaning, *political economy* refers to different, but related, approaches to studying economic and related behaviours, ranging from the combination of economics with other fields to the use of different, fundamental assumptions that challenge earlier economic assumptions:

- *Political economy* most commonly refers to interdisciplinary studies drawing upon economics, sociology, and political science in explaining how political institutions, the political environment, and the economic system—capitalist, socialist, or mixed—influence each other. The *Journal of Economic Literature* classification codes associate political economy with three subareas: the role of government and/or power relationships in resource allocation for each type of economic system, international political economy, which studies the economic impacts of international relations, and economic models of political processes. The last area, derived from public choice theory and dating from the 1960s, models voters, politicians, and bureaucrats as behaving in mainly self-interested ways, in contrast to a view, ascribed to earlier economists, of government officials trying to maximize individualutilities from some kind of social welfare function. An early and continuing focus of that research programme is what came to be calledconstitutional political economy.

Economists and political scientists often associate political economy with approaches using rational-choice assumptions, especially ingame theory, and in examining phenomena beyond economics' standard remit, such as government failure and complex decision making in which context the term "positive political economy" is common. Other "traditional" topics include analysis of such public policy issues aseconomic regulation, monopoly, rent-seeking, market protection, institutional corruption, and distributional politics. Empirical analysis includes the influence of elections on the choice of economic policy, determinants and forecasting models of electoral outcomes, thepolitical business cycles, central-bank independence, and the politics of excessive deficits.

A recent focus has been on modeling economic policy and political institutions as to interactions between agents and economic and political institutions, including the seeming discrepancy of economic policy and economist's recommendations through the lens of transaction costs. From the mid-1990s, the field has expanded, in part aided by new cross-national data sets that allow tests of hypotheses oncomparative economic systems and institutions. Topics have included the breakup of nations, the origins and rate of change of political institutions in relation to economic growth, development, backwardness, reform, and transition economies, the role of culture, ethnicity, and gender in explaining economic outcomes, macroeconomic policy, the environment, fairness, the relation of constitutions to economic policy, theoretical and empirical.

- New political economy may treat economic ideologies as the phenomenon to explain, per the traditions of Marxian political economy. Thus, Charles S. Maier suggests that a political economy approach "interrogates economic doctrines to disclose their sociological and political premises.... in sum, [it] regards economic ideas and behavior not as frameworks for analysis, but as beliefs and actions that must themselves be explained." This approach informs Andrew Gamble's *The Free Economy and the Strong State*(Palgrave Macmillan, 1988), and Colin Hay's *The Political Economy of New Labour* . It also informs much work published in *New Political Economy*, an international journal founded by Sheffield University scholars in 1996.

- International political economy (IPE) is an interdisciplinary field comprising approaches to the actions of various actors. In the United States, these approaches are associated with the journal *International Organization*, which in the 1970s became the leading journal of IPE under the editorship of Robert Keohane, Peter J. Katzenstein, and Stephen Krasner. They are also associated with the journal *The Review of International Political Economy*. There also is a more critical school of IPE, inspired by Karl Polanyi's work; two major figures are Matthew Watson and Robert W. Cox.
- Anthropologists, sociologists, and geographers use *political economy* in referring to the regimes of politics or economic values that emerge primarily at the level of states or regional governance, but also within smaller social groups and social networks. Because these regimes influence and are influenced by the organization of both social and economic capital, the analysis of dimensions lacking a standard economic value (e.g., the political economy of language, of gender, or of religion) often draws on concepts used in Marxian critiques of capital. Such approaches expand on neo-Marxian scholarship related to development and underdevelopment postulated by André Gunder Frankand Immanuel Wallerstein.
- Historians have employed *political economy* to explore the ways in the past that persons and groups with common economic interests have used politics to effect changes beneficial to their interests.

RELATED DISCIPLINES

Because political economy is not a unified discipline, there are studies using the term that overlap in subject matter, but have radically different perspectives:

- Sociology studies the effects of persons' involvement in society as members of groups, and how that changes their ability to function. Many sociologists start from a perspective of production-determining relation from Karl Marx. Marx's theories on the subject of political economy are contained in his book *Das Kapital*.
- Anthropology studies political economy by investigating regimes of political and economic value that condition tacit aspects of

sociocultural practices (e.g., the pejorative use of pseudo-Spanish expressions in the US entertainment media) by means of broader historical, political, and sociological processes. Analyses of structural features of transnational processes focus on the interactions between the world capitalist system and local cultures.

- Archaeology attempts to reconstruct past political economies by examining the material evidence for administrative strategies to control and mobilize resources. This evidence may include architecture, animal remains, evidence for craft workshops, evidence for feasting and ritual, evidence for the import or export of prestige goods, or evidence for food storage.
- Psychology is the fulcrum on which political economy exerts its force in studying decision making (not only in prices), but as the field of study whose assumptions model political economy.
- History documents change, often using it to argue political economy; some historical works take political economy as the narrative's frame.
- Human geography at times draws on theories of politico-economic processes. Typically under the moniker of political ecology, political ecology has been used by geographers to understand human systems and their relationship with the environment, broadly defined.
- Ecology deals with political economy, because human activity has the greatest effect upon the environment, its central concern being the environment's suitability for human activity. The ecological effects of economic activity spur research upon changing market economy incentives.
- Cultural studies examines social class, production, labor, race, gender, and sex.
- Communications examines the institutional aspects of media and telecommuncation systems. As the area of study focusing on aspects of human communication, it pays particular attention to the relationships between owners, labor, consumers, advertisers, structures of production, and the state, and the power relationships embedded in these relationships.

THE MEANING OF POLITICAL ECONOMY

MAN, HIS PLACE AND POWERS

We awake to consciousness to find ourselves, clothed in flesh, and in company with other like beings, resting on what seems to us a plane surface. Above us, when the clouds do not conceal them, the sun shines by day and the moon and stars by night. Of what this place is, and of our relations to it, the first men probably knew little more than is presented to us in direct consciousness, little more in fact than the animals know; and, individually, we ourselves could know little more. But the observations and reflections of many succeeding men, garnered and systematized, enable us of the modern civilization to know, and with the eyes of the mind almost to see, things to which the senses untaught by reason are blind.

By the light of this gathered knowledge we behold ourselves, the constantly changing tenants of the exterior of a revolving sphere, circling around a larger and luminous sphere, the sun, and beset on all sides by depths of space, to which we can neither find nor conceive of limits. Through this immeasurable space revolve myriads of luminous bodies of the nature of our sun, surrounded, it is confidently inferred from the fact that we know it to be the case with our sun, by lesser, non-luminous bodies that have in them their centers of revolution. Our sun, but one, and far from one of the largest, of countless similar orbs, is the center of light and heat and revolution to eight principal satellites (having in their turn satellites of their own), as well as to an indefinite number of more minute bodies known to us as asteroids and of more erratic bodies called comets. Of the principal satellites of the sun, the third in point of distance from it, and the fourth in point of size, is our earth. It is in constant movement around the sun, and in constant revolution on its own axis, while its satellite, the moon, also revolving on its own axis, is in constant movement around it.

The sun itself, revolving too on its own axis, is, with all its attendant bodies, in constant movement around some, probably moving, point in the universe which astronomers have not yet been able to determine. Thus we find ourselves, on the surface of a globe seemingly fixed, but really in constant motion of so many different kinds that it would be impossible with our present knowledge to make a diagram indicating its real movement through space at any point - a globe large to us, yet only as a grain of sand on the sea-shore compared with the bodies and spaces of the universe of which it is a part. We find ourselves on the surface of this ceaselessly moving globe, as passengers, brought there in utter insensibility, they know not how or whence, might find themselves on the deck of a ship, moving they know not where, and who see in the distance similar ships, whether tenanted or how tenanted they can only infer and guess. The immeasurably great lies beyond us, and about and beneath as the immeasurably small.

The microscope reveals infinitudes no less startling to our minds than does the telescope. Here we are, depth upon depth about us, confined to the bottom of that sea of air which envelops the surface of this moving globe. In it we live and breathe and are constantly immersed. Were our lungs to cease taking in and pumping out this air, or our bodies relieved of its pressure, we should die. Small as our globe seems in the light of astronomy, it is not really of the whole globe that we are tenants, but only of a part of its surface. Above this mean surface, men have found it possible only with the utmost effort and fortitude to ascend something less than seven miles; below it our deepest mining shafts do not pierce a mile. Thus the extreme limits in depth and height to which man may occasionally adventure, though not permanently live, are hardly eight miles. In round numbers the globe is 8000 miles in diameter. Thus the skin of the thinnest-skinned apple gives no idea of the relative thinness of the zone of perpendicular distance to which man is confined.

And three fourths of the surface of the globe at its junction with the air is covered by water, on which, though man may pass, he cannot dwell; while considerable parts of what remain are made inaccessible by ice. Like a bridge of hair is the line of temperature that we must keep. Investigators tell us of the existence of temperatures thousands of degrees above zero and thousands of degrees below zero. But man's body must maintain the constant level of a fraction over 98 degrees above zero. A rise or fall of seven degrees either way from this level and he dies. With the permanent rise or fall of a few more degrees in the mean temperature of the surface of the globe it would become uninhabitable by us. And while all about us, even what seems firmest, is in constant change and motion, so is it with ourselves. These bodies of ours are in reality like the flame of a gas-burner, which has continuous and defined form, but only as the manifestation of changes in a stream of succeeding particles, and which disappears the moment that stream is cut off. What there is real and distinctive in us is that to which we may give a name but cannot explain nor easily define - that which gives to changing matter and passing motion the phase and form of man.

But our bodies and our physical powers themselves, like the form and power of the gas-flame, are only passing manifestations of that indestructible matter and eternally pulsing energy of which the universe so far as it is tangible to us is made up. Stop the air that every instant is drawn through our lungs and we cease to live. Stop the food and drink that serve to us the same purpose as coal and water to the steam-engine, and, as certainly, if more slowly, the same result follows.

In all this, man resembles the other animals that with him tenant the superficies of the same earth. Physically he is merely such an animal, in form and structure and primary needs closely allied to the mammalia, with whose species he is zoologically classified. Were man only an animal he would be but an inferior animal. Nature has not given him the powers and weapons which enable other animals readily to secure their food. Nor yet has she given him the covering which protects them. Had he like them no power of providing himself with artificial clothing, man could not exist in many of the regions he now inhabits. He could live only in the most genial and equable parts of the globe. But man is more than an animal. Though in physical equipment he may in nothing surpass, and in some things fall below other animals, in mental

equipment he is so vastly superior as to take him out of their class, and to make him the lord and master of them all - to make him veritably, of all that we may see, "the roof and crown of things." And what more clearly perhaps than all else indicates the deep gulf which separates him from all other animals is that he alone of all animals is the producer, or bringer forth, and in that sense a maker. In this is a difference which renders the distinction between the highest animal and the lowest man one not of degree but of kind, and which, linked with the animals though he be, justifies the declaration of the Hebrew Scripture, that man is created in the likeness of the All-Maker.

Consider this distinction: We know of no race of men so low that they do not raise fruits or vegetables, or domesticate and breed animals; that do not cook food; that do not fashion weapons; that do not construct habitations; that do not make for themselves garments; that do not adorn themselves or their belongings with ornamentation; that do not show at least the rude beginnings of drawing and painting and sculpture and music. In all the tribes of animated nature below man there is not the slightest indication of the power thus shown. No animal save man ever kindled a fire or cooked a meal, or made a tool or fashioned a weapon.

It is true that the squirrel hides nuts; that birds build nests, that the beaver dams streams; that bees construct combs, in which they store the honey they extract from flowers; that spiders weave webs; that one species of ants are said to milk insects of another kind. All this is true, just as it is also true that there are birds whose melody far surpasses the best music of the savage, and that on tribes below man nature lavishes an adornment of attire that in taste as well as brilliancy surpasses the meretricious adornments of primitive man. But in all this there is nothing akin to the faculties which in these things man displays. What man does, he does by taking thought, by consciously adjusting means to ends. He does it by adapting and contriving and experimenting and copying; by effort after effort and trial after trial. What he does, and his ways of doing it, vary with the individual, with social development, with time and place and surroundings, and with what he sees others do.

But the squirrel hides its nuts; the birds after their orders build their nests, and in due time force their young to fly; the beaver constructs its dam; the bees store their honey; the spiders weave, and the ants do the work of their societies, without taking thought, without toilsomely scheming for the adapting of means to ends, without experimenting or copying or improving. What they do of such things, they do not as originators who have discovered how to do it; nor yet as learners or imitators or copyists. They do it, first as well as last, unfalteringly and unalteringly, forgetting nothing and improving in nothing. They do it, not by reason but by instinct; by an impulse inhering in their nature which prompts them without perplexity or trial on their part to go so far, but gives them no power to go farther. They do it as the bird sings or the dog barks, as

the hen sits on her eggs or the chick picks its way from the shell to scratch the ground. Nature provides for all living things beneath man by implanting in them blind, strong impulses which at proper times and seasons prompt them to do what it is necessary they should do. But to man she grants only such impellings of instinct as that which prompts the mother to press the newborn babe to her breast and the babe to suckle.

With exceptions such as these, she withdraws from man her guiding power and leaves him to himself. For in him a higher power has arisen and looks out on the world - a power that separates him from the brute as clearly and as widely as the brute is separated from the clod; a power that has in it the potency of producing, of making, of causing things to be; a power that seeks to look back into a past ere the globe was, and to peer into a future when it will cease to exist; a power that looks on Nature's show with curiosity like that with which an apprentice might scan a master's work, and will ask why tides run and winds blow, and how suns and stars have been put together; a power that in its beginnings lacks the certainty and promptness of instinct, but which, though infinitely lower in degree, must yet in some sort be akin to that from which all things proceed.

As this power, which we call reason, rises in man, nature withdraws the light of instinct and leaves him to his own devices - to rise or fall, to soar above the brute or to sink lower. For as the Hebrew Scriptures have phrased it, his eyes are opened and before him are good and evil. The ability to fall, no less than the ability to rise - the very failures and mistakes and perversities of man - show his place and powers. There is among the brutes no drunkenness, no unnatural vice, no waste of effort in accomplishing injurious results, no wanton slaughter of their own kind, no want amid plenty. We may conceive of beings in the form of man, who, like these animals, should be ruled by such clear and strong instincts that among them also there would be no liability to such perversions.

Yet such beings would not be men. They would lack the essential character and highest powers of man. Fitted perfectly to their environment they might be happy in a way. But it would be as the full-fed hog is happy. The pleasure of making, the joy of overcoming, the glory of rising, how could they exist for such beings? That man is not fitted for his environment shows his higher quality. In him is that which aspires - and still aspires. Endowed with reason, and deprived, or all but deprived, of instinct, man differs from other animals in being the producer. Like them, for instance, he requires food.

But while the animals get their food by taking what they find, and are thus limited by what they find already in existence, man has the power of getting his food by bringing it into existence. He is thus enabled to obtain food in greater variety and in larger quantity. The amount of grass limits the number of wild cattle, the amount of their prey limits the number of the carnivora; but man

causes grasses and grains and fruits to grow where they did not grow before; he breeds animals on which he feeds. And so it is with the fulfillment of all his wants; the satisfaction of all his desires. By the use of his animal powers, man can cover perhaps as much ground in a day as can a horse or a dog; he can cross perhaps about as wide a stream. But by virtue of the power that makes him the producer he is already spanning continents and oceans with a speed, a certainty and an ease that not even the birds of most powerful wing and swiftest flight can rival.

THE ECONOMY CALLED POLITICAL ECONOMY

The word economy, drawn from two Greek words, house and law, which together signify the management or arrangement of the material part of household or domestic affairs, means in its most common sense the avoidance of waste. We economize money or time or strength or material when we so arrange as to accomplish a result with the smallest expenditure. In a wider sense its meaning is that of a system or arrangement or adaptation of means to ends or of parts to a whole. Thus, we speak of the economy of the heavens; of the economy of the solar systems; the economy of the vegetable or animal kingdoms: the economy of the human body; or, in short, of the economy of anything which involves or suggests the adaptation of means to ends, the coordination of parts in a whole.

As there is an economy of individual affairs, an economy of the household, an economy of the farm or workshop or railway, each concerned with the adaptation in these spheres of means to ends, by which waste is avoided and the largest results obtained with the least expenditure, so there is an economy of communities, of the societies in which civilized men live — an economy which has special relation to the adaptation or system by which material wants are satisfied, or to the production and distribution of wealth.

The word political means, relating to the body of citizens or state, the body politic; to things coming within the scope and action of the commonwealth or government; to public policy.

Political economy, therefore, is a particular kind of economy. In the literal meaning of the words it is that kind of economy which has relation to the community or state; to the social whole rather than to individuals. But the convenience which impels us to abbreviate a long term has led to the frequent use of "economic" when "politico-economic" is meant, so that we may by usage speak of the literature of principles or terms of political economy as "economic literature," or "economic principles," or "economic terms." Some recent writers, indeed, seem to have substituted the term "economics" for political economy itself. But this is a matter as to which the reader should be on his guard, for it has been used to make what is not really political economy pass for political economy, as I shall hereafter show.

Adam Smith, who at the close of the last century gave so powerful an impulse to the study of what has since been called political economy that he is, not without justice, spoken of as its father, entitled his great book, *An Inquiry into the Nature and Cause of the Wealth of Nations;*and what we call political economy the Germans call national economy.

No term is of importance if we rightly understand what it means. But, both in the term "political economy," and in that of "national economy," as well as in the phrase "wealth of nations," lurk suggestions which may and in fact often do interfere with a clear apprehension of the ground they properly cover.

The use of the term "political economy" began at a time when the distinction between natural law and human law was not clearly made, when what I have called the body economic was largely confounded with what is properly the body politic, and when it was the common opinion in Europe, even of thoughtful men, that the production and distribution of wealth were to be regulated by the legislative action of the sovereign or state.

The first one to use the term is said to have been Antoine de Montchretien in his *Treatise on Political Economy* (*Traité de l'économie politique*), published in Rouen, France, 1615. But if not invented by them, it was given currency, some 130 or 140 years after, by those French exponents of natural right, or the natural order, who may today be best described as the first single-tax men. They used the term "political economy" to distinguish from politics the branch of knowledge with which they were concerned, and from this called themselves Economists.

The term is used by Adam Smith only in speaking of "this sect," composed of "a few men of great learning and ingenuity in France." But although these Economists were overwhelmed and have been almost forgotten, yet of their "noble and generous system" this term remained, and since the time of Adam Smith it has come into general use as expressive of — to accept the most common and I think sufficient definition — that branch of knowledge that treats of the nature of wealth, and the laws of its production and distribution.

But the confusion with politics, which the Frenchmen of whom Adam Smith speaks endeavored to clear away by their adoption of the term "political economy," still continues and is in fact suggested by the term itself, which seems at first apt to convey the impression of a particular kind of politics rather than of a particular kind of economy. The word political has a meaning which relates it to civil government, to the exercise of human sovereignty by enactment or administration, without reference to those invariable sequences which we call natural laws. An area differentiated from other areas with reference to this power of making municipal enactments and compelling obedience to them, we style a political division; and the larger political divisions, in which the highest sovereignty is acknowledged, we call nations. It is therefore important to keep in mind that the laws with which political economy primarily deals are not human enactments or municipal laws, but natural laws; and that they have no more reference to political divisions than have the laws of mechanics, the laws of optics or the laws of gravitation.

It is not with the body politic, but with that body social or body industrial that I have called the body economic, that political economy is directly concerned; not with the commonwealth of which a man becomes a member by the attribution or acceptance of allegiance to prince, potentate or republic; but with the commonwealth of which he becomes a member by the fact that he lives in a state of society in which each does not attempt to satisfy all of his own material wants by his own direct efforts, but obtains the satisfaction of some of them at least through the cooperation of others. The fact of participation in this cooperation does not make him a citizen of any particular state. It makes him a civilized man, a member of the civilized world — a unit in that body economic to which our political distinctions of states and nations have no more relation than distinctions of color have to distinctions of form.

The unit of human life is the individual. From our first consciousness, or at least from our first memory, our deepest feeling is, that what we recognize as "I" is something distinct from all other things, and the actual mergement of its individuality in other individualities, however near and dear, is something we cannot conceive of. But the lowest unit of which political economy treats often includes the family with the individual. For though isolated individuals may exist for a while, it is only under unnatural conditions. Human life, as we know it, begins with the conjuncture of individuals, and even for some time after birth can continue to exist only under conditions which make the new individual dependent on and subject to preceding individuality; while it requires for its fullest development and highest satisfactions the union of individuals in one economic unit.

While, then, in treating of the subject-matter of political economy, it will be convenient to speak of the units we shall have occasion to refer to as individuals, it should be understood that this term does not necessarily mean separate persons, but includes, as one, those so bound together by the needs of family life as to have, as our phrase is, "one purse."

An economy of the economic unit would not be a political economy, and the laws of which it would treat would not be those with which political economy is concerned. They would be the laws of personal or family conduct. An economy of the individual or family could treat the production of wealth no further than related to the production of such a unit. And though it might take cognizance of the physical laws involved in its agriculture and mechanics, of the distribution of wealth in the economic sense it could not treat at all, since any apportionment among the members of such a family of wealth obtained by it would be governed by the laws of individual or family life, and not by any law of the distribution of the results of socially conjoined effort.

But when in the natural course of human growth and development economic units come into such relations that the satisfaction of material desires is sought by conjoined effort, the laws which political economy seeks to discover begin to appear.

The system or arrangement by which in such conditions material satisfactions are sought and obtained may be roughly likened to a machine fed by combined effort, and producing joint results, which are finally divided or distributed in individual satisfactions — a machine resembling an old-time grist-mill to which individuals brought separate parcels of grain, receiving therefrom in meal, not the identical grain each had put in, nor yet its exact equivalent, but an equivalent less a charge for milling.

Or to make a closer illustration: The system or arrangement which it is the proper purpose of political economy to discover may be likened to that system or arrangement by which the physical body is nourished. The lowest unit of animal life, so far as we can see, is the single cell, which sucks in and assimilates its own food; thus directly satisfying what we may style its own desires. But in those highest forms of animal life of which man is a type, myriads of cells have become conjoined in related parts and organs, exercising different and complex functions, which result in the procurement, digestion and assimilation of the food that nourishing each separate cell maintains the entire organism. Brain and stomach, hands and feet, eyes and ears, teeth and hair, bones, nerves, arteries and veins, still less the cells of which all these parts are composed, do not feed themselves. Under the government of the brain, what the hands, aided by the legs, assisted by the organs of sense, procure, is carried to the mouth, masticated by the teeth, taken by the throat to the alembic of the stomach, where aided by the intestines it is digested, and passing into a fluid containing all nutritive substances, is oxygenized by the lungs; and impelled by the pumping of the heart, makes a complete circuit of the body through a system of arteries and veins, in the course of which every part and every cell takes the nutriment it requires.

Now, what the blood is to the physical body, wealth, as we shall hereafter see more fully, is to the body economic. And as we should find, were we to undertake it, that a description of the manner in which blood is produced and distributed in the physical body would involve almost, if not quite, a description of the entire physical man with all his powers and functions and the laws which govern their operations; so we shall find that what is included or involved in political economy, the science which treats of the production and distribution of wealth, is almost, if not quite, the whole body social, with all its parts, powers and functions, and the laws under which they operate.

The scope of political economy would be roughly explained were we to style it the science which teaches how civilized men get a living. Why this idea is sufficiently expressed as the production and distribution of wealth will be more fully seen hereafter; but there is a distinction as to what is called getting a living that it may be worthwhile here to note. We have but to look at existing facts to see that there are two ways in which men (i.e., some men) may obtain satisfaction of their material desires for things not freely supplied to them by nature.

The first of these ways is, by working, or rendering service.

The second is, by stealing, or extorting service.

But there is only one way in which man (i.e., men in general or all men) can satisfy his material desires — that is by working, or rendering service.

For it is manifestly impossible that men in general or all men, or indeed any but a small minority of men, can satisfy their material desires by stealing, since in the nature of things working or the rendering of service is the only way in which the material satisfactions of desire can be primarily obtained or produced. Stealing produces nothing; it only alters the distribution of what has already been produced.

Therefore, however it be that stealing is to be considered by an individual economy or by an economy of a political division, and with whatever propriety a successful thief who has endowed churches and colleges and libraries and soup — houses may in such an economy be treated as a public benefactor and spoken of as Antony spoke of Caesar — He hath brought many captives home to Rome, Whose ransoms did the general coffers fill.

A true science of political economy takes no cognizance of stealing, except in so far as the various forms of it may pervert the natural distribution, and thus check the natural production of wealth. Yet, at the same time, political economy does not concern itself with the character of the desires for which satisfaction is sought. It has nothing to do, either with the originating motive that prompts to action in the satisfaction of material desires, nor yet with the final satisfaction which is the end and aim of that action. It is, so to speak, like the science of navigation, which is concerned with the means whereby a ship may be carried from point to point on the ocean, but asks not whether that ship may be a pirate or a missionary barque, what are the expectations which may induce its passengers to go from one place to another, or whether or not these expectations will be gratified on their arrival. Political economy is not moral or ethical science, nor yet is it political science. It is the science of the maintenance and nutriment of the body politic.

Although it will be found incidentally to throw a most powerful light upon, and to give a most powerful support to, the teachings of moral or ethical science, its proper business is neither to explain the difference between right and wrong nor to persuade to one in preference to the other. And while it is in the same way what may be termed the bread-and-butter side of politics, it is directly concerned only with the natural laws which govern the production and distribution of wealth in the social organism, and not with the enactments of the body politic or state.

THE ELEMENTS OF POLITICAL ECONOMY

To understand a complex machine the best way is first to see what is the beginning and what the end of its movements, leaving details until we have mastered its general idea and comprehended its purpose. In this way we most easily see the relation of parts to each other and to the object of the whole, and readily come to understand to the minutest movements and appliances what without the clue of intention might have hopelessly perplexed us.

When the safety bicycle was yet a curiosity even in the towns of England and the United States, an American missionary in a far-off station received from an old friend, unaccompanied by the letter intended to go with it, a present of one of these machines, which for economy in transportation had not been set up, but was forwarded in its unassembled parts. How these parts were to be put together was a perplexing problem, for neither the missionary himself nor any one he could consult could at first imagine what the thing was intended to do, and their guesses were of almost everything but the truth, until at length the saddle suggested a theory, which was so successfully followed that by the time, months afterwards, another ship brought the missing letter, the missionary was riding over the hard sand of the beach on his wheel.

In the same way an intelligent savage, placed in a great industrial hive of our civilization before some enormous factory throbbing and whirring with the seemingly independent motion of pistons and wheels and belts and looms, might, with no guide but his own observation and reäson, soon come to see the what, the how and the why of the whole as a connected device for using the power obtained by the transformation of coal into heat in the changing of such things as wool, silk or cotton into blankets or piece goods, stockings or ribbons.

Now the reason which enables us to understand the works of man as soon as we discover the reason that has brought them into existence, also enables us to interpret nature by assuming a like reason in nature. The child's question, "What is it for?" — what is its purpose or intent? — is the master key that enables us to turn the locks that hide nature's mysteries.

It is in this way that all discoveries in the field of the natural sciences have been made, and this will be our best way in the investigation we are now entering upon. The complex phenomena of the production and distribution of wealth in the elaborate organization of modern civilization will only puzzle us, as the many confused and confusing books written to explain it show, if we begin, as it were, from the middle. But if we seek first principles and trace out main lines, so as to comprehend the skeleton of their relation, they will readily become intelligible.

The immense aggregate of movements by which, in civilization, wealth is produced and distributed, viewed collectively as the subject of political economy, constitute a system or arrangement much greater than, yet analogous to, the system or arrangement of a great factory. In the attempt to understand the laws of nature, which they illustrate and obey, let us avoid the confusion that inevitably attends beginning from the middle, by proceeding in the way suggested in our illustration — the only scientific way.

These movements, so various in their modes, and so complex in their relations, with which political economy is concerned, evidently originate in the exertion of human will, prompted by desire; their means are the material and forces that nature offers to man and the natural laws which these obey; their end and aim the satisfaction of man's material desires. If we try to call to mind as many as we can of the different movements that are included in the production and distribution of wealth in modern civilization — the catching and gathering, the separating and combining, the digging and planting, the baking and brewing, the weaving and dyeing, the sewing and washing, the sawing and planing, the melting and forging, the moving and transporting, the buying and selling — we shall see that what they all aim to accomplish is some sort of change in the place, form or relation of the materials or forces supplied by nature so as better to satisfy human desire.

Thus the movements with which political economy is concerned are human actions, having for their aim the attainment of material satisfactions. And the laws that it is its province to discover are not the laws manifested in the existence of the materials and forces of nature that man thus utilizes, nor yet the laws which make possible their change in place, form or relation, but the laws of man's own nature, which affect his own actions in the endeavor to satisfy his desires by bringing about such changes.

The world, as it is apprehended by human reason, is by that reason resolvable, as we have seen, into three elements or factors — spirit, matter and energy. But as these three ultimate elements are conjoined both in what we call man and in what we call nature, the world regarded from the standpoint of political economy has for its original elements, man and nature.

Of these, the human element is the initiative or active factor — that which begins or acts first. The natural element is the passive factor — that which receives action and responds to it. From the interaction of these two proceed all with which political economy is concerned — that is to say, all the changes that by man's agency may be wrought in the place, form or condition of material things so as better to fit them for the satisfaction of his desires.

Between the material things which come into existence through man's agency and those which come into existence through the agency of nature alone, the difference is as clear to human reason as the difference between a mountain and a pyramid, between what was on the shores of Lake Michigan when the caravels of Columbus first plowed the waters of the Caribbean Sea and the wondrous White City, beside which in 1893 the antitypes of those caravels, by gift of Spain, were moored. Yet it eludes our senses and can be apprehended only by reason.

Any one can distinguish at a glance, it may be said, between a pyramid and a mountain, or a city and a forest. But not by the senses uninterpreted by reason. The animals, whose senses are even keener than ours, seem incapable of making the distinction. In the actions of the most intelligent dog you will find no evidence that he recognizes any difference between a statue and a stone, a tobacconist's wooden Indian and the stump of a tree. And things are now manufactured and sold as to which it requires an expert to tell whether they are products of man or products of nature.

For the essential thing that in the last analysis distinguishes man from nature can, on the material plane that is cognizable by the senses, appear only in the garb and form of the material. Whatever man makes must have for its substance preexisting matter; whatever motion he exerts must be drawn from a preexisting stock of energy. Take away from man all that is contributed by external nature, all that belongs to the economic factor land, and you have, what? Something that is not tangible by the senses, yet which is the ultimate recipient and final cause of sensation; something which has no form or substance or direct power in or over the material world, but which is yet the originating impulse which utilizes motion to mold matter into forms it desires, and to which we must look for the origin of the pyramid, the caravel, the industrial palaces of Chicago and the myriad marvels they contained.

I do not wish to raise, or even to refer further than is necessary, to those deep problems of being and genesis where the light of reason seems to fail us and twilight deepens into dark. But we must grasp the thread at its beginning if we are to hope to work our way through a tangled skein. And into what fatal confusions those fall who do not begin at the beginning may be seen in current economic works, which treat capital as though it were the originator in production, labor as though it were a product, and land as though it were a mere agricultural instrument — a something on which cattle are fed and wheat and cabbages raised.

We cannot really consider the beginning of things, so far as a true political economy is forced to concern itself with them, without seeing that when man came into the world the sum of energy was not increased nor that of matter added to; and that so it must be today. In all the changes that man brings about in the material world, he adds nothing to and subtracts nothing from the sum of matter and energy. He merely brings about changes in the place and relation of what already exists, and the first and always indispensable condition to his doing anything in the material world, and indeed to his very existence therein, is that of access to its material and forces.

So far as we can see, it is universally true that matter and energy are indestructible, and that the forms in which we apprehend them are but transmutations from forms they have held before; that the inorganic cannot of itself pass into the organic; that vegetable life can only come from vegetable life; animal life from animal life; and human life from human life. Notwithstanding all speculation on the subject, we have never yet been able to trace the origin of one well-defined species from another well-defined species. Yet the way in which we find the orders of existence superimposed and related, indicates to us design or thought — a something of which we have the first glimpses only in man. Hence, while we may explain the world of which our senses tell us by a world of which our senses do not tell us, a world of what Plato vaguely called ideas, or what we vaguely speak of as spirit, yet we are compelled when we would seek for the beginning cause and still escape negation to posit a primary or all-causative idea or spirit, an all-producer or creator, for which our short word is God.

But to keep within what we do know. In man, conscious will — that which feels, reasons, plans and contrives, in some way that we cannot understand — is clothed in material form. Coming thus into control of some of the energy stored up in our physical bodies, and learning, as we may see in infancy, to govern arms, legs and a few other organs, this conscious will seeks through them to grasp matter and to set to work, in changing its place and form, other stores of energy.

The steam-engine rushing along with its long train of coal or goods or passengers, is in all that is evident to our senses but a new form of what previously existed. Everything of it that we can see, hear, touch, taste, weigh, measure or subject to chemical tests, existed before man was. What has brought preexisting matter and motion to the shape, place and function of engine and train is that which, prisoned in the engineer's brain, grasps the throttle; the same thing that in the infant stretches for the moon, and in the child makes mud-pies. It is this conscious will seeking the gratification of its desires in the alteration of material forms that is the primary motive power, the active factor, in bringing about the relations with which political economy deals. And while, whatever be *its* origin, this will is in the world as we know it an original element, yet it can act only in certain ways, and is subject in that action to certain uniform sequences, which we term laws of nature.

FUNDAMENTAL LAW OF POLITICAL ECONOMY

The only way man has of satisfying his desires is by action. Now action, if continued long enough in one line to become really exertion, a conscious putting forth of effort, produces in the consciousness a feeling of reluctance or weariness. This comes from something deeper than the exhaustion of energy in what we call physical labor; for whoever has tried it knows that one may lie on his back in the most comfortable position and by mere dint of sustained thinking, without consciously moving a muscle, tire himself as truly as by sawing wood; and that the mere clash and conflict of involuntary or undirected thought or feeling, or its continuance in one direction, will soon bring extreme weariness.

But whatever be its ultimate cause, the fact is that labor, the attempt of the conscious will to realize its material desire, is always, when continued for a little while, in itself hard and irksome. And whether from this fact alone, or from this fact, conjoined with or based upon something intuitive to our perceptions, the further fact, testified to both by observation of our own feelings and actions and by observation of the acts of others, is that men always seek to gratify their desires with the least exertion.

This, of course, does not mean that they always succeed in doing so, any more than the physical law that motion tends to persist in a straight line means that moving bodies always take that line. But it does mean the mental analogue of the physical law that motion seeks the line of least resistance — that in seeking to gratify their desires men will always seek the way which under existing physical, social and personal conditions seems to them to involve the least expenditure of exertion. Whoever would see this disposition of human nature exemplified in trivial things has only to watch the passers-by in a crowded street, or those who enter or depart from a frequented house. He will be instructed and perhaps not a little amused to note how slight the obstruction or semblance of obstruction that will divert their steps, and will see the principle observed by saint and sinner — by "wicked man on evil errand bent," and "Good Samaritan intent on works of mercy."

Whether it proceed from experience of the irksomenes of labor and the desire to avoid it, or further back than that, have its source in some innate principle of the human constitution, this disposition of men to seek the satisfaction of their desires with the minimum of exertion is so universal and unfailing that it constitutes one of those invariable sequences that we denominate laws of nature, and from which we may safely reason. It is this law of nature that is the fundamental law of political economy — the central law from which its deductions and explanations may with certainty be drawn, and, indeed, by which alone they become possible.

It holds the same place in the sphere of political economy that the law of gravitation does in physics. Without it there could be no recognition of order, and all would be chaos. Yet the failure clearly to apprehend this as the fundamental law of political economy has led to very serious and wide-spread mistakes as to the nature of the science; and has indeed, in spite of the vigorous assertions and assumptions of its accredited professors, prevented it from truly taking in popular esteem the place of a real science, or from long holding in scholastic circles the credit it had for a while gained.

For the principle that men always seek to satisfy their desires with the least exertion, there has been substituted, from the time that political economy began to claim the attention of thoughtful men, the principle of human selfishness. And with the assumption that political economy takes into its account only the selfish feelings of human nature, there have been linked, as laws of political economy, other assumptions as destitute of validity. To show how completely the idea has prevailed that the foundation of political economy is the assumption of human selfishness, I shall not stop to quote from the accredited writers on the subject, nor yet from those who have made of it a ground of their repugnance to the political economy that has been with justice styled "the dismal science" — such as Carlyle, Dickens or Ruskin.

I take for that purpose a writer who, while he fully accepted what was at his time (1857 — 60) the orthodox political economy, deeming it "the only subject immediately connected with the art of government that has yet been raised to a science," and was well conversant with its literature, was not concerned with it as a controversialist, but only as a historian of the development of thought. Buckle's understanding of political economy was that it eliminated every other feeling than selfishness. In his "Inquiry into the Influence Exercised by Religion, Literature and Government", he says that in the *Wealth of Nations,* which he regards as "probably the most important book which has ever been written," Smith "generalizes the laws of wealth, not from the phenomena of wealth, nor from statistical statements, but from the phenomena of selfishness; thus making a deductive application of one set of mental principles to the whole set of economical facts."

And in his *Examination of the Scotch Intellect during the Eighteenth Century*, he returns in greater detail to the same subject. Adam Smith, he says, wrote two great books, with an interval of seventeen years between them. In both he employed the same method, that form of deduction "which proceeds by an artificial separation of facts in themselves inseparable." In the first of these, the *Theory of Moral Sentiments,* he "so narrowed the field of inquiry as to exclude from it all consideration of selfishness as a primary principle, and only to admit its great antagonist, sympathy." In the second, the Wealth of Nations, which Buckle regards as a correlative part of Smith's one great scheme, though still greater than its predecessor, Smith, on the contrary, "assumes that selfishness is the main regulator of human affairs, just as in his previous work he had assumed sympathy to be so." Or, as Buckle, later on, repeats:

He everywhere assumes that the great moving power of all men, all interests and all classes, in all ages and in all countries, is selfishness. The opposite power of sympathy he entirely shuts out; and I hardly remember an instance in which even the word occurs in the whole course of his work. Its fundamental assumption is, that each man exclusively follows his own interest, or what he deems to be his own interest.... In this way Adam Smith completely changes the premises he had assumed in his earlier work. Here, he makes men naturally selfish; formerly, he had made them naturally sympathetic. Here, he represents them pursuing wealth for sordid objects, and for the narrowest personal pleasures; formerly, he represented them as pursuing it out of regard to the sentiments of others, and for the sake of obtaining their sympathy. In the *Wealth of Nations* we hear no more of this conciliatory and sympathetic spirit; such amiable maxims are altogether forgotten, and the affairs of the world are regulated by different principles. It now appears that benevolence and affection have no influence over our actions. Indeed, Adam Smith will hardly admit common humanity into his theory of motives. If a people emancipate their slaves, it is a proof, not that the people are acted on by high moral considerations, nor that their sympathy is excited by the cruelty inflicted on these unhappy creatures. Nothing of the sort. Such inducements to conduct are imaginary and exercise no real sway. All that the emancipation proves, is, that the slaves were few in number, and, therefore, small in value. Otherwise they would not have been emancipated.

So, too, while in his former work he had ascribed the different systems of morals to the power of sympathy, he, in this work, ascribes them entirely to the power of selfishness.

This presumption, so well stated and defended by Buckle, that political economy must eliminate everything but the selfish feelings of mankind, has continued to pervade the accredited political economy up to this time, whatever may have been the effects upon the common mind of the attacks made upon it by those, who, not putting their objections into logical and coherent form, could be spoken of as sentimentalists, but not political economists. Yet, however generally the accepted writers on political economy may have themselves supposed the assumption of universal selfishness to be the fundamental principle of political economy, or how much ground they may have given for such a supposition on the part of their readers, a true political economy requires no such assumption. The primary postulate on and from which its whole structure is built is not that all men are governed only by selfish motives, or must for its purposes be considered as governed only by selfish motives; it is that all men seek to gratify their desires, whatever those desires may be, with the least exertion. This fundamental law of political economy is, like all other laws of nature, so far as we are concerned, supreme. It is no more affected by the selfishness or unselfishness of our desires than is the law of gravitation. It is simply a fact.

The irksomeness or weariness that inevitably attends all continued exertion caused earlier men to look on the necessity of labor to production as a penalty imposed upon our kind by an offended Deity. But in the light of modern civilization we may see that what they deemed a curse is in reality the impulse that has led to the most enormous extensions of man's power of dealing with nature. So true is it that good and evil are not in external things or in their laws of action, but in will or spirit.

METHODS OF POLITICAL ECONOMY

A misconception of the fundamental law on which a science is based must lead to divergences and confusions as the attempt to develop that science proceeds. In the case of political economy, the result of the assumption that its fundamental principle is human selfishness is shown in disputes and confusions as to its proper method. These began shortly after it was recognized as deserving the attention of the institutions of learning, and are an increasingly noticeable feature in economic literature for some sixty or seventy years. Adam Smith and the most prominent of his successors followed the deductive method. But ere long there began to be questionings as to whether the inductive method was not the proper one. Having on their side the weight of authority, the defenders of the deductive method, or "old school" political economy, as it began to be called, held for a long time their formal position, though compelled by the incongruities of the system they were endeavoring to uphold to make damaging deductions and weakening admissions; while the opposition to them, called by various names, but generally known as inductive or "new school" economists, gathered strength.

What lay beneath this contest, which was largely verbal, and in which there was confusion on both sides, I shall have occasion to speak of hereafter; but as to how it seemed to stand in the scholastic world at the beginning of the seventh decade of our century I quote from the article "Political Economy" in the *New American Cyclopedia* (1861), which, as written by an opponent of the then orthodox school (Henry Carey Baird), with an evident desire to be entirely fair, will I think better show the actual situation at that time than anything else I can find:

The progress thus far made in political economy has been slow and uncertain, and there is in its entire range hardly a doctrine or even the definition of an important word which is universally or even generally accepted beyond dispute. . . . Amid all their discords and disagreements it is possible to divide political economists under two general heads: those who treat the subject as a deductive science, "in which all the general propositions are in the strictest sense of the word hypothetical;" and those who treat it by the inductive or Baconian method. Of the first — named school are all the English economists and most of those of continental Europe who have acquired any reputation. As the representatives of the last, Mr. Henry C. Carey and his followers are most prominent.

Thus, in 1861, the deductive method, even to the view of an adherent of the opposing school, still formally held sway in the scholastic world. But at present, as the century nears its close, it has so utterly lost its hold that so far as I can discover, there is not now a prominent college or university anywhere in which the professed teachers of what is reputed to be political economy adhere to what was then called the deductive method. Yet this triumph in scholastic opinion of the advocates of what is called the inductive method is in reality but the triumph of one set of confusions over another set of confusions, in which the determining element has been the vague consciousness that the previously authoritative political economy was not a true political economy. Where a new set of confusions is pitted against an old set of confusions, the victory must finally and for a time remain with the new; for the reason that on the old lies the burden of defending what is indefensible, while the new has for a while only the easier task of attack. What this passing phase of economic thought really shows is the utter confusion into which the whole scholastic political economy has fallen from lack of care as to first principles. In my view of the matter those who have said that the deductive method was the proper method of political economy have been right as to that, but wrong in principles from which they have made deductions; while those who contended for the inductive method have been wrong as to that, but right as to the weaknesses of their opponents.

As to the course of what has been called the science of political economy and the destructive revolution which it has of late years undergone, I shall have occasion to speak in the next book. I am here concerned in clearing only what might be a perplexity to the reader in regard to the proper methods of the real science. The human reason has two ways of ascertaining truth. The first of these is that of reasoning from particulars to generals in an ascending line, until we come at last to one of those invariable uniformities that we call laws of nature. This method we call the inductive, or *a posteriori.* But when we have reached what we feel sure is a law of nature, and as such true in all times and places, then an easier and more powerful method of ascertaining truth is open to us — the method of reasoning in the descending line from generals to particulars. This is the method that we call the deductive, or *a priori* method. For knowing what is the general law, the invariable sequence that we call a law of nature, we have only to discover that a particular comes under it to know what is true in the case of that particular.

In the relation of priority the two methods stand in the order in which I have named them — induction being the first or primary method of applying human reason to the investigation of facts, and deduction being the second or derivative. So far as our reason is concerned, induction must give the facts on which we may proceed to deduction.

Deduction can safely be based only on what has been supplied to the reason by induction; and where the validity of this first step is called in question, must apply to induction for proof. Both methods are proper to the careful investigation that we speak of as scientific: induction in its preliminary stages, when it is groping for the law of nature; deduction when it has discovered that law, and is thus able to proceed by a short cut from the general to the particular, without any further need for the more laborious and, so to speak, uphill method of induction, except it may be to verify its conclusions. There is a further method of investigation, which consists in a combination of these two original methods of the reason, and which has been found most effective in the discovery of truth in the physical sciences. When our inductions so point to the existence of a natural law that we are able to form a surmise or suspicion of what it may prove to be, we may tentatively assume the existence of such a law, and proceed to see whether particulars will fall into place in deductions made from it. This is the method of tentative deduction, or hypothesis.

The inductive method is sometimes, as in the last quotation I have made, spoken of as the Baconian method, and the great name of Bacon has been freely used to give plausibility to what the advocates of the "new school" in political economy have called the inductive method. But whatever originality there may have been in his classifications and devices, Bacon did not invent the inductive method. It was by that method that man's reason has from the first enabled him to apprehend laws of nature that he has subsequently used as bases for deduction. It was thus that he must have learned what we are accustomed to think the simplest of nature's uniformities — such as, that after an interval a new moon succeeds the old moon; that the sun, after apparently tending to the south for a while, turns again to the north; that fire will burn, and that water will quench fire.

What Bacon did was not to invent or discover the inductive method, but to formulate some rules for its application and to apply it to the investigation of fields of knowledge from which it had been long shut out by a blind reliance upon authority — by a false assumption that wiser men who had gone before had taught all there was worth knowing on certain subjects, and that there remained for those who came after nothing further to do than to make deductions from premises their predecessors had supplied.

Where the application of the inductive method was really needed in what is now called by the "new lights" the "classical" political economy was to test the premises from which its deductions were made, and to clear them of what had no better warrant than a disposition to use political economy to justify existing social arrangements. It was not needed to take the place of the deductive method, where that was applicable. For the deductive method, when applied to the further extension of what has already been validly ascertained, constitutes the most powerful means of extending knowledge that the human mind can avail itself of.

In its use of the deductive method after its premises had been settled, the classical political economy was not in error. The error that gave insecurity to its whole structure lay deeper still, in the insufficient inductions on which those premises rested. But, instead of addressing themselves to these flaws in its accepted premises, the various schools of economists generally classed as inductive have denied that there were any general principles that could with certainty be laid down as the basis for deduction. Thus, if such a question be asked them as, does free trade or protection best promote a general prosperity? or, what is the best system of land-tenure? or, what is the best system of taxation? or, what are the limits of governmental interference with industry, or trade — union regulations? no general answer can be given. It can only be said that one thing may be best in one place and time, and another in another place and time, so that the matter can be determined only by special investigations. In other words, to quote the phrase of Professor James, of the University of Pennsylvania, an adherent of the "new school", they have opposed "the theory which seeks eternally valid natural laws in economics, and which considers the natural condition of unlimited personal freedom as the only justifiable one, without regard to the needs of special times and nations."

The result, therefore, of the triumph of the "inductionists" over the "deductionists" in the accredited organs of economic teaching, has been to destroy in the "new" political economy even the semblance of coherency that it had in the "old," and to decompose it into a congeries of unrelated doctrines and unverified speculations which only its professors can presume to understand, and as to which they can dispute and quarrel with each other in the wild abandon that results from the absence of any recognized common principle.

But to me it seems clear that if political economy can be called a science at all, it must as a science, that is to say from the moment the laws of nature on which it depends are discovered, follow the deductive method of examination, using induction only to test the conclusions thus obtained. For the particulars which are included in its province are too vast and too complex to admit of any hope of bringing them into order and relation by direct induction.

To quote from the latest elementary text-book of logic of which I know, Professor Noah K. Davis's *Elements of Inductive Logic*:

The great object of the scientist is to obtain by rigid induction the laws of nature, and to follow them by rigid deduction to their consequences. A science at first wholly inductive becomes, as soon as a law has been proved, more or less deductive, and as it progresses, rising to higher and wider but fewer inductions, the deductive processes increase in number and importance, until it is no longer properly an inductive, but a deductive science. Thus, hydrostatics, acoustics, optics and electricity, commonly called inductive sciences, have passed under the dominion of mathematics, from inductive to deductive sciences and mechanics has a like history. Celestial mechanics as founded in the *Principia* of Newton is mainly inductive, as elaborated in the *Mécanique Céleste* of Laplace, is mainly deductive. By pursuing this latter process it has multiplied its matter and reached its present high perfection. A revolution is quietly progressing in all the natural sciences. Bacon changed their method from deductive to inductive, and it is now rapidly reverting from inductive to deductive. The task of logic is to explicate and regulate these methods.

Now the law of nature which forms the postulate of a true science of political economy is not, as has been erroneously assumed, that men are invariably and universally selfish. As a matter of fact, this is not true. Nor can we abstract from man all but selfish qualities in order to make as the object of our thought on economic matters what has been called the "economic man," without getting what is really a monster, not a man.

The law of nature which is really the postulate of a true science of political economy is that men always seek to gratify their desires with the least exertion, whether those desires are selfish or unselfish, good or bad. That this is a law of nature we have the highest possible warrant, wider in fact than we can have for any of the laws of external nature, such for instance as the law of gravitation. For the laws of external nature can be apprehended only objectively. But that it is a law of nature that men seek to gratify their desires with the least exertion, we may see both subjectively and objectively.

Since man himself is included in nature, we may subjectively reach the law of nature that men seek to gratify their desires with the least exertion, by an induction derived from consciousness of our own feelings and an analysis of our own motives of action; while objectively we may also reach the same law by an induction derived from observation of the acts of others.

Proceeding from a law of nature thus doubly assured, the proper method of a political economy which becomes really a science by its correct apprehension of a fundamental law, is the method of deduction from that law, the method of proceeding from the general to the particular; for this is the method which will enable us to attain incomparably greater results. To abandon that method and resort to what the "new lights" of political economy seem really to mean by induction, would be as though we were to discard the rules of arithmetic and endeavor by direct inquiries in all parts of the world to discover how much one number added to another would make, and what would be the quotient of a sum divided by itself.

Thus, in the main, the science of political economy resorts to the deductive method, using induction for its tests. But in its more common investigations its most useful instrument is a form of hypothesis which may be called that of mental or imaginative experiment, by which we may separate, combine or eliminate conditions in our own imaginations, and thus test the working of known principles. This is a most common method of reasoning, familiar to us all, from our very infancy. It is the great working tool of political economy, and in its use we have only to be careful as to the validity of what we assume as principles.

NEW POLITICAL ECONOMY

New Political Economy (NPE) is a relatively recent sub-school within the field of political economy. NPE scholars treat economic ideologies as the relevant phenomena to be explained by political economy. Thus, Charles S. Maier suggests that a political economy approach: "interrogates economic doctrines to disclose their sociological and political premises [...] in sum, [it] regards economic ideas and behavior not as frameworks for analysis, but as beliefs and actions that must themselves be explained". This approach informs Andrew Gamble's *The Free Economy and the Strong State* , and Colin Hay's *The Political Economy of New Labour* . It also informs much work published in *New Political Economy*, an international journal founded by Sheffield University scholars in 1996.

Matthew Watson with Richard Higgott, in explicit response to Benjamin Cohen's approach, seek to move International Political Economy away from Cohen's division of the subject into American and British camps, and to promote their own vision of a 'New Political Economy'. NPE, they propose:

1. transgresses conventional social science boundaries;
2. explicitly rejects the loaded connotations of the 'rigour' that Cohen espouses, as this engenders unhelpful methodological competition;
3. resists the abstractionism of postmodernism in favour of the progressive principle that life might be made better.

This 'new political economy' attempts to combine the approach of the classical political economists (from Smith to Marx) with more recent "analytical advances". Authors adopting this approach include Gamble (1996), Watson himself, and a series of authors in the work edited by Higgott and Payne (2000). The approach "rejects the old dichotomies – between agency and structure, between ideas and material interests, and between states and markets". The approach seeks to make explicit the normative assumptions that lie behind its analysis, and to be a "hosting metaphor" that will encourage political debate about societal preferences. It considers that different levels of abstraction are needed to "deeply ground" work in historical, cultural and social detail, thereby fostering a 'real world' political economy able to explain the influence of social meanings - of both actions and objects - on economic choices.

Watson and Higgott argue that practitioners of this approach are gradually increasing in number. They note the prevalence of NPE not only among "Third World economic nationalists and academic critics of the neo-liberal policy agenda who find little comfort in the turn instead to anti-foundationalist theories associated with postmodernism", but also among many "mainstream" economists who have become disillusioned with neoclassical theory. In this second category they list Dani Rodrik (1998), Paul Krugman(1999) and Joseph Stiglitz (2002).

2

Principles of Political Economy

In common discourse, wealth is always expressed in money. If you ask how rich a person is, you are answered that he has so many thousand pounds. All income and expenditure, all gains and losses, everything by which one becomes richer or poorer, are reckoned as the coming in or going out of so much money. It is true that in the inventory of a person's fortune are included, not only the money in his actual possession, or due to him, but all other articles of value. These, however, enter, not in their own character, but in virtue of the sums of money which they would sell for; and if they would sell for less, their owner is reputed less rich, though the things themselves are precisely the same. It is true, also, that people do not grow rich by keeping their money unused, and that they must be willing to spend in order to gain.

Those who enrich themselves by commerce, do so by giving money for goods as well as goods for money; and the first is as necessary a part of the process as the last. But a person who buys goods for purposes of gain, does so to sell them again for money, and in the expectation of receiving more money than he laid out: to get money, therefore, seems even to the person himself the ultimate end of the whole. It often happens that he is not paid in money, but in something else; having bought goods to a value equivalent, which are set off against those he sold.

But he accepted these at a money valuation, and in the belief that they would bring in more money eventually than the price at which they were made over to him. A dealer doing a large amount of business, and turning over his capital rapidly, has but a small portion of it in ready money at any one time. But he only feels it valuable to him as it is convertible into money: he considers no transaction closed until the net result is either paid or credited in money: when he retires from business it is into money that he converts the whole, and not until then does he deem himself to have realized his gains: just as if money were the only wealth, and money's worth were only the means of attaining it. If it be now asked for what end money is desirable, unless to supply the wants or pleasures of oneself or others, the champion of the system would not be at all embarrassed by the question. True, he would say, these are the uses of wealth, and very laudable uses while confined to domestic commodities, because in that case, by exactly the amount which you expend, you enrich others of your countrymen. Spend your wealth, if you please, in whatever indulgences you have a taste for; but your wealth is not the indulgences, it is the sum of money, or the annual money income, with which you purchase them.

While there were so many things to render the assumption which is the basis of the mercantile system plausible, there is also some small foundation in reason, though a very insufficient one, for the distinction which that system so emphatically draws between money and every other kind of valuable possession. We really, and justly, look upon a person as possessing the advantages of wealth, not in proportion to the useful and agreeable things of which he is in the actual enjoyment, but to his command over the general fund of things useful and agreeable; the power he possesses of providing for any exigency, or obtaining any object of desire. Now, money is itself that power; while all other things, in a civilized state, seem to confer it only by their capacity of being exchanged for money.

To possess any other article of wealth, is to possess that particular thing, and nothing else: if you wish for another thing instead of it, you have first to sell it, or to submit to the inconvenience and delay (if not the impossibility) of finding some one who has what you want, and is willing to barter it for what you have. But with money you are at once able to buy whatever things are for sale: and one whose fortune is in money, or in things rapidly convertible into it, seems both to himself and others to possess not any one thing, but all the things which the money places it at his option to purchase. The greatest part of the utility of wealth, beyond a very moderate quantity, is not the indulgences it procures, but the reserved power which its possessor holds in his hands of attaining purposes generally; and this power no other kind of wealth confers so immediately or so certainly as money.

It is the only form of wealth which is not merely applicable to some one use, but can be turned at once to any use. And this distinction was the more likely to make an impression upon governments, as it is one of considerable importance to them. A civilized government derives comparatively little advantage from taxes unless it can collect them in money: and if it has large or sudden payments to make, especially payments in foreign countries for wars or subsidies, either for the sake of conquering or of not being conquered (the two chief objects of national policy until a late period), scarcely any medium of payment except money will serve the purpose.

All these causes conspire to make both individuals and governments, in estimating their means, attach almost exclusive importance to money, either *in esse* or *in posse*, and look upon all other things (when viewed as part of their resources) scarcely otherwise than as the remote means of obtaining that which alone, when obtained, affords the indefinite, and at the same time instantaneous, command over objects of desire, which best answers to the idea of wealth. An absurdity, however, does not cease to be an absurdity when we have discovered what were the appearances which made it plausible; and the Mercantile Theory could not fail to be seen in its true character when men began, even in an imperfect manner, to explore into the foundations of things, and seek their premises from elementary facts, and not from the forms and phrases of common discourse. So soon as they asked themselves what is really meant by money—what it is in its essential characters, and the precise nature of the functions it performs—they reflected that money, like other things, is only a desirable possession on account of its uses; and that these, instead of being, as they delusively appear, indefinite, are of a strictly defined and limited description, namely, to facilitate the distribution of the produce of industry according to the convenience of those among whom it is shared.

Further consideration showed that the uses of money are in no respect promoted by increasing the quantity which exists and circulates in a country; the service which it performs being as well rendered by a small as by a large aggregate amount. Two million quarters of corn will not feed so many persons as four millions; but two millions of pounds sterling will carry on as much traffic, will buy and sell as many commodities, as four millions, though at lower nominal prices. Money, as money, satisfies no want; its worth to any one, consists in its being a convenient shape in which to receive his incomings of all sorts, which incomings he afterwards, at the times which suit him best, converts into the forms in which they can be useful to him.

Great as the difference would be between a country with money, and a country altogether without it, it would be only one of convenience; a saving of time and trouble, like grinding by water power instead of by hand, or (to use Adam Smith's illustration) like the benefit derived from roads; and to mistake money for wealth, is the same sort of error as to mistake the highway which may be the easiest way of getting to your house or lands, for the house and lands themselves.1

Money, being the instrument of an important public and private purpose, is rightly regarded as wealth; but everything else which serves any human purpose, and which nature does not afford gratuitously, is wealth also. To be wealthy is to have a large stock of useful articles, or the means of purchasing them. Everything forms therefore a part of wealth, which has a power of purchasing; for which anything useful or agreeable would be given in exchange. Things for which nothing could be obtained in exchange, however useful or necessary they may be, are not wealth in the sense in which the term is used in Political Economy. Air, for example, though the most absolute of necessaries, bears no price in the market, because it can be obtained gratuitously: to accumulate a stock of it would yield no profit or advantage to any one; and the laws of its production and distribution are the subject of a very different study from Political Economy. But though air is not wealth, mankind are much richer by obtaining it gratis, since the time and labour which would otherwise be required for supplying the most pressing of all wants, can be devoted to other purposes. It is possible to imagine circumstances in which air would be a part of wealth. If it became customary to sojourn long in places where the air does not naturally penetrate, as in diving-bells sunk in the sea, a supply of air artificially furnished would, like water conveyed into houses, bear a price: and if from any revolution in nature the atmosphere became too scanty for the consumption, or could be monopolized, air might acquire a very high marketable value. In such a case, the possession of it, beyond his own wants, would be, to its owner, wealth; and the general wealth of mankind might at first sight appear to be increased, by what would be so great a calamity to them. The error would lie in not considering, that however rich the possessor of air might become at the expense of the rest of the community, all persons else would be poorer by all that they were compelled to pay for what they had before obtained without payment.

This leads to an important distinction in the meaning of the word wealth, as applied to the possessions of an individual, and to those of a nation, or of mankind. In the wealth of mankind, nothing is included which does not of itself answer some purpose of utility or pleasure. To an individual anything is wealth, which, though useless in itself, enables him to claim from others a part of their stock of things useful or pleasant. Take, for instance, a mortgage of a thousand pounds on a landed estate. This is wealth to the person to whom it brings in a revenue, and who could perhaps sell it in the market for the full amount of the debt. But it is not wealth to the country; if the engagement were annulled, the country would be neither poorer nor richer.

The mortgagee would have lost a thousand pounds, and the owner of the land would have gained it. Speaking nationally, the mortgage was not itself wealth, but merely gave A a claim to a portion of the wealth of B. It was wealth to A, and wealth which he could transfer to a third person; but what he so transferred was in fact a joint ownership, to the extent of a thousand pounds, in the land of which B was nominally the sole proprietor. The position of fundholders, or owners of the public debt of a country, is similar. They are mortgagees on the general wealth of the country.

The cancelling of the debt would be no destruction of wealth, but a transfer of it: a wrongful abstraction of wealth from certain members of the community, for the profit of the government, or of the tax-payers. Funded property therefore cannot be counted as part of the national wealth. This is not always borne in mind by the dealers in statistical calculations. For example, in estimates of the gross income of the country, founded on the proceeds of the income-tax, incomes derived from the funds are not always excluded: though the tax-payers are assessed on their whole nominal income, without being permitted to deduct from it the portion levied from them in taxation to form the income of the fundholder. In this calculation, therefore, one portion of the general income of the country is counted twice over, and the aggregate amount made to appear greater than it is by almost1 thirty millions. A country, however, may include in its wealth all stock held by its citizens in the funds of foreign countries, and other debts due to them from abroad. But even this is only wealth to them by being a part ownership in wealth held by others. It forms no part of the collective wealth of the human race. It is an element in the distribution, but not in the composition, of the general wealth.

Another example of a possession which is wealth to the person holding it, but not wealth to the nation, or to mankind, is slaves. It is by a strange confusion of ideas that slave property (as it is termed) is counted, at so much per head, in an estimate of the wealth, or of the capital, of the country which tolerates the existence of such property. If a human being, considered as an object possessing productive powers, is part of the national wealth when his powers are owned by another man, he cannot be less a part of it when they are owned by himself. Whatever he is worth to his master is so much property abstracted from himself, and its abstraction cannot augment the possessions of the two together, or of the country to which they both belong.

In propriety of classification, however, the people of a country are not to be counted in its wealth. They are that for the sake of which its wealth exists. The term wealth is wanted to denote the desirable objects which they possess, not inclusive of, but in contradistinction to, their own persons. They are not wealth to themselves, though they are means of acquiring it.

It has been proposed to define wealth as signifying "instruments:" meaning not tools and machinery alone, but the whole accumulation possessed by individuals or communities, of means for the attainment of their ends. Thus, a field is an instrument, because it is a means to the attainment of corn. Corn is an instrument, being a means to the attainment of flour.

Flour is an instrument, being a means to the attainment of bread. Bread is an instrument, as a means to the satisfaction of hunger and to the support of life. Here we at last arrive at things which are not instruments, being desired on their own account, and not as mere means to something beyond. This view of the subject is philosophically correct; or rather, this mode of expression may be usefully employed along with others, not as conveying a different view of the subject from the common one, but as giving more distinctness and reality to the common view. It departs, however, too widely from the custom of language, to be likely to obtain general acceptance, or to be of use for any other purpose than that of occasional illustration.

Wealth, then, may be defined, all useful or agreeable things which possess exchangeable value; or, in other words, all useful or agreeable things except those which can be obtained, in the quantity desired, without labour or sacrifice.

To this definition, the only objection seems to be, that it leaves in uncertainty a question which has been much debated—whether what are called immaterial products are to be considered as wealth: whether, for example, the skill of a workman, or any other natural or acquired power of body or mind, shall be called wealth, or not: a question, not of very great importance, and which, so far as requiring discussion, will be more conveniently considered in another place.

These things having been premised respecting wealth, we shall next turn our attention to the extraordinary differences in respect to it, which exist between nation and nation, and between different ages of the world; differences both in the quantity of wealth, and in the kind of it; as well as in the manner in which the wealth existing in the community is shared among its members.

There is perhaps, no people or community, now existing, which subsists entirely on the spontaneous produce of vegetation. But many tribes still live exclusively, or almost exclusively, on wild animals, the produce of hunting or fishing. Their clothing is skins; their habitations, huts rudely formed of logs or boughs of trees, and abandoned at an hour's notice. The food they use being little susceptible of storing up, they have no accumulation of it, and are often exposed to great privations.

The wealth of such a community consists solely of the skins they wear; a few ornaments, the taste for which exists among most savages; some rude utensils; the weapons with which they kill their game, or fight against hostile competitors for the means of subsistence; canoes for crossing rivers and lakes, or fishing in the sea; and perhaps some furs or other productions of the wilderness, collected to be exchanged with civilized people for blankets, brandy, and tobacco; of which foreign produce also there may be some unconsumed portion in store. To this scanty inventory of material wealth, ought to be added their land; an instrument of production of which they make slender use, compared with more settled communities, but which is still the source of their subsistence, and which has a marketable value if there be any agricultural community in the neighbourhood requiring more land than it possesses. This is the state of greatest poverty in which any entire community of human beings is known to exist; though there are much richer communities in which portions of the inhabitants are in a condition, as to subsistence and comfort, as little enviable as that of the savage.

The first great advance beyond this state consists in the domestication of the more useful animals; giving rise to the pastoral or nomad state, in which mankind do not live on the produce of hunting, but on milk and its products, and on the annual increase of flocks and herds. This condition is not only more desirable in itself, but more conducive to further progress: and a much more considerable amount of wealth is accumulated under it. So long as the vast natural pastures of the earth are not yet so fully occupied as to be consumed more rapidly than they are spontaneously reproduced, a large and constantly increasing stock of subsistence may be collected and preserved, with little other labour than that of guarding the cattle from the attacks of wild beasts, and from the force or wiles of predatory men. Large flocks and herds, therefore, are in time possessed, by active and thrifty individuals through their own exertions, and by the heads of families and tribes through the exertions of those who are connected with them by allegiance.

There thus arises, in the shepherd state, inequality of possessions; a thing which scarcely exists in the savage state, where no one has much more than absolute necessaries, and in case of deficiency must share even those with his tribe. In the nomad state, some have an abundance of cattle, sufficient for the food of a multitude, while others have not contrived to appropriate and retain any superfluity, or perhaps any cattle at all. But subsistence has ceased to be precarious, since the more successful have no other use which they can make of their surplus than to feed the less fortunate, while every increase in the number of persons connected with them is an increase both of security and of power: and thus they are enabled to divest themselves of all labour except that of government and superintendence, and acquire dependents to fight for them in war and to serve them in peace.

One of the features of this state of society is, that a part of the community, and in some degree even the whole of it, possess leisure. Only a portion of time is required for procuring food, and the remainder is not engrossed by anxious thought for the morrow, or necessary repose from muscular activity. Such a life is highly favourable to the growth of new wants, and opens a possibility of their gratification. A desire arises for better clothing, utensils, and implements, than the savage state contents itself with; and the surplus food renders it practicable to devote to these purposes the exertions of a part of the tribe. In all or most nomad communities we find domestic manufactures of a coarse, and in some, of a fine kind. There is ample evidence that while those parts of the world which have been the cradle of modern civilization were still generally in the nomad state, considerable skill had been attained in spinning, weaving, and dyeing woollen garments, in the preparation of leather, and in what appears a still more difficult invention, that of working in metals. Even speculative science took its first beginnings from the leisure characteristic of this stage of social progress. The earliest astronomical observations are attributed, by a tradition which has much appearance of truth, to the shepherds of Chaldea.

From this state of society to the agricultural the transition is not indeed easy (for no great change in the habits of mankind is otherwise than difficult, and in general either painful or very slow), but it lies in what may be called the spontaneous course of events. The growth of the population of men and cattle began in time to press upon the earth's capabilities of yielding natural pasture:

and this cause doubtless produced the first tilling of the ground, just as at a later period the same cause made the superfluous hordes of the nations which had remained nomad precipitate themselves upon those which had already become agricultural; until, these having become sufficiently powerful to repel such inroads, the invading nations, deprived of this outlet, were obliged also to become agricultural communities.

But after this great step had been completed, the subsequent progress of mankind seems by no means to have been so rapid (certain rare combinations of circumstances excepted) as might perhaps have been anticipated. The quantity of human food which the earth is capable of returning even to the most wretched system of agriculture, so much exceeds what could be obtained in the purely pastoral state, that a great increase of population is invariably the result. But this additional food is only obtained by a great additional amount of labour; so that not only an agricultural has much less leisure than a pastoral population, but, with the imperfect tools and unskilful processes which are for a long time employed (and which over the greater part of the earth have not even yet been abandoned), agriculturists do not, unless in unusually advantageous circumstances of climate and soil, produce so great a surplus of food, beyond their necessary consumption, as to support any large class of labourers engaged in other departments of industry. The surplus, too, whether small or great, is usually torn from the producers, either by the government to which they are subject, or by individuals, who by superior force, or by availing themselves of religious or traditional feelings of subordination, have established themselves as lords of the soil.

The first of these modes of appropriation, by the government, is characteristic of the extensive monarchies which from a time beyond historical record have occupied the plains of Asia. The government, in those countries, though varying in its qualities according to the accidents of personal character, seldom leaves much to the cultivators beyond mere necessaries, and often strips them so bare even of these, that it finds itself obliged, after taking all they have, to lend part of it back to those from whom it has been taken, in order to provide them with seed, and enable them to support life until another harvest. Under the régime in question, though the bulk of the population are ill provided for, the government, by collecting small contributions from great numbers, is enabled, with any tolerable management, to make a show of riches quite out of proportion to the general condition of the society; and hence the inveterate impression, of which Europeans have only at a late period been disabused, concerning the great opulence of Oriental nations.

In this wealth, without reckoning the large portion which adheres to the hands employed in collecting it, many persons of course participate, besides the immediate household of the sovereign. A large part is distributed among the various functionaries of government, and among the objects of the sovereign's favour or caprice. A part is occasionally employed in works of public utility. The tanks, wells, and canals for irrigation, without which in many tropical climates cultivation could hardly be carried on; the embankments which confine the rivers, the bazars for dealers, and the seraees for travellers, none of which could have been made by the scanty means in the possession of those using them, owe their existence to the liberality and enlightened self-interest of the better order of princes, or to the benevolence or ostentation of here and there a rich individual, whose fortune, if traced to its source, is always found to have been drawn immediately or remotely from the public revenue, most frequently by a direct grant of a portion of it from the sovereign.

The ruler of a society of this description, after providing largely for his own support, and that of all persons in whom he feels an interest, and after maintaining as many soldiers as he thinks needful for his security or his state, has a disposable residue, which he is glad to exchange for articles of luxury suitable to his disposition: as have also the class of persons who have been enriched by his favour, or by handling the public revenues. A demand thus arises for elaborate and costly manufactured articles, adapted to a narrow but a wealthy market. This demand is often supplied almost exclusively by the merchants of more advanced communities, but often also raises up in the country itself a class of artificers, by whom certain fabrics are carried to as high excellence as can be given by patience, quickness of perception and observation, and manual dexterity, without any considerable knowledge of the properties of objects: such as some of the cotton fabrics of India.

These artificers are fed by the surplus food which has been taken by the government and its agents as their share of the produce. So literally is this the case, that in some countries the workman, instead of taking his work home, and being paid for it after it is finished, proceeds with his tools to his customer's house, and is there subsisted until the work is complete. The insecurity, however, of all possessions in this state of society, induces even the richest purchasers to give a preference to such articles as, being of an imperishable nature, and containing great value in small bulk, are adapted for being concealed or carried off. Gold and jewels, therefore, constitute a large proportion of the wealth of these nations, and many a rich Asiatic carries nearly his whole fortune on his person, or on those of the women of his harem.

No one, except the monarch, thinks of investing his wealth in a manner not susceptible of removal. He, indeed, if he feels safe on his throne, and reasonably secure of transmitting it to his descendants, sometimes indulges a taste for durable edifices, and produces the Pyramids, or the Taj Mehal and the Mausoleum at Sekundra. The rude manufactures destined for the wants of the cultivators are worked up by village artisans, who are remunerated by land given to them rent-free to cultivate, or by fees paid to them in kind from such share of the crop as is left to the villagers by the government. This state of society, however, is not destitute of a mercantile class; composed of two divisions, grain dealers and money dealers. The grain dealers do not usually buy grain from the producers, but from the agents of government, who, receiving the revenue in kind, are glad to devolve upon others the business of conveying it to the places where the prince, his chief civil and military officers, the bulk of his troops, and the artisans who supply the wants of these various persons, are assembled.

The money dealers lend to the unfortunate cultivators, when ruined by bad seasons or fiscal exactions, the means of supporting life and continuing their cultivation, and are repaid with enormous interest at the next harvest; or, on a larger scale, they lend to the government, or to those to whom it has granted a portion of the revenue, and are indemnified by assignments on the revenue collectors, or by having certain districts put into their possession, that they may pay themselves from the revenues; to enable them to do which, a great portion of the powers of government are usually made over simultaneously, to be exercised by them until either the districts are redeemed, or their receipts have liquidated the debt.

Thus, the commercial operations of both these classes of dealers take place principally upon that part of the produce of the country which forms the revenue of the government. From that revenue their capital is periodically replaced with a profit, and that is also the source from which their original funds have almost always been derived. Such, in its general features, is the economical condition of most of the countries of Asia, as it has been from beyond the commencement of authentic history, and is still [1848], wherever not disturbed by foreign influences.

In the agricultural communities of ancient Europe whose early condition is best known to us, the course of things was different. These, at their origin, were mostly small town-communities, at the first plantation of which, in an unoccupied country, or in one from which the former inhabitants had been expelled, the land which was taken possession of was regularly divided, in equal or in graduated allotments, among the families composing the community. In some cases, instead of a town there was a confederation of towns, occupied by people of the same reputed race, and who were supposed to have settled in the country about the same time.

Each family produced its own food and the materials of its clothing, which were worked up within itself, usually by the women of the family, into the coarse fabrics with which the age was contented. Taxes there were none, as there were either no paid officers of government, or if there were, their payment had been provided for by a reserved portion of land, cultivated by slaves on account of the state; and the army consisted of the body of citizens. The whole produce of the soil, therefore, belonged, without deduction, to the family which cultivated it. So long as the process of events permitted this disposition of property to last, the state of society was, for the majority of the free cultivators, probably not an undesirable one; and under it, in some cases, the advance of mankind in intellectual culture was extraordinarily rapid and brilliant.

This more especially happened where, along with advantageous circumstances of race and climate, and no doubt with many favourable accidents of which all trace is now lost, was combined the advantage of a position on the shores of a great inland sea, the other coasts of which were already occupied by settled communities. The knowledge which in such a position was acquired of foreign productions, and the easy access of foreign ideas and inventions, made the chain of routine, usually so strong in a rude people, hang loosely on these communities. To speak only of their industrial development; they early acquired variety of wants and desires, which stimulated them to extract from their own soil the utmost which they knew how to make it yield; and when their soil was sterile, or after they had reached the limit of its capacity, they often became traders, and bought up the productions of foreign countries, to sell them in other countries with a profit.

The duration, however, of this state of things was from the first precarious. These little communities lived in a state of almost perpetual war. For this there were many causes. In the ruder and purely agricultural communities a frequent cause was the mere pressure of their increasing population upon their limited land, aggravated as that pressure so often was by deficient harvests, in the rude state of their agriculture, and depending as they did for food upon a very small extent of country. On these occasions, the community often emigrated *en masse*, or sent forth a swarm of its youth, to seek, sword in hand, for some less warlike people, who could be expelled from their land, or detained to cultivate it as slaves for the benefit of their despoilers.

What the less advanced tribes did from necessity, the more prosperous did from ambition and the military spirit: and after a time the whole of these city-communities were either conquerors or conquered. In some cases, the conquering state contented itself with imposing a tribute on the vanquished: who being, in consideration of that burden, freed from the expense and trouble of their own military and naval protection, might enjoy under it a considerable share of economical prosperity, while the ascendant community obtained a surplus of wealth, available for purposes of collective luxury or magnificence. From such a surplus the Parthenon and the Propylaea were built, the sculptures of Pheidias paid for, and the festivals celebrated, for which AEschylus, Sophocles, Euripides, and Aristophanes composed their dramas. But this state of political relations, most useful, while it lasted, to the progress and ultimate interest of mankind, had not the elements of durability.

A small conquering community which does not incorporate its conquests, always ends by being conquered. Universal dominion, therefore, at last rested with the people who practised this art—with the Romans; who, whatever were their other devices, always either began or ended by taking a great part of the land to enrich their own leading citizens, and by adopting into the governing body the principal possessors of the remainder. It is unnecessary to dwell on the melancholy economical history of the Roman empire. When inequality of wealth once commences, in a community not constantly engaged in repairing by industry the injuries of fortune, its advances are gigantic; the great masses of wealth swallow up the smaller.

The Roman empire ultimately became covered with the vast landed possessions of a comparatively few families, for whose luxury, and still more for whose ostentation, the most costly products were raised, while the cultivators of the soil were slaves, or small tenants in nearly servile condition. From this time the wealth of the empire progressively declined. In the beginning, the public revenues, and the resources of rich individuals, sufficed at least to cover Italy with splendid edifices, public and private; but at length so dwindled under the enervating influences of misgovernment, that what remained was not even sufficient to keep those edifices from decay. The strength and riches of the civilized world became inadequate to make head against the nomad population which skirted its northern frontier; they overran the empire, and a different order of things succeeded.

In the new frame in which European society was now cast, the population of each country may be considered as composed, in unequal proportions, of two distinct nations or races, the conquerors and the conquered: the first the proprietors of the land, the latter the tillers of it. These tillers were allowed to occupy the land on conditions which, being the product of force, were always onerous, but seldom to the extent of absolute slavery. Already, in the later times of the Roman empire, predial slavery had extensively transformed itself into a kind of serfdom: the *coloni* of the Romans were rather villeins than actual slaves; and the incapacity and distaste of the barbarian conquerors for personally superintending industrial occupations, left no alternative but to allow to the cultivators, as an incentive to exertion, some real interest in the soil. If, for example, they were compelled to labour, three days in the week, for their superior, the produce of the remaining days was their own.

If they were required to supply the provisions of various sorts, ordinarily needed for the consumption of the castle, and were often subject to requisitions in excess, yet after supplying these demands they were suffered to dispose at their will of whatever additional produce they could raise. Under this system during the Middle Ages it was not impossible, no more than in modern Russia (where, up to the recent measure of emancipation, the same system still essentially prevailed),1 for serfs to acquire property; and in fact, their accumulations are the primitive source of the wealth of modern Europe.

In that age of violence and disorder, the first use made by a serf of any small provision which he had been able to accumulate, was to buy his freedom and withdraw himself to some town or fortified village, which had remained undestroyed from the time of the Roman dominion; or, without buying his freedom, to abscond thither. In that place of refuge, surrounded by others of his own class, he attempted to live, secured in some measure from the outrages and exactions of the warrior caste, by his own prowess and that of his fellows. These emancipated serfs mostly became artificers; and lived by exchanging the produce of their industry for the surplus food and material which the soil yielded to its feudal proprietors.

This gave rise to a sort of European counterpart of the economical condition of Asiatic countries; except that, in lieu of a single monarch and a fluctuating body of favourites and employés, there was a numerous and in a considerable degree fixed class of great landholders; exhibiting far less splendour, because individually disposing of a much smaller surplus produce, and for a long time expending the chief part of it in maintaining the body of retainers whom the warlike habits of society, and the little protection afforded by government, rendered indispensable to their safety.

The greater stability, the fixity of personal position, which this state of society afforded, in comparison with the Asiatic polity to which it economically corresponded, was one main reason why it was also found more favourable to improvement. From this time the economical advancement of society has not been further interrupted. Security of person and property grew slowly, but steadily; the arts of life made constant progress; plunder ceased to be the principal source of accumulation; and feudal Europe ripened into commercial and manufacturing Europe. In the latter part of the Middle Ages, the towns of Italy and Flanders, the free cities of Germany, and some towns of France and England, contained a large and energetic population of artisans, and many rich burghers, whose wealth had been acquired by manufacturing industry, or by trading in the produce of such industry.

The Commons of England, the Tiers-Etat of France, the bourgeoisie of the Continent generally, are the descendants of this class. As these were a saving class, while the posterity of the feudal aristocracy were a squandering class, the former by degrees substituted themselves for the latter as the owners of a great proportion of the land.

This natural tendency was in some cases retarded by laws contrived for the purpose of detaining the land in the families of its existing possessors, in other cases accelerated by political revolutions. Gradually, though more slowly, the immediate cultivators of the soil, in all the more civilized countries, ceased to be in a servile or semi-servile state: though the legal position, as well as the economical condition attained by them, vary extremely in the different nations of Europe, and in the great communities which have been founded beyond the Atlantic by the descendants of Europeans. The world now contains several extensive regions, provided with the various ingredients of wealth in a degree of abundance of which former ages had not even the idea. Without compulsory labour, an enormous mass of food is annually extracted from the soil, and maintains, besides the actual producers, an equal, sometimes a greater number of labourers, occupied in producing conveniences and luxuries of innumerable kinds, or in transporting them from place to place; also a multitude of persons employed in directing and superintending these various labours; and over and above all these, a class more numerous than in the most luxurious ancient societies, of persons whose occupations are of a kind not directly productive, and of persons who have no occupation at all.

The food thus raised supports a far larger population than had ever existed (at least in the same regions) on an equal space of ground; and supports them with certainty, exempt from those periodically recurring famines so abundant in the early history of Europe, and in Oriental countries even now not unfrequent. Besides this great increase in the quantity of food, it has greatly improved in quality and variety; while conveniences and luxuries, other than food, are no longer limited to a small and opulent class, but descend, in great abundance, through many widening strata in society. The collective resources of one of these communities, when it chooses to put them forth for any unexpected purpose; its ability to maintain fleets and armies, to execute public works, either useful or ornamental, to perform national acts of beneficence like the ransom of the West India slaves; to found colonies, to have its people taught, to do anything in short which requires expense, and to do it with no sacrifice of the necessaries or even the substantial comforts of its inhabitants, are such as the world never saw before.

But in all these particulars, characteristic of the modern industrial communities, those communities differ widely from one another. Though abounding in wealth as compared with former ages, they do so in very different degrees. Even of the countries which are justly accounted the richest, some have made a more complete use of their productive resources, and have obtained, relatively to their territorial extent, a much larger produce, than others; nor do they differ only in amount of wealth, but also in the rapidity of its increase. The diversities in the distribution of wealth are still greater than in the production.

There are great differences in the condition of the poorest class in different countries; and in the proportional numbers and opulence of the classes which are above the poorest. The very nature and designation of the classes who originally share among them the produce of the soil, vary not a little in different places. In some, the landowners are a class in themselves, almost entirely separate from the classes engaged in industry. in others, the proprietor of the land is almost universally its cultivator, owning the plough, and often himself holding it. Where the proprietor himself does not cultivate, there is sometimes, between him and the labourer, an intermediate agency, that of the farmer, who advances the subsistence of the labourers, supplies the instruments of production, and receives, after paying a rent to the landowner, all the produce: in other cases, the landlord, his paid agents, and the labourers, are the only sharers. Manufactures, again, are sometimes carried on by scattered individuals, who own or hire the tools or machinery they require, and employ little labour besides that of their own family; in other cases, by large numbers working together in one building, with expensive and complex machinery owned by rich manufacturers. The same difference exists in the operations of trade. The wholesale operations indeed are everywhere carried on by large capitals, where such exist; but the retail dealings, which collectively occupy a very great amount of capital, are sometimes conducted in small shops, chiefly by the personal exertions of the dealers themselves, with their families, and perhaps an apprentice or two; and sometimes in large establishments, of which the funds are supplied by a wealthy individual or association, and the agency is that of numerous salaried shopmen or shopwomen.

Besides these differences in the economical phenomena presented by different parts of what is usually called the civilized world, all those earlier states which we previously passed in review, have continued in some part or other of the world, down to our own time. Hunting communities still exist in America, nomadic in Arabia and the steppes of Northern Asia; Oriental society is in essentials what it has always been; the great empire of Russia is[1] even now, in many respects, the scarcely modified image of feudal Europe. Every one of the great types of human society, down to that of the Esquimaux or Patagonians, is still extant.[2]

These remarkable differences in the state of different portions of the human race, with regard to the production and distribution of wealth, must, like all other phenomena, depend on causes. And it is not a sufficient explanation to ascribe them exclusively to the degrees of knowledge possessed at different times and places, of the laws of nature and the physical arts of life. Many other causes co-operate; and that very progress and unequal distribution of physical knowledge are partly the effects, as well as partly the causes, of the state of the production and distribution of wealth.

In so far as the economical condition of nations turns upon the state of physical knowledge, it is a subject for the physical sciences, and the arts founded on them. But in so far as the causes are moral or psychological, dependent on institutions and social relations, or on the principles of human nature, their investigation belongs not to physical, but to moral and social science, and is the object of what is called Political Economy.

The production of wealth; the extraction of the instruments of human subsistence and enjoyment from the materials of the globe, is evidently not an arbitrary thing. It has its necessary conditions. Of these, some are physical, depending on the properties of matter, and on the amount of knowledge of those properties possessed at the particular place and time. These Political Economy does not investigate, but assumes; referring for the grounds, to physical science or common experience. Combining with these facts of outward nature other truths relating to human nature, it attempts to trace the secondary or derivative laws, by which the production of wealth is determined; in which must lie the explanation of the diversities of riches and poverty in the present and past, and the ground of whatever increase in wealth is reserved for the future.

Unlike the laws of Production, those of Distribution are partly of human institution: since the manner in which wealth is distributed in any given society, depends on the statutes or usages therein obtaining. But though governments or nations have the power of deciding what institutions shall exist, they cannot arbitrarily determine how those institutions shall work. The conditions on which the power they possess over the distribution of wealth is dependent, and the manner in which the distribution is effected by the various modes of conduct which society may think fit to adopt, are as much a subject for scientific enquiry as any of the physical laws of nature.

CONSEQUENCES OF THE TENDENCY OF PROFITS TO A MINIMUM

The theory of the effect of accumulation on profits, laid down in the preceding chapter, materially alters many of the practical conclusions which might otherwise be supposed to follow from the general principles of Political Economy, and which were, indeed, long admitted as true by the highest authorities on the subject.

It must greatly abate, or rather, altogether destroy, in countries where profits are low, the immense importance which used to be attached by political economists to the effects which an event or a measure of government might have in adding to or subtracting from the capital of the country. We have now seen that the lowness of profits is a proof that the spirit of accumulation is so active, and that the increase of capital has proceeded at so rapid a rate, as to outstrip the two counter-agencies, improvements in production, and increased supply of cheap necessaries from abroad: and that unless a considerable portion of the annual increase of capital were either periodically destroyed, or exported for foreign investment, the country would speedily attain the point at which further accumulation would cease, or at least spontaneously slacken, so as no longer to overpass the march of invention in the arts which produce the necessaries of life.

In such a state of things as this, a sudden addition to the capital of the country, unaccompanied by any increase of productive power, would be but of transitory duration; since by depressing profits and interest, it would either diminish by a corresponding amount the savings which would be made from income in the year or two following, or it would cause an equivalent amount to be sent abroad, or to be wasted in rash speculations. Neither, on the other hand, would a sudden abstraction of capital, unless of inordinate amount, have any real effect in impoverishing the country. After a few months or years, there would exist in the country just as much capital as if none had been taken away. The abstraction, by raising profits and interest, would give a fresh stimulus to the accumulative principle, which would speedily fill up the vacuum. Probably, indeed, the only effect that would ensue, would be that for some time afterwards less capital would be exported, and less thrown away in hazardous speculation.

In the first place, then, this view of things greatly weakens, in a wealthy and industrious country, the force of the economical argument against the expenditure of public money for really valuable, even though industriously unproductive, purposes. If for any great object of justice or philanthropic policy, such as the industrial regeneration of Ireland, or a comprehensive measure of colonization or of public education, it were proposed to raise a large sum by way of loan, politicians need not demur to the abstraction of so much capital, as tending to dry up the permanent sources of the country's wealth, and diminish the fund which supplies the subsistence of the labouring population.

The utmost expense which could be requisite for any of these purposes, would not in all probability deprive one labourer of employment, or diminish the next year's production by one ell of cloth or one bushel of grain. In poor countries, the capital of the country requires the legislator's sedulous care; he is bound to be most cautious of encroaching upon it, and should favour to the utmost its accumulation at home, and its introduction from abroad. But in rich, populous, and highly cultivated countries, it is not capital which is the deficient element, but fertile land; and what the legislator should desire and promote, is not a greater aggregate saving, but a greater return to savings, either by improved cultivation, or by access to the produce of more fertile lands in other parts of the globe.

In such countries, the government may take any moderate portion of the capital of the country and expend it as revenue, without affecting the national wealth: the whole being either drawn from that portion of the annual savings which would otherwise be sent abroad, or being subtracted from the unproductive expenditure of individuals for the next year or two, since every million spent makes room for another million to be saved before reaching the overflowing point. When the object in view is worth the sacrifice of such an amount of the expenditure that furnishes the daily enjoyments of the people, the only well-grounded economical objection against taking the necessary funds directly from capital, consists of the inconveniences attending the process of raising a revenue by taxation, to pay the interest of a debt.

The same considerations enable us to throw aside as unworthy of regard, one of the common arguments against emigration as a means of relief for the labouring class. Emigration, it is said, can do no good to the labourers, if, in order to defray the cost, as much must be taken away from the capital of the country as from its population. That anything like this proportion could require to be abstracted from capital for the purpose even of the most extensive colonization, few, I should think, would now assert: but even on that untenable supposition, it is an error to suppose that no benefit would be conferred on the labouring class.

If one-tenth of the labouring people of England were transferred to the colonies, and along with them one-tenth of the circulating capital of the country, either wages, or profits, or both, would be greatly benefited, by the diminished pressure of capital and population upon the fertility of the land. There would be a reduced demand for food: the inferior arable lands would be thrown out of cultivation, and would become pasture; the superior would be cultivated less highly, but with a greater proportional return; food would be lowered in price, and though money wages would not rise, every labourer would be considerably improved in circumstances, an improvement which, if no increased stimulus to population and fall of wages ensued, would be permanent; while if there did, profits would rise, and accumulation start forward so as to repair the loss of capital. The landlords alone would sustain some loss of income; and even they, only if colonization went to the length of actually diminishing capital and population, but not if it merely carried off the annual increase.

From the same principles we are now able to arrive at a final conclusion respecting the effects which machinery, and generally the sinking of capital for a productive purpose, produce upon the immediate and ultimate interests of the labouring class. The characteristic property of this class of industrial improvements is the conversion of circulating capital into fixed: and it was shown in the first Book, that in a country where capital accumulates slowly, the introduction of machinery, permanent improvements of land, and the like, might be, for the time, extremely injurious; since the capital so employed might be directly taken from the wages fund, the subsistence of the people and the employment for labour curtailed, and the gross annual produce of the country actually diminished.

But in a country of great annual savings and low profits, no such effects need be apprehended. Since even the emigration of capital, or its unproductive expenditure, or its absolute waste, do not in such a country, if confined within any moderate bounds, at all diminish the aggregate amount of the wages fund — still less can the mere conversion of a like sum into fixed capital, which continues to be productive, have that effect. It merely draws off at one orifice what was already flowing out at another; or if not, the greater vacant space left in the reservoir does but cause a greater quantity to flow in. Accordingly, in spite of the mischievous derangements of the money-market which were at one time occasioned by the sinking of great sums in railways, I was never able to agree with those who apprehended mischief, from this source, to the productive resources of the country. Not on the absurd ground (which to any one acquainted with the elements of the subject needs no confutation) that railway expenditure is a mere transfer of capital from hand to hand, by which nothing is lost or destroyed.

This is true of what is spent in the purchase of the land; a portion too of what is paid to parliamentary agents, counsel, engineers, and surveyors, is saved by those who receive it, and becomes capital again: but what is laid out in the bona fide construction of the railway itself, is lost and gone; when once expended, it is incapable of ever being paid in wages or applied to the maintenance of labourers again; as a matter of account, the result is that so much food and clothing and tools have been consumed, and the country has got a railway instead. But what I would urge is, that sums so applied are mostly a mere appropriation of the annual overflowing which would otherwise have gone abroad, or been thrown away unprofitably, leaving neither a railway nor any other tangible result.

The railway gambling of 1844 and 1845 probably saved the country from a depression of profits and interest, and a rise of all public and private securities, which would have engendered still wilder speculations, and when the effects came afterwards to be complicated by the scarcity of food, would have ended in a still more formidable crisis than was experienced in the years immediately following.

In the poorer countries of Europe, the rage for railway construction might have had worse consequences than in England, were it not that in those countries such enterprises are in a great measure carried on by foreign capital. The railway operations of the various nations of the world may be looked upon as a sort of competition for the overflowing capital of the countries where profit is low and capital abundant, as England and Holland. The English railway speculations are a struggle to keep our annual increase of capital at home; those of foreign countries are an effort to obtain it.

It already appears from these considerations, that the conversion of circulating capital into fixed, whether by railways, or manufactories, or ships, or machinery, or canals, or mines, or works of drainage and irrigation, is not likely, in any rich country, to diminish the gross produce or the amount of employment for labour.

How much then is the case strengthened, when we consider that these transformations of capital are of the nature of improvements in production, which, instead of ultimately diminishing circulating capital, are the necessary conditions of its increase, since they alone enable a country to possess a constantly augmenting capital without reducing profits to the rate which would cause accumulation to stop. There is hardly any increase of fixed capital which does not enable the country to contain eventually a larger circulating capital, than it otherwise could possess and employ within its own limits; for there is hardly any creation of fixed capital which, when it proves successful, does not cheapen the articles on which wages are habitually expended. All capital sunk in the permanent improvement of land, lessens the cost of food and materials; almost all improvements in machinery cheapen the labourer's clothing or lodging, or the tools with which these are made; improvements in locomotion, such as railways, cheapen to the consumer all things which are brought from a distance.

All these improvements make the labourers better off with the same money wages, better off if they do not increase their rate of multiplication. But if they do, and wages consequently fall, at least profits rise, and, while accumulation receives an immediate stimulus, room is made for a greater amount of capital before a sufficient motive arises for sending it abroad. Even the improvements which do not cheapen the things consumed by the labourer, and which, therefore, do not raise profits nor retain capital in the country, nevertheless, as we have seen, by lowering the minimum of profit for which people will ultimately consent to save, leave an ampler margin than previously for eventual accumulation, before arriving at the stationary state.

We may conclude, then, that improvements in production, and emigration of capital to the more fertile soils and unworked mines of the uninhabited or thinly peopled parts of the globe, do not, as appears to a superficial view, diminish the gross produce and the demand for labour at home; but, on the contrary, are what we have chiefly to depend on for increasing both, and are even the necessary conditions of any great or prolonged augmentation of either. Nor is it any exaggeration to say, that within certain, and not very narrow, limits, the more capital a country like England expends in these two ways, the more she will have left.

POLITICAL ECONOMY AS SCIENCE AND ART

There is found among economic writers much dispute not only as to the proper method of political economy, but also as to whether it should be spoken of as a science or as an art. There are some who have styled it a science, and some who speak of it as both science and art. Others again make substantially the same division, into abstract or theoretical or speculative political economy, upon the one side, and concrete, normative or applied political economy, on the other side.

Into this matter, however, it is hardly worthwhile for us to enter at any length, since the reasons for considering a proper political economy as a science rather than an art have been already given. It is only necessary to observe that where systematized knowledge may be distinguished, as it sometimes is, into two branches, science and art, the proper distinction between them is that one relates to what we call laws of nature; the other to the manner in which we may avail ourselves of these natural laws to attain desired ends. There may be disputes as to whether there is yet a science of political economy, that is to say, whether our knowledge of the natural economic laws is as yet so large and well digested as to merit the title of science. But among those who recognize that the world we live in is in all its spheres governed by law, there can be no dispute as to the possibility of such a science.

When we have worked out the science of political economy — when we shall have discovered and related the natural laws which govern the production and distribution of wealth, we shall then be in a position to see the effect of human laws and customs. But it does not seem to me that such knowledge can be properly spoken of as an art of political economy. There is a science of astronomy, which has its applications in such arts as those of navigation and surveying; but no art of astronomy; and there is a science of chemistry, which has its applications in many arts; but no art of chemistry. And so the science of political economy finds its applications in politics and its various subdivisions. But these applications can hardly be spoken of as constituting an art of political economy.

Yet if we choose, as some have done, to speak of political economy as both science and art, then the art of political economy is the art of securing the greatest production and the fairest distribution of wealth; the art whose proper object is to abolish poverty and the fear of poverty, and so lift the poorest and weakest of mankind above the hard struggle to live. For if there be an art of political economy, it must be the noble art that has for its object the benefit of all members of the economic community.

But just as when men believed in magic they held that there was both white magic and black magic — an art which aimed at alleviating suffering and doing good, and an art which sought knowledge for selfish and evil ends — so, in this view, it may be said that there is a white political economy and a black political economy.

Where a knowledge of the laws of the production and distribution of wealth is used to enrich a few at the expense of the many, or even when a reputed knowledge of those laws is used to bolster up such injustice, and by darkening counsel to prevent or delay the reform of it, such art of political economy, real or reputed, is truly a black art. This is the art of which the great Turgot spoke.

For our part, having seen the nature and scope of the science of political economy, for which we adopt the older definition — the science that investigates the nature of wealth and the laws of its production and distribution — let us proceed in this order, endeavoring to discover: 1) the nature of wealth; 2) the laws of its production; and then 3) the laws of its distribution. When this is done we shall have accomplished all that is necessary for a true science of political economy as I understand it.

DEVELOPMENT OF THE SCHOLASTIC POLITICAL ECONOMY

When the first few copies of my *Progress and Poverty* were printed in an author's edition in San Francisco, a large landowner (the late Gen. Beale, proprietor of the Tejon Ranch, and afterwards the United States Minister to Austria), sought me to express the pleasure with which he had read it as an intellectual performance. This, he said, he had felt at liberty to enjoy, for to speak with the freedom of philosophic frankness, he was certain my work would never be heard of by those whom I wished it to affect.

In the same way, but to much greater degree, the small class whom alone the *Wealth of Nations* could first reach were able to enjoy its greatness as an intellectual performance that widened the circle of thought. Few of them were disturbed by any fear of its ultimate effect on special interests. At that time a popular press was not yet in existence, and books of this kind were addressed only to the "superior orders." The House of Commons, the nominal representative of the unprivileged in Great Britain, was filled by the appointees of the great landowners; and the oligarchy that ruled in the British Islands was really stronger than the similar class under the absolute monarchy of France.

Adam Smith had avoided arousing antagonism from the land interests. And in turning the aggressive side of the new science against the protective system, he found favor with, rather than excited prejudice among, the cultured class — the only class to which such a book as his could at that time be addressed. Such a class, under the conditions then existing in Great Britain, is apt to feel a contempt tinged with anger for traders beginning to aspire towards sharing the power and place of "Born masters of the soil."

The larger fact is that Adam Smith, opening the study of political economy at a lower level than the Physiocrats, found less resistance, and his book began to secure so permanent a recognition for the new science that its continuance to our time is properly traced to him as its founder rather than to them.

In 1798, eight years after the author of the *Wealth of Nations,* lamenting with his last breath that he had done so little, was laid to rest in the Edinburgh Cannongate, the English clergyman Malthus brought forward his famous theory of population. This at once, like "a long-felt want," took its place in the crystallizing system of political economy which Smith had brought into shape, and which, if it was lacking in a clear and consistent definition of wealth, was not on that account objectionable to the spirit of the learned institutions. A few years after Malthus came Ricardo, to correct mistakes into which Smith had fallen as to the nature and cause of rent, and to formulate the true law of rent; but to do this by laying stress on the fact that rent would increase as the necessities of increasing population forced cultivation to less and less productive land, or to lessen less productive points on the same land.

When Adam Smith, as though fearful of the radical conclusions to which it must lead, abandoned his true perception that "the produce of labor constitutes the natural recompense or wages of labor," he fell into a theory of wages which considered the master as providing from his capital the wages of his workman. This, together with the theory of the tendency of population to increase faster than subsistence, and the apprehension of the theory of rent as resulting from the forcing of exertion to less and less productive land, became cardinal doctrine. These, linking with and buttressing each other, in what soon became the accepted system of political economy as developed from the *Wealth of Nations,* did away effectually with any fear that the study of natural laws of the production and distribution of wealth might be dangerous to the great House of Have.

In textbooks and teachings from which Adam Smith's recurring perceptions of the natural equality of men were eliminated, it became indeed "the dismal science." It was held by its admirers that it needed only to be sufficiently taught them to convince even the "lower orders," that things as they are are things as they ought to be, except perhaps that "the monopolizing spirit of merchants and manufacturers," and "the sneaking arts of underling tradesmen" should no longer be permitted to be erected into maxims for governmental interferences with trade.

Thus as the system of political economy presented by Adam Smith began to attract the attention of the thoughtful and cultured, it did not meet the resistance it would have encountered had the special interests which it threatened really been those of the growing class of merchants and manufacturers. On the other hand, the apparent turning of its aggressive side against merchants and manufacturers prevented the powerful landed interest from perceiving fully its relation to their own monopoly until it had gained the weight of recognized philosophic authority.

The repeal of the English corn-laws passed in Great Britain for a victory of free trade as far as it was practicable to carry free trade. And in scholastic circles in that country and in the United States, and throughout the civilized world that took its intellectual impulse from England, it greatly increased the hopefulness of the professed economists.

Thus strengthened by this powerful impulse, there continued to grow up under the sanction and development of a series of able and authoritatively placed men, whose efforts were devoted to smoothing away difficulties and covering up incongruities, an accredited system of political economy which found its most widely accepted expounder in John Stuart Mill, and reached perhaps its highest point of authority in scholastic circles about or shortly after the centennial of the publication of the *Wealth of Nations*. Yet it was as wanting in coherence as the image that Nebuchadnezzar saw in his dream. It contained much real truth well worked out. But this was conjoined with fallacies which could not stand examination. The attempt to define its object-noun, wealth, and the sub-term of wealth, capital, made them much more indefinite and confused than they had been left by Adam Smith. And it was never attempted to bring together what were given as the laws of the distribution of wealth —

as that would have shown at a glance their want of relation. This political economy had no real hold on common thought, and was regarded even by ordinarily intelligent men as a scholastic or esoteric science. But it was spoken of by its professors with the utmost confidence as an assured science, and their belief in its success was greatly increased.

From the beginning until well past the middle of the nineteenth century the temper of the recognized expounders of the political economy which took shape from Adam Smith's foundation was hopeful and confident. They believed they had hold of a true science, which needed only development to be universally recognized. Thus Colonel Torrens, in the introduction to his *Essay on the Production of Wealth,* says in 1821:

In the progress of the human mind, a period of controversy among the cultivators of any branch of science must necessarily precede the period of unanimity. With respect to political economy, the period of controversy is passing away, and that of unanimity rapidly approaching. Twenty years hence there will scarcely exist a doubt respecting any of its fundamental principles.

With the great defeat of protection in 1846, the confidence of political economists became even greater than before. But the predictions that the example of Great Britain in abolishing protective duties would be quickly followed throughout the civilized world were not realized; and fostered by such tremendous political events as the great fight between the American States and the Franco-German war, the wave of reaction in favor of protection seemed to sweep over pretty nearly all the civilized world.

And while in the scholastic world, of the English-speaking countries at least, the triumph of Adam Smith's opposition to the principles of the mercantile system seemed to have established firmly an accepted science of political economy, and chairs for its teaching formed an indispensable adjunct of every institution of education, the real incoherencies which had been slurred over began more and more to show themselves.

The reason for the constantly increasing confusion of the scholastic political economy has lain in the failure of the so-called science to define its subject-matter or object-noun. Statistics cannot aid us in the search for things until we know what it is we want to find. It is the Tower of Babel over again. Men who attempt to develop a science of the production and distribution of wealth without first deciding what they mean by wealth cannot understand each other or even understand themselves.

3

Character and Logical Method of Political Economy

WHAT POLITICAL ECONOMY

Political Economy, or Economics, is the name of that body of knowledge which relates to wealth.Political Economy has to do with no other subject, whatsoever, than wealth. Especially should the student of economics take care not to allow any purely political, ethical or social considerations to influence him in his investigations. All that he has, as an economist, to do is to find out how wealth is produced, exchanged, distributed and consumed. It will remain for the social philosopher, the moralist, or the statesman, to decide how far the pursuit of wealth, according to the laws discovered by the economist, should be subordinated to other, let us say, higher, considerations. The more strictly the several branches of inquiry are kept apart, the better it will be for each and for all. The economist may also be a social philosopher, a moralist, or a statesman, just as the mathematician may also be a chemist or a mechanician; but not, on that account, should the several subjects be confounded.

POLITICAL ECONOMY DOES NOT INCULCATE LOVE OF WEALTH

Because political economy confines itself to discovering the laws of wealth, it has by some been called, derisively, the Gospel of Mammon. In reply to this sneer it would be enough to say that, while wealth is not the sole interest of mankind, it is yet of vast concern, of vital concern, to individuals and to communities. As such, it deserves to be studied. Now, if it is to be studied at all, it will best be studied by itself. The easiest and surest way to increase our knowledge of any subject is to isolate it, and investigate it, to the strict exclusion, for the time, of all other subjects.

But more may be said. Political Economy does not inculcate love of wealth. It simply inquires how that passion, or propensity, in the degree in which it exists, does, in fact, influence the actions of men. Political Economy has no quarrel with passions or propensities which may, in a greater or less degree, supplant the love of wealth. It does not assume to sit in judgment on human conduct; It exercises no choice among human motives; It simply undertakes to follow causes to their effects in one single department of human activity, *viz.*, the pursuit of wealth.

POLITICAL ECONOMY TEMPERS THE PASSION FOR WEALTH

So far from ministering to greed, it would be easy to prove that the study of Political Economy has tended, by showing how wealth is really best gained and kept, to banish a ravening, ferocious greed which seeks to snatch its objects of desire by brutal violence, at whatever cost of misery to others, and to replace this by an enlightened sense of self-interest, which seeks its objects through exchanges mutually beneficial, and which supports social order and international peace as the conditions of general well-being.

Political Economy does not plant the love of wealth in human minds. It finds it there, a strong, native passion, which, but for enlightened views, is likely to break out into private rapine and public war. A little more than one hundred years ago, before Adam Smith published his great work, "The Wealth of Nations," it was a maxim of public policy, that only one party to trade could profit by a transaction, and that all which one party might gain, the other must lose. Out of this root grew wars and commercial restrictions which set man against man, and nation against nation, making the intercourse of even the most civilized states a game of deceit and violence. Adam Smith left the love of wealth in human minds, not rebuked but enlightened. Little more than a century has elapsed, yet mankind have made greater progress toward humane and mutually advantageous international relations in that time than during all the other centuries of human history.

But What is Wealth?

Economists have found much difficulty in defining Wealth; and not a few writers, especially of late, have chosen to abandon the word altogether.

Several of these have called Political Economy the Science of Exchanges. But the use of this term only removes the essential difficulty of the subject one stage further away. Exchanges of what? All human life, in society, is made up of exchanges, in feeling, word and act. The family relation, the neighborhood, the State, the Church, imply an unceasing exchange of sympathies, activities and incentives, only a portion of which are within the view of the economist.

If we say exchanges of wealth, we have not escaped the difficulty of defining Political Economy, since we have, all the same, to tell what wealth is. If we say exchanges of services, we must further explain what sort of services we mean, since there is an infinitude of services of man to man, in a great variety of relations, with which Political Economy can claim to have nothing to do. The services of parents to children, of children to parents, of children to each other, of friend to friend, do not form any part of the subject matter of Political Economy. If we say economic services, we have still to define the scope of the word economic: that is, we are back again at the point from which we started.

The Term a Popular One

The substitute offered for the term wealth, in describing the field of Political Economy, proving thus defective, let us see what we can do with the word so long in use. Wealth is, as Prof. Price justly observes, "the word which belongs to the world which Political Economy addresses." It would, therefore, be a matter of regret, were it to be abandoned unnecessarily. When the man of business, the laboring man, even the man of leisure, is told that Political Economy is the science of wealth, he at once feels drawn to the subject. No one is above, few are below, an interest in the subject. But the term, science of exchanges, is not especially attractive. A banker, deeming that "foreign exchanges" are meant, may at first think himself concerned; but will discover his misapprehension when he opens the book. The great majority of people will doubt, on hearing the title, whether they care much or any thing about the science of exchanges. Since, then, so great popular interest attaches to the word, wealth, it would be a pity to lose the use of it without good reason.

Yet Subject to Scientific Uses

And we note that the conception of wealth formed by men who are not students of Political Economy, is clear and well-defined. It is only scholars, when they begin to talk and write about wealth, who find any difficulty in the use of the word. Stop a dozen men in succession, and ask them what constitutes wealth, and you will find an almost perfect agreement. "Every one," says Mr. John Stuart Mill, "has a notion sufficiently correct for common purposes of what is meant by wealth. The inquiries which relate to it are in no danger of being confounded with those relating to any other of the great human interests."

Moreover, if we inquire what is the difficulty attributed to the use of the term, we find that it relates, not so much to the definition of wealth, as to the formation of a catalogue of the articles which make up the wealth of an individual or community.

Now, it is not important that such a catalogue should be formed. It would not even be fatal to a definition of wealth that certain objects should be found which seemed to fall across the line of demarkation. All definitions in Political Economy, as, indeed, in the natural sciences, are subject to this condition. Few naturalists will presume to say just where the vegetable kingdom ends and the animal kingdom begins. There are objects in nature concerning which it would puzzle the most learned scholar to say whether they are animal or vegetable. Yet we do not, on that account, hesitate to say that a tree belongs to the vegetable, and an elephant to the animal kingdom.

Relation of Wealth to Value

Wealth comprises all articles of value and nothing else. If any thing have not value, it does not belong to this category. It may conceivably be better than wealth; but it certainly is other than wealth. It may become a means of acquiring wealth; but it is not wealth itself. In the language of Prof. N. W. Senior, "the words wealth and value differ as substance and attribute. All those things, and those only, which constitute wealth, are valuable."

But What is Value?

Value is the power which an article confers upon its possessor, irrespective of legal authority or personal sentiments, of commanding, in exchange for itself, the labor, or the products of the labor, of others. Briefly and somewhat elliptically speaking: Value is power in exchange.

We say: irrespective of legal authority. The Emperor of Germany can, by a word, call two millions of men from their homes and send them to distant fields, even to foreign lands, to work, to watch, to march, to fight and to die. Yet these services are not economic, because not voluntary. On the other hand, the services of a soldier in the British army are economic, as they are rendered under the terms of a voluntary enlistment, the result of a fair and open bargain between the crown and the subject.

We say also: irrespective of personal sentiments. The mother hangs over the sick bed, day and night, draining her very life blood to save her child. Her services are not economic, because dictated by a purely personal sentiment. On the other hand, the work of the hired nurse and of the feed physician comes fairly within the view of the economist.

TRANSFERABILITY ESSENTIAL TO VALUE

We note that exchange implies two exchangers. Value is, then, a social phenomenon. But exchange implies, also, the capability of detaching from the present possessor the articles to be exchanged, and making them over to another.

Do health, strength, intelligence, skill, possess this capability? Are they wealth? Have they value? Not a little of the difficulty which has attended the use, in economics, of the word wealth, has arisen from attributing value to such properties or possessions as these. Prof. Alfred Marshall, in his admirable work, "The Economics of Industry," even includes honesty in the "personal wealth" of a country.

But let us apply the test of our definition. Can these possessions or properties be exchanged? Can health, strength, intelligence, skill, be detached and become the property of another? No; they can be taken away from one, as by sickness or death; but they can not be made over to any one else. The gouty millionaire can not, with all that he has, purchase the robust health of the laborer by the wayside, or buy for his empty-headed son the learning or the trained faculties of the humblest scholar. Hence, all that which some economists have called intellectual capital, and all that which, by analogy, might be called physical capital, are to be excluded from the category of wealth.

BETTER THAN WEALTH, BUT NOT WEALTH

Those possessions or properties have seemed to be things so desirable in themselves, so much to be preferred, in any right view of human welfare, that excellent writers have not been able to bring themselves to leave them out of the field of economics. But Political Economy is the science, not of welfare, but of wealth. There may be many things which are better than wealth, which are yet not to be called wealth. A good name is rather to be chosen than riches, and loving favor than silver and gold; yet a good name is not riches, and loving favor is neither silver nor gold. Here the popular understanding of the word coincides with the definition given for scientific purposes. Plain men do not speak of such qualities, or endowments, as being wealth. No merchant or manufacturer or laboring man would include any one of these items in an account of his wealth, however precious he might esteem them.

And it is to be noted that it does not matter whether the incapacity to detach and make over a possession to another, arises from the nature of things, as in the case of personal health and strength, skill and intelligence, or from the constraints of law or public opinion. In Circassia, a beautiful daughter is wealth, and is popularly so accounted. No one in making up the list of his wealth would omit this item, any more than he would leave out his horses or his fields. In Christian countries, a daughter is not wealth, though she is far better than wealth. The Proclamation of Emancipation, in the United States and in Russia, annihilated a vast mass of wealth; it created what was better than much wealth—a body of free men.

But while strength, skill and intelligence can not be detached, and transferred, and thus can not be said to be wealth, the present use of them can be assigned to another, and hence may become the subject of exchange. The rich valetudinarian may command the services of the robust laborer, in waiting on his person; he may hire the poor scholar to be tutor to his son. The usufruct of all such qualities and endowments, therefore, properly constitutes an item of wealth, and, by the force of contract, the capability of transferring this species of wealth may be extended beyond the present moment to considerable periods of time, as when a man is hired by the month or year.

RELATION OF WEALTH TO COMMUNITY OF GOODS

But it may be objected that, inasmuch as exchange implies a present individual possessor, were community of goods or of labor to be universally established, there would no longer be such a thing as wealth, or such a department of human inquiry as Political Economy. To this it is sufficient to reply, that community of labor or of enjoyment is simply impossible, from the very nature of mankind.

Were a hundred persons to unite in such a society, each would have to work by himself: the exertion must be his; the pain and weariness would be all his. On the other hand, what he received from the common stock, would be his own; the food would nourish him alone; the clothing and the food would warm only him; none of his fellows would share in the pleasure or the benefit of what he consumed. The so-called community of labor and of goods, then, amounts simply to a mode of roughly apportioning exertion and enjoyment, on the basis of an assumed equality of abilities and of needs. Subject to all the injustice involved in such an assumption, each one of the hundred members would still part with his services to his fellows, and receive from them his remuneration, in the form of food, clothing, fuel and shelter.

RELATION OF VALUE TO GRATUITY

It will have been gathered from what has been said respecting value, that wealth and well-being are not synonymous. Much which is essential to the latter is no element of the former. Wealth may be increased at the expense of well-being, as in the case of the reduction of free laborers to the grade of chattel slavery. Wealth may be diminished temporarily by causes which minister to the advancement of the community and the State, as in the case of inventions which throw out of use large amounts of material and apparatus, or of ameliorating changes in nature which allow costly contrivances to be dispensed with. "If," wrote Prof. Senior, "the climate of England could suddenly be changed to that of Bogota, and the warmth which we extract imperfectly and expensively from fuel were supplied by the sun, fuel would cease to be useful, except as one of the productive instruments employed by art; we should want no more grates or chimney-pieces in our sitting-rooms; what had previously been a considerable amount of property, in the fixtures of houses, in stock in trade and materials, would become valueless; coals would sink in price; the most expensive mines would be abandoned; those which were retained would command smaller rents."

CONTINUOUS DISPLACEMENT OF VALUE BY GRATUITY

We are now called further to notice that there is a constant tendency to this diminution of the sum of wealth, and even to the annihilation of individual items, from age to age. So rapid and persistent is that tendency that, but for the increase of population, and the multiplication and diversification of human desires, due to increasing civilization and refinement, the subject matter with which Political Economy has to deal would be continually diminishing. How small the sum of wealth which would suffice for a community, in our stage of knowledge and skill, which should aspire to live only as well as a tribe of savages! The boats, the nets, the huts, the clothing and the domestic utensils of a primitive community represent an incredible amount of exertion and sacrifice; possess a vast amount of purchasing power. A like outfit would require but an insignificant part of the labor power of a modern community, and would have but little purchasing power.

The tendency which has been noted arises out of the progress of mankind in the chemical and mechanic arts, by which operations formerly difficult are made easy; by which materials naturally scarce are made plentiful; by which human necessities once urgently felt are wholly obviated, and, finally, by which things once costing labor are made to produce themselves spontaneously.

GROWTH OF HUMAN WANTS

In fact, however, while, in any community, this displacement of value by gratuity is continually in progress, the increase of population and the multiplication and diversification of human wants may be operating as steadily and strongly in the other direction. The labor that is made free by discoveries and inventions is applied to overcome the difficulties which withstand the gratification of newly-felt desires. The hut is pulled down to make room for the cottage; the cottage gives way to the mansion; the mansion to the palace. The rude covering of skins is replaced by the comely garment of woven stuffs; and these, in the progress of luxury, by the most splendid fabrics of human skill. In a thousand forms wealth is created by the whole energy of the community, quickened by a zeal greater than that which animated the exertions of their rude forefathers to obtain a scanty and squalid subsistence.

DISTINCTION BETWEEN WEALTH AND PROPERTY

A further distinction is that between wealth and property. The neglect of this has caused great confusion, especially in discussions of the principles and methods of taxation. Mr. J. S. Mill affords an example of the confusion of these terms when he says, respecting a mortgage on a landed estate, "this is wealth to the person to whom it brings in a revenue, and who could, perhaps, sell it in the market for the full amount of the debt. But it is not wealth to the country; if the engagement were annulled, the country would be neither poorer nor richer."

A more accurate statement of the case would be this: The landed estate is wealth, that is, possesses value; that is, confers upon its possessor the power of commanding, in exchange for itself, the labor, or the products of the labor, of others. The mortgage is property, or a right to wealth; in this case, a right to an undivided portion of the landed estate. The amount of the property of the owner of the estate is the value of the estate less the mortgage. There is but one body of wealth; there are two properties, that of the owner, and that of the mortgagee. The wealth of the community is no greater and no less, whether the ownership of the estate be entire, or divided into two or half a dozen properties. Indeed, we might say that "property" is not a word with which the political economist has any thing to do. It is legal, not economic, in its significance.

"The wealth," says Prof. Senior, "which consists merely of a right or credit, on the part of A., with a corresponding duty or debt on the part of B., is not considered by the Political Economist. He deals with the things which are the subjects of the right, or the credit, not with the claims or liabilities which may affect them. In fact, the credit amounts merely to this: that B. has in his hands a part of the property of A."

THE PREMISES OF POLITICAL ECONOMY

What are the proper premises of Political Economy? that is, what facts and principles should the economist take to reason from? Are they many or few? Shall the economist take into account all the facts, mental or physical, which influence the phenomena of wealth; or shall he confine himself to certain principal facts?

Shall we take man, for the purpose of economic reasoning, precisely as he is found to be, with all his appetencies and characteristics, so far as they affect the power and the disposition to labor, or so far as they increase or impair the ability of individuals to secure their share in the distribution of the product of industry? or shall we create, for the purposes of our reasoning, an economic man, assumed to be impelled by certain motives in respect to wealth, from whose actions men in general, knowing themselves to be more or less fully controlled by similar motives, may derive instruction?

Instead of seeking to extend our knowledge of the actual conditions under which wealth is produced by man, shall we content ourselves with certain leading conditions, such as that food is produced without human labor only in small quantities and very precariously; that the soils of every country vary widely in fertility; and that of no soil can the produce be increased indefinitely without a more than proportional expenditure of labor and capital?

Shall we take account of the various endowments, in the way of soil and climate, mineral resources and water power, of different countries? Shall we study their institutions and the predominant traits of character manifested by their people, so far as these appear to influence their actions in respect to wealth? Or shall we, on the other hand, disregard all that makes one nation to differ from another, caring to learn nothing of any which would not hold good of all.

Upon the answer to these questions depends the character and logical method of Political Economy. Upon that answer depends also much of the usefulness of this department of inquiry and the interest it may be expected to arouse in the public mind.

TWO SCHOOLS OF POLITICAL ECONOMY

The differences of opinion which exist regarding the proper extent of the premises of Political Economy have given rise to two schools which are commonly called the English and the German school.

The economists of the former school insist that the proper premises of pure Political Economy consist of a few certain facts of human nature, of human society, and of the physical constitution of the earth. That these, not more than five or six in number, constitute all the premises proper to the inquiry. That the scope of economic reasoning can not be extended beyond these without destroying the purity and simplicity of the science, and introducing error and confusion.The economists of the latter school hold that it is the province of Political Economy to explain the phenomena of wealth. That, in order to do this, the economist must inquire how men do, in fact, behave in regard to wealth, constituted as they are, and under the conditions and circumstances in which they are placed.

In this view, nothing that importantly influences the production and distribution of wealth can be neglected by the economist. All human history becomes his domain. The other sciences, alike the physical and the moral, become tributary to the science he cultivates.

With its premises thus enlarged, Political Economy ceases to be something which one man of superior intellect could, with a definite exertion of his faculties, work completely out at a sitting, as Beckford wrote "Vathek"; and that too without having visited any community beyond the one in which he was born, or knowing a page of history. Political Economy, as thus comprehended, becomes a work to which many men and successive ages must contribute; the material of which is accumulated in human experience, and is thus continually on the increase. It becomes a work which never is, but is always to be done, growing with the growing knowledge of the race.

Prof. Cairnes' Statement

It has been said that the two schools of Political Economy are known as the English and the German school. The terms are not fortunate, inasmuch as some of the economists who have labored most fully in the spirit of the so-called German school, have been natives of the British Isles. The best statement known to me of the true scope of economic inquiry is that given by Prof. Cairnes, from whose admirable lectures I abridge the following paragraphs, preserving the author's phraseology:

The desires, passions and propensities which influence mankind in the pursuit of wealth are almost infinite. Yet among these are some principles of so marked and paramount a character as both to admit of being ascertained, and when ascertained, to afford the data for determining the most important laws of the production and distribution of wealth. To possess himself of these is the first business of the political economist. He has then to take account of some leading physiological facts connected with human nature; and, lastly, to ascertain the principal physical characteristics of those natural agents of production on which human industry is exercised.

But it must not be thought that when these cardinal facts have been ascertained, and their consequences duly developed, the labors of the political economist are at an end. Many subordinate influences will intervene to disturb, and occasionally to reverse, the operation of the more powerful principles, and thus to modify the resulting phenomena.

SUBORDINATE CAUSES IN ECONOMICS

The next step, therefore, in his investigations will be to endeavor to ascertain the character of those subordinate causes, whether mental or physical, political or social, which influence human conduct in the pursuit of wealth. These, when he has found them, and is enabled to appreciate them with sufficient accuracy, he will incorporate among the premises of the science.

Thus, the political and social institutions of a country, in particular, the laws affecting the tenure of land, will be included among such subordinate agencies. It will be for the political economist to show in what way causes of this kind modify the operation of more fundamental principles. Again, any great discovery in the arts of production, such, *e. g.*, as the steam engine, will be a new fact for the consideration of the political economist. It will be like the discovery of a new planet, the attraction of which, operating on all the heavenly bodies within the sphere of its influence, will cause them more or less to deviate from the path which had been previously calculated for them.

In the same way, also, those motives and principles of action which may be developed in the progress of society, so far as they may be found to affect the phenomena of wealth, will also be taken account of by the political economist. He will consider, *e. g.*, the influence of custom in modifying human conduct in the pursuit of wealth. He will consider how, as civilization advances, the estimation of the future in relation to the present is enhanced, and the desire for immediate enjoyment is controlled by the increasing efficacy of prudential restraint. He will also observe how ideas of decency, comfort and luxury are developed as society progresses, modifying the natural force of the principle of population, influencing the mode of expenditure of different classes, and affecting thereby the distribution of industrial products. Even moral and religious considerations are to be taken account of by the economist precisely in so far as they are found, in fact, to affect the conduct of men in the pursuit of wealth.

Remarks on Prof. Cairnes' Statement

Nothing could be added to this statement of the logical method of Political Economy, as it is pursued by those who hold that it is the province of the science to explain the phenomena of wealth; and that, to this end, all causes which, whether primarily, or principally social, ethical, physical or physiological, do, in fact, enter to affect the actions of men respecting wealth, should be identified and determined, so far as may be, both in their direction and in the degree of their influence.

In this view the economist who omits any cause, structural or dynamic, physical or moral, which affects the production, exchange, distribution or consumption of wealth, must justify himself, not by the plea that such a cause has no relevancy to his investigation, but by some plea which would excuse an admittedly less than complete treatment of the subject, *e. g.*, the lack of information, the limitations of the human faculties, or the need, for popular instruction, of very brief and very general statements of principle.

Mr. Mill on the Economic Man

On the other hand, perhaps the best statement of the view taken by the economists of the so-called English school, as to the proper premises of Political Economy, is that given by Mr. J. S. Mill, in his work published in 1844.

"Political Economy," says Mr. Mill, "is concerned with man solely as a being who desires to possess wealth and who is capable of judging of the comparative efficacy of means to that end. It makes entire abstraction of every other human passion or motive, except those which may be regarded as perpetually antagonizing principles to the desire of wealth, namely, aversion to labor and desire of the present enjoyment of costly indulgences. These it takes, to a certain extent, into its calculations, because these do not merely, like other desires, occasionally conflict with the pursuit of wealth, but accompany it always, as a drag or impediment, and are, therefore, inseparably mixed up in the consideration of it. Political Economy considers mankind as occupied solely in acquiring and consuming wealth."

We have here all the elements of the economic man. He is taken as a being perfectly capable of judging of the comparative efficacy of means to the end of wealth. That is, he will never fail, whoever he may be, or wherever he may live, whether a capitalist or a laborer, rich or poor, taught or untaught, to know exactly what course will secure his highest economic interest, that is, bring him the largest amount of wealth.

Moreover, that end of wealth he never fails to desire, with a steady, uniform, constant passion. Of every other human passion or motive, Political Economy "makes entire abstraction." Love of country, love of honor, love of friends, love of learning, love of art, pity, shame, religion, charity, will never, so far as Political Economy cares to take account, withstand the effort of the economic man to amass wealth.

There are, however, two human passions and motives, of which Political Economy takes account, as "perpetually antagonizing principles to the desire of wealth," namely, "aversion to labor and desire of the present enjoyment of costly indulgences," that is, indolence and gluttony.

As by this view of Political Economy all men are taken as equally absorbed in the passion for wealth, so all men are taken as equally lazy and self-indulgent. The South Sea Islander and the large-brained European are equally averse to exertion; equally subject to the impulses of immediate appetite.

Ricardo the Master of the English School

Such are the features of the economic man, as delineated by Mr. Mill. Not a few treatises have been written mainly according to this method. The ablest body of doctrine ever composed from this point of view is that of David Ricardo. Hence this school of Political Economy may not inaptly be called the Ricardian. Mr. Ricardo, indeed, modified those assumptions so far as to recognize the difference in economic quality existing between men of different countries, not only between the East Indian and the Englishman, but also between the Englishman and the Portuguese. Within the same country, however, he recognized no such differences; but held rigorously to the few and simple postulates which have been stated. The acuteness of his intellect, the tenacity of his logical grasp, make him easily the master of all the economists of this school.

Relations of the Two Schools

It need not be a matter of surprise that so wide a difference of opinion as to the proper scope of economic inquiry should have led to much passionate controversy. The economists of the so-called German school have been disposed to deny, not only the universality of principles deduced from assumptions so arbitrary and falling so far short of the real facts of life and society, but also the significance, for any purpose whatever, of conclusions thus obtained. The economists of the so-called English, or Ricardian school, have treated the method of their opponents as unscientific, giving scope to charlatanry, and at the best tending to mere sentimentality.

The mutual contempt entertained by the two schools is not justified by a large view of the progress of economics in the past, or by a consideration of the history of other social sciences. Political Economy should begin with the Ricardian method. A few simple assumptions being made, the processes of the production, exchange and distribution of wealth should be traced out and be brought together into a complete system, which may be called pure Political Economy, or arbitrary Political Economy, or, *a priori* Political Economy, or by the name of its greatest teacher, Ricardian Political Economy. Such a scheme should constitute the skeleton of all economic reasoning; but upon this ghastly frame-work should be imposed the flesh and blood of an actual, vital Political Economy, which takes account of men and societies as they are, with all their sympathies, apathies, and antipathies; with every organ developed, as in life; every nerve of motion or of sensibility in full play.

THE TRUE LABOR OF PHILOSOPHY

On this subject what could be more pregnant with meaning than the aphorism of Bacon, "Those who have treated of the sciences have been either empirics or dogmatical.

"The former, like ants, only heap up and use their store; the latter, like spiders, spin out their own web.

"The bee, as a mean between both, extracts matter from the flowers of the garden and the field; but works and fashions it by its own efforts.

"The true labor of philosophy resembles hers; for it neither relies entirely or principally on the powers of the mind, nor yet lays up in the memory the matter afforded by the experiments of natural history and mechanics, in its raw state, but changes and works it in the understanding."

Is Political Economy indeed a Science?

The answer to this question depends rather upon the definition imposed on the word science, than upon the view we take of Political Economy itself. If we give the word no wider extension than Dr. Whewell gave it, when he spoke of "those bodies of knowledge which we call sciences," Political Economy indubitably ranks as a science. It forms a body of knowledge, constantly growing, it is true, from the outside, and undergoing not a little change from time to time within, yet still embracing, in the present, a vast collection of related facts, with the reason of their succession, one to another, more or less clearly seen, and allowing many practical rules and precepts of great importance in determining human conduct to be deduced with all needed assurance. In this sense, then, Political Economy is a science.

Whether it be a science in the highest sense given that word, may be disputed. M. Comte, the great positivist philosopher, denied the claim of Political Economy to this title. In his view, it is an attribute of a true social science that it results in establishing a rational filiation between events, so as to allow of systematic prevision respecting their occurrence in a certain succession. Prediction—forecast of the future—is, according to M. Comte, the fruit of all true science. Of this, he asserts, political economy has not shown itself capable.

Prof. Cairnes rejoins that the economic prevision is a prevision not of events, but of tendencies. Admitting the incapacity of forecasting events, Prof. Cairnes urges that "it argues no imperfection in economic science. The imperfection is not here, but in those other cognate sciences, to which belongs the determination of the non-economic quàntities in the problem, etc. Meanwhile it is no slight gain, in speculating on the future of society, to have it in our power to determine the direction of an order of tendencies exercising so wide, constant and potent an influence on the course of human development, as the conditions of wealth. So much for the highest form of scientific fruit, 'forecast of the future.' The principle, however, of establishing a filiation in events may take the more modest form of explaining the past. That political economy, assuming that it fulfills its limited purpose of unfolding the natural laws of wealth, is capable of throwing light on the evolutions of history, will scarcely be denied."

THE PRACTICAL IMPORTANCE OF POLITICAL ECONOMY

We can not stay to discuss the question. Whether Political Economy be or be not a science in the high sense attributed to that word by M. Comte, it assuredly is, as a branch of social inquiry, worthy the earnest attention of every publicist and every citizen. It deals with some of the most important subjects which concern society. Whether the degree of assurance that may be attained in the study of these questions be higher or be lower, the questions can not but be more justly decided by reason of such study.

If Political Economy have not yet reached the standing of a true science, in the high sense in which that word is used by M. Comte; if political economists are still at disagreement on many points of theoretical or practical importance, it can not be denied that the investigation of the conditions of wealth by Adam Smith and his successors has already resulted in the removal of monstrous delusions which a century ago profoundly affected the legislation of every civilized country, to the inexpressible injury of the commonwealth of nations. The first fruits of Political Economy have been worth a million times the intellectual effort that has been bestowed upon the subject.

DISTINCTION BETWEEN A SCIENCE AND AN ART

Before proceeding to inquire whether Political Economy should be dealt with as a science or as an art, it seems desirable strongly to emphasize the distinction between a science and an art. This is the more needed because of the strangely persistent habit of economic writers in confusing these two things, which should be kept clearly distinct.

A science, whether the science of mathematics, or physics, or mechanics, or chemistry, or geology, or physiology, or economics, deals only with the relations of cause and effect within its own field. It assumes nothing to be a good and nothing to be an evil. It does not start with the notion that something is desirable or undesirable; nor does it arrive at any such conclusion as its result. It has no business to offer precepts or prescriptions. Its sole single concern is to trace effects back to their causes; to project causes forward to their effects.

An art, on the other hand, starts with the assumption that a certain thing is desirable or that a certain other thing is undesirable; that something is a good or that something is an evil. The object it seeks is to ascertain how the good may be attained, or the evil avoided. In pursuing this inquiry, it makes use of the principles, or laws, governing the relations of cause and effect, which have been ascertained in the cultivation of any and all sciences that have in any way to do with its own subject matter. As a result, it issues with certain precepts and prescriptions for the guidance and assistance of those who would gain the good or avoid the evil which that particular art has in contemplation, whether it be the art of navigation, or of cookery, of painting, of gunnery, of architecture, of mining, or of weaving.

The Distinction Illustrated

This distinction between a science and an art ought to be sufficiently clear; but the inveterate disposition of economic writers, which has been referred to, will perhaps justify an illustration which I shall make familiar, even at the risk of appearing coarse.

Suppose I am in my laboratory and a man enters who says that he desires to consult me, as a professor of chemistry, as to whether he had better swallow the contents of a vial which he holds in his hand. I reply to him: "Sir, I have no advice, as a professor of chemistry, to offer you as to what you shall swallow or refrain from swallowing. I perceive that the liquid contained in your vial is prussic acid. I will cheerfully state to you the action of prussic acid on any substance about which you may choose to inquire; but probably you had better, for your apparent purpose, go to Prof. S., the physiologist, who can more fully and readily than myself explain the precise action of prussic acid when taken into the stomach of a living being."

The inquirer now goes to Prof. S., and says that he desires to consult him, as a professor of physiology, as to whether he had better swallow the liquid which the chemist has told him is undilute prussic acid. Prof. S. replies: "Sir, should you consult me as a fellow being, I would not stand on ceremony, but frankly advise you to empty the contents of your vial into the sink. But if you insist on consulting me as a professor of physiology, I must reply that I have no advice to give. Physiology, sir, is a science; as such, it has nothing to do with precepts or prescriptions, but only with the relations of cause and effect within the field of animal life.

As a student of that science, I inform you that, if you swallow the liquid, you will experience such and such sensations, and, at about such a time, you will be dead. Since you still insist upon having advice as to whether you had better do this or not, I refer you to my neighbor, Dr. G., who is the professor, not of a science, but of an art. As such, it is his business to give advice regarding conduct. As such, he has a right to entertain the notion that certain things are good, and certain things evil; that the means calculated (as shown by the appropriate science or sciences) to bring about the good, are desirable; that the courses which (as shown by the appropriate science or sciences) lead to the evil, are undesirable. He would not be a physician unless he held that pain and death were evil; life and the absence of pain, good. What he is a physician for is to help his patients to avoid the evil and obtain the good. In doing this he will naturally seek to apply the largest and latest results of the *science* of physiology to the *art* of healing."

DISTINCTION BETWEEN POLITICAL ECONOMY AS A SCIENCE AND AS AN ART

"If," says Prof. Senior, "Political Economy is to be treated as a science, it may be defined as the science which states the laws regulating the production and distribution of wealth, so far as they depend on the action of the human mind. If it be treated as an art, it may be defined as the art which points out the institutions and habits most conducive to the production and accumulation of wealth; or, if the teacher ventures to take a wider view, as the art which points out the institutions and habits most conducive to that production, accumulation and distribution of wealth which is most favorable to the happiness of mankind."

Prof. Senior goes on to remark that, in the eighteenth century, political economy was treated as an art, a branch of statesmanship. Sir James Steuart so treated it. The French Physiocrats so regarded it. Even with Adam Smith, "the scientific portion of his work is merely an introduction to that which is practical."

Oddly enough, the statesman Turgot must be made an exception to the remark respecting the French Physiocrats. "It is remarkable," says Prof. Senior, "that the only man among the disciples of Quesnay who was actually practicing political economy as an art, is the only one who treated its principles as a science. His 'Réflexions sur la formation et la distribution des richesses,' published in 1774, is a purely scientific treatise. It contains not a word of precept, and might have been written by an ascetic, who believed wealth to be an evil."

Prof. Senior continues: "The English writers who have succeeded Adam Smith have generally set out by defining political economy as a science, and proceeded to treat it as an art. Mr. Ricardo is, however, an exception. His great work is little less scientific than that of Turgot. His abstinence from precept, and even from illustrations drawn from real life, is the more remarkable, as the subject of his treatise is 'Distribution,' the most practical branch of political economy, and 'Taxation,' the most practical branch of Distribution. The modern economists of France, Germany, Spain, Italy and America, so far as I am acquainted with their works, all treat political economy as an art."

We shall deal with Political Economy as a Science

The inveterate disposition, which Prof. Senior thus notes, to abandon the investigation of principles for the formulation of precepts, has doubtless retarded greatly the progress of political economy. It can not be too strongly insisted on, that the economist, as such, has nothing to do with the questions, what men had better do; how nations should be governed; or what regulations should be made for their mutual intercourse. His business simply is to trace economic effects to their causes, leaving it to the philosopher of everyday life, to the moralist or the statesman, to teach how men and nations should act in view of the principles so established. The political economist, for example, has no more call to preach free trade, as the policy of nations, than the physiologist to advocate monogamy as a legal institution.

Throughout this work until we reach Part VI, which will be in terms devoted to Some Applications of Economic Principles, the effort will be made to treat political economy strictly as a science. If at any point the writer lapses into expressions only suitable to the teacher of an art, it will be partly because of that strong predisposition which has been noted in almost all writers on this subject, and partly to the influence of example.

Is There a National Political Economy?

This is a question which has been much debated. The so-called protectionists have favored the view that each country has a political economy of its own. One writer of our own country has entitled his work "American Political Economy." The controversy over this question arises out of the confusion produced, first, by the failure to distinguish between the science of political economy and the use of political economy in the art of statesmanship; secondly, by the different views taken of the proper premises of the science of political economy by the two schools before referred to.

Those who say that there is an American Political Economy, for example, mean that the precepts derived from political economy, whether addressed to the legislator, or to the body of the people, should not be applied to America without reference to the peculiar constitution, conditions and needs of America. But a science has nothing to do with precepts or prescriptions. Rules of conduct belong to an art.

NATIONAL AND RACE CHARACTERISTICS

Moreover, the notion that there is a political economy for each race of men, and even for each nation, has been fostered by the arbitrary character of the assumptions of what we have called the Ricardian school, and by the refusal to pay a reasonable regard to some of the most characteristic features of human nature and some of the most prominent facts of industrial society, embracing institutions and laws which vitally affect the production and distribution of wealth.

Thus, the *à priori* economist, in discussing the question of wages, assumes, for the purposes of his reasoning, a body of laborers who are wholly intent on getting the largest remuneration; who will, for any advantage, however slight, change their occupation, and with equal readiness their place of abode, at least within their own country; who, moreover, are so intelligent and well-informed that no preference, economically, can exist on behalf of any other occupation or place of abode, without their knowing it, and, of course, acting at once upon it. The economist having created such a race of beings, whose likeness is found nowhere upon earth, proceeds to point out,' it may be with great acuteness and accuracy, what the individual members thereof would do in various supposed cases, under the impulse of this or that economic force. His conclusions are put forth as "laws" of political economy.

Is it strange that an intelligent East Indian, reading these conclusions, should say, if this is political economy, it must be European political economy, and there should be a separate political economy for the East, since here, over vast regions, social and religious feelings absolutely prohibit multitudes of workmen from changing their occupation, for any reason; while the almost uniform penury of the laboring class, their ignorance, superstition, and fear of change, combine to render movement from place to place tardy and difficult, if not, as in most cases, practically impossible?

Relation of Political Economy to other Sciences

Political Economy does not ascertain for itself a single one of the facts which form the premises of the economist. These are all derived from other sciences as data, *i. e.*, things given. From the physiologist, for instance, is obtained the fact of man's need of food to sustain life, from which is deduced the economic doctrine of minimum wages.

From the physiologist, again, is obtained the fact of a strong disposition, arising from the sexual passion, to carry population beyond the limits of decent or comfortable subsistence, from which is deduced the much-abused doctrine known as Malthusianism. From the agricultural chemist is obtained the fact that, beyond a certain point, the application of capital and labor to land yields a continually diminishing return, from which is deduced the doctrine of Rent. None of these facts does the economist ascertain for himself. He takes them, as the realized results of other sciences, and makes them the premises, the starting point, of his own.

Even the fact of the indisposition of men to strenuous exertion, from which is deduced the principle that they will, so far as they are intelligent and are left free to act, always buy in the cheapest market, is not found by the economist. It is furnished, ready to his hand, by the moral philosopher. The economist takes from all sciences, by turns, all facts which bear upon the one subject, wealth; considers them only so far as they bear thereon; and puts them together and builds them up into a "body of knowledge" which he calls the Science of Wealth, or Political Economy. Even in the field of prices and wages, the distinction should always be observed between the economic statistician, who finds the facts, and the economist, who puts the facts into their place in the industrial system.

POLITICAL ECONOMY AND NATURAL THEOLOGY

Prof. Cliffe Leslie has shown the powerful influence exerted upon the economic views of Adam Smith, who, as Professor of Moral Philosophy in the University of Glasgow, had occasion to teach both Political Economy and Natural Theology, by the assumption of a beneficent natural order of society, to the disturbance of which by human institutions are due all the economic evils that afflict mankind. To this order-of-nature it should, according to Dr. Smith, be the unceasing effort of mankind to return; and the political economist will fully discharge himself of his mission as an investigator and teacher when he points out the path by which mankind may make their way back to that state in which all things economic will work together for the good of the race.

Now, this subjection of political economy to the interests of natural theology is wrong. I do not say that good natural theology will make bad political economy. I content myself with asserting that political economy has just as much right to be independent of natural theology, as have astronomy and geology. There was a time when the students of those sciences were deemed to be bound to restrain themselves within the supposed requirements not only of natural theology, but also of revealed religion. We know how mischievous were the consequences of that subjection.

Political economy owes nothing to natural theology. The economist is under no obligation to any assumptions derived from that source. He has no more right to start with the theory of an order of nature which is purely beneficent, than he would have to start with the opposite theory of an order of nature wholly maleficent. As economist, he has no mission to "vindicate the ways of God to man." He is to investigate the laws of wealth. That duty he will best discharge by reasoning as justly as his mental powers enable him to do, from economic premises which have been established by adequate induction, and from such only.

POLITICAL ECONOMY AND POLITICAL EQUITY

The boundary line between ethical and economic inquiry is perfectly clear, if one will but regard it. Great confusion has been engendered by writers in economics wandering off into discussions of political equity. The economist, as such, has nothing to do with the question whether existing institutions, or laws, or customs, are right or wrong: why right, or how far right: why wrong, or how far wrong. His only concern with them is to ascertain how they do, in fact, affect the production and distribution of wealth.

It is true that if the sense of injustice be awakened in the mass of the people, or in any considerable class in the community, industry, frugality, and sobriety are likely to be in a greater or less degree impaired, and thus the production and distribution of wealth will be affected. But it is wholly because of the effect last indicated, and not at all because of its ethical character, that any social arrangement or political institution comes within the consideration of the economist.

Indeed there is reason to believe that such arrangements and institutions do not necessarily produce economic evils in proportion to the degree in which they violate political equity. A custom or law might conceivably be inequitable in the degree to be flagrantly iniquitous, yet exert only a slight influence upon the production or distribution of wealth. Another, presenting so great an array of reasons in its favor that many ethical writers would strongly approve it, might, by crossing popular prejudices, or through some wholly adventitious feature of its own, become a mighty economic force for mischief. Indeed, it is not at all because a social arrangement or political institution is wrong, but because people think it wrong, that it does harm in the domain of wealth. The system of land tenure against which the peasantry of Ireland are so largely in revolt does an amount of mischief which is wholly independent of the consideration whether the Irish people or the English Parliament be at fault in the matter.

RESPECT THE LIMITS OF ECONOMIC INQUIRY

Hence we say that the limits of strictly economic inquiry should be scrupulously respected. The writer on ethics who deems the greatest good of the greatest number the ultimate rule of right, may make excursions into economics, in order to judge of the moral quality of an act, or a system, by its effects on the production and distribution of wealth; but the economist, on his part, has no occasion to cross the boundary line. The French writers, who have, in general, been singularly just in their apprehension of the character and logical method of political economy, have, more than all others, erred on this side. Many of them write throughout with a side glance at the existing social system. They profess to be intent on the solution of economic problems, while directing their efforts toward the vindication of political arrangements. The writings of the admirable Frederic Bastiat are deeply infected with this error. He strives incessantly to prove that the institution of property is just; whereas the only concern which, as an economist, he has with that institution, is to inquire how it influences the action of mankind in respect to wealth.

SENTIMENT AND POLITICAL ECONOMY

Holding rigidly to the same view of the nature and scope of economic inquiry, we see that those who allow their opinions to be in any degree shaped by what is called sentiment, are equally wrong with those who sneer at any recognition of sentiment by the economist. The economist's own sentiments should be put completely out of sight; he has only to do with the sentiments of others, and with these only so far as they affect the actions of men in respect to wealth. We shall have occasion to observe that feelings of justice, of compassion, of respect, of kindly regard, may greatly influence the rents paid in any country, by tenants to landlords, or the wages paid by employers to workingmen or working-women. So far as such sentiments produce these effects, they require to be recognized as economic forces.

RELATION OF POLITICAL ECONOMY TO SOCIOLOGY

M. Comte, whom we have already quoted, as denying to political economy the character of a true science, because its history did not, as he esteemed it, bear the tests of continuity and fecundity, also held that the phenomena of wealth should not, and could not advantageously, be considered apart from the facts of the intellectual, moral and political order with which they are closely interwoven. Society, he held, must be considered in the totality of its elements. All isolated theory of a particular aspect of social life, such as wealth, or of a single order of relations, *e. g.*, the economic, he regarded as essentially vicious. The laws and conditions of wealth, in the view of this writer, are a single thread in a closely knit web of social interests and concerns, from which no one can be disconnected, to be contemplated by itself alone.

To this opinion, Mr. J. S. Mill has made what seems to be a conclusive reply:

"Notwithstanding," he says, "the universal *consensus* of the social phenomena, whereby nothing which takes place in any part of the operations of society, is without its share of influence on every other part, and notwithstanding the paramount ascendency which the general state of civilization and social progress in any given society must hence exercise over all the partial and subordinate phenomena, it is not the less true that different species of social facts are, in the main, dependent, immediately, and in the first resort, on different kinds of causes, and, therefore, not only may with advantage, but must be studied apart, just as, in the natural body, we study separately the physiology and pathology of each of the principal organs and tissues, though every one is acted on by the state of all the others, and though the peculiar conditions and general health of the organism co-operate with and often predominate over, the local causes, in determining the state of any particular organ."

OBSTACLES WHICH POLITICAL ECONOMY ENCOUNTERS

It is worth while to note certain obstacles which the economist encounters in his efforts to secure the popular recognition and acceptance of the laws of wealth, as he discerns them in his study of man and society. Two of these may be regarded as wholly peculiar in kind, or highly peculiar in the degree in which political economy encounters them.

The first is well expressed by Prof. Cairnes: "Its close affinity to the moral sciences brings it constantly into collision with moral feelings and prepossessions, which can not fail to make themselves felt in the discussion of its principles; while its conclusions, intimately connected as they are with the art of government, have a direct and visible bearing upon human conduct, in some of the most exciting pursuits of life." Archbishop Whately had the same in view when he remarked that the demonstrations of Euclid would not have commanded universal assent had they been applicable to the pursuits and fortunes of individuals.

Another of the obstacles referred to is found in the fact that political economy has to do with affairs so ordinary and familiar that men, in general, feel themselves competent, irrespective of study or of special experience, to form opinions regarding them. The more closely men are concerned with any matter, the harder it is to maintain the authority of the learned body which assumes to engross scientific knowledge on the subject.

Few are presumptuous enough to dispute with the chemist or mechanician upon points connected with the studies and labors of his life; but almost any man who can read and write feels at liberty to form and maintain opinions of his own upon trade and money.

Now, this is not wholly of evil. The plain common-sense of unlettered men has not infrequently served as a corrective to economic doctrines too finely drawn for the purposes of legislation, perhaps based upon a partial and disparaging view of human nature. But while thus, in the application of political economy to the art of statesmanship, the self-assertion of the uninstructed mind has not been without its advantages, this disposition has certainly hindered the development of political economy as a science.

The economic literature of every succeeding year embraces works conceived in the true scientific spirit, and works exhibiting the most vulgar ignorance of history and the most flagrant contempt for the conditions of economic investigation. It is much as if astrology were being pursued side by side with astronomy, or alchemy with chemistry.

A third obstacle which political economy encounters arises from the use of terms derived from the vocabulary of every-day life, such as value, exchange, wealth, rent, profits—with some of which are associated in the popular mind conceptions inconsistent with, or, at times, perhaps antagonistic to, those which are in the view of the writer on economics. Thus, as we have seen, the economist uses the word, value, in the single sense of power-in-exchange. Common speech makes every thing valuable which is useful, desirable or meritorious, irrespective of the consideration whether, by reason of its scarcity or the difficulty of securing it, this or that article so spoken of confers upon its possessor the power of commanding in exchange the labor, or the products of the labor, of others.

The chemist, the geologist, the botanist, on the other hand, invents terms for the classes of objects or the classes of phenomena which he is to discuss. The reader carries with him into the discussion only the idea of the thing which the author has created for the purpose. If the writer be clear, and the reader be careful, there is no danger of a failure of understanding. But, no matter how precise the one may be in definition, or how close the attention of the other, it is inevitable that the use, in economic discussion, of terms taken from the vocabulary of common life, should engender confusion, from the practically irresistible tendency of the mind of the reader, and even, in a degree, of the writer, to slip back to the habitual meanings of the words employed.

So strongly has this last disadvantage pressed upon some writers, that they have been impelled to resort to strange and foreign terms to obviate the difficulty. Thus, Archbishop Whately, treating political economy as the science of exchange, introduced the Greek word, Catallactics, to express the scope of his inquiry; and Prof. Hearn has given to his admirable book the name, Plutology, to escape the vagueness of meaning which he thought he saw in the popular use of the word wealth.

THE DEPARTMENTS OF POLITICAL ECONOMY

All the questions of political economy are both conveniently and appropriately discussed under four titles: Production, Exchange, Distribution and Consumption.

Of late, a disposition has been manifested, on the part of many writers, in England and America, to drop these familiar titles; to decline to admit any departments in political economy; and to treat of production and distribution, *e. g.*, as not separable in economic discussion.

This has unquestionably been stimulated, if, indeed, it has not been generated, by the wish to bring political economy into a strictly scientific form, with which the recognition of distinct departments has been deemed incompatible. It may be doubted whether our knowledge of the laws of wealth has yet reached the degree of completeness and assurance which would allow a science to be constituted after the lofty ideal of these writers. Meanwhile there seems reason to believe that the abandonment of the familiar and useful terms, production, exchange, distribution and consumption, has caused some very important considerations to be overlooked. "Nothing," said Edmund Burke, "is so great an enemy to accuracy of judgment as a coarse discrimination; a want of such classification and distribution as the subject admits of."

Now, clearly the subject, wealth, admits of being considered, first, with respect to the motives which lead to its production and the conditions under which production takes place; secondly, with respect to the laws which govern the exchange of products in the market; thirdly, with respect to the forces which distribute the product of industry, in larger or smaller shares, among the several classes of persons who take part in production; fourthly, with respect to the influences which the different modes of consumption exert upon the disposition and the ability to take part in the future production of wealth.

And if wealth admits of being considered in these several aspects, it seems to me clear that such a classification will conduce both to completeness of view and to accuracy of judgment. We shall have occasion to note, a very striking instance of the mischief that has arisen from the neglect of this classification by recent writers in economics.

MENTAL AND PHYSICAL PREMISSES OF POLITICAL ECONOMY

The expressions 'physical' and 'mental,' as applied to science, have generally been employed to designate those branches of knowledge of which physical and mental phenomena respectively form the subject-matter. Thus, Chemistry is considered as a physical science because the subject-matter on which chemical inquiry is exercised, viz., material elements and combinations, is physical. Psychology, on the other hand, is a mental science; the subject-matter of it being mental states and feelings. And as the office of the chemist consists in observing and analyzing material objects with a view to discovering the laws of their elementary constitution; so, that of the psychologist consists in endeavouring, by means of reflection on what passes in his own, or appears to pass in the minds of others, to ascertain the laws by which the phenomena of our mental constitution succeed and produce each other. If this be a correct statement of the principle on which the designations 'mental' and 'physical' are applied to the sciences, it seems to follow that Political Economy does not find a place under either category.

Neither mental nor physical nature forms the *subject-matter* of the investigations of the political economist. He considers, it is true, physical phenomena, as he also considers mental phenomena, but in neither case as phenomena which it belongs to his science to explain. The subject-matter of that science is wealth; and though wealth consists in material objects, it is not wealth in virtue of those objects being material, but in virtue of their possessing value—that is to say, in virtue of their possessing a quality attributed to them by the mind. The subject-matter of Political Economy is thus neither purely physical nor purely mental, but possesses a complex character, equally derived from both departments of nature, and the laws of which are neither mental nor physical laws, though they are dependent, and, as I maintain, dependent equally on the laws of matter and on those of mind.

Let us consider, for example, the causes which determine the rate of wages. This, it will be admitted on all hands, is an economic problem. It is evident that the objects which the labourer receives are material objects, but those material objects are invested by the mind with a peculiar attribute in consequence of which they are considered as possessing value; and it is in their complex character, as physical objects invested with the attribute of value, that the political economist considers them. The subject-matter, therefore, of the wages-problem possesses qualities derived alike from physical and from mental nature; consequently, if it is to be denominated from the nature of its subject-matter, it is equally entitled or disentitled to the character of a physical or mental problem.

But it is said that Political Economy considers the problem no further than as it depends on the action of the human mind. The food and clothing which the labourer consumes have, no doubt, physical properties, as the labourer himself has a physical as well as a mental nature; but with the physical properties, we are told, the political economist has no concern: he considers those objects so far forth only as they possess value, and value is a purely mental conception. But is this true? Does the political economist—does Mr. Senior, *e.g.,* in his purely scientific treatment of this question—entirely put out of consideration the physical properties of the commodities which the labourer consumes, or the physiological conditions on which the increase of the labouring population depends? What is the solution of the wages-problem? Wages, it will be said, depend on demand and supply; or, more explicitly, on the relation between the amount of capital applied to the payment of wages, and the number of labourers seeking employment. But the amount of capital employed in the payment of wages depends, amongst other causes, on the productiveness of industry in raising the commodities of the labourer's consumption—a circumstance which is equally dependent on the laws of physical nature and on the mental qualities which the workman brings to his task. The number of labourers seeking employment, again, depends, amongst other causes, on the laws of population; while these are determined as much by the physiological laws of the body, as the psychological laws of the mind; the political economist taking equal cognizance of both.

It thus appears that, as the subject-matter of Political Economy, viz., wealth, possesses qualities derived equally from the world of matter and from that of mind, so its premisses are equally drawn from both these departments of nature. The latter point, indeed, is admitted by the authorities to whom I have referred, who nevertheless, by what I must deem a strange oversight, represent the science as investigating the laws of wealth no further than as they depend on the laws of the human mind.

But perhaps this point will be made more clear—the equal dependence, namely, of the science of Political Economy on the laws of the physical world and on those of the human mind—if we consider that a change in the character of the former laws will equally affect its conclusions with a change in that of the latter. The physical qualities of the soil, *e.g.,* under the present constitution of nature are such, that, after a certain quantum of cultivation has been applied to a limited area, a further application is not attended with a proportionate return.

The proof of this is, that, instead of confining cultivation to the best soils, and forcing them to yield the whole amount of food that may be required, it is found profitable to resort to soils of inferior quality.

This physical fact, as every political economist knows, and as shall be explained on a future occasion, leads, through the play of human desires in the pursuit of wealth, to the phenomenon of rent, to the fall of profits as communities advance, and to a retardation in the advance of population. If the fact were otherwise, if the physical properties of the soil were such as to admit of an indefinite increase of produce in undiminished proportion to the outlay by simply increasing the outlay—if, *e.g.*, it were found that by doubling the quantity of manure upon a given acre and by ploughing it twice as often, a farmer could obtain a double produce, and by a quadruple outlay, a quadruple produce, and so on *ad infinitum;* if this were so, the science of Political Economy, as it at present exists, would be as completely revolutionized as if human nature itself were altered—as if benevolence, for example, were so strengthened at the expense of self-love, that human beings should refuse to avail themselves, at the expense of their neighbours, of those special advantages with which nature or fortune may happen to endow them; under such a change in the physical qualities of the soil rent would disappear, profits would have no tendency permanently to fall, and population in the oldest countries might advance as rapidly as in the newest colonies.

The position of Political Economy, as just described, may be illustrated by that of Geology in relation to the sciences of Mechanics, Chemistry, and Physiology. The complex phenomena presented by the constitution of the earth's crust form the subject-matter of the science of the geologist; they are the complex result of mechanical, chemical, and physiological laws, and the business of the geologist is to trace them to these causes; but having done this, his labours as a geologist are at an end: the further investigation of the problem belongs not to Geology, but to Mechanics, Chemistry, and Physiology.

The premisses, or ultimate facts, of Political Economy being thus drawn alike from the world of matter and from that of mind, it remains that I should indicate the character of those facts, physical and mental, from which the conclusions of the science are derived; in other words, that I should show in what manner the facts which are pertinent to economic investigations are to be distinguished from those which are not. The answer to this question must in general be determined by considering what the science proposes to accomplish. This, as you are aware, is the discovery of the laws of the production and distribution of wealth. The facts, therefore, which constitute the premisses of Political Economy are those which influence the production and distribution of wealth; and in order that the science be absolutely perfect, so that an economist might predict the course of economic phenomena with the same accuracy and certainty with which an astronomer predicts the course of celestial phenomena, it would be necessary that these premisses should include every fact, mental and physical, which influences the phenomena of wealth.

It does not, however, seem possible that this degree of perfection should ever be attained. In Political Economy, as in all those branches of inquiry which include amongst their premisses at once the moral and physical nature of man, the facts to be taken account of are so numerous, their character so various, and the laws of their sequence so obscure, that it would seem scarcely possible to ascertain them all, much less to assign to each its exact value. And even if this were possible, the task of tracing these principles to their consequences, allowing to each its due significance, and no more than its due significance, would present a problem so complex and difficult as to defy the powers of the most accomplished reasoners.

But although this is so, and although, therefore, neither Political Economy nor any of the class of inquiries to which it belongs may ever be expected to reach that perfection which has been attained in some of the more advanced physical sciences, yet this does not forbid us to hope that, by following in our economic investigations the same course which has been pursued with such success in physical science, we may attain, if not to absolute scientific perfection, at least to the discovery of solid and valuable results.

The desires, passions, and propensities which influence mankind in the pursuit of wealth are, as I have intimated, almost infinite; yet amongst these there are some principles of so marked and paramount a character as both to admit of being ascertained, and when ascertained, to afford the data for determining the most important laws of the production and distribution of wealth, in so far as these laws are affected by mental causes. To possess himself of these is the first business of the political economist; he has then to take account of some leading physiological facts connected with human nature; and, lastly, to ascertain the principal physical characteristics of those natural agents of production on which human industry is exercised.

Thus he will consider, as being included amongst the paramount mental principles to which I have alluded, the general desire for physical well-being, and for wealth as the means of obtaining it; the intellectual power of judging of the efficacy of means to an end, along with the inclination to reach our ends by the easiest and shortest means,—mental facts from which results the desire to obtain wealth at the least possible sacrifice: he will further duly weigh those propensities which, in conjunction with the physiological conditions of the human frame, determine the laws of population; and, lastly, he will take into account the physical qualities of the soil and of those other natural agents on which the labour and ingenuity of man are employed. These facts, whether mental or physical, he will consider, as I have already stated, not with a view to explain them, but as the data of his reasoning, as leading causes affecting the production and distribution of wealth. But it must not be thought that, when these cardinal facts have been ascertained and their consequences duly developed, the labours of the political economist are at an end, even supposing that his treatment of them has been exhaustive and his reasoning without a flaw. Though the conclusions thus arrived at will, in the main, correspond with the actual course of events, yet great and glaring discrepancies will frequently occur. The data on which his speculations have been based include indeed the grand and leading causes which regulate the production and distribution of wealth, but they do not include all the causes.

Many subordinate influences will intervene to disturb, and occasionally to reverse, the operation of the more powerful principles, and thus to modify the resulting phenomena. The next step, therefore, in his investigations, will be to endeavour as far as possible to ascertain the character of those subordinate causes, whether physical or mental, political or social, which influence human conduct in the pursuit of wealth, and these, when he has found them and is enabled to appreciate them with sufficient accuracy, he will incorporate amongst the premisses of the science, as data to be taken account of in his future speculations.

Thus the political and social institutions of a country, and in particular the laws affecting the tenure of land, will be included among such subordinate agencies; and it will be for the political economist to show in what way causes of this kind modify the operation of more fundamental principles in relation to the phenomena which it belongs to his science to investigate.

Again, any great discovery in the arts of production, such, *e.g.*, as the steam-engine, will be a new fact for the consideration of the political economist; it will be for him to consider its effect on the productiveness of industry or the distribution of its products; how far and in what directions it is calculated to affect wages, profits, and rent, and to modify those conclusions to which he may have been led by reasoning from the state of productive industry previous to its introduction. It will be like the discovery to an astronomer of a new planet, the attraction of which, operating on all the heavenly bodies within the sphere of its influence, will cause them more or less to deviate from the path which had been previously calculated for them. It is a new force, which, in speculating on the tendencies of economic phenomena, the political economist will include as a new datum amongst his premisses.

In the same way, also, those motives and principles of action which may be developed in the progress of society—so far as they may be found to affect the phenomena of wealth—will also be taken account of by the political economist. He will consider, *e.g.*, the influence of custom in modifying human conduct in the pursuit of wealth; he will consider how, as civilisation advances, the estimation of the future in relation to the present is enhanced, and the desire for immediate enjoyment is controlled by the increasing efficacy of prudential restraint; he will also observe how ideas of decency, comfort, and luxury are developed as society progresses, modifying the natural force of the principles of population, influencing the mode of expenditure of different classes, and affecting thereby the distribution of industrial products.

The question is sometimes asked—How far should moral and religious considerations be admitted as coming within the purview of Political Economy? and the doctrine now under exposition enables us to supply the answer. Moral and religious considerations are to be taken account of by the economist precisely in so far as they are found in fact to affect the conduct of men in the pursuit of wealth. In so far as they operate in this way, such considerations are as pertinent to his inquiries as the desire for physical well-being, or the propensity in human beings to reproduce their kind; and they are only less important as premisses of his science than the latter principles, because they are far less influential with regard to the phenomena which constitute the subject-matter of his inquiries.

As we have already remarked, it is scarcely possible that all these circumstances should be ascertained, or accurately appreciated; but it seems quite possible that some of the most important of them may, with sufficient accuracy at least to be made available as data for subsequent deductions, and be entitled to a place among the premisses of the science. And in proportion as this is done, in proportion to the completeness of its premisses, and to the skill with which they are reasoned upon, will the science of Political Economy approximate towards that perfection which has been attained in other branches of knowledge; in the same degree will its conclusions correspond with actual events, and its doctrines become safe and trustworthy guides to the practical statesman and the philanthropist.

Having now considered the character and limits of Political Economy, we shall conclude this lecture by adverting briefly to a point—not, as might at first sight seem, of purely theoretic importance, on which some high authorities are at variance. We allude to the question whether Political Economy be a positive or a hypothetical science. It does not appear that the meaning of the terms 'positive' and 'hypothetical,' as they have been used in this controversy, has been precisely fixed, and I am disposed to think that the difference of opinion which prevails may, in a great measure, be resolved into an ambiguity of language. Let us consider, then, what is to be understood by the terms 'positive' and 'hypothetical' when applied to a science.

In the first place, we may describe a science as 'positive' or 'hypothetical' with reference to the character of its premisses. It is in this sense that we speak of Mathematics as a hypothetical science, its premisses being arbitrary conceptions framed by the mind, which have nothing corresponding to them in the world of real existence; and it is in this sense that we distinguish it from the positive physical sciences, the premisses of which are laid in the existing facts of nature. But 'positive' and 'hypothetical' may also be used with reference to the conclusions of a science; and in this sense all the physical sciences which have advanced so far as to admit of deductive reasoning must be considered hypothetical, in contradistinction to those less advanced sciences which, being still in the purely inductive stage, express in their conclusions merely observed and generalized facts.

The conclusions, *e.g.*, of a mechanician or of an astronomer, though correctly deduced from premisses representing concrete realities, may have nothing accurately to correspond with them in nature. The mechanician may have overlooked the disturbing influence of friction. The astronomer may have been ignorant of the existence of some planet, the attractive force of which may be an essential element in the solution of his problem.

The conclusions of each, therefore, when applied to facts, can only be said to be true *in the absence of disturbing causes;* which is, in other words, to say that they are true on *the hypothesis* that the premisses include all the causes affecting the result. The correspondence of such deductions with facts may, according to the circumstances of each case, possess any degree of probability, from a mere presumption in favour of a particular result to a probability scarcely distinguishable from absolute certainty. This will depend on the degree of perfection which the science has attained; but whatever be that degree of perfection, from the limited nature of man's faculties he can never be sure that he is in possession of all the premisses affecting the result; and therefore can never be certain that his conclusions represent positive realities. Speaking, therefore, with reference to the conclusions of those physical sciences in which deductive reasoning is employed, such sciences must be regarded as hypothetical.

On the other hand, in those sciences which have not advanced far enough to admit of deductive reasoning, such laws as they have arrived at, being mere generalized statements of observed phenomena, represent not hypothetical but positive truth. Such are the generalized facts in geology and in many of the natural sciences.

Now Political Economy seems in this respect plainly to belong to the same class of sciences with Mechanics, Astronomy, Optics, Chemistry, Electricity, and, in general, all those physical sciences which have reached the deductive stage. Its premisses are not arbitrary figments of the mind, formed without reference to concrete existences, like those of Mathematics; nor are its conclusions mere generalized statements of observed facts, like those of the purely inductive natural sciences. But, like Mechanics or Astronomy, its premisses represent positive facts; whilst its conclusions, like the conclusions of these sciences, may or may not correspond to the realities of external nature, and therefore must be considered as representing only hypothetical truth. It is positively true, *e.g.*, to assert that men desire wealth, that they seek, according to their lights, the easiest and shortest means by which to attain their ends, and that consequently they desire to obtain wealth with the least exertion of labour possible; and it is a logical deduction from this principle, that, where perfect liberty of action is permitted, labourers will seek those employments, and capitalists those modes of investing their capital, in which, *ceteris paribus,* wages and profits are highest.

It is further a necessary consequence of this principle, that, were it universally and constantly acted upon, the rate of profit and the rate of wages over the whole world would not indeed be the same, but would stand, or tend to stand, in the same relation to the actual sacrifices undergone by the recipients of these two kinds of remuneration. Yet so far is this from being the case, that there are scarcely two countries in which wages and profits (meaning thereby the average rate of each) are not permanently different. The French labourer will content himself with the rate of wages which prevails in France, rather than cross the Atlantic for a double remuneration. The English capitalist will prefer eight or ten per cent. profit with English society to the quadruple returns of California or Australia.

The same inequality which we find in the average rates of wages and profits prevailing in different countries, we find also in a less degree in the different departments of productive industry in the same country. What in the former case is done by the love of country to control the simple desire for wealth and aversion to labour, and to modify the resulting phenomena, is done in the latter by the ignorance and poverty of large classes which disable them for competing for the more lucrative employments, and by opinions and prejudices respecting the degree of credit or respectability attaching to particular trades and employments, such as prevail in every civilized community.

It is evident, therefore, that an economist, arguing from the unquestionable facts of man's nature—the desire of wealth and the aversion to labour—and arguing with strict logical accuracy, may yet, if he omits to notice other principles also affecting the question, be landed in conclusions which have no resemblance to existing realities. But he can never be certain that he does not omit some essential circumstance, and, indeed, it is scarcely possible to include all: it is evident, therefore, that, as is the case in those deductive physical sciences to which I have alluded, his conclusions will correspond with facts *only in the absence of disturbing causes,* which is, in other words, to say that they represent not positive but hypothetic truth.

It thus appears that Political Economy, according as we consider it with reference to its premisses or to the doctrines deduced from them, must be regarded in the one case as a positive, in the other as a hypothetical science. It is, however, to be remarked that that portion of the science which represents positive truth—its premisses, namely, or the facts mental and physical upon which it rests—belongs to it in common with many other sciences and arts. All that is properly speaking Political Economy is that system of doctrines which has been, or may be, deduced from those premisses; and all this represents, as I have shown, hypothetical truth. It appears to me, therefore, clearly proper that Political Economy should be classed as a hypothetical science.

PROBLEMS OF LOGICAL METHOD IN POLITICAL ECONOMY

The development of statistical data and technique, and the marked tendency toward the broadening of the scope of economic inquiry, have again made the problem of economic method an appropriate theme for discussion. This discussion cannot be left entirely to the logician, partly because he shows little interest in it and partly because there are many phases of it on which the economist can best throw light.

There is a tendency among economists to fear overmuch for the integrity of their science and to try to maintain its borders intact by carefully avoiding encroachment on the fields of other sciences. Specialization has its advantages, as the economist has good occasion to know, but unorganized specialization means confusion instead of co-operation. If any body of scientists fail to adapt the subject matter of their particular science to the needs of other sciences, each of the other sciences must appropriate from it such of its data as it needs for its own purposes, and even, if necessary, retain for itself the right of judgment on disputes within that science which have bearing on its own problems. And in no other of its border-line problems does political economy so urgently require a recasting and reanalysis of its principles as in the problems of logical method in political economy.

The logical doctrines of the average economist are antiquated and inadequate for his needs. Furthermore, the literature of economic method is dominated by the writings of a group of economists who were at the same time logicians of a narrow and largely discredited school. These economists, influenced by their general logical dogmas, either rejected induction *in toto*as a possible method of economic research, or gave it only grudging admission as the veriest handmaid to the deductive method. Contemporary logic has thrown new light on the character and possibilities of the inductive method and has conceded it a much more generous scope.

If the economist follows the old economic logicians in their rejection of induction, his own practice, generally better than his precepts, forces him into contradictions from which he finds only partial escape by belated and inconsistent concessions to a method of whose value he would at first admit nothing. It is the purpose of this paper to set forth the differences between the two methods as they concern the economist, to state and examine the case which has been made against the use of the inductive method in economic research, and to outline the possibilities and the limitations of the method. The discussion of such logical problems and the use of such technical terminology as do not seem absolutely essential to the presentation of the argument will be carefully avoided. Deduction and induction are the two logical processes of thought, and are the reverse of each other in character, the former being the process of analyzing a generalization into its particular propositions, the latter the process of building up a generalization from a number of particular propositions.

The deductive inference must start with a generalization, and generalizations are obtainable only in three ways: by complete enumeration of the individual propositions comprising the generalization, by hypothesis or assumption, or by inductive inference from incomplete enumeration. The first method is not a method of reasoning, since it merely supplies us with a collective expression for a number of known identical propositions; the second becomes inductive as soon as an attempt is made to bring it into touch with reality, since the generalization derives what validity it may thus obtain from the particular instances found to support it; the third is of course pure induction. Unless a science is wholly abstract or hypothetical, it must therefore rely on inductive inferences for its fundamental general propositions, and must consist largely of inductive inference and the deductive application of such inference to narrower groups of instances. Only the mathematical sciences are purely deductive, and they have remained so by remaining purely abstract.

Inductive reasoning has its psychological basis in our instinctive tendencies to believe in the existence of a uniformity of causation in nature, and to argue from analogy and the association of ideas. In its fully developed scientific form it is of course much more. True induction is never merely the inference, from a few or many observed instances of the coexistence of two phenomena, of the universal necessity of such a correlationship. It demands the intuitive belief, obtainable only through knowledge and insight of the phenomena, that the coexistence was a necessary one in each instance of its discovery. It demands, also, the careful examination of new instances, before we may conclude that they resemble the old in the characteristics which seem to be essential to the existence of the supposed relationship.

Furthermore, it demands the absence of known contrary instances, and the assurance that such contrary instances would have been discovered did they exist. Only after these conditions have been fulfilled may we be reasonably certain of the truth of our conclusion. Inductive reasoning can never bring absolute certainty, but it may bring any degree of conviction from a mere probability to what may be accepted as certainty for all practical purposes. But the deductive method cannot bring more certain positive results, since its conclusions are either hypothetical or are derived from inductive premises of uncertain truth in the logical sense. The academic logician, whether he be economist or not, who demands absolute certainty as the canon of research, who sees no pause in the descent from absolute certainty to random guesswork, is therefore setting up a standard impossible of attainment in any but the purely abstract sciences. The nature of the methodological problem in political economy is not, therefore, whether induction can or must be entirely dispensed with—unless there is any sound argument in favor of making economics a purely abstract, hypothetical science. Nor need it necessarily be conceived as a comparison of the relative importance of the two methods. The important problem for the economist is rather the question of the possibility of an extended use of the inductive method in research in other than a fashion purely subsidiary to deduction.

The economists have surpassed the logicians, as is perhaps natural, in the looseness with which they have used the term induction. Thus, by Pierson the value of induction in economic research has been contrasted with the value of reasoning, as if the two terms were opposites. By many writers of the "historical school" induction was asserted to be the principal and even the only method of political economy, although they often used the term as if it meant the simple observation of particular phenomena without any attempt at the inference of general principles therefrom.

It is no longer necessary to spend time in refuting the claim that the mere record of the historical sequence of facts can be made to reveal an enlightening philosophy of history or to disclose without further analysis or interpretation an explanation of contemporary economic phenomena. But the identification of the historical with the inductive methods is a mistaken one, and the weakness of the former in nowise involves the latter.

The cause of induction has been further weakened by the excessive claims made for it and of it. Thus Mayo-Smith's contention that by a simple process of analogy we can reason "from the prosperity of England to the principle of free trade, at least for industrially developed nations," is an exaggeration of the ease of research regardless of the methods employed, and is based on an inadequate notion of the nature and limitations of the inductive method, derived largely from his intellectual connections with the "historical school." Similarly the critics of the inductive method have chosen their illustration of its inefficacy from just those problems which are the last to which the inductive economist would attempt to apply his methods. Mill offers, as tests of the possibility of the use of induction in political economy, such problems as the determination of "the effect of a particular circumstance in education upon the formation of character," and believes that the failure of the inductive economist to solve such problems demonstrates the futility of his method.

The objections to the use of the inductive method which have proved to be of most weight are those made by that group of English economists who were at the same time logicians of considerable authority, and were thus peculiarly able to impose their logical doctrines on economic literature. Most important of these was John Stuart Mill, and it is to his criticism of the method that we shall chiefly direct our attention. Mill defined induction more broadly than do most logicians and did not demand for its successful application the fulfilment of all those conditions which we have put forth as essential to the true inductive method. Furthermore, he interpreted induction as a method bringing conclusions of absolute certainty.

As a result of the breadth of his definition and the extent of his demands of the method, he was led to limit the possible application of the method to the fields in which the difficulties were fewest and of least importance. What these alleged limitations are, we cannot grasp until we have examined Mill's exposition of the technique of induction.

The technique of induction, first developed by Herschel, was given its most elaborate treatment by Mill in his *System of Logic.* His analysis of the methods of induction has been severely criticized by logicians, but the main points have remained intact, and it is mainly on questions of interpretation and formulation that his treatment has received any very important modifications. I shall follow Mill's treatment, except where the revisions suggested by modern logicians are of significance to the problem of economic method.

The purpose of an induction being supposed to be the proof that A is a cause of B, the problem of induction is, What are the possible methods of obtaining this proof? They all resolve themselves into a demonstration that B is present wherever A is present, and that B is absent wherever A is absent. If, in a number of otherwise diverse situations, B is always found to be present when A is present, we may conclude that A and B are causally connected—the method of agreement. If the addition of A to a situation from which it was formerly absent causes B to appear in the situation, and if the subtraction of A from the situation causes B to disappear, we may conclude that A and B are causally connected—the method of difference.

Each of these methods may be improved if in each case we examine all the negative instances of A, and find that B is always absent when A is absent—the methods of double agreement and of double difference. These are the primary methods, from which are derived two other methods, the methods of residues and of concomitant variations. These latter Mill seems to thinly of quite minor importance, and in his discussion of the scope of the inductive method in political economy he practically ignores them. We will reserve further consideration of them until we have dealt with Mill's treatment of the primary methods.

The method of (single) agreement is applicable where experimentation is not possible. Mill asserts, however, that the method is unreliable for ascertaining causal sequences, because of the so-called plurality of causes to be found in nature. The method of (single) difference, on the other hand, almost always demands experiment, since it is very rarely that one finds in nature several situations resembling one another in every possible respect except the presence in some and the absence in others of a single cause and its effect. The "double methods" both require experiment for their application, since in no other way can we make sure that we have exhausted all the instances in which the cause to be studied is absent. Because of the existence of the plurality of causes, the use of the inductive method as an independent method of research is therefore impossible unless resort can be had to experiment and the artificial manipulation of material. Since the plurality of causes is most prominent in the phenomena with which the social sciences deal, and since experiment is practically impossible in these sciences, Mill is finally led to conclude that the inductive method is of no value in these sciences.

The plurality of causes, of which Mill makes so much, is not nearly so important as he supposed. Mill does not distinguish between the doctrine that different causes may produce the same effect, to which alone the term may properly be applied, and the entirely independent doctrine that different causes may combine to produce a joint effect, but gives his adherence to both without any discrimination. Plurality of causation, if it were really existent in nature, would place serious obstacles in the way of scientific research not only by means of the inductive method, but by means of any of the methods of thought with which we are acquainted.

But it seems to be the consensus of modern opinion, both among logicians and among the physical scientists, that the plurality of causes is apparent rather than real; that the belief in the plurality of causes is the result, not so much of its actual existence in nature, as of our inability to reduce nature to its simpler elements. The apparent plurality vanishes before exact investigation, wherever such investigation is possible. But the concurrence of causes, the combination of causes to produce a joint effect, is to be found in all actual situations. The doctrine of plurality, therefore, is only a practical working caution. Until we definitely discover the *immediate* cause, we must remember that what are apparently different causes may bring about the same event. If we can extend our investigation, we shall always discover, however, that the same immediate cause is contained in all these combinations of causes.

The problem of induction is to analyze these combinations of causes and of effects into their separate elements, and then to proceed to the attempt at discovery of necessary relationships between the individual causes and the individual effects. Is isolation of factors for observation and experiment as impossible for the economist as Mill believes it to be?

And is isolation of factors the only possible method of analysis of complex economic situations? To answer these questions and to explain Mill's affirmative answers, we must examine his statement of the nature of the subject matter and the problems of political economy. Mill conceives political economy to be a psychological science. Political economy is "the science relating to the moral or psychological laws of the production and distribution of wealth." The laws of political economy, according to Mill, are laws of mind. And the methods applied to the investigation of laws of matter cannot be used in the determination of the laws of mind, since "laws of matter and laws of mind are so dissimilar in their nature, that it would be contrary to all principles of rational arrangement to mix them up as part of the same study. In all scientific methods, therefore, they are placed apart." Human psychology is not available for inductive study, because of the differences between individual minds, the immense multitude of the influencing circumstances, the practical difficulty of experiment upon human beings.

Even in operating upon an individual mind, which is the case affording greatest room for experimenting, we cannot often obtain a crucial experiment. The effect for example of a particular circumstance in education, upon the formation of character, may be tried in a variety of cases, but we can hardly ever be certain that any two of those cases differ in all their circumstances except the solitary one of which we wish to estimate the influence. In how much greater a degree must this difficulty exist in the affairs of states.

Political economy, therefore, is conceived by Mill as a study of human psychology. But not of all human psychology, or even of real human psychology, but only of an assumed psychology.

Geometry presupposes an arbitrary definition of a line, "that which has length but not breadth." Just in the same manner does Political Economy presuppose an arbitrary definition of man as a being who invariably does that by which he may obtain the greatest amount of necessaries, conveniences and luxuries, with the smallest quantity of labour and physical self-denial with which they can be obtained in the existing state of knowledge.... Political Economy, therefore, reasons from *assumed*premises—from premises which might be totally without foundation in fact, and which are not pretended to be universally in accordance with it.

But the assumptions are not confined to the "economic man." They are extended, although less explicitly, to the environment to which this creature is supposed to react. Private property, perfect competition, *laissez faire,* the English land-tenure system, are assumed to be as universal as the "economic" psychology. A hypothetical psychology and a hypothetical environment cannot, of course, be subjected to anything but hypothetical examination or experimentation. So long as the science is built upon such a basis, Mill is justified in claiming deduction as its only possible logical method, and that not a positive but an "a priori" or hypothetical deduction.

It was in this way that the English economists hoped to build an abstract economic science, closely resembling the mathematical sciences, and indeed with these sciences as their model. From the limited number of hypothetical propositions of human psychology and of the social environment accepted as the fundamental postulates of the science, there was to be derived the whole body of economic doctrine. The validity of this doctrine was conditional upon the validity of the postulates upon which it was built. If anyone chose to compare these doctrines with reality, he was at perfect liberty to do so, but in doing so he was stepping beyond the bounds of economic science, and indeed of any science. "To verify the hypothesis itself a posteriori, that is, to examine whether the facts of any actual case are in accordance with it, is no part of the business of science at all, but of the *application* of science." When the abstract economists concede that the work of testing and verifying the hypotheses, and of bringing them into agreement with reality, is to be done by induction—as they often do—this does not therefore involve the concession of a place for induction in economic research.

The abstract economists exaggerate the possibility of obtaining a vast deal of knowledge from a system of deductions derived from an initial set of four or five propositions. Even the mathematical sciences, although they have the advantage of a completely abstract set of fundamental propositions, could not advance very far were it not that they start either with an infinite series of such propositions, as does algebra, or, like geometry, are continually introducing new material in the form of postulates, axioms, definitions, and hypotheses. The possibility of drawing out new knowledge in an endless stream from a given set of initial propositions, as a magician draws endless ribbons of paper from an empty hat, is a purely fictitious one.

And of the two alternatives to the economist, of either relying on his imagination or resorting to a study of economic facts for his new material, the latter method is probably less subject to exhaustion.

The contentions for such heroic abstraction as was advocated by the English economists seem to be as follows: Men are motivated by such conflicting desires, and the possibility of direct observation of these desires in isolated operation is so limited that only by abstraction from all the motives which actuate men except the "economic" one, and only by deduction from our knowledge of the action of this desire obtained through our introspective examination of its operation within ourselves, and our inference—induction!—that it operates likewise within other individuals, can we get sweeping generalizations of universal application.

Similarly, only by assuming a uniform environment, and again relying on our introspection for the discovery of how the "economic" motive would operate in such an environment, can we save our generalizations, which apply to all men, from limitations by differences in the situations in which these men find themselves. To modify or reduce the extension of our generalizations, as differences appear in the psychology and environment of different individuals or groups, is to step beyond the bounds of economic science into the field of application of science. This reasoning does not seem very convincing. Almost always the value of very wide generalizations lies in their being broken up into narrower ones. We have in actual life to deal with special, and not general, situations, and the value of general principles consists in their provision of starting-points from which to derive less general principles, covering fewer instances, but telling us more of each instance. The old knowledge in each such case is obtained from the wider generalization, the new knowledge is the product of an inductive inference. In order to derive any benefit from our knowledge of how the "economic motive" operates in a handpicked selection of more or less hypothetical situations, we must compare that knowledge with what additional knowledge we can obtain from an examination of the actual situations in their multiform variety.

How much of the reduction of generalizations, to apply to narrower and more completely described groups of instances, may be left safely to the individual practicing the art built upon that science, how near we may approach to particularism, at what stage the scientist may assume that he has obtained sufficient insight into the situations and their problems to make uneconomical and unwise a still further analysis, only individual practice and experience can reveal. The scientist, developing methods and tools of research, must confine himself to fairly extensive generalizations. The individual, practicing the art derived from that science, must start where the scientist leaves off, and end finally at the handling of particular facts.

We have been too much dominated by the reasoning of Mill and his school, to the effect that application begins and political economy ceases as soon as we depart from the romantic generalizations of widest possible scope—generalizations as thin as they are broad. As a result, we are accustomed to regard the fields of money, or of labor, or of commerce, as "applied economics," lying outside the field of economic theory. Occasionally we even meet a worker in these fields who claims freedom from the necessity of using economic "theory" or any theory. These critics of economic "theory" are, let us hope, really critics of those excessive generalizations of the pure deductive school, which are not always capable of being brought into closer touch with actual phenomena, and which, even if capable of comparison with reality, remain either extremely devoid of content or extremely removed from direct relevance to the problems of this world. But theory, generalization, the systematization and organization of facts and the inference of causal laws therefrom, they must resort to, even in their "applied" fields, or they cease to be scientists, and become either descriptive artists or plyers of trades.

The abstract economists justify their method by appeal to the example set by the mathematical sciences, a case of faulty inductive inference. For the abstractions of the a priori economists, particularly if these economists conformed in practice to the precepts dictated by their methodological theories, would be extremely heroic, while those of the mathematician are for ordinary purposes of little practical import. The areas contained in points and lines do not trouble the carpenter, unless he is using a blunt pencil; and the relations between ten and twenty which are only postulated by the mathematician for ten in the abstract and twenty in the abstract seem to work equally well when the ten or twenty are pounds or cabbages or dollars.

But the "postulates" of the classical political economy, while restricted and scanty enough, were not as hypothetical or "assumed" as was supposed by the economists who formulated them. The psychology of the "economic man," faulty and unsatisfactory as it was, in the one characteristic essential to the economist above all others was not nearly as remote from reality as his creators supposed. In fact it may almost be said that the "economic man" was an actual Englishman of the commercial world, the description of whose behavior was correctly obtained by inductive inference from observation, but marred and distorted by faulty deductions from an inaccurate introspective, speculative psychology, in an attempt to obtain a rational explanation of the motivation of his behavior. In his commercial activity, with which the economist is primarily concerned, man is thoroughly economic.

As economists we are concerned with his ends and not with his motives. His motives may be numerous enough and complex enough to merit the abstractions of the old economists, but in his ends he is simple enough for inductive investigation. The bottle of medicine for a dying child, or of wine for himself; the tools for his trade; the supplies for a home for the aged, bought as a contribution to the home from a future inmate—all are bought with the same end of getting the most for the least, whatever the motive for the purchase may be. Nor in asserting that the ordinary individual, in his economic activity, of his possible alternatives follows the one he most desires to follow—which is all the economist need assert—do we preclude ourselves from the admission that a laborer will not necessarily seek the higher wage if it involves the harder work or the longer day.

It is of course allowable in the interests of science to start from such a fiction as that a number of persons are ruled only by egoism, and from the further fiction that the means of satisfying this egoism are seen and applied by them reasonably and consistently. But because a reality corresponding to these hypotheses can nowhere be ascertained, the deductions of this exact process cannot be confronted with reality.

It seems a more fruitful way, and one more easily compared with reality, to start from ends. To obtain the greatest possible value with the least possible outlay of labour and capital is an end, which is not only quite comprehensible, but is extensively present and acknowledged; from what motives individuals place this end before them is a further question which is not necessary to take into immediate consideration for the consequences of the end.... It is this end which must logically determine the behavior of man to a large extent. Whatever follows this end under given actual conditions can be constructed and can be directly compared with reality.... In construction from motives we must work from the fictitious normal man. In commercial activity the economic end fails to act in isolation only to the extent to which one party to an economic transaction concerns himself with the motives or welfare of the other. With the growing degree of impersonality this moral factor becomes negligible; and the economic transaction becomes non-moral in the sense that each party excludes the other from his moral situation.

The parties may not know each other, may deal only through an intermediary, human or mechanical, and except for the plane of competition as dictated by the various relevant forms of social control neither is influenced by anything but his immediate economic end. The plane of competition is always, at least in commercially advanced countries, a lower one morally than that on which man's more personal contact with man takes place. Commercial transactions were not always impersonal—and therefore non-moral—nor are they completely so in special instances in advanced countries, or generally in backward countries.

One cannot argue toward the determination of contract rents paid by tenant farmers in England on the basis of a deductive theory of rent resting on the complete dominance of the economic end—as one may perhaps for urban rents in New York City. But if an inductive examination of the situation studied should lead us to believe that the economic end is dominant there in so far as concerns economic transactions, we are not driven to abstractions to discover what are the reactions of the group of individuals to the various economic phenomena within that situation.

The economist is concerned with human behavior, and with human psychology only in so far as it is necessary for an explanation of human behavior in its economic aspects. In order to learn how men will act in a given situation, or how a change in the situation will modify their behavior, it is surely more practical to observe their behavior than to attempt to discover by introspection or otherwise what they might be supposed to do if actuated by a certain motive operating alone. Both methods are inductive, but the former seems to meet the canons of induction much more satisfactorily than the latter. Even the psychologist as such is beginning to rely less and less upon abstract, speculative propositions, and to explain human psychology by the acts of men under given circumstances rather than by the mental processes behind these acts, which are not subject to inductive examination.

The modern trend in psychology is decidedly away from introspection and the attempt to explain behavior by rational motives revealed by introspection. The psychologist looks rather to the systematic observation of behavior as the source of psychological generalizations, and uses the inductive method—experimental only in part—as a means of obtaining his general principles. The part which consciousness plays cannot be so revealed, of course, and here the method of inference from specific observation fails, but the economist as such is concerned only with the external aspects of human psychology, and can well afford to leave the analysis of motives to the speculative psychologist. The bonds which tie political economy to an out-of-date rational hedonistic psychology and its appropriate logical method of investigation are not indissoluble.

But of even more importance to the fixation of economic method than the shortcomings of their psychology is the failure of the English classical economists, in their writings on methodology, to realize that political economy is not wholly or even predominantly psychological in character. One would be justified in concluding from Mill's definition and description of the science that political economy is a subdivision of psychology, concerned with the workings of one human motive.

The economist is not only concerned with man's reactions to his environment in their objective manifestations, but he must also examine and analyze the environment and study the effects upon it of man's reactions to it. Political economy has been too often described as if it were merely a "pure" or a priori psychological theory of value and distribution. Of much greater importance to the economist than any "pure" theory are the knowledge and understanding of the concrete facts of production, distribution, consumption, of the whole economic situation with all its causal processes. To most of this material the processes of specific observation, systematization, and inductive inference are applicable. To much of it, particularly in its dynamic processes, or processes of change, no other method is of any service.

That the great field for research in political economy lies in the analysis of that vast proportion of economic phenomena which are predominantly objective in character, recent tendencies in economic literature and in the scientific activities of economists amply demonstrate. Objective economic phenomena not only can be subjected to specific observations, but can even be submitted to that further process of analysis which consists of the classification, enumeration, and weighing of phenomena.

If this is possible, analysis of complex situations into their constituent causes and effects, which Mill maintained was possible only abstractly by deduction, has been made capable of accomplishment by the direct method of induction. Psychological quantities themselves, though not at yet subject to direct measurement, can be measured with some approximation to accuracy through their objective manifestations. Wealth in terms of commodities, for instance, while far from being an accurate measure of welfare, may, for certain problems involving large masses of mankind in varying degrees of prosperity, indicate accurately enough for the purposes of the economist what changes have taken place in conditions of welfare.

Of the methods of induction which we have already described, the method of agreement is always qualitative, and the method of difference when used quantitatively is only rudimentary, and is simply an undeveloped form of a more valuable quantitative method. It was to these two methods in their qualitative forms that Mill and the other writers on economic method have directed most of their attention.

This was due in part to their narrow definition of political economy, which would make of it an intensive study of the operations of one psychological motive, and in part to the belief that all the objective phenomena of real importance, at least to the abstract science, were matters of common knowledge and experience, not demanding systematic observation and analysis. If not immediately present to consciousness, the information was obtainable in predigested form from other sciences.

With the accumulation of quantitative data, inference from the facts of common experience and knowledge gives way in importance to the method of inference from facts not discoverable except by methodical and scientific investigation of economic phenomena. Jevons, in arguing against the use of induction in political economy, asserts that the data of the economist are either the results of investigation by other sciences, or else are "old inductions" belonging to the collective experience of mankind.

He derives from this contention the conclusion that "specific" or systematic investigation of phenomena is not of value to the economist. But Jevons' facts merely describe political economy as it was when he wrote; they do not detract from the value of the more scientific and productive methods of acquiring data followed by other sciences, unless we grant that political economy has, with such data as it has otherwise secured, already reached a stage of perfection.

The methods of qualitative induction can be applied only to situations where changes in kind have occurred, where a cause and a resultant effect different in kind from those already present are suddenly introduced, or make a sudden appearance in an economic situation. In actual economic situations causes rarely disappear entirely, and as rarely make entirely new appearances. Thus with the narrow limitations on such experiment as consists in the addition or subtraction of causes in their entirety, the qualitative methods are scarcely ever completely applicable to economic problems and can be used with any approach to certainty only where the appearances or disappearances, whether natural or contrived, are so great that the original or the persistent elements can be safely disregarded as minor and negligible quantities.

While these methods have limited scope in political economy, they are far, however, from being altogether inapplicable. Even those economists who were most decided in their contention that the abstract deductive method was the only one available to the economist made considerable use of these inductive methods in their economic researches. In some cases, their chief contributions to political economy were predominantly inductive in character. Thus Mill's entire theory of production his discussion of the effectiveness of the various systems of land tenure, his analysis of large-scale production and of the laws of increase of labor, capital, and productiveness from land, his explanation of the differences of wages in different employments, his chapter on the future conditions of the working classes, his discussion of the problems of taxation, are characteristically inductive. Cairnes, who was even more extreme than Mill in his belief in the futility of economic inductions, based his theory of non-competing groups on inductive reasoning, supported his theory of international trade by an inductive examination of gold movements and price levels in Australia, and made an entire volume of an inductive examination of the economics of slavery. Bagehot was equally inconsistent, since his work was almost entirely inductive—much of it quantitative induction, however—while Jevons made an inductive examination of the coal industry and also tried to establish, by an application of the inductive method of agreement, the existence of a causal relationship between the recurrence of sunspots and the recurrence of business crises.

But the quantitative methods give promise of a much wider scope to induction in political economy. Quantitative induction—inference from measured or statistical data—is always preferable to qualitative induction, where the data have been gathered with sufficient accuracy of enumeration and classification, and in sufficient quantity. The mere fact that the factors in a situation have been measured and classified indicates a high degree of analysis of the situation and of knowledge of its significant elements, and makes it less difficult to avoid overlooking any essential elements.

The quantitative methods of induction are the methods of residues and of concomitant variations, of which the latter will undoubtedly prove to be by far the more important to the economist. The canon of the method of residues is thus stated by Mill: "Subduct from any phenomena such part as is known by previous *inductions* to be the effect of certain antecedents, and the residue of the phenomenon is the effect of the remaining antecedents." Thus stated, the method assumes that we have already successfully performed several inductions. The method is applicable where a number of causes combine to produce a joint effect, and all the causes but one can be submitted to specific inspection. If we wish to learn how much of the effect is to be attributed to this cause, we can do so by subtracting from the total effect all that is attributable to the other causes.

If all the causes are subject to specific inspection, it is a safer and less burdensome method to examine directly the cause whose effect we wish to learn. This method can only disclose a correlationship existing at a given moment and can use statistical material covering a period of time only through separate inferences for each statistical time unit. The method of residues is, in fact, of value, not so much in demonstrating the existence of a certain causal relationship, as in pointing out an as yet unexplained effect, or portion of an effect, the cause of which is to be sought. The method of concomitant variations, on the other hand, is a direct method of discovering causal relationships where measurement of variations in phenomena over a period of time is possible. It may be stated simply as follows: Wherever some correspondence can be found between the variations of two phenomena in the same situation, we may conclude that these phenomena are causally connected.

It is not essential to this method that exact measurement of the phenomena be possible, but only that the intensities, or directions and degrees of change, of the two phenomena shall be comparable. If mortality from consumption varies with the amount of house-room per person, or if output per hour varies with the amount of light in the workshop or the length of the working day, we may in each case conclude that these phenomena are causally connected.

Where several causes combine to produce a given effect, the effect may not vary with variations in one of the causes if these are offset by variations in the remainder of the causal situation. The method is applicable with a great deal of certainty where one element in the situation varies greatly, while the remainder of the situation is fairly constant. Under such circumstances, which among economic phenomena are by no means rare, the minor variations may be disregarded, especially since exact results are not required in political economy.

Even where several of the concurrent causes vary considerably, the method is often applicable, although with a lesser degree of certainty. Artificial elimination of the disturbing cause may be possible, although this resource is of course very limited to the economist. Or it may be possible to discover the amount of influence exercised by the other factors by their examination in other fields. If the variations in the other factors follow a regular ascertainable order of change, the comparative importance of these factors at the different moments of time can be gauged, and allowance made with some accuracy for the amount of change in the effect to be attributed to the variations in these factors. If a great number of situations be studied, and most of the causes combining to produce the effect are minor ones, it will often be found that the changes in these minor causes tend to neutralize each other. Since in all these cases precise results are not demanded, the permissible degree of error may be considerable, without destroying the value of the results if the variations in the essential factors have been great.

For preliminary induction by the method of concomitant variations, it is sufficient to know that A varies as B, without further knowledge of the data which these symbols represent, to infer a causal relationship between A and B. It is on the basis of preliminary induction that many of the statistical tests of correlation and methods of allowance for error find their logical justification. But for true induction, the fact that a correlationship of phenomena is found, and persists throughout the period of investigation and throughout all the situations studied, would not be accepted even in the absence of contrary evidence or of the expectation of the discovery of contrary evidence, as a sufficient demonstration of the necessity of such a concurrence. For true induction, there is further demanded a direct acquaintance with the data and the situation, and an intuitive belief arising from the insight obtained through such acquaintance, that in each instance of the concurrence, such concurrence seemed a necessity of the situation, and not a possible coincidence. In concluding from an observed concurrence between two statistically measured phenomena that the concurrence is a necessary one, our inference obtains greater scientific validity when we discover that the phenomena we knew as A and B are congestion and mortality, or fatigue and output, or similar phenomena which by their known characteristics suggest the possibility of correlationship.

Correlationships in statistical data do not demonstrate themselves automatically. Some hypothesis is a preliminary to every inductive investigation. What elements of the situation shall be measured, and which of the measured elements are to be compared in the search for causal correlationship, cannot be determined by any set rules. Discovery, whether direct discovery of the correlationship within a mass of accidentally contiguous data, or, what is more probable, indirectly through the flash of insight which suggests a possible hypothesis, confirmation of which is to be sought in the data, is an essential preliminary of the inductive method; and discovery, in all its phases, is never automatic, or the simple result of formulated rules of discovery mechanically followed. But direct knowledge of, and keen insight into, the situation to be analyzed is necessary, not only as a preliminary to the discovery of causal relationships between constituent elements, but for the knowledge of what are its constituent elements.

4

Economic Models for Political Analysis

SOCIAL AND POLITICAL ANALYSIS

At the dawn of the 21st century, neoliberalism is the predominant political and economic model in the world, impacting every level of society. While giving the appearance of dominance, the neoliberal model is built on increasingly shaky ground, including shrinking democratic spaces, unsuccessful attempts at cultural hegemony under the guise of "modernization," and a distorted distribution of wealth that has no historic precedent. The majority of the world's people are in a savage "race to the bottom" - poorer today than they were three decades ago - and no amount of propaganda can hide this stark reality. For the past four decades, the US-Mexico relationship has been the most important laboratory for the neoliberal model, a sort of proving grounds for corporate-centered globalization. The implications of this experiment will be felt for generations to come, both North and South.

The neoliberal era began four decades ago on the US-Mexico border with the Border Industrialization Programme, a "free trade zone" that ushered in the era of maquiladoras. Factories that paid decent wages in the US moved south of the border, where wages are typically less than $1 an hour, labor laws are lax, and environmental standards are not enforced. The result is huge profits for transnational corporations, but declining standards of living for the Mexican and the US working classes, and an environmental disaster that affects both sides of the border.

The maquiladora/free trade model is now the predominant economic development model throughout Latin America. In 1981, under pressure from the Latin American debt crisis, Mexico signed the first IMF-sponsored Structural Adjustment Programme (SAP) in exchange for bailout loans. Today, SAPs are standard fair throughout the South, forcing governments with progressive tendencies to adopt neoliberal economic policies (or providing more conservative elites with political cover to do the same). The North America Free Trade Accord (NAFTA), signed on January 1, 1994, is defining future US economic relations with the rest of Latin America - free flows of capital and goods across international borders but strict control of people. NAFTA has meant a loss of democracy in Mexico and the US, and an economic disaster for workers on both sides of the border.Neoliberal policies have had a dramatic impact in rural areas throughout Latin America, particularly in Mexico. Highly subsidized corn exports from the US destroyed the internal corn market, placing nearly one-quarter of the Mexican population in dire circumstances. The result is massive migration, either to urban centers in Mexico or as undocumented workers to the United States.

Neoliberal policies are directly responsible for this historically unprecedented migration, yet they barely enter the discussion on immigration policy. The neoliberal model represents a globalization of class alliances. The wealthiest 5 or 10% on both sides of the border, those who control the economies and political systems, have more in common with each other than they do with their fellow citizens, and the resulting neoliberal policies reflect their interests. The elites enjoy increasingly strong institutional links, while the rest of us are left with less democracy, fewer economic options, more repression, increased poverty and less sovereignty.

In a world of growing globalization, international grassroots alliances become increasingly important in the struggle for democracy, sovereignty, and economic and political justice. The US-Mexico relationship is central in defining the ties between elites, and it is also central in defining increasingly important grassroots connections within civil society on both sides of the border. The Mexico Solidarity Network is a community-based organization dedicated to fundamental social change that challenges existing power relationships, builds horizontal relations in directly affected communities and promotes autonomous alternatives.

LEGAL POSITIVISM AND POLICY ANALYSIS IN ECONOMIC ANALYSIS OF LAW

The policy analysis strand of economic analysis of law often implicitly adopts some variant of legal positivism as its understanding of the concept of law. Recall that the policy analysis treats the behavior of judges in particular (and sometimes public officials generally) differently from the behavior of those subject to the legal rules.

An economic analysis of the behavioral effects of a legal rule generally begins with the assumption that the legal rule is clearly known not only to judges and other public officials but also to those subject to the legal rule. This knowledge of private citizens might amount simply to the knowledge of what consequences follow from each possible action the agent might take. Actions that provoke a response from public officials generally, or judges in particular, have no special character to them; the citizen in her deliberations treats the consequences of rule-following or rule-breaking as she treats any other price.

On Hart's account of legal positivism, however, a private citizen may adopt this detached attitude towards legal rules. The concept of law inherent in policy analysis is thus consistent with positivism.

The typical model in economic analysis of law, however, assumes that public officials conscientiously apply the legal rule under study. The public official does not identify the rule that would best promote her own preferences and then apply (or not apply) that rule; rather she "conscientiously" applies the rule that "ought" to govern the event. Conscientious application here simply implies that the official may uncontroversially apply an identified legal rule to the events in question.

This assumption might reflect a "partial equilibrium" approach to the analysis of the problem at hand. If the effects of the legal rule are the central focus of inquiry, the incentives and behavior of public officials who enforce that rule may be of less interest. The analysis of the institutional structures and processes that insure the "conscientious" application of law by public officials are left for later analysis.

Other aspects of the economic analysis of law are consistent with this positivist approach to the law. Economic analysis of social norms, for example, often provides a characterization of social norms that largely coincides with Hart's own scheme for distinguishing social rules that are legal rules from social rules that are not. Specifically, economic analysts of law point to the decentralized character of the promulgation and enforcement of legal rules as the properties that distinguish social norms from legal rules.

TOWARDS A SOCIAL SCIENTIFIC CONCEPT OF LAW?

Two positions dominate philosophical debates over the concept of law. One set of positions, advanced by legal positivists such as Raz [1994] and Coleman [2001] argues that the articulation of a concept of law is an exercise in self-understanding. They pursue their position through conceptual analysis. Call this approach the self-understanding approach. The second position, advanced in a number of variants that differ significantly in substance, for example, by Dworkin [2004], Murphy [2001], and Perry [2001], contends that we should adopt the concept of law that best advances our political aims. Call this the political approach.

Though the two positions disagree on the methodology for determining the concept of law, they apparently agree that a concept of law should provide a unitary answer to three distinct questions. Two of these questions are internal to any legal practice but the third is not, or, at least, not necessarily internal. The first internal question — the professional or doctrinal question — asks: which public, collectively chosen norms ought public officials and citizens use to guide their actions? The second internal question — the adjudicatory question — asks: how ought (or, occasionally, do) judges decide cases? The third question

— the differentiation question — asks: what is the nature of law? What distinctive characteristics of law distinguish it essentially from other social phenomena such as coercion, morality, and politics?

Legal positivists generally have sought to answer the third question. Their answer, however, often connects the first professional question with the third differentiation question. H.L.A. Hart [1961] articulated his project as the differentiation question. The book, though, largely addresses the professional question, arguing that the governing legal rules in the community are identified not by reference to the commands of a sovereign but by reference to rule of recognition used by the legal officials to identify the set of norms that governs their (public) actions. This answer to the professional question provides at least a partial answer to the second, adjudicatory question. After all, legal adjudication must rely at least in part on legal norms and the rule of recognition clearly demarcates legal norms from other norms and grounds of decision. Notice, however, that the the answer to the professional question links it to the differentiation question. What counts as law depends upon the internal perspectives of (some)individuals.

More recently, however, positivists have argued more directly that the answer to the differentiation question rests on law's claim to authority. Raz [1979, 1986], for example, advances this argument. The claim to authority has, as Soper [2002] clearly expresses, two aspects. First, the law claims that it has the right to punish those who violate its prescriptions. Second, the law claims that individuals have a correlative duty to obey the law's prescriptions. Raz argues, somewhat paradoxically, that, though law claims this authority, it generally does not have it.

Characterizing law by its claim to authority does not immediately implicate the content of the law. One need not necessarily answer the professional question in order to answer to the differentiation question.

The Razian answer to the differentiation question may arguably rely on the internal attitudes of individuals and hence provide an internal account. Raz identifies two conditions that the law must meet to make a claim of authority. The second of these, as characterized by Marmor (2011), requires legal authority to be "personal" by which one means that the norm by authored. This reference to authorship apparently implicates the intentional attitudes of individuals within the legal system.

Dworkin, by contrast to the positivists, begins with the second, adjudicatory question. He provides an account of how judges decide cases. He then generalizes this account to an account of law through the recognition that all citizens, not only judges, must apply law. Each must answer the same questions that confront a judge in resolving a case. His theory of adjudication thus also answers the first, professional question; it identifies the legal rules that are in force within the community. Finally, this account distinguishes law from other phenomena because law so identified promotes a distinct political virtue, legality or, as Dworkin terms it, integrity. Dworkin thus offers a fully unitary answer to the three questions. His answer, moreover, adopts an internal perspective on all questions.

Political economy, by contrast, pursues a substantially different project. It seeks to understand the ways in which society structures its political, economic and legal institutions. This project suggests neither a self-conscious nor a political concept of law but a social-scientific one that would help us understand the social world in general, the emergence and persistence of social groups over time and the causes and consequences of different governmental structures. Political economy, or a general sociology, then seeks to answer a question similar to the third, external question of differentiation posed by the philosophical discussion of the concept of law. How do we differentiate structures of social governance from other phenomena within a society such as gangs and games? Similarly, to discover cross cultural and intertemporal regularities, the analyst must identify comparable structures within different societies. That is, our criteria for differentiation must work cross culturally and intertemporally.

An understanding of society and social phenomena, of course, may not require anything akin to the concept of law at issue in the philosophical debates. Two different reasons, however, suggest some relation between the philosophical debate and the social-scientific inquiry. One should recall that Hart [1961] characterized, perhaps off-handedly, his project as one in the descriptive sociology of law. Such a sociological project presumably requires a social scientific concept of law. Moreover, once one had articulated a viable and useful set of social scientific concepts one might ask what relation they bear to the issues at the center of the philosophical inquiries of the value of legality and of articulating the criterion that distinguishes legal from other grounds of decision.

Adopting Hart's discussion as a starting point, we shall in the rest of this subsection, sketch a social-scientific concept of a governance structure and suggest how it might relate both to the project of political economy and to the philosophical debate over the concept of law. (Kornhauser [2004] provides a more extended account.)

One of Hart's rhetorical devices provides a useful starting point for the development of a social scientific concept. To introduce the concept of a secondary rule, Hart [1961 recounts a fable concerning the emergence of a legal system in a small community. He suggests that a small, homogeneous, stable and closely knit society requires no differentiated structures of governance. These structures emerge to resolve problems that arise in societies that are large, heterogeneous, or subject to environmental uncertainty. Though Hart identifies only three such problems, we shall identify four distinct functions that might be distributed across societal structures: (1) the characterization of socially acceptable (or unacceptable) behavior, a task the importance of which grows as the rate of change in society increases. (2) Policing of behavior to identify likely instances of deviant behavior; more anonymous societies may require more institutionalized policing; (3) Definitive adjudication of non-conformity to social norms; again, when society is no longer face-to-face, such adjudication may be necessary to trigger sanctions. And (4) Sanctioning of deviant behavior.

Governance within a society requires that the society somehow accomplish each of these four tasks. A society might do so in a number of different ways. A governance structures is the set of institutional structures within a society that address one or more of the four problems of adaptation, detection, application, and sanction that are the central elements of governance. An institutional structure is a decision-making protocol that specifies procedures relevant to the resolution of one or more of the problems of adaptation, detection, application, and sanction. Clear understanding requires a distinction here between institutional structures, realized institutions, and functioning institutions. This distinction parallels the distinction between game forms, games, and plays of a game in the theory of games. As noted before, an institutional structure is simply the basic rules or protocol for governance; a realized institution is an institutional structure situated in a given society and populated by particular individuals; a functioning institution is a realized institution as it operates in a society in actual conditions.

A crude taxonomy of governance structures might distinguish them along two dimensions: the degree of institutional differentiation in the structure and the mechanism of internal, "bureaucratic" control.

A governance structure may be more or less differentiated from other institutions (such as those governing exchange or reproduction) in a society. Hart considered two extremes: a simple society with no differentiation of governance from other institutions and modern, municipal legal systems that have distinct institutions for adaptation, policing, adjudication, and sanctioning. Indeed, a society such as the United States has multiple legislative, executive and judicial institutions that relate in complex ways.

We may follow Hart in elaborating the second dimension of the mechanism of internal bureaucratic control. Hart contrasted two motivations for compliance with law or legal obligations: incentives that rely on the self-interest of individuals and acceptance of rules as guides to action. For Hart, law required that a core set of public officials had to accept the rule of recognition as an authoritative guide to action.

Political economy, by contrast, aims to explain all legal phenomena in terms of the self-interest of agents. This analytic strategy precludes a Hartian account of law; legal rules cannot play any role in the explanation of behavior of either private individuals or public officials because no agent has the relevant internal attitude towards the rule. An individual faced with a choice considers the costs and benefits that each option presents to her. These costs and benefits will include "legal costs and benefits" but these costs and benefits are not determined by rules; they are the result of the incentives that private and public officials face. Rules are only rules of thumb that express the response of average individuals under normal circumstances to particular events. Which rules of thumb are used, of course, may greatly affect the social equilibrium achieved in a particular jurisdiction.

Political economy thus seeks a concept of governance that relies only on incentives; it consequently denies the existence of legal systems in Hart's sense. It might nonetheless acknowledge a different concept of law. Some political economists, for example, suggest that legality in the sense of an impartial "rule of law" promotes economic growth. The political economist then might identify law or legal systems with governance structures that realize such a rule of law (in given circumstances). The political economist, then, might adopt two related concepts. The first concept of a governance structure is an explanatory one; it characterizes the mechanisms of social governance in terms of the degree of institutional differentiation and the mechanism of bureaucratic control within these institutions. The second related concept is normative. It identifies a value that a governance structure might realize. Call this value *legality*. The concept of law is thus a normative one; it identifies the value of legality. The social scientist then seeks to identify conditions under which specific governance structures will realize the value of legality.

ADJUDICATION IN POLITICAL ECONOMY

As noted earlier the political economy strand of economic analysis of law itself contains two strands that are in tension with each other. On the one hand, the political economy strand seeks only to explain legal phenomena rather than to prescribe either the structure of legal institutions or the content of particular legal rules. One might find within this strand of political economy a positive theory of adjudication but not a normative theory. Indeed, the positive theory advanced argues that judges seek to promote their interests. Usually, these interests are defined as policy interests, that is, an interest to promote particular policies.

The second strand of political economy, *constitutional political economy*, does have normative aims. It assumes that political actors will act in a self-interested fashion *within* existing political institutions but that agents will act more impartially in the *design* of the political institutions within which they will work. A normative theory of adjudication does emerge from this strand of political economy but it differs significantly from the normative theory endorsed by the policy analysis strand of economic analysis of law. For constitutional political economy, a normative theory of adjudication must be a structural one; it should describe the structure of adjudication. The theory thus cannot dictate directly judicial motivation because, according to political economy, judges will always act self-interestedly. Adjudicative institutions, however, can be designed to align better the interests of judges with the interests of the designer of the constitution.

In 1975, Landes and Posner offered a justification for the independence of the judiciary that is often understood as a normative theory of adjudication within the tradition of constitutional political economy. On the account of Landes and Posner, an independent judiciary serves the interest of legislators who seek to impose their policies on the jurisdiction for periods that exceed the length of their majority in the legislature. As a consequence, they find it in their interest to have the judiciary enforce the original bargain struck in all legislation.

This argument contains a normative theory of statutory interpretation. Judges ought to enforce the bargains reached by the legislature that enacted the statute. On this account, a judge ignores the views of the current legislative majority. She also eschews interpretation of the statute in terms of her own policy preferences.

One should note that, from the perspective of constitutional political economy, the argument of Landes and Posner is incomplete. They ground their theory of judicial independence in the interests of legislators. The interests of legislators within extant legislative institutions may not coincide with the interests of the constitutional designer.

ADJUDICATION IN POLICY ANALYSIS

A normative theory of adjudication was among the earliest claims advanced in the economic analysis of law. Posner [1973, 1979, 1980, 1985, 1990, 1995] asserted claim II in the introduction: the common law *ought* to be efficient. He interpreted efficiency as "wealth maximization" but then interpreted wealth maximization as "willingness to pay." This interpretive stance yielded an argument that judges in (common law) cases ought to choose the legal rule that maximized the ratio of benefits to costs as measured by the sum of individual willingnesses to pay.

Posner's claim evoked great controversy in the late 1970s and early 1980s. Twenty years later, Kaplow and Shavell [2001] revived and revised Posner's claim. The revision had two components. First, and most important, they chose *welfarism* generally rather than cost-benefit analysis in particular as the normative basis for adjudication. Welfarism requires that evaluation depend solely on the well-being of individuals. Cost-benefit analysis is thus a form of welfarist evaluation; but Kaplow and Shavell's argument allows them to avoid various criticisms of cost-benefit analysis. Second, Kaplow and Shavell do not argue primarily for a normative theory of adjudication. Rather they contend that evaluation of legal rules and institutions by scholars ought to be welfarist. They suggest however that judges by and large have the same evaluative obligation as the third party analyst.

A Brief Critique of Cost-Benefit Analysis as a Theory of Adjudication

Cost-benefit analysis attempts to implement a Kaldor-Hicks evaluative criterion. According to the Kaldor-Hicks criterion, a distribution of goods (broadly understood) *X* is superior to a distribution of goods *Y* if and only if there exists a third distribution of goods *Z* such that (a) *Z* is a redistribution of the distribution *X*; and (b) *Z* is Pareto preferred to *Y*.

Cost-benefit analysis proceeds in two steps. First, for each individual, it identifies a particular representation of the individual's ordinal ranking of the options open to the policy maker. Second, it aggregates these representations of each individual's preferences into a social ranking.

The first step is unproblematic. Consider agent *K*. *K* has preferences over states of the world. A representation of these preferences assigns a number to each state of the world such that *K* prefers state *X* to state *Y* if and only if the number assigned to state *X* is higher than the number assigned to state *Y*. Cost-benefit analysis assigns as numbers the agent's willingness to pay. This procedure thus links the range of numbers that the agent may assign to the agent's wealth as willingness to pay is defined in part in terms of the agent's ability to pay. The procedure for assigning numbers on the basis of an individual's willingness to pay in fact yields a representation of that agent's preferences. Willingness to pay is a utility function that accurately represents the agent's (ordinal) preferences over states.

The second step of cost-benefit analysis is more problematic. To aggregates the individual willingnesses to pay, cost-benefit analysis simply sums the individual willingnesses to pay. One can see immediately several difficulties with this procedure. First, each ranking is ordinal; the numbers have no significance beyond the order. If *K* assigns a number 2 to state *X*, a number 4 to state *Y* and a number 16 to state *Z*, we cannot conclude anything about *K*'s intensity of preference; she does not prefer *Z* to *Y* six times as much as she prefers *Y* to *X*. It therefore seems odd that one can add agent*K*'s willingness to pay to agent J's willingness to pay.

Second, cost-benefit analysis adopts a method of interpersonal comparisons of well-being that is particularly unconvincing. Interpersonal comparison of well-being requires that one identify the appropriate representation of each individual's preference ordering and compare those representations. Cost-benefit analysis however does not identify representations on moral or political grounds; rather it chooses the representations that contingently arise from the actual distribution of wealth and income in the society. If Tom is poor while Bill is wealthy, it is unclear why the representations of the well-being of each that derives from willingness to pay provide interpersonally comparable measures. Equally, if Tom and Bill are equally wealthy but Tom is disabled and Bill is not, the willingness to pay of each may still not be interpersonally comparable.

A Structural Critique of Welfarist Theories of Adjudication

One might construct a normative theory of adjudication at either of two levels. First, one might take as given the general structure of adjudication within a particular judicial system and ask what obligations the judges within that system ought to have. Second, one might more fundamentally design the judicial system from scratch. On this second account, the institutional environment in which judges act as well as the obligations of judges within that institutional environment would be subject to evaluation.

Most normative theories of adjudication are of the first type. They take the institutional structure in which adjudication occurs largely as given and then identify the obligations of judges within that system. Phrased differently, normative theories of adjudication are interpretive of an ongoing practice rather than efforts to design a practice from scratch. Welfarist theories of adjudication face several difficulties when understood as interpretive theories of existing (common law) practice.

First, the structure of adjudication does not generally provide adequate or appropriate information for the selection of rules that maximize social welfare. Adjudication in a common law system usually focuses on a past transaction between particular parties. This transaction may not be typical of transactions that were litigated; it certainly will not be typical of the entire population of transactions that a rule would govern. Under a given rule, for instance, the set of transactions that do not lead to litigation are likely to differ systematically from the set of transactions that do give rise to litigation. Equally important, different legal rules are apt to generate different sets of transactions. The current structure of adjudication does not provide any information that would help a decision maker assess these differences across potential legal rules.

Second, the selection procedure for judges does not identify individuals with the appropriate training and background to make accurate calculations of social welfare. Judges in common law countries have generally not been trained systematically in economics and statistics, two disciplines necessary (but not sufficient) for the determination of social welfare under alternative legal rules.

Third, and related, judges usually face severe constraints in the set of legal rules they may consider in any adjudication. When confronted by a tort case, for example, the court usually considers a limited number of legal regimes; perhaps it will reformulate the standard of care or shift from a regime of negligence to one of strict liability. A court, however, is unlikely to adopt a complex scheme of no-fault insurance or to impose a different insurance scheme even though these more radical transformations of social institutions would provide higher overall welfare.

EVALUATION OF LEGAL RULES AND INSTITUTIONS

The evaluative tradition in economics is resolutely welfarist. That tradition extends to the policy analysis branch of economic analysis of law. We considered the manifestation of this tradition in the advocacy of cost-benefit analysis as a normative theory of adjudication. We consider arguments for welfarism as the sole evaluative standard against which to appraise legal rules and institutions.

The arguments were directed against cost-benefit analysis, a specific and concrete form of welfarism developed to implement the more abstract evaluative ideas underlying welfarism. Objections to the specific instantiation of welfarism do not necessarily run against the more general class of evaluative criteria. Similarly, the argument focused on the institutional structure of adjudication; we argued that this structure was hostile to an implementation of a welfarist theory of adjudication.

The arguments in this chapter address the claim that we evaluate legal rules and institutions *only*against welfarist criteria. This argument has several elements. The first element identifies an individual's well-being with her preferences. Thus, an individual *K* has greater well-being in state *X*than in state *Y*, if and only if she prefers state *X* to state *Y*. The second, key element of the argument welfarism interprets the agent's preferences as her all-things-considered ranking of alternatives. This step thus incorporates within the agent's preference ordering anything that the agent considers relevant to her decisions. Consequently, the claim about an agent's well being now becomes: *K*prefers state *X* to state *Y* if and only if *K* believes, all things considered, that state *X* is better than (or ought to be promoted rather than) state *B*.

K's all-things-considered judgments, of course, will included many considerations that, in ordinary language, are not usually considered as in *K*'s self-interest or even as contributing to her well-being. So, for example, her all-things-considered judgments will incorporate concerns for the well-being of others as well as considerations of justice and deontological constraints on action. Subsection 1 argues that an individual's concerns for justice and her endorsement of deontological constraints cannot be integrated into an adequate concept of well-being.

The argument for the exclusivity of welfarism as an evaluative criterion rests on a third leg. The argument contends that use of any non-welfarist criterion is incompatible with the Pareto criterion. We then point out that the Pareto criterion conflicts with principles of rationality, valuation, liberty and responsibility that have an equally strong appeal. It is thus not clear that we should accept the Pareto criterion and reject these others principles.

PREFERENCE AND WELL-BEING

Call an ordering that incorporates every consideration that the agent views as relevant to her decision "an extended preference ordering". Kaplow and Shavell include the agent's moral concerns in this extended preference ordering. We shall call this approach the "strategy of incorporation."

A complete argument that the extended preference ordering does not correspond to a morally compelling conception of well-being would require articulation of the concept of well-being, a task well beyond the scope of this entry. Here we outline two formal arguments against the strategy of incorporation that treats the agent's moral concerns, her views about equality, fairness and distributive and corrective justice more generally, as elements of well-being.

We broached the first formal argument. There we noted that not every norm could be integrated with self-interested concerns into an all-things-considered set of judgments that satisfied the formal conditions of a preference. To succeed, the strategy of incorporation must show that each of the agent's moral "tastes" or concerns have a normative structure that is compatible with her underlying, self-interested preferences. The strategy of incorporation thus might fail because of the structure of the obligations that the agent endorses.

Second, a welfarist theory distinguishes between the well-being of each agent and the criteria that determine the structure of the social welfare function. The theory, that is, distinguishes what makes an individual's life go better and the concerns that determine how one integrates the well-being of individuals into "social welfare." These latter concerns weigh the well-being of individual *J* against the well-being of individual *K*. Consider two states of the world *s* and *t*. Agent *J*'s well-being is higher in state *s* than in state *t* while agent *K*'s well-being is higher in state *t* than in state *s*. To rank the two states, society must determine the relative importance of the well-being of the two individuals.

Moral norms perform precisely this function. A moral norm determines when the well-being of agent *J* should take precedence over the well-being of agent *K*. Indeed, we say that agent *J* has a *right* against agent *K* precisely when we think that the decisions or choices of agent *J* should prevail over the decisions or choices of agent *K*. The moral concerns of each agent thus reflect the agent's views about the structure of the social choice function not (necessarily) her views about what constitutes her own well-being.

Of course, an agent might believe that her life goes better if she lives in a more egalitarian society. But she might also believe to the contrary that her life would go better if she lived in a more hierarchical society. Then, the social structure would affect the agent's well-being. The choice of social structure, however, is not dependent on the agent's well-being. The structure of the social choice function rather determines the social structure. Thus, an agent may believe that an egalitarian social welfare function is appropriate (or perhaps even "better than" a hierarchical social welfare function) but she may nonetheless believe that her own well-being would be higher in a hierarchical society than in an egalitarian one.

The social welfare function resolves conflicts of "interest" between individuals. Moral disagreements, however, reflect not conflicts of interest but a dispute over how such conflicts should be resolved. The resolution of a moral conflict determines whose well-being counts not how much well-being the agent has. The strategy of incorporation confuses these two concepts.

Many of the concerns that, under the strategy of incorporation, are included in an individual's extended preference ordering thus bear on the structure of the social choice function; they do not necessarily make the agent's life go better. Concerns for distributive justice, for example, reflect moral judgments about how to integrate different distributions of well-being. They do not reflect judgments about how well-off each agent is. Similarly, respect for deontological constraints on action reflect the judgment that the effects on the well-being of the constrained agent do not bear on our assessment of the social state.

The social welfare function aggregates or integrates the well-being of each individual in society into a social ranking of states. It does not integrate or aggregate the differing views of the individuals concerning the appropriate social welfare function. Conflicts over the appropriate social welfare function must be resolved through some separate process. Society for example might vote on which social welfare function to adopt. Such a vote might be justified on epistemic grounds; it cannot be justified on social welfare grounds. We do not choose our social welfare function in order to maximize social welfare.

THE PARETO CRITERION

Let us first define the Pareto Criterion. Consider a society of n individuals, each of whom has a well-defined preference over all possible states of the world. The Pareto criterion states that a state of the world x is socially better than a state of the world y if and only if each individual considers state x at least as preferred as state y and at least one person strictly prefers x to y. It follows from this definition, of course, that, if each individual prefers x to y then x is socially better than y.

The Pareto criterion has the strong intuitive appeal. If everyone agrees that a state x is preferred to a state y, certainly the collective assessment must rank x more highly than y. The Pareto criterion moreover appears to be weak, i.e. to impose few constraints on social choice. After all, each member of the society will only rarely rank two alternatives as every other member of the society. Nevertheless, the Pareto criterion has strong implications for the aggregation of individual judgments. Indeed, as summarized below, the Pareto criterion is inconsistent with a large number of other principles, each of which also has strong intuitive appeal.

Perhaps the inconsistency that would most disconcert an economist arises between the Pareto criterion and the demand for aggregate rationality under uncertainty. Consider again our society of n individuals. Assume now though that society must choose among a number of policies, the consequences of which will depend on the underlying but unknown state of the world. Each individual has preferences over these policies that satisfy the axioms of subjective expected utility theory. Consequently, one may represent each individual's preference over actions by a set of preferences over consequences and a set of beliefs (that satisfy the probability axioms) over states of the world; moreover, the individual prefers policy p to policy q if and only if the expected utility from policy p exceeds the expected utility from policy q.

Aggregate rationality demands the construction of a collective preference over policies that also satisfies the axioms of subjective expected utility theory. Suppose, in addition, that we demand that the collective preference satisfy the Pareto criterion. That is, if each individual in society prefers policy p to policy q then society collectively must prefer p to q. Unfortunately, Seidenfeld, Kadane, and Schervish [1989] have proven that, if at least two individuals both rank two consequences differently and assess the likelihood of some state of the world differently, then society cannot simultaneously satisfy the Pareto criterion and the demands of aggregate rationality.

The Pareto criterion also conflicts with substantive moral claims. Larry Temkin [1993], for example, has argued that the Pareto criterion is inconsistent with the existence of communal goods. A communal good is one that provides social value but does not improve the well-being of any individual. A communal good, that is, is good for *us* even though it is good for *no* individual. He offers equality as an example. A society with equality of well-being, for instance, might be better than a society in which individuals have highly unequal levels of well-being even if each person in the unequal society has higher well-being than she has in the more equal society.

Communal goods often seem scarce or improbable; how could something that is good for us be good for none of us in particular? Many people, for example, reject either the claim that equality is a communal good or that it is valuable at all. Our prior discussion, however, suggests a host of potential other communal "goods". There is a sense in which each of the determinants of the structure of the social welfare function is good for us without necessarily being good for anyone. At least for a welfarist, the structure of the social welfare function is constitutive of the good. Everyone might be "better off" under a regime of slavery but that regime would nevertheless remain worse than a free society.

The Pareto criterion is also inconsistent with three different aspects of the value of autonomy: liberty, responsibility, and self-governance. A formal argument underlies each of these claims. Amartya Sen [1971] first articulated the conflict between the Pareto criterion and liberty. He began from the standard social choice framework developed by Arrow [1963] in which each agent has preferences over final states of the world.

He imposed two of the Arrovian conditions, universal domain and the Pareto criterion, but substituted the condition of minimal liberty for the other two (non-dictatorship and independence of irrelevant alternatives). Minimal liberty is indeed minimal; Sen required only that each member in society was decisive over two alternatives. He then proved that one could not construct a social preference that satisfied all three axioms; the Pareto criterion and minimal liberty conflict.

The Arrovian framework, however, does not present the ideal environment in which to study minimal liberty. An agent may have the right (or in Hohfeldian terms a privilege) to determine a social decision. Typically, though, he need not exercise his right. Or the agent may be willing to trade or waive his right in exchange for some benefit. Gibbard [1974] argued that the power to waive one's rights undermined Sen's claim. Subsequent authors then reformulated Sen's argument within a more suitable, game theoretic framework. The conflict thus persists in a more plausible and appealing formal framework.

In Hohfeld's taxonomy of legal rights, a legal duty is the jural correlate of a legal right. We might similarly consider responsibility the ethical correlate of liberty within the conceptual framework of autonomy. Recent formal work has shown that this aspect of autonomy also conflicts with the Pareto criterion.

Sen defined autonomy as liberty understood as freedom to choose. Autonomy as responsibility for one's choices and actions represents the obverse side of this freedom to choose. Political philosophers have examined this issue in their study of distributive justice. Rawls [1971] famously argued that individuals were not responsible for their innate talents. Dworkin [1981] extended this argument through his distinction between "brute luck" and "option luck". Distributive justice in both arguments required insurance against bad realization of risks of "brute luck" but responsibility for the bad realizations of option luck.

Within economics, the study of responsibility has emerged from the literature initiated by Duncan Foley [1967] and Hal Varian [1974] on fairness. An allocation is fair if and only if it is Pareto efficient and envy-free. An allocation is envy-free if no individual would prefer the outcome assigned to another individual to the outcome assigned to her. In an exchange economy, a competitive equilibrium that results from an initial, equal allocation of resources is both Pareto efficient and envy-free because each individual has the same set of options available to her. The competitive equilibrium is thus fair.

In a production economy, however, a similar argument will fail if individuals have different talents. The argument fails for two reasons. First, talents are not transferable though, of course, we may transfer money between agents. Second, when two individuals have unequal talents, they face different sets of feasible options. The more talented have better options and hence do better. The less talented may envy them. As a consequence, no efficient and envy-free equilibrium exists.

These arguments apply to the more abstract concerns of distributive justice and responsibility. The no-envy test outlined above combines two distinct ideas. First, individuals with identical attributes for which they are responsible should have identical well-being. Second, individuals with identical characteristics for which they are not responsible should receive identical compensation for their losses. The first condition addresses option luck; the second brute luck.

Fleurbaey [2008] comprehensively explores the tensions between these two aspects of the no-envy test and between the no-envy test and the Pareto criterion. The compatibility of these two conditions depends on the nature of the correlation of these effects of brute and option luck on the agent's well-being. If the well-being of agents with bad luck is unusually responsive to their bad luck, no fair allocation exists. The requirements of no-envy and Pareto again conflict. We now turn to a third aspect of autonomy, self-governance. In the context of collective action, self-governance refers to democratic governance. The vast literature on social choice theory investigates the relation of self-governance to the Pareto criterion in this context.

Various assumptions reflect the value of democratic governance in this literature. The most minimal assumption is non-dictatorship. We may interpret Arrow's initial result as demonstrating, for direct democracy, a complex incompatibility between the Pareto criterion and several other axioms including non-dictatorship, the axiom of minimal self-governance. The complexity arises because we cannot easily determine which of the several axioms is most fundamental. The literature, for example, has investigated the importance of the axiom of independence of irrelevant alternatives more thoroughly than the Pareto criterion. This emphasis perhaps reflects the strong appeal of the Pareto criterion.

Representative democracy, however, presents the conflict more starkly. In modern society, communal self-governance generally operates through representative institutions. Individuals do not directly enact substantive legislative programmes. Rather, they elect representatives to legislatures that then enact substantive legislative programmes. Phrased differently, election procedures are candidate-based rather than assembly-based or programme based. Notice that this distinction persists even in those states that have adopted party-list proportional representation schemes. In these schemes, an individual votes for a party rather than an individual candidate that has endorsed a specific programme. The election determines the party composition of the legislature. Each contesting party then constitutes a candidate.

These candidate-based procedures, however, are inconsistent with the minimal demands of communal self-governance. Benoit and Kornhauser [2010] have proven that the only Pareto efficient, candidate-based procedure is a dictatorship. Again the Pareto criterion conflicts with a (minimal) requirement of communal self-governance or autonomy.

THE ARGUMENT FOR WELFARISM REVISTED

We should reject welfarism as the sole evaluative criterion for legal rules and institutions. We have argued only that arguments that rest on the intuitive appeal of the Pareto criterion are insufficient to establish the welfarist claim. The Pareto criterion has great intuitive appeal but it also has strong implications that bring it into conflict with other principles that also have strong intuitive appeal.

Legal rules and institutions offer a comprehensive guide to and regulation of social life. The intuitive appeal of various principles may vary with the range of activity governed by the legal rule or institution. The intuitive appeal of the Pareto criterion is strongest in those areas of law that regulate corporate and commercial behavior. Perhaps here indeed welfarist considerations should provide the sole guide to the structure of legal rules and institutions. Election law and laws regulating political speech, by contrast, may be legal domains in which the appeal of principles of communal self-governance dominate. In these areas, evaluation based exclusively on welfarist considerations seems less appropriate.

Controversies in many areas of law, however, implicate many of our values. Environmental regulation, for example, clearly implicates welfarist concerns. Regulation determines in part the relative costs of production of various goods and services that contribute to individual well-being. Environmental regulation, however, also clearly implicates questions of autonomy. Productive activities may impose unwanted risks on individuals that limit the exercise of the individual's autonomy. Tort law perhaps raises these issues more starkly.

Similarly, we may understand conflicts over the appropriate tax and social welfare policy as raising questions not only of efficiency but also of autonomy as responsibility. Exclusive focus on welfarist concerns distorts these policy debates by ignoring fundamental issues that divide us.

THE SOCIO-POLITICAL ANALYSIS OF ECONOMIC DECLINE

The evolution of the Argentinean economy in the 20th century is disconcerting. In the first decades of the 20th century, Argentina was in an outstanding position among the most promising economies of the world. The economy was growing at a sustained rate; overseas investment in the railroad transportation system was linking the whole country; immigrants were arriving from all over the globe providing the necessary labor force to explode a rich soil; the educational system, under the impulse of the "80s generation", expanded and translated to a huge reduction in illiteracy rate, placing the country among the most educated nations in the world. In summary, the perspectives for the country in the long run were favorable. If someone had affirmed at that time that the situation of Argentina was going to be exactly the opposite at the beginning of the 21st century, this could have been considered delusional.

Nevertheless, the results during the second half of the 20th century were disappointing. Economic growth stopped while a reverse process started. As a consequence, the medium and long term perspectives fell apart. The combination of bad circumstances and bad decisions translated to persistently high inflation rate, growing government debt, an oversized -and most of the time, very ineffective- government, a weak and poorly regulated financial system, and a non-competitive economy which progressively lost relevance in the international market. Short expansive processes followed by crisis and devaluation of the currency, the so-called stop-and-go cycles deteriorated the living condition of the low income population.

The goal of this project is to study the factors that led Argentina to its current situation. We will explore the political economy during the period that goes from the end of the 19th century to the beginning of the 21st century. The study will address both economic and political aspects that are, more so than in any other country, intimately intertwined in the case of Argentina.

SPECIFIC AIMS

We will answer the following research questions:

Economic structure:

Why was Argentina not able to diversify the economy towards an advanced industrial base?

Welfare State:

1. Which were the historical approaches taken towards the welfare state in Argentina: France, Italy or the Nordic countries?
2. The failure of the welfare state why and how?
3. Why was the welfare state in Argentina involved in the production of goods and services beyond the distributional aspects? Was ideology involved in such choices? Why did the society disregard the inefficiencies in the Argentinean welfare state?
4. The vicious circle: Did the Welfare State create social classes that depended on Gov't monies. Did the Gov't crowd-out private initiative?
5. Which was the role of labor unions in the evolution of the welfare state? Was the labor union a winner in the income pie? Did it have consequences on labor market and the competitiveness of the economy?

Political Story:

How was Peronism born? Which was the underlying ideology? Which was the Peronist role in the welfare state? Is there any parallel with other populist movements in Latin America?

Economic growth and redistribution:

Are income growth and income redistribution incompatible or does some variant of populism have the chance to succeed?

BACKGROUND AND MOTIVATION

Throughout its history, Argentina's economy varied due to successive changes and crises. Though Argentina was always referred to as an agricultural country its economics history could be characterized by the permanent search for alternatives to the agricultural-based economy; the conflicts between the federal and the state's government regarding the distribution of economic resources; and the close ties between economic models and political ideology.

In general terms, the economic history of Argentina of the 20th century could be divided into 3 periods. 1880 to 1930 known as the agriculture exporter period; 1930 to 1976 or the import-substitution period; and 1976 to 2010 usually referred as the openness phase.

1880 to 1930: the conquest of the desert facilitated the integration of large extensions of land to productive activities, land that previously belonged to almost exterminated indigenous population. The economic model was characterized by the ranch system that produced commodities such as grains and meat. The country established strong commercial ties to England, a country that was the main lender and investor in Argentina, especially in the railroad industry. Rosario and Buenos Aires were the ports. Most industrial products were imported, but the substitution began in some light industries, especially in areas such as refrigeration, food, beverages, construction materials, soap, and some textiles. The economic expansion caused a labor shortage which was filled with the large influx of European immigrants, mostly Spanish and Italian who concentrated in the coastal areas.

This economic model had ups and downs, generally linked to the terms of trade. In the 1920 the first labor unions were born, influenced by anarchist ideologies that came with the European immigrants, but these movements were often suppressed in a bloody fashion. During the First World War there was a period of industry growth favored to the decrease in imports from Europe due to the War. In 1929 the produced the stock market crash on Wall Street led to a large economic downturn in the country. The economic crisis caused the overthrow of democratic government that had failed to respond to the crises and raised the need for a new economic model.

Import substitution period: Due to the economic crisis of 1929 to 1930 the country closed the main exports and sources of foreign exchange. A complete change in focus was taken: now the objective was the domestic market and the state switch from a passive to a more active role in the economy, intervening in currency and financial markets, setting higher tariffs and quotas on imports, and acting as a driver of demand by the expansion on public spending. Many State Owned Enterprises (SOEs) were established in this period as a legal form for the new activities of the State, the production of good and services. With all those stimuli the private sector channeled the effort to the production of industrial goods and away from the agricultural investment.

The victory of Peronism in the 1946 elections implied a boon for industrialization and the integration of the lower classes to consumption thanks to the redistributive policy of the government of Peron. However, the economic model chosen had a weakness: the lack of heavy industries as well as sufficient energy resources.

The characteristic of this period were cycles of growth with increasing purchasing power of wages, greater demand for imported inputs by the industry expansion that, later on, led to exchange rate adjustment which caused inflation and a fall in the real wage. When a new equilibrium was reached a new loop of expansion-crisis (or a "stop and go" cycle) started over again.

In this period the main purveyor of capital was the United States. The new industries concentrated in the coastal areas (Buenos Aires and Rosario) thus the state intervened actively to develop other areas such as Cordoba by giving incentives to the automotive and armed forces-related industries. The labor union activity was absorbed in this period by Peronism, when most collective bargaining agreements that persist –with minimum change- to these days were signed.

After the coup d'Etat of 1955 the Peronism was banned as a political movement and some intents to open up the economy were tried. These years were of intense political conflict as Peronism tried to return to government, which finally happened in 1973. This was an era marked by political violence with the unfavorable external situation (mainly due to the oil crisis) that led in 1976 to a new coup d'état.

Period of economic opening: With the arrival of the military government there was a change in the economic paradigm. The economy opened to imports. The state increasingly relied on foreign borrowing to finance its activities, and fixed exchange rate management which facilitated speculative capital inflows which instead of investing in productive activities searched only searched for the high rate of returns in the financial sector. This caused a decline in the industry employment and lowered the purchasing power of wages. The economy concentrated in export commodities and the country was exposed to the ups and downs of international financial markets that caused periodic crises and devaluations (and high inflation).

The return of democracy in 1983 did not change dramatically the scenario and later on, in 1989 a Peronist President (Carlos Menem) decided to turn to a more liberal approach by selling SOEs enterprises and introduce some flexibility in the labor-firm relationship with new "forms" of contracts modeled after the Spanish experience.

In 1998 it began a series of balance of payment crises that led to financial crisis, recession and unemployment. This ended in 2001 with the worst crisis in the history of the country: deposits were frozen and the financial systems and the economy collapsed. As the popular discontent erupted the government of radical President De la Rua was overthrown and the country declared default on its external debt few days later.

Looking back at the economic performance of Argentina in the 20th century leaves a sensation of frustration. There were times of growth as well as crisis and recoveries, though in none of the cases the growth was sustained for more than 5 years. There were many mistakes, bad decisions and adverse external circumstances. The country scarcely grew and is lagging well behind the advanced countries. Which were the causes? Whether the country will be able to recover and retake the path of growth is some of the questions we will explore in this project.

ANALYSIS OF CULTURAL PLANNING STRATEGIES: SOCIAL, ECONOMIC, CULTURAL AND POLITICAL FACTORS

SOCIAL ANALYSIS

The transformation from an industrial to a post industrial society has brought with it new social constellations with greater emphasis upon services and intangible things making culture from being a mere 'soft' into a 'hard' factor. At the same time, family and reproduction patterns change with many more women preferring to work rather than staying at home. Even though social policies vary throughout the European countries certainly the concern about the family as core social unit has intensified with shifts in demographic structures reflecting an ageing population with less and less new borns who could sustain once they have entered permanent employment the ever more expensive social security systems.

ECONOMIC ANALYSIS

Economic conditions are best described by policy being directed towards growth rather than retaining an economic development which fulfils social conditions. Here cities need to look at development in terms as to who has the economic force to alter things and redirect the flow of goods and commodities. No longer the private sector as such can demand things but more so the combination of the private with the public sector can lead to overt development patterns which harm the rest of the urban development possibilities. This is certainly the case in Metropolitan cities in which subdistricts differ greatly from another in both economic base and investments made out of earnings gained from having some very specific economic activities in the area. For this can lead to the demand of having a new access road, a demand differing greatly from developing the public transportation system.

CULTURAL PREDICAMENTS

Culture communicates in many even subversive ways lead models which people have identified as the successful ones in such a system and which they tend to imitate. This is because culture is largely determined by the media. As a matter of fact the media culture is such that it makes everything else into its own tool. Crucial is, therefore, whether or not a city and its social and economic groups can come to agree on keeping free some areas of their culture from over commercialization while still giving in to such money based activities as they mean a net return for the city in terms of cultural investments made. The accounting system of a city has here a special task.

It starts with measuring the non-measurable and does not end there but demands a clear trans-sensitivity from economic costs to political gains out of each and every cultural action and event.

That there are special tasks added such as preserving and promoting identity is not put into doubt but rather adds to the kind of cultural administration set up in order to bring some practical routines into what is doing business with culture.

POLITICAL REALITIES: THE HIDDEN 'IRRATIONALITIES'

Politics reflects what constellations of interests favour which model of development, including just an economic growth model. Lately politics has come under the increasing influence by a certain rich class which has powerful links to business, media and politics e.g. Berlusconi.

That leaves ever more the cultural sector, including artists, writers, cultural workers etc. without a clear voice to be heard at all levels. More so, the creative artistic directors are vanishing from leading cultural institutions and are replaced by people disposed in quite another direction as funding and therefore success criteria are changing. Certainly a director of a National Gallery would in the past hesitate to invite artists in relation to national categories since such markations they know will harm these artists while today art exhibitions in a global business aim for quite another show casing of block buster types of exhibitions with high publicity value.

And always there are prestige, equally functional values which drive decisions in a highly symbolic direction to satisfy certain inherent interests e.g. to have a musical hall in the city. Such a demand is made more out of prestige reasons than out of recognition what culture does bring to a city.

When considering all of these various ingredients, it should be said oddly enough culture is not perceived as something in need of consistency. Despite consistency having a prime value when it comes to working through the conditions for cultural development, most of the cultural planning strategies think of everything else but of how to maintain consistency over time. They are often born out of frustration and the need to do something completely new, novel and innovative as if what happened before is irrelevant, old fashioned and derelict.

By seeking only value in the new it optimises the dilemma of a society seeking only the radical new without anticipating that such a society will due to the cultural created out of a loss of continuity stumble into the same old questions which society has yet to resolve. Consequently it should not be overlooked that very often cultural strategies are developed at the height of a cultural crisis with everyone agreeing the neglect of culture can no longer continue. Something has to be done but what is not clear.

This is when the next mistake is being made by imitating marketing strategies, by branding culture as if a product, by making the creative sector more efficient, operatively speaking, when in fact it is reduced to mostly high level restaurants and suggestions of high life, so as to leave culture to become equally functional e.g. the woman playing at the piano in a night bar in order to give just that touch needed to make the atmosphere for those dining and enjoying themselves a bit more magical than usual. It is good for business and if the artist can earn a living from it, why not. Then it is also good for the arts and culture. It is made to appear that simple: the equation between things that are in reality not equal.

The Cultural Capacity to Overcome Incompatibilities by Bringing About Consistency in Order to Sustain Cultural Development

Out of it follows a true strategic cultural plan has to relate first of all to all incompatibilities between the arts and culture when linked to a world wishing to operate under the premise 'business as usual'. The business norm is, however, not a cultural norm but if the latter is silenced, then the incompatibility will not be perceived.

Consequently to bring about an authentic cultural development, there is needed to see to it how the city's institutions can become more consistent by themselves.

When in London in July 2005 bombs went off in the London Tube, afterwards a report about museums pointed out how few artefacts of the cultural communities existing in England can be found in museums. It is not merely a matter of collecting these items to show the creative path a community has been taking, but also who shall interpret and narrate the stories linked to those items? If museums have only a volunteer staff, made up of over fifty, white, male, then it can be easily imagined that most of the museums in the UK have difficulties of becoming consistent with the needs of these cultural communities. The recommendation in that report was made that museums should open up their collections to these communities.

CARRYING CAPACITY ANALYSIS (CCA)

Besides the Cultural Calendar such planning tools as Cultural Impact Statements substantiated by Carrying Capacity Analysis (CCA) of a tourist destination. The CCA is a useful tool for development planners and decision makers.

It serves two levels: as tourist destination how it contributes to sustainable development and as feed back to the tourist market it gives orientation about how this local destination can and does respond to 'global trends'. In Greece a first shift away from wild campers and rucksack tourists was to forbid wild camping and to move them into camp sites which had provisions like water, sanitation (toilettes) and even some basic shelters.

At the same time, the capacity of local municipalities to cope with tourist influxes was severely tested once a critical mass was surpassed in the summer months. Here transportation, food, health services and accommodation must be able to sustain extra demand over and beyond a certain capacity if this means in the short term to meet extra demand; on the other hand, over investment leads to the sad sight of empty standing hotels reflecting badly back into the landscape as if not attractive enough as tourist destination.

People begin to wonder why and attempt to discover reasons for failures. This can lead to confirming negative experiences more than acknowledging positive experiences made. Capacity means also extra staff in case of need and at mass scale, such as the funeral of Pope John Paul II, it meant for Rom and the region around Rom to involve the civil protection services as crowd control and management of large number of people without accidents and/or delays. Here special kind of vulnerability studies in the field of tourism are required just as they are being prepared for natural and man made disaster scenarios.

Moving Towards Successful Cultural Planning Strategies: Specific Examples

Cultural Development Plan

When the city entered the cultural planning process, then it was seeking a specific qualification approach, in order that Linz would receive the designation of being the European Capital of Culture in 2009. The Cultural development Plan was developed in 2000. Its prime aims was to seek new forms of cooperation between local, regional and federal level, in order to act in unison in the interest of gaining the support from all sides to be the European Capital of Culture. Local level: working in neighbourhoods, providing services, better infrastructure until local people can use the city as stage to articulate themselves.

This can be reinforced by promoting participation in international events (promotion of city expertise and profile) and by bringing international networks to link up with local networks e.g. in Linz identifying local meeting places – market places, pubs – meant also making use of local traditions and customs within the larger cultural development strategy plan.

Approaching the city from a regional level – the UK policy

"The Regional Development Agencies in the UK have begun to give a valuable spatial dimension to economic development, as regional plans and economic strategies are being brought together."

Three concrete steps:

Setting the right tone - what initial papers on culture will set the right tone?

"The Planning Green Paper will be an important stimulus to this. The challenge now is to move on from thinking about structures – about design knowledge – to address the best ways in which to deliver policy – delivery knowledge."

Change in agenda: list of priorities and how they match together with a structured approach to issues of development (in which direction, what cohesion, economic and social ramifications?) "The link between the economic and social agendas was vital for the North East.

This could be seen in some of the achievements of One North East; in the establishment of Regional Venture Capital and Loan funds, and a Regional Education Forum for example.

Linkage to modern social and technological developments crucial for a successful cultural plan: "The creation of a 'learning society' in the region was paramount in the RDA's priorities."

First appraisal:

- By comparison the cultural dimension = region is doubtful if articulated at that level unless you take Germany with its federal system and culturally well defined regions
- Cultural planning and economic strategies are brought together

Cultural planning strategy as dissemination of culture (cultural information and knowledge)

Cultural dissemination of good practices and creating an audience should not be the first aim of any cultural plan. Instead, getting information to citizens and finding out when and how they will want to participate in cultural events, is more about the original involvement of people in the life of their city than about attending lectures, seeing movies, going to concerts. The cultural dissemination of information is has a primary function of valorizing what is going on. When people say that is an important event or an astonishing exhibition which should not be missed, then the impulse to go there is almost similar to compulsive thinking.

The next question is just as important, but what if everyone goes there, why should I or do I have to be as well a conformist in order to take in what everyone else seems to enjoy?

That sort of personal reflection indicates another paradigm: taste and what constitutes an aesthetical experience (with many dimensions involved e.g. what makes one laugh, happy, sad, remorseful, thoughtful etc. can be evaluated quite differently in terms of where that person finds him- or herself at e.g. at the beginning of a love relationship, after the break-up of the marriage, loosing a friend or job, etc.) in terms of real human experiences and what is needed to reflect upon them.

At a second level there is the question of sustainability and obviously this is connected to the creation of audiences or visitors. Any advisor for museums like Peter Higgins from land design studio knows that there are local inhabitants who will come to a museum but once if they think if they have seen it once then they have seen it all.

As a consequence he designed and advised the construction of a museum for sailing boats where the exhibition can be changed every year to allow many more and different sailing boats to be shown which otherwise would have been in storage, therefore out of sight.

Always museums will let this interplay between permanent and temporary exhibitions shape their visitor policy in order to attract newcomers but also retain a consistent profile over time with which visitors can identify themselves with and what would constitute their identification with that institution. Obviously there are still other methods on how to create and to keep an audience while new comers are welcomed by those who are participating already in organized guides and tours through the museum. The example shows that there are many practical questions in need of being resolved when wishing to bring about a sustainable cultural development.

Out of it follows that there does coincide quite often the search for more consistency with finding consistency in what one is doing as main off spring for a more mature cultural planning strategy. The moment that difference to seeking just the new is reached, that is once more mature concepts prevail, then the formulation of a sound cultural planning strategy has more promises of success.

Dissemination in Ancient Greece – a historical example

Ancient Greek theatres facilitated the dissemination of Greek values through plays and discussions with audiences meant to be given insights into human values. Culture differs from propaganda techniques and ideological indoctrinations as adaptation of plays requires constant re-interpretation and furthermore the writing of plays. Once this includes the chorus as representatives of the people on stage, wisdom, practical judgment and the power of common people is demonstrated. Moreover Ancient Greek dramas had beside the chorus the protagonists and the omnipotent Gods as a kind of human trilogy.

If one thinks of these in terms of the modern concepts of judicial, executive and legislative powers, or what the philosopher Kant conceived to be the differences between theoretical, practical and moral reasoning, then only in the combination of the three there may be told the story and the hubris of it all find an illustrative example as to where law, human folly and just fate sets the limits and determines finally the outcome of things.

It should not be concluded that the Polis based on the Agora as meeting place was spread, culturally speaking, for that required not only a political will but also and fore mostly the recognition as to who is a citizen of such a Polis. By definition, this excluded others and made the term 'stranger' become as important as the ones who know their law and the rituals which go with them in order to demonstrate that everyone is willing to observe them. Here then religion and the scheme of appearance which enters with religion city life.

Of interest is that the term 'citizens' was bounded by the Polis to the city itself. From there to the citizens of Calais as portrayed in the sculpture of Rodin, there is a notion that citizens are not only bounded by their respective cities but are representatives in a political sense of the mass of people who stand behind their representatives.

However, it is quite unclear where differences between citizens of a city and citizens of a nation was superseded by citizens being defined solely through the state and what kind of allegiance it demanded if the power of the state was to be upheld by all citizens. Thus from the Ancient Text beginning with "many words speak like the rain on stones long heated up by the sun" to "my fellow citizens" as expressed by politicians wishing to rally in first the citizens and then the troops for a certain cause.

Out of such reflections about the Ancient Past are born further going ideas but also it becomes for culture a strategic question but what audiences are to be created, if the creative process is to be sustained over time? And is it too simple to speak merely about a creative process if the invaluable lesson taught was in reality a morality one? Can that be compared with an audience going to the cinema instead of the theatre and what about music?

Certainly for the analysis it is necessary to establish out of the difference between there being already an audience which is receptive for a certain culture and the need to create an audience for new kinds of cultural interactions something like a barometer by which tastes and dispositions are established, in order to mediate between need to fulfill certain demands and the creation of new demands by bringing into play both a new form of expression and an audience which will accept such forms of expression. That may as well be reflected in debates about cultural policy in support of what cultural expressions, for if only traditional ones are accepted by the already existing audience, then the new forms of innovation may never be realized and thereby changes more passively experienced then really shaped consciously as part of the city's desire to go with the times.

LILLE

Linking up centre with peripheries through cultural routes based on the public transport systems. Since then the movement towards integration meant an attempt to bring together social, economic, political and cultural structures e.g. Munich – for the Olympics in 1972 – construction of metro system and opening up the city centre to pedestrian walks. This became known later as the agora concept.

In response to policy measures and given framework conditions.

Then, certain policies affect cities e.g. performance indicators in the UK makes cities attempt to fulfill also cultural targets. This means a cultural policy framework is in place e.g. 'creative regions' but these top down measures are monitored and finally administrated at various levels and not only at federal. Hence besides the regional and local level there are various institutional players e.g. MLA oversees policy implementation in the areas of museums, libraries and archives in the UK and can influence local actors while responding to the overall dynamic created especially in the museum sector due to funds being obtained through lottery while the digitalization process of the Information Society encompasses all three areas: museums, libraries and archives.

Major Assumptions About Cultural Planning Strategies

They are either developed due to the growing need to tackle issues within a certain time and after it has become obvious certain practiced models are no longer sufficient to resolve growing tensions between different cultures e.g. the model of multi culturalism as part of the immigration policy and method to integrate others into local communities.

Or else cultural planning strategies are developed in response to cultural needs having become generally recognized and desirable e.g. that the city is alive, open, vibrant while becoming more competitive in other than the traditional fields of the economy as managed up to now.

Cultural planning strategies are also developed when there is an impulse coming from some cultural initiative with its own success story e.g. Edinburgh festival, or else by a city wishing and becoming a European cultural capital.

The major assumption for promising to be a successful cultural planning strategy is when culture itself is in a flux and there is besides a movement of people and goods a lot of good ideas abounding to undertake cultural initiatives at all levels. Cities can seize upon local initiatives by providing them with space while on the other hand the willingness of all citizens to participate in a bid (e.g. all Leipzig citizens joined the city's effort to get the Olympic bid by bicycling in a marathon around the city and undertaking other actions to draw the attention of the Olympic Committee to the fact that the people of Leipzig support this effort.

One of the criterion for awarding the Olympic Games to any city) can make the city go for the whole revamping of its image and promise to be able to cope with a greater cultural demand upon its cultural and other infrastructures. In that case a success is directly linked to a cultural capacity to respond in a qualitative way to the challenge. It would mean the city can translate the tasks ahead in such a way that the organizational capacity amounts to a qualitative leap in the city's development and thereby stands to gain in profile.

5

Constitutional Economics

Constitutional economics is a research programme in economics and constitutionalism that has been described as extending beyond the definition of "the economic analysis of constitutional law" in explaining the choice "of alternative sets of legal-institutional-constitutional rules that constrain the choices and activities of economic and political agents." This is distinct from explaining the choices of economic and political agents within those rules, a subject of "orthodox" economics.

Constitutional economics studies the "compatibility of effective economic decisions with the existing constitutional framework and the limitations or the favorable conditions created by that framework." It has been characterized as a practical approach to apply the tools of economics to constitutional matters. For example, a major concern of every nation is the proper allocation of available national economic and financial resources. The legal solution to this problem falls within the scope of constitutional economics.

Constitutional economics takes into account the significant impacts of political economic decisions as opposed to limiting analysis to economic relationships as functions of the dynamics of distribution of "marketable" goods and services. "The political economist who seeks to offer normative advice, must, of necessity, concentrate on the process or structure within which political decisions are observed to be made. Existing constitutions, or structures or rules, are the subject of critical scrutiny."

ORIGINS

The term "constitutional economics" was coined in 1982 by the U.S. economist Richard McKenzie to designate the main topic of discussion at a conference held in Washington. D.C. McKenzie's neologism was then adopted by another American economist, James M. Buchanan, as a name for a new academic sub-discipline. It was Buchanan's work on this sub-discipline that brought him the Nobel Memorial Prize in Economic Sciences for his "development of the contractual and constitutional bases for the theory of economic and political decision-making" in 1986. Constitutionalism has been the subject of criticism for its previous ignorance of economic issues but this criticism was taken into account by the development of constitutional economics. Buchanan rejects "any organic conception of the state as superior in wisdom, to the individuals who are its members."

This philosophical position is, in fact, the very subject matter of constitutional economics. A constitutional economics approach allows for a combined economic and constitutional analysis, helping to avoid a one-dimensional understanding. Buchanan believes that a constitution, intended for use by at least several generations of citizens, must be able to adjust itself for pragmatic economic decisions and to balance interests of the state and society against those of individuals and their constitutional rights to personal freedom and private happiness.

Constitutional economics draws substantial inspiration from the reformist attitude which is characteristic of Adam Smith's vision, and that Buchanan's concept can be considered the modern-day counterpart to what Smith called "the science of legislation." According to Buchanan the ethic of constitutionalism is a key for constitutional order and "may be called the idealized Kantian world" where the individual "who is making the ordering, along with substantially all of his fellows, adopts the moral law as a general rule for behaviour".

Buchanan's Nobel lecture quoted the work of the late 19th century Swedish economist Knut Wicksell, who greatly influenced Buchanan's research: "If utility is zero for each individual member of the community, the total utility for the community cannot be other than zero." In epigraph to the chapter of Nobel lecture entitled "The Constitution of Economic Policy" Wicksell states that "whether the benefits of the proposed activity to the individual citizens would be greater than its cost to them, no one can judge this better than the individuals themselves."

A constitutional economics approach allows for a combined economic and constitutional analysis, helping to avoid a one-dimensional understanding. Buchanan believes that aconstitution, intended for use by at least several generations of citizens, must be able to adjust itself for pragmatic economic decisions and to balance interests of the state and society against those of individuals and their constitutional rights to personal freedom and private happiness.

Buchanan introduced rich cross-disciplinary concepts of "constitutional citizenship" and "constitutional anarchy". Constitutional anarchy is a modern policy that may be best described as actions undertaken without understanding or taking into account the rules that define the constitutional order. This policy is justified by references to strategic tasks formulated on the basis of competing interests regardless of their subsequent impact on political structure. At the same time Buchanan introduces the concept of "constitutional citizenship", which he designates as compliance of citizens with their constitutional rights and obligations that should be considered as a constituent part of the constitutional policy. Buchanan also outlines importance of protection of the moral principles underlying constitutional norms.

ETHICS OF CONSTITUTIONAL CITIZENSHIP

James Buchanan wrote that "the ethics of constitutional citizenship is not directly comparable to ethical behavior in interaction with other persons within the constraints imposed by the rules of an existing regime. An individual may be fully responsible, in the standard ethical sense, and yet fail to meet the ethical requirement of constitutional citizenship."Buchanan considered the term "constitutionality" in the broad sense and applied it to families, firms and public institutions, but, first of all, to the state.

Buchanan emphasised that public policy cannot be considered in terms of distribution, but is instead always a question of the choice over rules of the game that engender a pattern of exchange and distribution. Buchanan is largely responsible for the rebirth of political economy as a scholarly pursuit. Buchanan's work in public choice is often interpreted as the quintessential case of economic imperialism. However, as Amartya Sen has pointed out, Buchanan should not be identified with economic imperialism. Sen states that Buchanan has done more than most to introduce ethics, legal political thinking, and indeed social thinking into economics.

Crucial to understanding Buchanan's system of thought is the distinction he made between politics and policy. Politics is about the rules of the game, where policy is focused on strategies that players adopt within a given set of rules. "Questions about what are good rules of the game are in the domain of social philosophy, whereas questions about the strategies that players will adopt given those rules is the domain of economics, and it is the play between the rules (social philosophy) and the strategies (economics) that constitutes what Buchanan refers to as constitutional political economy".

In 1990, Buchanan, along with a few other budding constitutional economists, launched the journal *Constitutional Political Economy* with the purpose of further researching and developing the discipline. Buchanan wrote the vanguard article entitled "The Domain of Constitutional Economics", establishing the bounds of the emerging study and cementing the various topics he developed in 1962 and 1986. Buchanan gave a technical definition of constitutional economics as the research programme directed at the rules of institutions in which individuals make choices, along with the process of creating these rules. While ordinary economic inquiry focuses on the choices within the rules or the constraints imposed on the individuals, constitutional economics aims at the actual rules themselves, the choice among constraints. Individuals agree to place constraints on themselves in exchange for anticipated benefits, a similar to a social contract view of government. Just as a market transaction occurs through voluntary, mutually beneficial exchange, so with political "exchanges" of rights and authority. With this theory, politics becomes a form of exchange and is therefore worthy of economic analysis, thus establishing the formal beginning of constitutional economics.

By the end of the article, Buchanan enters philosophical territory, almost verging on skepticism, saying that each individual must perceive phenomena through his particular "window" and agreement is impossible when everyone views reality from different windows. Due to radical individualism, constitutional economics can include only people who view the world through economic paradigms or windows, not idealistic, goal-driven paradigms.

POSITIVE CONSTITUTIONAL ECONOMICS

Within positive constitutional economics, the tools or methods are unique from normal economic tools because of the cross-discipline nature of the programme. The main tool of positive constitutional economics is "comparative institutional analysis", with four main elements. The first element examines how certain constitutional rules arose and what factors caused the rules to be developed as a result of aggregated individual inputs. The second element looks at how rules are distinguishable between individual and collective factors, though Voigt acknowledges this research method is rarely used.

The third element is the possibilities of further constitutional (or rules) change. Any proposed change to constitutional constraints, or rules of constraints, are subject to economic scrutiny for their effects on efficiency and equity. The fourth element of positive constitutional economics examines the economic effects of developed or modified change to rules.

All economic analysis seeks to maximize efficiency, and constitutional economics is no exception. In the market, individuals maximize efficiency when both parties perceive a personal benefit, mutual exchange, and when resources go to their highest valued use. Market economy is today's reality, but it must be a "constitutional market economy" as a term introduced by Chief Justice of Indonesian Constitutional Court Jimly Asshiddiqie ini his "Economic Constitution". The political process is one of exchange, only unlike the market, the resources exchanged are political, not material or financial. Therefore, political efficiency is political consent, or when all individuals in the community agree to the political structures. Constitutional economics mimics a traditional contractarian political economy in its focus on the contract, or consent, between the governed and government. However, consent follows efficiency in markets while efficiency follows consent in politics.

NORMATIVE CONSTITUTIONAL ECONOMICS

Normative constitutional economics focuses on legitimizing the state and its actions as the best means of maximum efficiency and utility, judging conditions or rules that are efficient, and discerning and studying the political systems to maximize efficiency, where the outcome of collective choices are considered "fair", "just", or "efficient". Once again, Buchanan dominates the normative discussion of constitutional economics, specifically how methodological individualism affects economic analysis.

By 1988, Buchanan's thought had matured since his speech in 1986. Both Buchanan and Stefan Voigt argue the foundational assumption of normative constitutional economics is that no single individual's goals or values can supersede the value of another's. Therefore, a universal, absolute social norm or goal is impossible. Since politics is a form of exchange, when individuals agree to exchange goods, they are acting rationally in their own perceived self-interest if the decision is voluntary and informed. With these criteria, any such agreement is "efficient" and therefore normatively ought to occur.

Methodological individualism leads Buchanan to the normative claim that a political theory very similar to that of John Rawls in his seminal 1971 work, *A Theory of Justice*, would best realize individuals' unique goals. Complete with a veil of ignorance and *a priori* decisions of social goals, Buchanan says political economy does not have a social engineer or moral purpose but only assists individuals in their search for rules that best serve their individual purposes. For Buchanan, the "good" society is one that furthers the interests of individuals, not some independent moral or teleological end.

HAYEK

Buchanan is not the only contributor to normative constitutional economics. Economic polymath Friedrich Hayek also wrote extensively on the topic of constitutional economics, even if he did not name constitutional economics specifically. Hayek defends a representative constitutional democracy as the best structure of government. Hayek's main project was the vindication of freedom and establishing criteria for a regime of freedom.

Hayek was worried by the kind of state that Buchanan/Rawls deemed normative. Hayek thought it necessary for a return to the traditional views of government, human nature, political philosophy, and economics. He believed the Buchanan/Rawls state had the almost inevitable propensity to totalitarianism as the state seeks to maximize individual utility. People would soon be at the mercy of para-government bureaucracy of the provision-state.

Hayek cautions his readers against rashly launching into the kind of state Rawls and Buchanan conceive, saying individual choice cannot be the only determining factor in the choices of constraints, and the actual structure of the rules or constraints (the constitution) must conform to what Buchanan would label a supra-individual goal. For Hayek, liberal constitutional democracies are the best way to achieve the goal of individual freedom, equality, opportunity, and efficiency for three reasons. First, constitutions codify pre-existing (presumably efficient) law. Second, they place explicit constraints on government to prevent totalitarianism. Finally, they preserve law and order for the polis. All of this is within the framework of a moral and teleological order.

ECONOMIC ANALYSIS OF THE US CONSTITUTION

The generally accepted birth of constitutional economic analysis of US Constitution was Charles Austin Beard's landmark 1913 book *An Economic Interpretation of the Constitution of the United States*. While most scholars today reject Beard's overall thesis, he initiated a new method of economic and political thought that would evolve into contemporary constitutional economics analysis. Beard's main thesis was that the U.S. Constitution was an economic document created by men who were economically motivated.

Writing in 1987 for the Yale Law School, Jonathan Macey synthesizes the history of constitutional economic analysis applied to the US Constitution. Macey offers a different analysis of the US Constitution and responds critically to Beard's view of the Constitution.

Beard said the US Constitution was the product of a wealthy bourgeois class seeking the retention of personal wealth, even to the point of exploiting the lower classes. Beard even goes so far as to say that a famous and crucial part of the Constitution, separation of powers, was actually a means of allowing hegemony of resources in the hands of the rich few. Macey could not disagree more; he argues that the Constitution and separation of powers were created to hinder aggregate political and economic power. He points toFederalist No. 10, James Madison's famous description of the necessity of factions due to the truths of human nature.

SEPARATION OF POWERS

Macey says this conception of human nature is essentially economic. If government is not separated into distinct powers, the possibility of extensive rent-seeking threatens the efficiency of the government. Self-interested groups or individuals will lobby to political powers for their goals, possibly leading to injustice or inefficiency. In Macey's interpretation of Madison, the separation of powers channels lobbyists into the competitive, more efficient market by raising transaction costs so much that private market means are less expensive than appealing to the various separate powers of government.

Macey demonstrates how constitutional economics can be applied to constitutions. Rather than looking at the political or philosophic intentions of the founders, the constitutional economist looks at a constitution through economic eyes, considering the incentives, choices, allocations, and other economics factors within the political rules of a constitution. Traditionally, the creation of factions has been interpreted as a brilliant political move to separate power and prevent hegemony of the state. Macey agrees but adds a caveat. He maintains a real economic incentive to factions existed which compelled the Founders to separate government.

Factions and separated powers raise transaction costs of mobilizing political support beyond what interest groups can pay if they rely on private, non-governmental means. Macey even graphs the quantity of legislation on a standard supply-demand curve, where the demand is the interest groups' desire for laws and the supply is the legislation's provision. Separation of powers shifts the supply curve left, raising the price and decreasing the quantity of legislation. Macey admits that though the US Constitution is imperfect, he does vindicate it from the purely material accusations of Beard. He examines a political system of constraints using standard economic methods.

LEGAL APPROACH

Judge Richard Posner emphasized the importance of a constitution for economic development. He examines the interrelationship between a constitution and the economic growth. Posner approaches constitutional analysis mainly from the perspective of judges, who constitute a critical force for interpretation and implementation of a constitution, thus — *de facto* in common law countries — creating the body of constitutional law. He emphasizes the importance of constitutional provisions "in setting broader outer bounds to the exercise of judicial discretion". Thus, a judge, when trying a case, is guided firstly by the spirit and letter of the constitution. The role of economics in this process is to help "identify the consequences of alternative interpretations" of the constitution.

He then explains that "economics may provide insight into questions that bear on the proper legal interpretation." In the end, as Posner emphasizes, "the limits of an economic approach to deciding constitutional cases [are] set by the Constitution." In addition, he argues that "effective protection of basic economic rights promotes economic growth."

Concurrently with the rise of academic research in the field of constitutional economics in the US in the 1980s, the Supreme Court of India for almost a decade had been encouraging public interest litigation on behalf of the poor and oppressed by using a very broad interpretation of several articles of the Indian Constitution. The former Chief Justice of Indonesian Constitutional Court, Jimly Asshiddiqie, also published his book "Konstitusi Ekonomi" (2010) in promoting the idea of Economic Constitution. This is a vivid example of a *de facto* practical application of the methodology of constitutional economics.

The President of the Constitutional Court of the Russian Federation, Valery Zorkin, made a special reference to the educational role of constitutional economics: "In Russia, the addition of such new academic disciplines as constitutional economics to the curricula of university law and economics departments becomes critically important."

RUSSIAN SCHOOL

The Russian school of constitutional economics was created in the early twenty-first century with the idea that constitutional economics allows for a combined economic and constitutional analysis in the legislative (especially budgetary) process, thus helping to overcome arbitrariness in the economic and financial decision-making.

For instance, when military expenses (and the like) dwarf the budget spending on education and culture. Constitutional economics studies such issues as the proper national wealth distribution. This also includes the government spending on the judiciary, which in many transitional and developing countries is completely controlled by the executive.

The latter undermines the principle of checks and balances, instrumental in the separation of powers, as this creates a critical financial dependence of the judiciary. It is important to distinguish between the two methods of corruption of the judiciary: the state corruption (through budget planning and various privileges being the most dangerous), and the private corruption. The former makes it almost impossible for any business to facilitate the optimal growth and development of national market economy. In the English language, the word "constitution" possesses a whole number of meanings, encompassing not only national constitutions as such but also charters of corporations, unwritten rules of various clubs, informal groups, etc.

The Russian model of constitutional economics, originally intended for transitional and developing countries, focuses entirely on the concept of constitution of a state. This model of the constitutional economics is based on the understanding that it is necessary to narrow the gap between practical enforcement of the economic, social, and political rights granted by the constitution and the annual (or midterm) economic policy, budget legislation and administrative policies conducted by the government. In 2006, the Russian Academy of Sciences officially recognized constitutional economics as a separate academic sub-discipline.

Since in many countries with transitional political and economic systems, their constitutions are often treated by the ruling elite as abstract legal documents totally disconnected from the economic policy of the state, the practice of constitutional economics becomes there a decisive prerequisite for the democratic development of both the state and society.

CRITICISM

Not all scholars embrace constitutional economics. Walter Block and Thomas DiLorenzo make a strong criticism of constitutional economics as even a possible science. They maintain that politics cannot be equated with the market and, therefore, as a study, it cannot exist. They maintain that unlike the market, consent is not the foundation of politics, and that politics is driven by violent, historically bellicose, coercion. Therefore, they believe that the CE method only clouds the discussion of public choice and political economy. Buchanan, Voigt, Macey, and even Beard all at least implicitly assume that politics is the exchange of political "goods", a strong social contract view.

But for Block and DiLorenzo, politics is one powerful group coercing free rides from a weaker group. From the Roman Empire to the present, they trace how the state always comes from conquest and exploitation, never consent. *The Calculus of Consent*, a foundational text for constitutional economics, bears much of their attack. If they are correct that no state has been or can be voluntary and that voluntary government is inherently contradictory, constitutional economics as a discipline cannot exist.

William Campbell explains the weakness of constitutional economics in its assumption that the goal of a regime must be efficiency, individual liberty, and libertarian rights, not morality or super-individual good.

CONSTITUTIONAL ECONOMICS AND ETHICS

Fundamental to the economic approach to human behavior is the notion that people are motivated by self-interest in the sense that, if faced with a choice among alternative courses of action, they do what, in their view, best serves their own interests. Ethics, on the other hand, is based on the idea that there exist rules of moral conduct, and that people are not permitted simply to pursue their own interests, but are obliged to conform to these rules.

It seems evident that what serves people's self-interest need not always coincide, in fact, often clashes with what they ought to do from a moral point of view. Such conflicts between morality and self-interest are presumably the key reason for the often encountered view that economics and ethics not only have little in common, but that there exists a "categorical difference between the ethical and economic perspective" (P. Ulrich 1996:30).

In what follows, I hope to show that this notion of a "categorical difference" needs to be revised, at least in regard to the kind of economic perspective that has been advanced, in somewhat different but compatible ways, by the research programme of the Freiburg School, founded by economist Walter Eucken and jurist Franz Boehm as well as by the paradigm of Constitutional Political Economy, initiated by James M. Buchanan. The perspective that they share is, to be sure, not entirely novel in economics. It can actually be traced back to Adam Smith's concept of political economy as a "science of legislation," a science that can provide guidance to those who are to choose the rules for a society.

Like the political economy of Adam Smith, the constitutional economics approaches of Eucken and Buchanan essentially focus on the development of desirable rules for human coexistence and cooperation, which inevitably brings them into systematic proximity with the domain of social ethics, which is concerned with the moral rules people should observe in their dealings with one another. When it comes to assessing these rules we find that constitutional economics arguments, which refer to individuals' interests, and ethical arguments, being based on criteria of moral desirability, are far more closely related than the common perception of a conflict between morality and self-interest suggests. In fact, what may appear as an irreconcilable conflict at the level of particular actions appears in a different light if we look at the level of rules and relate the question which rules are desirable from an ethical perspective to the question which rules are desirable from the self-interest perspective of the individuals whose coexistence and cooperation is to be governed by them.

ACTION INTERESTS, DISPOSITION INTERESTS, AND CONSTITUTIONAL INTERESTS

Based on a set of conceptual distinctions summarized in the table below, I shall show how, in their respective approaches to the issue of what are desirable rules of human coexistence and cooperation, the constitutional economics perspective and the ethical perspective can be compared to each other. The table distinguishes three levels, at which an ethical and economic perspective can be applied: 1) the level of particular action, 2) the level of individual rules of conduct or behavioral dispositions, and 3) the level of social rules. In columns 1 and 2 the relevant ethical and economic issues are specified for each level. Column 3 refers to the constitutional issue of how to create conditions which make ethics and self-interest compatible.

Ethical perspective Economic (self-interest) perspective Constitutional perspective Level of particularactions Which choice of action is morally right? Which choice of action serves the agent's interests? Can conditions be created in which the morally right choice always coincides with the agent's interests? (unsolvable problem)

Level of individual behavioral dispositions Which behavioral dispositions can be defined as ethical? Which behavioral dispositions serve the agents' interests in the environment in which they live? Can conditions be created in which adopting ethical dispositions serves the agents' interests? (solvable problem)

Level of social rules What rules of social conduct are ethically desirable? Which social rules serve agents' constitutional interests? Can conditions be created in which the agents' constitutional interests coincide with moral rules? (solvable problem)

The definitions in the table are based on the idea that the key to clarifying the relationship between self-interest and morality, or between economics and ethics, is to distinguish various interest levels. If, as in the table, we distinguish between *action* interests, *disposition* interests, and *constitutional* interests, it should become apparent that, while a conflict between morality and self-interest may be inevitable at the level of particular behavioral choices, this is no longer so when we look at the level of dispositions and social rules, asking the question: which dispositions may serve a person's interest, and under which social rules may a person wish to live?

It is easy to envisage specific choice situations where an action that directly serves a person's own interests contradicts what he should do from an ethical point of view. Indeed, it is scarcely possible to envisage a world in which this conflict between morality and self-interest would not exist. Yet, things appear somewhat different at the level of general behavioral dispositions, and very different at the level of constitutional interests.

The evidently accurate observation that individuals may face conflicts between self-interest and ethical imperatives in particular choice situations, often leads to the rash conclusion that a willingness to put one's own interests last is the sign of moral behavior.

If, like this, we assume from the start that morality is a question of *motivation*, there is no point to further investigating the relationship between the economic perspective, which is based on the assumption that behavior is generally self-interested, and the ethical perspective. If morality is defined in motivational terms, an unbridgeable gap between morality and self-interest is created by definition, with the effect that economic and ethical perspectives must seem inherently irreconcilable.

The issue of the relationship between self-interest and morality is only worth exploring if one adopts a *behavioral* view of morality, i.e. a view that does not focus on an action's underlying (and unobservable) *motivation*, but on whether the empirically observable behavior coincides with specifiable norms of ethical conduct. According to the behavioral view, morality does not require the individual to abandon the pursuit of self-interest, but only to abandon the pursuit of self-interest by immoral means. Although a behavioral concept of morality does not eliminate the potential conflict between self-interest and morality, it does not exclude by definition alone the possibility that self-interested behavior can be moral and vice versa. By insisting on the distinction between the motivation and the factual consequences of human actions, it also alerts us to the fact that non-self-interested or altruistic motivation by no means guarantees a behavior that, in terms of its actual consequences, we would consider morally desirable.

If we regard the function of morality as providing a desirable frame for human coexistence and cooperation, the behavioral concept of morality is surely the more appropriate alternative. According to such a concept, persuading people to abandon self-interest is neither necessary nor sufficient for solving the problem of moral order. Rather, the problem can only be solved by creating structural conditions which induce people to act morally out of their own interest, conditions which reconcile self-interested behavioral *motivation* and ethical behavioral *conduct*. To be sure, the problem of creating a moral order would in fact be an unsolvable task if conditions first had to be created (row 1, column 3 of the table), whereby - in concrete decision-making situations - the most personally advantageous alternative always coincided with the morally required one.

The nature of the problem changes, however, if instead of asking whether, in particular choice situations, it is in the interest of an individual to behave morally, we ask whether it promotes his own interests to be *generally disposed* towards complying with moral rules, i.e. not to calculate in each single case if moral behavior is advantageous or not.

The comparison that at this level is of relevance for the relationship between morality and self-interest is no longer concerned with the consequences of single, specific choices, but with the total sum of personal advantages and disadvantages that result from a "moral disposition" over a relevant period of time, i.e. from the general willingness to respect the rules of moral conduct, independently of the specific circumstances of particular choice situations. In other words, the relevant comparison is between the overall pattern of payoffs that results from a moral disposition, compared to the pattern of payoffs a person would experience if she had *other general dispositions* or simply behaved in a discretionary manner in every single case.

In everyday language we refer to behavioral dispositions when we talk of a person's character. Accordingly, the issue at hand can also be expressed in terms of the question whether - and if so, under which conditions - a moral character can be to a person's advantage. This, of course, raises the further question of how the implied notion of a "calculus of advantage" can be theoretically defined at the level of behavioral dispositions. Obviously, we can hardly speak of a genuine "choice" between alternative behavioral dispositions (or character traits) in the normal sense in which we speak of a choice between alternative courses of action. Behavioral dispositions are much more the product of subconscious learning processes than a subject of deliberate choice. They can, therefore, not simply be adopted or rejected as a result of a conscious calculation of their advantages and disadvantages, even though a person may, of course, wish to adopt certain dispositions and make efforts to develop the respective character traits.

If we assume, as certainly we must, that some kind of "calculus of advantage" occurs at the level of dispositions, the "accounting" of the advantages and disadvantages of relevant alternatives at that level must clearly be based on something other than deliberate calculation. In order to allow for such a modified notion of a "calculus of advantage," the conventional economic model of rational choice will have to be expanded or revised, for instance along the lines of Ronald Heiner's theory of "rule-governed behavior" (1990).

An "economic," in the sense of interest-based, explanation of moral dispositions developed along these lines would proceed in two steps. The first step would be to explain, as Heiner's theory dos, why rule-following behavior can produce greater long-term benefits than discretionary decisions from case to case. The second step would consist of determining the conditions in which a *moral* disposition can yield greater rewards than potential alternative dispositions.

MORAL ORDER AND CONSENSUAL CONSTITUTIONAL INTERESTS

The crucial point in the distinction between the level of behavioral choices and the level of general behavioral dispositions is the following: It is noticeably easier to create and sustain a moral order if one is not dealing with "homines oeconomici," who in every single instance choose the most personally profitable course of action, but with rule-following individuals who, even though they do, indeed, pursue their own interests, do so on the basis of general behavioral dispositions which they have found to work to their overall advantage. It would go beyond the scope of this paper to discuss the issue of what kind of learning process is required to process information on the relative benefits of alternative behavioral dispositions. What matters here is that the conditions which render it profitable for rule-following agents to possess *moral* dispositions (row 2, column 3 of the table) are far easier to create than conditions that ensure that for discretionary case-by-case maximizers the most profitable course of action generally coincides with what is morally required.

To be sure, the potential conflict between morality and self-interest continues to exist at the level of general behavioral dispositions, since moral dispositions are by no means always "rational," in all kinds of environment. However, the problem of creating an environment in which people can be "rationally" moral is a solvable problem. Indeed, it is a problem that every society must solve if a moral order is to be sustained.

The relationship between morality and interests appears in yet a different light if we turn to the third level, i.e. the level of social rules, and examine people's *rule* or *constitutional interests*, i.e. their preferences with regard to the "rules of the game" that they wish to see enforced in the society in which they live. One can meaningfully speak of constitutional interests only in relation to specific, definable communities or social units, which a person belongs to and where she can want certain rules to be enforced. People are generally affiliated to a variety of overlapping groups or communities, each one internally governed by specific rule systems (formal and/or informal): these range from the family and private associations, various kinds of polities at the sub-national, national or supranational level, to the largest group of all, i.e. the world community. For each of these units, we can ask which general rules reflect the constitutional interests of its members.

As regards the constitutional interests that people hold in their various groups, associations or communities, a distinction of key significance in the present context is that between *consensual* constitutional interests and interests in *privileges*. When people consider which rules serve their own interests, the first to spring to mind are likely to be rules that grant them some privilege or other, i.e. offer special personal advantages. And, as far as they are in a position to choose and enforce social rules without considering the interests of other members, we should expect self-interested individuals to be tempted by their interests in privileges. Interests in privileges are by their very nature non-consensual. They may be enforced by means of fraud or coercion, but are no basis for a constitutional order to which all participants can voluntarily agree, with a clear understanding of their own interests.

In contrast to non-consensual interests in privileges, *consensual constitutional interests* aim at rules that are desirable and acceptable to all parties involved. The key contention of this article can be stated as follows: the informed constitutional interests shared by all members of a group or community define the very rules which, from an ethical perspective, are morally desirable for that group.

The adjective "informed" is added in order to account for the fact that the relationship between the enforcement of specific social rules and the resulting pattern of outcomes may be complex and not immediately obvious, and that, because they are not fully aware of the real relationships, people may be prompted to endorse rules they would reject if they were better informed about their factual working properties. What must be assumed to be of normative significance, therefore, is their informed agreement.

Just as the question of which rules are the subject of consensual constitutional interests can be meaningfully discussed only in relation to specified groups, the question of which behavioral rules qualify as moral rules can, according to the interpretation proposed here, properly be answered only if we specify the relevant group of reference.

The (group-) relativity of morality implied in such a notion is of less impact than it may first appear. It implies no limitation or restriction whatsoever with respect to what one may consider the relevant level of moral commitment, be it a local community or humankind. It only requires that one specifies with regard to what group or community a rule is claimed to qualify as a moral rule. How the appropriate reference group is to be defined depends on the nature of the issue one is interested in.

The argument that rules reflecting the consensual constitutional interests of all members of a group correspond to the rules that are morally desirable for that group, must be understood in a dual sense. On the one hand, it is meant as a proposed definition, i.e. it implies that the term morality can thus be meaningfully interpreted and expressed in operational terms. On the other hand, it is meant as the empirical hypothesis that both our general understanding of morality and major philosophical concepts of morality, as far as they are concerned with the issue of desirable rules for human coexistence and cooperation, can essentially be interpreted in terms of this concept or are at least compatible with it.

I suppose that many of the major ethical doctrines do in fact, with their respective definitions of the attributes of moral rules, refer to criteria which are identical or very similar to what has been defined here in terms of consensual constitutional interests. This evidently applies to concepts which see the essential criterion of moral rules in their impartiality and universal applicability or, as the discourse ethics of H.O. Apel and J. Habermas, in the "Konsensfahigkeit für alle Betroffenen" (acceptability to all parties) (Apel 1997:191). This is also true for all concepts which - like the moral philosophy of David Gauthier (1986) - in one form or another, view moral rules as behavioral constraints, which enable people to realize mutual gains from cooperation in cases where an unconstrained pursuit of self-interest would exclude such gains, or would even result in direct mutual damage.

Donald Campbell (1986: 171) similarly focuses on the issue of constitutional interests when he states that the rules of morality reflect our preferences with respect to the behavior of *others*, i.e. our interests in how they should behave. Obviously, the direct implication of this interest is only that we wish *others* to be bound by such rules. Yet, where rules cannot be unilaterally imposed but have to find agreement among equally rational agents, these interests in how others should behave can be implemented only as mutual or reciprocal commitments.

CONSTITUTIONAL INTERESTS AND "ORDNUNGSPOLITIK" (CONSTITUTIONAL POLITICS)

The constitutional economics concept of consensual constitutional interests is based on the idea that people can reap mutual benefits by jointly committing to suitable rules of the game. The key idea of this approach is that the notion of "gains from trade," familiar from the economic concept of voluntary market exchange, is generalized to agreements on rules, interpreted as voluntary "exchanges" of self-binding commitments. To be sure, the constitutional interests referred to here merely entail the desire to live in a community in which the rules in question are enforced.

This desire alone does not per se generate an interest in personally conforming to these rules. In other words, the *constitutional* interest in seeing rules *enforced* in one's community does not automatically generate an *action*-interest in *conforming to* them. Rational agents will recognize, however, that their constitutional interest in living in a community where certain rules are enforced can become effective only if conditions are in place that ensure a sufficient direct interest in rule-compliance among the parties involved. Therefore, they should have a common interest in creating such conditions where necessary. It is the task of *Ordnungspolitik* (constitutional politics), on the one hand, to identify and implement rules which serve the consensual constitutional interests of the members of a community and, on the other hand, to create conditions which generate sufficient interest in complying with these rules. This is what Walter Eucken (1990: 366) had in mind when he argued that the "coordination of individual and collective interests is the task of *Ordnungspolitik*."

As noted before, to ensure sufficient interest in adhering to moral rules does not require that the utility-maximizing and the moral course of action coincide for all agents in every single choice situation. This would in fact be an unsolvable task. What is required is that conditions are created which allow people to be "rationally" moral in the sense that they can trust that by respecting moral rules they serve their own overall interests and do not systematically and permanently put themselves at a disadvantage.

Eucken (2990: 368) refers to this issue when he notes that "it is unfair to require people to do what can only be accomplished by the economic constitution: to create a harmonious relationship between individual and collective interests." If people are systematically and constantly penalized for behaving "morally," i.e. in a socially desirable manner, it means that the general system contains flaws that cannot be offset by appealing to people's willingness to make personal sacrifices. In fact, people who are particularly open to such appeals would only expose themselves to exploitation by more cynical agents. And even if everyone could be motivated to make moral sacrifices, a moral system based on this type of willingness would always be vulnerable, since it would not have any defense against "immoral invaders," to whose exploitative tendencies it would only provide a particularly profitable niche.

According to what has been argued above, the ethical question concerning the rules of a moral order is essentially the same as the constitutional economics question concerning rules that reflect the consensual constitutional interests of the parties concerned. If one accepts this argument, one must regard behavior as moral as long as it is in accordance with rules of the game that are desirable for, i.e. in the consensual constitutional interest of, all persons involved. This fact is of special significance since the moral intuitions of people may not always correspond with their consensual constitutional interests.

Constitutional, that is rule-related interests are *derived* interests, in the sense that it is not the rules per se that interest us, but their working properties or their effects, i.e. the pattern of outcomes that result from alternative rule systems. The connection between the "order of rules" and the resulting "order of actions" is often complex and not at all obvious. Which rules people believe to serve their interests depends on their explicit and tacit, more or less adequate theories about what outcomes will result from potential alternative rules, and how they will be personally affected. Accordingly, people's understanding of what is in their consensual constitutional interest depends on their explicit or implicit expectations concerning the working properties of alternative rule regimes. This means that there is no guarantee for their moral intuitions always to coincide with their "informed" constitutional interests, i.e. the interests that they would hold if aware of the actual functional characteristics of the rules in question. It seems that discrepancies between spontaneous moral intuitions and informed constitutional interests are one of the main causes of the widespread moral distrust by which the competitive order of the market if often met.

THE MARKET AND MORALITY

The rules of the market system are rules for the interaction of an - in principle, unlimited - number of people, who are not related by personal ties or mutual attachment, but nevertheless wish to enjoy the mutual benefits that can be reaped from voluntary exchange and cooperation. By contrast, people's moral intuitions must be expected to be primarily shaped by the experience of living together in small groups, where "experience" is to be interpreted in a double sense, as the "experience" that, in a metaphorical sense, the species "homo sapiens" has undergone over its evolutionary history, and the experience that, in the ordinary sense, an individual person undergoes through his life time. The evolutionary history of the species was, up to roughly ten thousand years ago, marked for countless generations by the conditions of life in small hunter/gatherer groups.

Ten thousand years are too short a time span for significant changes to occur in biological evolution. We may conclude, therefore, that our *genetic* makeup - including our "moral instincts" - is adapted to these primordial conditions, and not to the conditions of life in modern extended societies. As regards the socialization history of individual persons, that too is predominantly shaped by the conditions of life in small groups - the family, school, the workplace, so that we must assume that the acquired behavioral dispositions of human beings - including their learned moral intuitions – are primarily adapted to the conditions of life in such intimate groups.

Yet, the "moral instincts" and "moral intuitions" that are essential for cooperation in such groups are by no means necessarily adapted to the problems that have to be solved in order to sustain a mutually advantageous system of cooperation among a large number of virtual strangers. The creation of such a system is, however, precisely the function of the rules of the market. Needless to say, some of the behavioral rules governing cooperation in small groups will also be essential for market cooperation as well.

Yet, some of the moral principles (Hayek refers specifically to notions of "distributive justice") that may be functional in the context of small groups may well prove totally dysfunctional when transferred to a market context. The moral qualities of a market order – as of any other constitutional order - cannot be judged appropriately just by applying the moral instincts or intuitions referred to above. They should be judged according to whether their defining rules correspond to the (informed) consensual constitutional interests of the persons concerned. In other words, responsible moral criticism of the market system should prove its case by explicitly stating which of the rules of a market order are supposedly in conflict with the consensual, constitutional interests of the people concerned, and by specifying which alternative rules of the game are supposed to serve these interests better than the rules that are considered deficient.

Since Adam Smith's days, advocates of the competitive market order have, explicitly or implicitly, argued their case from the conviction that the order they favor serves the common interests of all, that it corresponds - in the terminology used here – to people's consensual constitutional interests. In his critique of the mercantilist system of privileges and in his appeal for what he termed the "simple system of natural liberty" Adam Smith was clearly concerned with the ethical nature of the competitive market order as a privilege-free system, a concern which has been restated most emphatically by Franz Böhm, co-founder of the Freiburg School, in an article on "Private law society and the market economy" (1966).

Yet, the message of the ethical value of the competitive market order as a privilege-free system has almost been drowned out by the choir of voices of those who, even if they are prepared to concede the "economic efficiency" of the market economy, nevertheless suggest that it is somehow a morally deficient system. In reference to such "resentment against economic liberty," as it emerged in the final decades of the 19th century, Franz Böhm (1980: 260) noted: "It was less the socialist critique than various diverse intellectual trends which have rapidly gained ground within the sciences - including economics - since the turn of the century that reinforced this prejudice: the conviction that the free market was an ethically reprehensible and socially amoral system gradually became an almost universally shared view among all intellectuals."

A preferred target of moral criticism is the link between market competition and profit-seeking, or, more precisely, the fact that the sanctioning mechanism of competition forces market participants to be guided in their economic decisions by anticipated profits. There can, of course, be no doubt about the fact that economic profit is the principal indicator of success in the "game of catallaxy," as Hayek has called the market exchange game. The "market game" works to reward those who succeed in producing goods or services for which others are willing to pay a price that exceeds the costs of providing them, i.e. the opportunity costs of the resources used. Profits simply constitute the difference between revenue and (opportunity-) costs. Profit-seeking thus means nothing other than striving for success in the "market game." If this is the case, what sense does it make to view striving for profit as immoral? What sense is there in reproaching the participants in a competitive game for simply attempting to play the game well? To be sure, one may well ask whether the game itself is desirable, i.e. whether it is at all in the common interest of all participants to play the game in its current form, i.e. as defined by the set rules, or whether they might not be better off playing a different game, one defined by better rules? Yet, if there is no reason to doubt that the game itself is a desirable game, then it is absurd to morally criticize people for seeking to play the game successfully, as long as they do so within the rules. And, if there are reasons to believe that a better game could be played, then the appropriate response is to seek a change in the rules of the game, not to require the players to disregard their own interests.

What is true for other games applies, of course, no less to the "market game," namely that players, or market participants, are morally obliged to comply with the rules that are binding for all. Market competition does not take place in an anarchic vacuum; it operates within specific rules of the game, within the constitutional framework of a competitive order, a *Wettbewerbsordnung*. The participants are not at liberty to strive for success using any means available. They are expected to seek success only by employing means and strategies that comply with the rules of the game, rules which may include, in addition to what is explicitly codified and formally sanctioned, certain generally accepted standards of fair and honorable behavior, which, even if they are not sanctioned formally, one cannot violate without damaging one's reputation. However, it does not make sense to regard not only unfair striving for success, but the striving for success per se as morally suspect.

Nor does it make sense to require market participants to compensate for deficiencies in the rules of the game by sacrificing their ambition to play the "market game" successfully. Ensuring that the competitive market process is a worthwhile and desirable game for all, as long as it is actually played according to the rules, is a matter of appropriate constitutional framing, the task of *Ordnungspolitik* or constitutional politics. To play the game within the rules is the obligation of the players. But it cannot be their role, to compensate, by their way of playing the game, for what Ordnungspolitik fails to do. Nor could they ever succeed in doing so.

CONSENSUS AND THE CHOICE OF RULES

If we assume that the attribute "moral" applies to rules which are in the *consensual* constitutional interests of the parties concerned, and if, on the other hand, we take into account that people generally have incentives to pursue their respective interests in *privileges*, a critical question arises with regard to the processes by which rules are selected. The question is whether conditions exist, or whether one can create or promote such conditions, in which people's consensual constitutional interests are likely to prevail. The remainder of this paper is about this issue.

Where people are in a position to affect the choice of rules in a community without regard for the interests of other parties, they will be tempted to opt for rules that put them in a privileged position, i.e. for rules that work to their differential advantage. Similar to what Eucken and Böhm had to say in their critique of what they described as "refeudalisation," the economic theory of rent-seeking has pointed to the problem that, by their simultaneous efforts to secure privileges for themselves, people tend to bring about, as an unintented but inevitable aggregate outcome, an overall constitutional regime that is less desirable for all parties - including the "beneficiaries" of privileges - than a privilege-free rule system would be that reflects the consensual constitutional interests of all. Therefore, the vital issue is how a constitutional order that serves the consensual interests of all can be established, and how it can be protected from being eroded by privilege-seeking or rent-seeking activities that induce a progressive decline towards a system which, in the end, serves nobody's interests.

If the aim is to structure or frame the process of constitutional choice in ways that allow the consensual constitutional interests of the members of a community to prevail, and to "filter out" interests in privileges as far as possible, two basic approaches can be adopted. On the one hand, we can attempt to create conditions that *motivate* individuals to demand "fair" or consensual rules. On the other hand, we can attempt to create conditions which leave people with *no other choice* than to opt for consensual rule systems, i.e. conditions which exclude or at least effectively curb opportunities for successful privilege-seeking.

The first alternative is the theme of approaches that model the agreement on rules as a choice behind a veil of uncertainty or ignorance. The essence of this concept is that people will be led, from their own self-interest, to choose fair or consensual rules, if they are ignorant or sufficiently uncertain about how alternative rules will affect them personally.

Under such conditions, they need to consider the various possible ways in which they might be affected by the rules in question. Since they cannot know what their own position will be, they will have to assess the merits of alternative rules in terms of their predictable *general* working properties, i.e. in terms of how desirable they are irrespective of what one's particular position is. Stated differently, the effect of the veil of uncertainty or ignorance it to transform potential *inter*-personal conflicts of interest into *intra*-personal conflicts, causing individuals to opt for "unbiased" or fair rules out of self-interest. For the framing or structuring of constitutional choice processes this implies: To the extent that these processes can be organized in ways that increase uncertainty about how one will be personally affected by the rules under consideration, the incentives for privilege-seeking will be lessened, and the prospects will be enhanced for consensual constitutional interests to prevail.

As regards the second alternative, two basic methods can in turn be distinguished by which opportunities for successful privilege-seeking may be reduced. The first method is to explicitly constrain legislative processes by a non-discrimination or equal-treatment requirement, i.e. to exclude discriminatory and privilege-granting rules as inadmissible. This has been the purpose of the classical principle of the rule of law, or the generality principle, as the constitutional ideal of what Franz Böhm (1980) has called the "private or civil law society." Yet, efforts to implement this ideal by explicit constitutional constraints on governments and legislative powers have only had limited success. Especially in the area of economic legislation, all kinds of privileges have been, and are, commonly granted by governments and legislators of all modern democracies, be it in the form of subsidies, protectionist regulations, tax exemptions or other special treatments.

The second strategy for restricting privilege-seeking and improving the prospects for consensual constitutional orders consists of promoting competition between political communities or "jurisdictions." What constitutes a privilege for one party (e.g. the recipient of subsidies) has as its mirror-image a discriminating, differential burden imposed on other parties (e.g. as taxpayers or consumers). The easier it is for members of a jurisdiction to evade discriminating treatment by moving mobile resources or by migrating in person to an alternative jurisdiction, the narrower the scope for successful privilege-seeking and for sustaining existing privileges becomes. In the limiting case of cost-free mobility between jurisdictions, the only constitutional regimes that can be sustained will be those that command the voluntary cooperation of all parties involved. Under such conditions, attempts at privilege-seeking cannot be assured long-term success.

Whatever their respective potential interests in privileges might be, in the absence of willing counterparts who would have to carry the burden of their privileges, individuals will have no other option than to choose among consensual constitutional regimes.

Real-life conditions are, of course, far removed from this theoretical borderline case, but every change in technology, institutional structure or other relevant factors that facilitates mobility between jurisdictions makes it more difficult to gain and to sustain privileges, and it improves the prospects for consensual constitutional interests to prevail. The developments currently being discussed widely under such headings as globalization and jurisdictional competition may turn out to be more effective in implementing the classical liberal ideal of a privilege-free constitutional order than the traditional efforts at implementing the generality principle have been. Of course, what applies to competition in general, is no less true at the level of competition between jurisdictions, namely, that in order for competition to work beneficially it has to be governed by appropriate rules. To address this issue is a challenge for the theory and politics of constitutional order.

MODERN CONSTITUTIONAL ECONOMICS

What is meant by constitutional economics today? It sounds like a very delimited term describing the economic problems of money, tariffs, and commerce that one might find as particular parts of the U.S. Constitution. It may include those items, but it is much more ambitious. The phrase "constitutional economics" primarily means a system of fundamental laws or rules which will tie down government in order to promote economic liberty. The free market is the ideal if not always the end result of constitution making. A list of several key books in the classical liberal and libertarian tradition is appended at the end of the lecture for the inquiring reader.

Constitutional economics has derived from several discontents with the piecemeal approach to public policy. For example, in monetary policy, discretionary rules have often led to disastrous results which would have been avoided by a fixed monetary rule.

In the area of fiscal policy, the excessive spending of Congress results from legislators looking only to short-run considerations in getting reelected. Balanced budget amendments to -theWilliam Campbell is Professor of Economics at Louisana State University. He spoke on July 27, 1988, during his appointment as a Bradley Resident Scholar at The Heritage Foundation. ISSN 0272-1155.

Constitution would serve as a constraining rule of the game, one step removed from the concrete policies. In sum, there are problems with unlimited modern democratic institutions. The strength of modem constitutional economics is its valuable insights on the themes of economic liberty, private property, and voluntary exchange.

The whole model is driven by equating social good or betterment with voluntary exchange. Confronting the Egalitarian Hydra. T he weakness of modern constitutional economics lies in the fact that it assumes that the nature of the regime is efficiency, individual liberty, or absolute libertarian rights - depending on the branch it stems from. Chicago school law and economics, Virginia public choice, and libertarian legal theory are some of the different branches. As do most conservatives, they tend to squabble among themselves. If they restricted economics to economics, there would be no problem. But they do not. Economic constitutionalism would be a more descriptive phrase than constitutional economics.

One of the advantages of ancient social science is that it was always aware that there were different regimes that claimed to be the best. Each regime had ruling principles, some of which were similar to the ruling principles of today's regimes or ideologies. A constitution was apoliteia or way of life and was ultimately to be judged by the kind of character it produced. When they are not squabbling among themselves, modem constitutional economists tend to recognize this only when they confront the egalitarian hydra.

FEDERALISM

The endowment of federalism has not always been used wisely. Federalism has been misunderstood and perverted by both the socialists and the liberals who wish to centralize and increase the powers of the central government. They have a constitution or way of life in mind, but it is a vision that oscillates between the society of no limits, the world turned perpetually upside down, and the perfect security of a padded cell. They go back and forth between the two sides of the famous Brueghel painting of "The Fight between Carnival and Lent." Federalism also has been truncated by modern constitutional economists. They are sensitive to the attempts to reduce federalism to a computational or administrative problem by mainstream economists. But it still comes down to being an amoral machine, which allows people to refuse consent to government by voting with their feet.

They wish to posit the solitary individual holding his trump cards against any social arrangements he does not consent to. The trump cards may be unanimous consent, absolute property rights, or natural rights as defined by libertarians. Keeping Man in Solitary. If the liberals and collectivists wish to keep man in solitary in his padded cell, the modern constitutional economists wish to keep him in solitary out of his padded cell. He may be as convivial as he can be, but any entangling alliances are purely of his own making. At the beginning of the game of creating a social contract or at the level of constitutional choice, he has no natural obligations to anyone else except for the libertarian duty of not invading someone else's property.

Let me illustrate the idea of constitutional economics by comparing three different approaches, which we can call the home making, the home breaking, and the home constructing models. The home making and household management of the Great Tradition correspond most closely with modem conservatism. The home breaking communism of Lycurgus in Sparta is very close in spirit to modem communism and liberalism. Finally, there is the home construction analogy used by James Buchanan in his modem constitutional economics.

HOMEMAKING

The ancients understood the essential task of economics to be household management, which included the proper ordering of the material side of life as well as its proper end, character formation. Because of certain limitations of the family in achieving i t s natural end, politics was required. But politics and constitutions flowed from the family and not from abstract, autonomous individuals. There were natural limits to the size of the po& or city-state if it was to hope to achieve its moral ends. This was the beginning of small republics and the fear of empire.

American federalism with its reliance on state and local self-government married virtue to the economic freedom of the extended commercial republic. The science of American politics was improved by holding to these principles simultaneously, even though they are in a state of tension.

HOME BREAKING

In both the ancient and modem world there has existed an egalitarian constitutional economics. Because of the fact that its adherents are disdainful of economic liberties, they are not usually included among the constitutional economists. But they have been the dominant influence in 20th century jurisprudence.

The modem liberal-socialist-communist view is built on the desire of bringing down the house. No matter how solid the construction, if the world is turned upside down, no house can stand. The liberal view is that the family who built the house is simply an obstruction because it is the perennial cause of inequality. The family needs to be destroyed and replaced by the onmicompetent state who will not allow such inequalities to be created. Incompetent parents must surrender the education of their children to the experts, whether in public schools or day care centers.

Public Virtue to the Point of Fanaticism. It is for these reasons that Sparta and its great lawgiver, Lycurgus, have been the prototypical communists. He understood that to bring about an egalitarian society, the springs of motivation that existed in the family must be replaced by other motives such as public virtue or enthusiasm to the point of fanaticism where they would gather about him like bees.

The modem liberal view might also be called the federal bulldozer approach. Wherever inequalities exist, they are evil and have to be leveled. Egalitarianism says knock down the imperfect states and communities as we know them and replace them according to new egalitarian blueprints.

HOME CONSTRUCTING

Our last homey image is James Buchanan's comparison of the process of making a social con tract or constitution to the process of making a home construction. contract; we are to assume the builder is a moral reprobate, a shirker, who will engage in acts of postcontractual opportunism. The goal of all this is self-protection from the lLeviathan state and not the literal creation of good households. Realism does not demand quite such a gloomy outlook. The

Federalist Number 55 hits the proper balance: "As there is a degree of depravity in mankind which requires a certain degree of circumspection a n d distrust, so there are other qualities in human nature which justify a certain portion of esteem and confidence. Republican government presupposes the existence of these qualities in a higher degree than any other form." Elaborate edifices are built aro u nd private property rights and gains from exchange.

The public choice variant of constitutional economics builds these structures ex nihilo if not ex nihilism; the legal variants simply attribute libertarian ideas to the Founding Fathers on the basis of a few legal maxims or statements commending private property. But at its normative core, modem constitutional economics is built around the autonomy or liberty of the individual, who has no natural obligations to anyone else. The free man, defined only in terms of the absence of coercion, becomes the autonomous man.

James Buchanan, as usual, is clearer and more explicit than most: "If we remain within the presuppositions of methodological individualism, the state or the polity must ultimately be justified i n terms of its potential for satisfying individuals' desires, whatever these might be.

The state is necessarily an artifact, an instrument that has evolved or is designed for the purpose of meeting individual needs that cannot be readily satisfied under alternative arrangements. In this sense, the great game of politics must be a positive-sum game. If this fact is recognized while also acknowledging the potential for conflict among differing individual interests, the basic exchange model of the economist is immediately suggested."

Pitfalls of Methodological Individualism. At the end of his Nobel lecture, he expressed the heart of his constitutional endeavors: "How can we live together in peace, prosperity and harmony, while retaining our liberties as autonomous individuals who can, and must, create our own values?" There is a fundamental conflict between the religious view of man as created in God's image and this autonomous view of man.

My experience leads me to Christian beliefs. I know that there are some , perhaps even many, constitutional economists who do not share the Enlightenment view of man's autonomy. I wish to persuade them and warn others, who are just starting their journey, of the pitfalls of a methodological individualism that does not stick to its business but attempts to become a complete political philosophy.

To reject these extreme normative formulations of the public choice approach to economic constitutionalism is neither to reject the positive analysis of how the world works if it is found useful nor to reject the free market. Preserving the free market is a proper concern of American conservatives. But instead of continuing to dwell on the limitations of modern constitutional economics and public choice in a full-blown abstract way, let me "accentuate the positive."

THE GIFT OF REASON IN THE GOSPELS

Let me begin by embellishing the Gospel account of Jesus and the Gadarene Swine. I wish to paint an imaginative picture to capture the themes of substantive reason, voice, and gratitude. A painting of pigs voting with their feet down a steep hillside will stick in your mind much longer than many thousands of my abstract words. A careful reading of the story will per m it me to touch briefly on Plato, Aristotle, and Edmund Burke, who are key figures in the economy of gratitude that I do not have sufficient space to deal with here. The Great Tradition is based on the rock of reality, and is not true because it has been handed down, but is handed down because it is true.

The Greek, Jewish, and Christian understandings of human nature are based on the same realistic experiences of human ingratitude and foolishness. One does not become an optimist about the plasticity of hum a n nature from reading Greek philosophy, the Old Testament, or the New Testament, as we shall see. But there are exceptions, and there is hope. The story of the Gadarene Swine in the Gospels is significant for helping us think through the connections between the problems of God's gifts, family and community, our feelings of gratitude and ingratitude, and the nature of human reason. It is also a cautionary tale about the nature of modern democracy which has lost its moral bearings.

The Man Possessed by Demon s. The description of the man possessed by demons in Luke sounds like a ringer for the present homeless: "a man from the city who had demons; for a long time he had wom no clothes, and he lived not in a house but among the tombs." If you live in Washington , D.C., the Metro stops often take on the feeling of a great tomb. Accosted by the homeless at the top of the escalator, one often feels as though "Abandon all hope ye who enter here" should be emblazoned on the portal. The demoniac's problem was of long standing.

He had been seized by unclean spirits many times before and had previously been kept "under guard, and bound with chains and fetters, but he broke the bonds and was driven by the demon into the desert." Notice the oscillating extremes are similar to those of modem liberalism. The problem is not dissimilar to the origins of many of the homeless today. We still need to separate out those who are truly possessed with demons, i.e the insane, and those who are shiftless. In our society, many of the mad men were freed by the American Civil Liberties Union rather than by their own native strength.

Edmund Burke's response to a similar problem in the 18th century is still relevant: "Should I felicitate a madman who has escaped from the protecting restraint and wholesome darkness of his cell on his restoration to the enjoyment of light and liberty? Am I to congratulate a highwayman and murderer who has broke prison upon the recovery of his natural rights?" Jesus then asks the demoniac the primary question : "What is your name?" If a man knows his name, he remembers his family, where he came from, and has his bearings. He knows who he is. But the demoniac has many demons, and his name is Legion. He has forgotten his family and who he is. The change of identities, life as a perpetual costume ball, is similar to the behavior of the crowd in Plato's description of democracy.

And what precisely is the character of the many? They did not wish to be tormented and "they begged him not to command them to depart into the abyss." The language here takes on the tone of the fear of last judgment. The multitude finds it difficult to live in the shadow of that.

The Time of Judgment. The version of the story in Matthew reinforces this interpretation. There were two demoniac s in that version and they cried out, "What have you to do with us, 0 Son of God? Have you come here to torment us before the time?" They may have been crazy, but they weren't dumb. The time, the crucial time, is the time of judgment. The last (value) judgment has no time for values clarification. The Gospel account then tells us that a "large herd of swine was feeding there on the hillside." The many demons begged Jesus "to let them enter these." The many can think of no more than living a pleasant existence filling their bellies like grazing pigs. Mere existence rather than human existence is the goal for the many. Plato's and Aristotle's understanding of 'the many is not significantly different. According to Aristotle, the life of pleasure is mistakenly identified as the good by the common run of people. They betray their "utter slavishness in their preference for a life suitable to cattle; but their views seem plausible because many people in high places share the feelings of Sardanapallus".

Voting With Their Feet. Jesus gave them what they asked for: "He gave them leave." One is reminded of the proper prayer, which says in effect, "Give me Lord not what I ask for, but what is good for me." The demons left the man, entered the herd of swine, and "the herd rushed down the steep bank into the lake and were drowned." They voted with their feet. Remember that H.L. Mencken once defined democracy as the theory that the people know what they want and deserve to get it good and hard.

Jo hn Stuart Mill once asked if you would rather be a pig satisfied or a Socrates dissatisfied. The obvious answer seems to be a pig satisfied. At least he fulfills his nature. But here we find the natural end of those humans who try to live like pigs: a suicidal plunge toward death.

The herdsmen fled and proceeded to tell everyone in sight what had happened. If they had told any economic libertarians, they were probably upset with the destruction of private property involved. The people were amazed an d wanted to know what had happened. When they found Jesus, they also found the man who had been healed, "sitting at the feet of Jesus, clothed and in his right mind; and they were afraid." They were afraid? Shouldn't they have been happy that this madman would no longer bother them with his bellowing and shouting? But they had been told by those who had seen it, "how he who had been possessed with demons was healed." The many are indeed many. They do not wish to give up their divided spirits and their animal appetites. Some problems are intractable when people do not really wish to be cured. Just let them graze on the hillside and leave them alone. Fear of Good News. As so often happens in the Scriptures when good news appears: "All the people of the surrounding country of the Gerasenes asked him to depart from them; for they were seized with great fear ...... Jesus gives them what they ask for, gets in his boat, and returns.

The natural condition of man is to be ungrateful. He is wary or suspicious of gifts because he knows that the freest gift still has strings of obligation or proper response attached to it. Milton Friedman's law of Tanstaafl, "There ain't no such thing as a free lunch," was refuted by the arch-empiric i st George Stigler, who modestly added a corollary, "But there are a lot of people eating them." Campbell's law is more universally true: "There ain't no such thing as a free gift." I would' only add as a corollary, "But there are a lot of people trying to receive them."

The demoniac wanted to be able to go with Jesus, but Jesus tells him to "Return to your home, and declare how much God has done for you." The ex-demoniac goes away "proclaiming throughout the whole city how much Jesus had done for him." Thin k of how difficult that must have been in an environment so hostile to the good news. We all know that prophets do much better in foreign lands. Not only does the story of the Gadarene Swine provide a searing indictment of modern constitutional economics and relativist democracy, but it provides the goals of sanity, right reason, family, homes, friends and one's own community as the context for dealing with the problems of tyranny and isolation in the modem world. These are the natural bases for dealing with the elderly, the young, and the homeless.

THE DECLARATION OF INDEPENDENCE

Let us now return to the early days of the Republic to see how these themes we have discussed set the stage for the later developments of substantive due process and police powers. We can compare and contrast the way in which the Declaration of Independence handles certain concepts and the way modern constitutional economics would treat the same concepts. The roots of the Declaration are in the ancient traditions and not a product of the rationalist enlightenment.

Consent of the Governed

Voice, rational discussion, and consent are an essential part of the American regime. Public choice dismisses voice and rational discussion as epiphenomena designed to take in the gullible. All people pursue self-interest, so let us have no foolishness about a disinterested public good. Don't listen to what people say, only observe what they do. Iron triangles replace golden triangles. But it would be interesting to know the number of successful deregulation efforts actually predicted by public choice theories in advance. How well did they predict the behavior of such government bureaucrats as Jim Miller, Alfred Kahn, and Dan Oliver?

The consent required is not just a mere act of will, but a rational, informed consent. The Declaration of Independence indicates this in its own language and procedures: self-evident truths, decent respect to the opinions of mankind, and submitting facts to a candid world. All of these require rationality and freedom of speech to make and to appreciate. The calculus of consent was not enacted by Mr. Jefferson's Declaration of Independence. There is neither a mathematical calculus nor a mere affirmation of raw will with individual veto power to drop in and drop out at random.

The signers said, "We... appealing to the Supreme Judge of the world for the rectitude of our intentions, do, in the Name, and by Authority of the good People of these Colonies solemnly publish and declare ......

Endowed by our Creator

In economics we like to refer to an "initial endowment" which is the same as talking about the "status quo." Each household (when we really should say "individual," but habits of the older tradition of household economics die hard) has a stock of wealth and resources, which we do not feel obligated to explain or justify. We certainly do not attribute them to the providence or goodness of our Creator or even our ancestors. But the Declaration treats these as gifts given to us for good uses for which we should be grateful.

Jefferson states in his Notes on Virginia: "And can the liberties of a nation be thought secure when we have removed their only firm basis, a conviction in the minds of the people that these liberties are the gift of God?" Walter Berns goes on to point out that modern libertarians would not accept such a gift because of the strings of right usage which might come with it.

Equality

The constitutional status of the idea of being created equal in the Declaration of Independence is the most fiercely debated topic in American history among conservatives. Following hard on its heels is the status of the 14th Amendment to the Constitution .

Although I am quite willing to allow the gnostic utopian nature of modern liberalism and its egalitarian drives, We are not willing to admit that that is what the writers of the Declaration intended. There is no reason to give to the liberals equality of result for any purpose. They may claim it, they may have imposed it on modern jurisprudence, but why let them keep it?

We have much further thinking to do on this complicated issue, but I would affirm that, on the level of constitutional economics, substantive due process jurisprudence was not illegitimate judicial activism, but was the proper reading of the original intent of the 14th Amendment. The right of labor, both black and white, to freely enter trades, own property, and establish contracts me ant that state and local legislation was subject to legitimate judicial review.

Unalienable Rights

The idea of unalienable rights in the Declaration refers to moral categories of good and evil that are not fit items of commerce. Inalienable means something that cannot be detached from something else. It is not a thing to be sold on the marketplace. All cultures and societies have prohibited certain types of things from appearing on the marketplace.

Commerce was subjected to "lawful commerce" in the same ways as callings were subjected to lawful callings - that is, within the purview of the police powers of state and local governments. The doctrine of "entrepreneurial freedom," as it has been labeled by its critics, was always hedged in by the concept of " lawful callings." The 14th Amendment assumed this police power for slavery on the national level. This was no longer a tolerable "domestic" institution.

Campbell and Justice Field argued their case and dissent respectively in the Slaughter-House Cases, 16 Wall. 36 (U.S., 1872), in terms of the relationship between the 14th Amendment and the Declaration of Independence. Field quoted from Adam Smith about the right of free labor, but stressed that the amendment was "intended to give particular effect to that declaration of 1776 of inalienable rights, rights which are the gift of the Creator, which the law does not confer, but only recognizes."

The Pursuit of Happiness

Did the Founding Fathers equate the pursuit of happiness with doing your own thing or some other modem vulgarity? Was happiness defined purely subjectively? The whole tradition of public choice and many libertarians is firmly based on the privatization of happiness that one finds in Hobbes and Locke.

Among political philosophers Walter Berns makes the same point. The government "they are instituting will have the limited purpose of securing their rights - including emphatically their right to pursue a happiness each of them defines for himself - and otherwise leaving them alone." But nowhere does he give justification for the crucial phrase "each of them defines for himself."

It has been suggested by E.S. Corwin that the phrase "pursuit of happiness" was indebted to Blackstone's statement that the law of nature boils down to "one paternal precept, that man should pursue his own true and substantial happiness." Paternal precept? True and substantial happiness? Does this not suggest that Blackstone is no friend of license? Could one imagine Blackstone saying that happiness is defined subjectively by each individual in a do-your-own-thing kind of fashion?

The spirit of ordered liberty is what permeates Blackstone. He defines "natural liberty" as "the power of acting as one thinks fit, without any restraint or control, unless by the law of nature." It is "inherent in us by birth" and is that gift of God which corresponds with "the faculty of free will." Yet every man, he continues, "when he enters into society, gives up a part of his natural liberty a s the price of so valuable a purchase," receiving in return "civil liberty," which is natural liberty "so far restrained by human laws (and no further) as is necessary and expedient for the general advantage of the public." Although we do not have the tim e to consider the Constitution in depth, in the light of our discussion above about Blackstone, we must wonder what Richard Epstein means when he argues that "The Lockean system was dominant at the time when the Constitution was adopted. His theory of the state was adopted in Blackstone's Commentaries, and the protection of property against its enemies was a central and recurrent feature of the political thought of the day." If you wish to take Blackstone, take all of him and not just a fragment.

WHAT CAN BE SALVAGED?

The legal wing of the constitutional economics movement has much that can be salvaged from its libertarian political philosophy. The attempts of Siegan, Epstein, and others to ground the protections of property rights, economic liberty, and freedom of competition in the Constitution are not vitiated by their oversimplification of the American political tradition.

Principled judicial activism and the "old" substantive due process tradition cut down laws restricting individuals' civil rights to own and use property. The affirmation of economic liberties and freedom of entry, the skepticism of the misuses of licensing and zoning are bringing together such powerful thinkers and activists as Thomas Sowell, Walter Williams, Robert Woodson, and most recently Clint Bolick. These should be a part of the conservative agenda. They offer hope and opportunity for the poor and minorities to lead productive lives and escape the poverty trap created by the liberal victim mentality. Activity should take place at both the legislative and judicial levels to promote economic freedom.

Dividing the Pie. But the substantive due process tradition is not the whole of American jurisprudence. American federalism also saw state and local governments with major responsibilities for their domestic institutions. Certainly the key to the Constitution is the complicated structure of federalism. The delegation of limited, restricted powers to the federal government and the retention of fairly broad, extensive powers to promote t he general good at the state and local level was the original intention and the one to which we ought to return. In the Declaration of Independence the several states were given the full "Power to levy War, conclude Peace, contract Alliances, establish Commerce, and to do all other Acts and Things which Independent States may of right do." In essence the Constitution divides up the pie and delegates the former to the national government and the "all other Acts and Things" to the state and local governments .

The legitimate and prudential use of police powers establishes the distinction between liberty and license. Pure laissez-faire doctrine must occasionally be restricted by substantive morality. The common sense of a John Howard and the Rockford Institute were recently echoed by George Gilder in Crisis magazine: "To the extent capitalists produce depraved goods, they destroy the moral conditions of capitalist progress, they undermine the families from which all true natural resources flow. It is largely liberal culture that refuses to ban pornography, or effectively suppress vice, or uphold the moral values of family life."

Even in the heyday of substantive due process, when the Supreme Court was protecting freedom of entry, it could still distinguish between occupations which were "lawful" and those which were not. State and local governments could regulate certain occupations on health and moral grounds. Prostitution, gambling, or drug running could be prohibited as a legitimate function of the police powers.

Promoting Domestic Tranquflity. What was the purpose behind the police powers? The American tradition of police powers - the reasonable and prudent use of coercion - was designed to defend and encourage the physical, moral, and spiritual health of the family. Blue laws, keeping the Sabbath, restrictions on drugs, alcohol, and pornography, and zoning were thought to contribute to the promotion of domestic tranquility and the control of license.

The same John Archibald Campbell who articulated and developed the case for substantive due process also summarized very eloquently the true American tradition of the police powers. They were designed to maintain the family with its concomitant freedoms and moral responsibilities. These remarks come from Campbell's address to the Alabama State Bar Association on August 7, 1884. He appealed to the members of the Bar "to stand fast in the liberty wherewith you became free, and which the Constitution has been the witness.

Be constant and firm to insist that the State [Alabama] shall be maintained in the fullness of the po w ers reserved by the Constitution which was made by the people of the States. The State is the repository where the family is formed, and with this, the source of domestic peace, where religion, morality, reverence, honor, human affections are implanted an d instruction most purely imbibed. It is the State that more surely defends life, liberty, property, family obligations and rights; it is the State that teaches primary duties of manhood and which shields and protects womanhood in her purity and holiness."

All of these types of legislation have undoubtedly been used imprudently at one time or another or for self-interested motives (what we now call rent-seeking). It is precisely the abuse of police powers beyond their reasonable purpose which the substantive due process tradition tried to prevent.

WHERE DO WE GO FROM HERE?

A substantive federalism rather than an administrative federalism will contain elements of both the substantive due process and police powers traditions. This is the balance and original intent which applies to the American experience.

One of the hallmarks of the Reagan Administration has been words and deeds devoted to the reconstruction of federalism. Reagan's ideal was of a "good neighbor" society based on local government (not federal and for that matter not even the state). Back in 1981 Reagan observed in his Address to the National Conference of State Legislatures that "this nation has never fully debated the fact that over the-past 40 years federalism - one of the underlying principles of our Constitution - has nearly disappeared as a guiding force in American politics and government." He also promised that the Administration intended to "initiate such a debate" and inaugurate a "quiet federalist revolution." It has been altogether too quiet.

Reagan also emphasized at the time that "Our recent emphasis on voluntarism, the mobilization of private groups to deal with our social ills, is designed to foster [a] spirit of individual generosity and our sense of communal values." Notice that the tone of this is vastly different from a public choice or economic approach to federalism which rests on the sanctity of individual tastes and preferences being assumed. Reagan assumes that the government, albeit at the state and local level, is responsible for educating the citizenry and fostering a certain spirit of duty or obligation in them which may not already exist.

Even though conservatives have grounds for being disappointed, there is no reason to give up on the ideals of economic liberty and moral virtue. I am optimistic that disillusionment with the bloated federal government and the re-assumption of responsibility by private citizens and their state and local governments bode well for the health of the Republic.

THE CONSTITUTION OF ECONOMIC POLICY

The science of public finance should always keep... political conditions clearly in mind. Instead of expecting guidance from a doctrine of taxation that is based on the political philosophy of by-gone ages, it should instead endeavor to unlock the mysteries of the spirit of progress and development.

On this of all occasions, I should be remiss if I failed to acknowledge the influence of that great Swede, Knut Wicksell, on my own work, an influence without which I should not be at this podium. Many of my contributions, and especially those in political economy and fiscal theory, might be described as varied reiterations, elaborations, and extensions of Wicksellian themes; this lecture is no exception.

One of the most exciting intellectual moments of my career was my 1948 discovery of Knut Wicksell's unknown and untranslated dissertation, *Finanztheoretische Untersuchungen*, buried in the dusty stacks of Chicago's old Harper Library. Only the immediate post-dissertation leisure of an academic novice allowed for the browsing that produced my own dramatic example of learning by serendipity. Wicksell's new principle of justice in taxation gave me a tremendous surge of self-confidence.

Wicksell, who was an established figure in the history of economic ideas, challenged the orthodoxy of public finance theory along lines that were congenial with my own developing stream of critical consciousness. From that moment in Chicago, I took on the determination to make Wicksell's contribution known to a wider audience, and I commenced immediately a translation effort that took some time and considerable help from Elizabeth Henderson, before final publication.

Stripped to its essentials, Wicksell's message was clear, elementary, and self-evident. Economists should cease proffering policy advice as if they were employed by a benevolent despot, and they should look to the structure within which political decisions are made. Armed with Wicksell, I, too, could dare to challenge the still-dominant orthodoxy in public finance and welfare economics. In a preliminary paper, I called upon my fellow economists to postulate some model of the state, of politics, before proceeding to analyse the effects of alternative policy measures. I urged economists to look at the "constitution of economic polity," to examine the rules, the constraints within which political agents act. Like Wicksell, my purpose was ultimately normative rather than antiseptically scientific. I sought to make economic sense out of the relationship between the individual and the state before proceeding to advance policy nostrums.

Wicksell deserves the designation as the most important precursor of modern public-choice theory because we find, in his 1896 dissertation, all three of the constitutive elements that provide the foundations of this theory: methodological individualism, *homo economicus*, and politics-as-exchange. I shall discuss these elements of analytical structure in the sections that follow. I integrate these elements in a theory of economic policy.

This theory is consistent with, builds upon, and systematically extends the traditionally accepted principles of Western liberal societies. The implied approach to institutional-constitutional reform continues, however, to be stubbornly resisted almost a century after Wicksell's seminal efforts. The individual's relation to the state is, of course, the central subject matter of political philosophy. Any effort by economists to shed light on this relationship must be placed within this more comprehensive realm of discourse.

METHODOLOGICAL INDIVIDUALISM

If utility is zero for each individual member of the community, the total utility for the community cannot be other than zero. The economist rarely examines the presuppositions of the models with which he works. The economist simply commences with individuals as evaluating, choosing, and acting units. This starting point for analysis necessarily draws attention to the choice or decision environment for the individuals who must make selections from among the alternatives. Regardless of the possible complexity of the processes or institutional structures from which outcomes emerge, the economist focusses on individual choices. In application to market or private-sector interactions, this procedure is seldom challenged. Individuals, as buyers and sellers of ordinary (legally tradable) goods and services are presumed able to choose in accordance with their own preferences, whatever these may be, and the economist does not feel himself obliged to inquire deeply into the content of these preferences (the arguments in individuals' utility functions). Individuals themselves are the sources of evaluation, and the economist's task is to offer an explanation-understanding of the process through which these unexamined preferences are ultimately translated into a complex outcome pattern.

The eighteenth century discovery that, in an institutional framework that facilitates voluntary exchanges among individuals, this process generates results that might be evaluated positively, produced "economics", as an independent academic discipline or science. The relationship between the positivelyvalued results of market processes and the institutional characteristics of these processes themselves emerged as a source of ambiguity when "the market" came to be interpreted functionally, as if something called "the economy" existed for the purpose of value maximization. Efficiency in the allocation of resources came to be defined independently of the processes through which individual choices are exercised.

Given this subtle shift toward a teleological interpretation of the economic process, it is not surprising that politics, or governmental process, was similarly interpreted. Furthermore, a teleological interpretation of politics had been, for centuries, the dominating thrust of political theory and political philosophy. The interpretations of "the economy" and "the polity" seemed, therefore, to be mutually compatible in the absence of inquiry into the fundamental difference in the point of evaluation. There was a failure to recognize that individuals who choose and act in the market generate outcomes that, under the specified constraints, can be judged to be value-maximizing for participating individuals, without the necessity of introducing an external evaluative criterion. The nature of the process itself insures that individual values are maximized. This "value maximization" perspective cannot be extended from the market to politics since the latter does not directly embody the incentive compatible structure of the former. There is no political counterpart to Adam Smith's invisible hand. It is not, therefore, surprising that the attempts by Wicksell and other continental European scholars to extend economic theory to the operation of the public sector remained undeveloped for so many years.

An economic theory that remains essentially individualistic need not have become trapped in such a methodological straight jacket. If the maximization exercise is restricted to explanation-understanding of the individual who makes choices, and without extension to the economy as an aggregation, there is no difficulty at all in analyzing individual choice behavior under differing institutional settings and in predicting how these varying settings will influence the outcomes of the interaction processes. The individual who chooses between apples and oranges remains the same person who chooses between the levers marked "Candidate A" and "Candidate B" in the polling booth. Clearly, the differing institutional structures may, themselves, affect choice behavior. Much of modern public choice theory explains these relationships. But my point here is the more basic one to the effect that the choice behavior of the individual is equally subject to the application of analysis in all choice environments. Comparative analysis should allow for predictions of possible differences in the characteristics of the results that emerge from market and political structures of interaction. These predictions, as well as the analysis from which they are generated, are totally devoid of normative content.

HOMO ECONOMICUS

... neither the executive nor the legislative body, and even less the deciding majority in the latter, are in reality ... what the ruling theory tells us they should be. They are not pure organs of the community with no thought other than to promote the common weal.

... members of the representative body are, in the overwhelming majority of cases, precisely as interested in the general welfare as are their constituents, neither more nor less.

This analysis can yield a limited set of potentially falsifiable hypotheses without prior specification of the arguments in individual utility functions. If, however, predictions are sought concerning the effects of shifts in constraints on choice behavior, some identification and signing of these arguments must be made. With this step, more extensive falsifiable propositions may be advanced. For example, if both apples and oranges are positively valued "goods," then, if the price of apples falls relative to that of oranges, more apples will be purchased relative to oranges; if income is a positively valued "good," and, then, if the marginal rate of tax on income source A increases relative to that on income source B, more effort at earning income will be shifted to source B; if charitable giving is a positively valued "good," then, if charitable gifts are made tax deductible, more giving will be predicted to occur; if pecuniary rents are positively valued, then, if a political agent's discretionary power to distribute rents increases, individuals hoping to secure these rents will invest more resources in attempts to influence the agent's decisions. Note that the identification and signing of the arguments in the utility functions takes us a considerable way toward operationalization without prior specification of the relative weights of the separate arguments. There is no need to assign net wealth or net income a dominating motivational influence on behavior in order to produce a fully operational economic theory of choice behavior, in market or political interaction.

In any extension of the model of individual rational behavior to politics, this difference between the identification and signing of arguments on the one hand and the weighting of these arguments on the other deserves further attention. Many critics of the "economic theory of politics" base their criticisms on the presumption that such theory necessarily embodies the hypothesis of net wealth maximization, an hypothesis that they observe to be falsified in many situations. Overly zealous users of this theory may have sometimes offered grounds for such misinterpretation on the part of critics.

The minimal critical assumption for the explanatory power of the economic theory of politics is only that identifiable economic self-interest (*e.g.*, net wealth, income, social position) is a positively valued "good" to the individual chooses.

This assumption does not place economic interest in a dominating position and it surely does not imply imputing evil or malicious motives to political actors; in this respect the theory remains on all fours with the motivational structure of the standard economic theory of market behavior. The differences in the predicted results stemming from market and political interaction stem from differences in the structures of these two institutional settings rather than from any switch in the motives of persons as they move between institutional roles.

POLITICS AS EXCHANGE

It would seem to be a blatant injustice if someone should be forced to contribute toward the costs of some activity which does not further his interests or may even be diametrically opposed to them.

Individuals choose, and as they do so, identifiable economic interest is one of the "goods" that they value positively, whether behavior takes place in markets or in politics. But markets are institutions of *exchange*; persons enter markets to exchange one thing for another. They do not enter markets to further some supra-exchange or supra-individualistic result. Markets are not motivationally functional; there is no conscious sense on the part of individual choosers that some preferred aggregate outcome, some overall "allocation" or "distribution" will emerge from the process.

The extension of this exchange conceptualization to politics counters the classical prejudice that persons participate in politics through some common search for the good, the true, and the beautiful, with these ideals being defined independently of the values of the participants as these might or might not be expressed by behavior. Politics, in this vision of political philosophy, is instrumental to the furtherance of these larger goals.

Wicksell, who is followed in this respect by modern public choice theorists, would have none of this. The relevant difference between markets and politics does not lie in the kinds of values/interests that persons pursue, but in the conditions under which they pursue their various interests. Politics is a structure of complex exchange among individuals, a structure within which persons seek to secure collectively their own privately defined objectives that cannot be efficiently secured through simple market exchanges. In the absence of individual interest, there is no interest. In the market, individuals exchange apples for oranges; in politics, individuals exchange agreed-on shares in contributions toward the costs of that which is commonly desired, from the services of the local fire station to that of the judge.

This ultimately voluntary basis for political agreement also counters the emphasis on politics as power that characterizes much modern analysis. The observed presence of coercive elements in the activity of the state seems difficult to reconcile with the model of voluntary exchange among individuals. We may, however, ask: Coercion to what purpose? Why must individuals subject themselves to the coercion inherent in collective action? The answer is evident. Individuals acquiesce in the coercion of the state, of politics, only if the ultimate constitutional "exchange" furthers their interests. Without some model of exchange, no coercion of the individual by the state is consistent with the individualistic value norm upon which a liberal social order is grounded.

THE CONSTITUTION OF ECONOMIC POLICY

... whether the benefits of the proposed activity to the individual citizens would be greater than its cost to them, no one can judge this better than the individuals themselves.

The exchange conceptualization of politics is important in the derivation of a normative theory of economic policy. Improvement in the workings of politics is measured in terms of the satisfaction of that which is desired by individuals, whatever this may be, rather than in terms of moving closer to some externally-defined, supra-individualistic ideal. That which is desired by individuals may, of course, be common for many persons, and, indeed, the difference between market exchange and political exchange lies in the sharing of objectives in the later. The idealized agreement on the objectives of politics does not, however, allow for any supersession of individual evaluation. Agreement itself emerges, again conceptually, from the revealed choice behavior of individuals. Commonly shared agreement must be carefully distinguished from any externally-defined definition or description of that "good" upon which persons "should agree".

The restrictive implications for a normative theory of economic policy are severe. There is no criterion through which policy may be directly evaluated. An indirect evaluation may be based on some measure of the degree to which the political process facilitates the translation of expressed individual preferences into observed political outcomes. The focus of evaluative attention becomes the process itself, as contrasted with end-state or outcome patterns. "Improvement" must, therefore, be sought in reforms in process, in institutional change that will allow the operation of politics to mirror more accurately that set of results that are preferred by those who participate.

One way of stating the difference between the Wicksellian approach and that which is still orthodoxy in normative economics is to say that the *constitution* of policy rather than policy itself becomes the relevant object for reform. A simple game analogy illustrates the difference here. The Wicksellian approach concentrates on reform in the rules, which may be in the potential interest of *all* players, as opposed to improvement in strategies of play for particular players within defined or existing rules.

In the standard theory of choice in markets, there is little or no concern with the constitution of the choice environment. We simply presume that the individual is able to implement his preferences; if he wants to purchase an orange, we presume that he can do so. There is no institutional barrier between the revealed expression of preference and direct satisfaction. Breakdown of failure in the market emerges, not in the translation of individual preferences into outcomes, but in the possible presentation of some choosers with alternatives that do not correspond to those faced by others in the exchange nexus. "Efficiency" in market interaction is insured if the participants are faced with the same choice options.

In political exchange, there is no decentralized process that allows "efficiency" to be evaluated deontologically, akin to the evaluation of a market. Individuals cannot, by the nature of the goods that are collectively "purchased" in politics, adjust their own behavior to common terms of trade. The political analogue to decentralized trading among individuals must be that feature common over all exchanges, which is *agreement* among the individuals who participate. The unanimity rule for collective choice is the political analogue to freedom of exchange of partitionable goods in markets.

It is possible, therefore, to evaluate politics independently of results only by ascertaining the degree of correspondence between the rules of reaching decisions and the unique rule that would guarantee "efficiency," that of unanimity or agreement among all participants. If, then, "efficiency" is acknowledged to be the desired criterion, again as interpreted here, normative improvement in process is measured by movement toward the unanimity requirement. It is perhaps useful to note, at this point, that Wicksell's own characterization of his proposals in terms of "justice" rather than "efficiency" suggests the precise correspondence of these two norms in the context of voluntary exchange.

Politics as observed remains, of course, far from the idealized collective-cooperative exchange that the unanimity rule would implement. The political equivalent to transactions cost makes them pursuit of idealized "efficiency" seem even more out of the bounds of reason than the analogous pursuit in markets. But barriers to realization of the ideal do not imply rejection of the benchmark definition of the ideal itself. Instead, such barriers are themselves incorporated into a generalized "calculus of consent".

Wicksell himself did not go beyond advocacy of reform in legislative decision structures. He proposed a required linking of spending and financing decisions, and he proposed that a quasi-unanimity rule be introduced for noncommitted outlays. Wicksell did not consciously extend his analysis to constitutional choice, to the choice of the rules within which ordinary politics is to be allowed to operate. His suggested reforms were, of course, constitutional, since they were aimed to improve the process of decision making. But his evaluative criterium was restricted to the matching of individual preferences with political outcomes in particularized decisions, rather than over any sequence.

It is perhaps worth noting that Wicksell himself did not look upon his suggested procedural reforms as restrictive. By introducing greater flexibility into the tax-share structure, Wicksell predicted the potential approval of spending programmes that would continue to be rejected under rigid taxing arrangements. Critics have, however, interpreted the Wicksellian unanimity constraint to be restrictive, and especially as compared to the extended activity observed in ordinary politics. This restrictive interpretation was perhaps partially responsible for the continued failure of political economists to recognize his seminal extension of the efficiency norm to the political sector.

Such restrictiveness is very substantially reduced, and, in the limit, may be altogether eliminated, when the unanimity criterion is shifted one stage upward, to the level of potential agreement on constitutional rules within which ordinary politics is to be allowed to operate. In this framework, an individual may rationally prefer a rule that will, on particular occasions, operate to produce results that are opposed to his own interests. The individual will do so if he predicts that, on balance over the whole sequence of "plays," his own interests will be more effectively served than by the more restrictive application of the Wicksellian requirement in-period. The in-period Wicksellian criterion remains valid as a measure of the particularized efficiency of the single decision examined. But the in-period violation of the criterion does not imply the inefficiency of the rule so long as the later is itself selected by a constitutional rule of unanimity.

As noted, the shift of the Wicksellian criterion to the constitutional stage of choice among rules also serves to facilitate agreement, and, in the limiting case, may remove altogether potential conflicts among separate individual and group interests. To the extent that the individual reckons that a constitutional rule will remain applicable over a long sequence of periods, with many in-period choices to be made, he is necessarily placed behind a partial "veil of uncertainty" concerning the effects of any rule on his own predicted interests. Choice among rules will, therefore, tend to be based on generalizable criteria of fairness, making agreement more likely to occur than when separable interests are more easily identifiable.

The political economist who operates from within the Wicksellian research programme, as modified, and who seeks to offer normative advice, must, of necessity, concentrate on the process or structure within which political decisions are observed to be made. Existing constitutions, or structures or rules, are the subject of critical scrutiny. The conjectural question becomes: Could these rules have emerged from agreement by participants in an authentic constitutional convention? Even here, the normative advice that is possible must be severely circumscribed. There is no external set of norms that provides a basis for criticism. But the political economist may, cautiously, suggest changes in procedures, in rules, that may come to command general assent. Any suggested change must be offered only in the provisional sense, and, importantly, it must be accompanied by a responsible recognition of political reality. Those rules and rules changes worthy of consideration are those that are predicted to be workable within the politics inhabited by ordinary men and women, and not those that are appropriate only for idealized, omniscient, and benevolent beings. Policy options must remain within the realm of the feasible, and the interests of political agents must be recognized as constraints on the possible.

CONSTITUTIONALISM AND CONTRACTARIANISM

The ultimate goal ... is equality before the law, greatest possible liberty, and the economic well-being and peaceful cooperation of all people. As the basic Wicksellian construction is shifted to the choice among rules or constitutions and as a veil of uncertainty is utilized to facilitate the potential bridging of the difference between identifiable and general interest, the research programme in political economy merges into that of contractarian political philosophy, both in its classical and modern variations. In particular, my own approach has affinities with the familiar construction of John Rawls, who utilizes the veil of ignorance along with the fairness criterion to derive principles ofjustice that emerge from a conceptual contractual agreement at a stage prior to the selection of a political constitution.

Because of his failure to shift his own analytical construction to the level of constitutional choice, Wicksell was confined to evaluation of the political process in generating current allocative decisions. He was unable, as he quite explicitly acknowledged, to evaluate political action involving either prior commitments of the state, for example, the financing of interest on public debt, or fiscally implemented transfers of incomes and wealth among persons and groups. Distributional questions remain outside the Wicksellian evaluative exercise, and because they do so, we locate another source of the long-continued and curious neglect of the fundamental analytical contribution. With the shift to the constitutional stage of politics, however, this constraint is at least partially removed.

Behind a sufficiently thick veil of uncertainty and/or ignorance, contractual agreement on rules that allow for some in-period fiscal transfers seems clearly to be possible. The precise features of a constitutionally-approved transfer structure cannot, of course, be derived independently because of the restriction of evaluative judgment to the process of constitutional agreement. In this respect, the application is fully analogous to Wicksell's unwillingness to lay down specific norms for tax sharing independently of the process of agreement. *Any* distribution of tax shares generating revenues sufficient to finance the relevant spending project passes Wicksell's test, provided only that it meets with general agreement. Analogously, *any* set of arrangements for implementing fiscal transfers, in-period, meets the constitutional stage Wicksellian test, provided only that it commands general agreement.

This basic indeterminacy is disturbing to political economists or philosophers who seek to be able to offer substantive advice, over and beyond the procedural limits suggested. The constructivist urge to assume a role as social engineer, to suggest policy reforms that "should" or "should not" be made, independently of any revelation of individuals' preferences through the political process, has simply proved too strong for many to resist. The scientific integrity dictated by consistent reliance on individualistic values has not been a mark of modern political economy.

The difficulty of maintaining such integrity is accentuated by the failure to distinguish explanatory and justificatory arguments, a failure that has described the position of almost all critics of social contract theories of political order. We do not, of course, observe the process of reaching agreement on constitutional rules, and the origins of the rules that are in existence at any particular time and in any particular polity cannot satisfactorily be explained by the contractarian model. The purpose of the contractarian exercise is not explanatory in this sense. It is, by contrast, justificatory in that it offers a basis for normative evaluation. Could the observed rules that constrain the activity of ordinary politics have emerged from agreement in constitutional contract? To the extent that this question can be affirmatively answered we have established a legitimating linkage between the individual and the state. To the extent that the question prompts a negative response, we have a basis for normative criticism of the existing order, and a criterion for advancing proposals for constitutional reform.

It is at this point, and this point only, that the political economist who seeks to remain within the normative constraints imposed by the individualistic canon may enter the ongoing dialogue on constitutional policy. The deficitfinancing regimes in modern Western democratic polities offer the most dramatic example. It is almost impossible to construct a contractual calculus in which representatives of separate generations would agree to allow majorities in a single generation to finance currently-enjoyed public consumption through the issue of public debt that insures the imposition of utility losses or later generations of taxpayers. The same conclusion applies to the implicit debt obligations that are reflected in many of the intergenerational transfer programmes characteristic of the modern welfare state.

The whole contractarian exercise remains empty if the critical dependence of politically-generated results upon the rules that constrain political action is denied. If end states are invariant over shifts in constitutional structure, there is no role for constitutional political economy. On the other hand, if institutions do, indeed, matter, the role is well defined.

Positively, this role involves analysis of the working properties of alternative sets of constraining rules. In a game theoretic analogy, this analysis is the search for solutions of games, as the latter are defined by sets of rules. Normatively, the task for the constitutional political economist is to assist individuals, as citizens who ultimately control their own social order, in their continuing search for those rules of the political game that will best serve their purposes, whatever these might be.

DEMOCRACY, CITIZEN SOVEREIGNTY AND CONSTITUTIONAL ECONOMICS

Its purpose is to explore the contribution that constitutional economics can make to the theory of democracy. Constitutional economics as the *economics of rules* is concerned with the study of how the choice of rules in the social, economic and political realm affects the nature of the processes of human interaction that evolve within these rules.

The theory of democracy is concerned with institutional-organizational problems of self-governing polities. The purpose of the paper is to examine some of the fundamental issues that are brought into focus by applying the perspective of constitutional economics to the rules and institutions of a democratic polity. General characteristics of the constitutional economics paradigm that are of particular significance to the study of democratic institutions.

CONSTITUTIONAL ECONOMICS AS APPLIED SCIENCE

Constitutional economics in the Buchanan-tradition is based on a methodological as well as a normative individualism. It starts from the presumptions that, firstly, social aggregate phenomena should be explained in terms of the behavior of individual human beings plus the combined effects of their interaction, and that, secondly, the values of the individuals involved should be regarded as the normative measuring rod against which the legitimacy of social institutions and collective arrangements is to be judged. Because of its normative individualism constitutional economics is often considered a "normative" branch of economics.

If this is meant to imply that, by contrast to "positive" economics, constitutional economics issues *value judgments* rather than refutable statements about matters of fact, it is a misleading description. It is misleading because it tends to blur the important distinction between what one might call "*genuine*" value judgments and the kind of "*conditional*" normative statements that *applied* sciences typically make. Or, in technical philosophical terms, it tends to blur the distinction between *categorical* and *hypothetical* imperatives.

Theoretical sciences provide insights into how the world works, and applied sciences make use of such theoretical insights in order to propose potential solutions to practical problems. As a *theoretical* science constitutional economics seeks to provide insights into how the framework of rules and institutions conditions the ways in which individuals interact with one another, and the social outcomes that result from their interaction. As an *applied* science constitutional economics seeks to provide knowledge for how the choice of suitable rules – or, respectively, suitable changes in the existing institutional framework – can help to solve problems in human interaction.

All applied sciences, including applied constitutional economics, make statements about what one "should" do or "ought" to do, if one wants to solve certain problems. By contrast to "genuine" value judgments or *categorical* imperatives, such "should" or "ought" statements are *hypothetical* imperatives that can be rationally discussed on empirical and theoretical grounds. They are false if the remedy that they suggest is in fact not a suitable means for solving the problem envisaged.

They are in need of further refinement if alternative and potentially preferable problem solutions can be shown to exist. And they provide irrelevant advice if the addressee at whom they are directed is not interested in solving the problem in question. Its normative individualism does not turn constitutional economics into a normative economics any more than its interest in solving human problems turns an engineering science into a normative physics. What its normative individualism does is to provide a selective focus to the kinds of questions that constitutional economics seeks to answer. It chooses to concentrate its analytical attention on exploring the *theoretical issue* of how alternative institutional arrangements affect the wellbeing of the individuals living under those arrangements, and the *practical issue* of how institutions may be designed so as to further the common interest of the individuals involved.

The arguments constitutional economics advances in answering these questions are, however, refutable statements about matters of fact, not value judgments. To be sure, such statements are of interest – and in this sense "of value" – only to someone who is interested in the questions that they are supposed to answer. But, again, the fact that their "value" depends on the interests of the addressee does not make them value judgments as long as they answer the noted questions purely in terms of refutable conjectures about matters of fact.

Another way of describing the analytical focus of *constitutional* economics – as compared to *standard* economics – is to say that its principal concern is with the issue of how individuals can realize mutual gains *by jointly committing to suitable rules*, rules that guide their interaction into socially more productive paths than would otherwise be the case.

If, as James Buchanan suggests, the "gains from trade" paradigm is indeed at the very essence of economics in general, constitutional economics can be said to systematically extend the "gains from trade" perspective from the study of voluntary exchange in markets to the "voluntary exchanges of commitments" that individuals may engage in at the *constitutional level* by jointly submitting to mutually beneficial rules. While the economics of markets is about how mutual gains can be realized through voluntary exchange of ordinary goods and services, constitutional economics explores the mutual gains that can be had from adopting better rules of the game, in all arenas – economic, social and political – in which individuals interact with each other.

It is instructive to contrast the perspective of constitutional economics with that of traditional welfare economics. Like constitutional economics welfare economics can be said to belong to the *applied* branch of economics in the sense that it uses theoretical economic insights in order to propose solutions to practical problems, specifically the problem of how a polity can improve its "welfare." In other words, both approaches advance conjectural advice about what kinds of policy measures promise to advance the "welfare" of the polity concerned. And, because welfare economics defines welfare in terms of individual utilities, i.e. the wellbeing of the individuals involved, it may appear to share the same normative individualism on which constitutional economics is based. Yet there is, as Buchanan has repeatedly stressed, a paradigmatic difference between the two approaches, a difference that he describes as the contrast between the constitutional economist's "gains from trade perspective" and the welfare economist's "allocational or maximizing perspective".

What is different about the two perspectives becomes apparent as soon as one takes a closer look at the way in which they model the individual and at the nature of the advice that they provide, specifically in regard to the question of who is, explicitly or implicitly, the addressee at whom the advice is directed. Arguing from a gains-from-trade perspective the constitutional economist looks at individuals as sovereign choosing agents who, by their actual choices, express what they judge to be in their interest and who, by their voluntary agreement, express what in social matters they consider to be in their *mutual* interest or, in this sense, to be "welfare enhancing."

Accordingly, as advisor in matters of "social welfare" the constitutional economist's analytical focus is on advancing conjectures about how, as politically organized groups, individuals may be able to realize mutual gains, in terms of their own judgment, and, in particular, conjectures about what kinds of collective choice procedures may better enable them to advance their common interests. The addressees of such advice are the individuals themselves, and the test of the adequacy and relevance of the advice is in whether the individuals addressed consider the constitutional economist's suggestions to serve, indeed, their interests, and in whether the factual assumptions implied in the respective conjectures are correct.

By contrast, arguing from an allocational, maximizing perspective the welfare economist looks at individuals as preference or utility functions from which he "reads" the utility values that serve as entries in the social welfare function upon which he, in turn, bases his judgment on what policy measures can be said to enhance the welfare of the respective polity. In this construction the individual disappears as a sovereign choosing agent and is reduced to the role of providing the utility-measurements that the welfare economist uses as informational input into his welfare calculations.

The analytical problems welfare economists encounter in deriving their social welfare functions (measuring utility, interpersonal comparison of utility) are well known and need not be recounted here. Even if we assume that all these problems could be satisfactorily solved, the issue that is of principal interest in the present context would still remain, namely, who is supposed to be the addressee of the welfare economist's advice or, in other terms, who – apart from those interested in the theoretical exercise as such – might be interested in being advised about how the welfare economist's aggregate function of "social welfare" may by maximized. Put in still another way, since, as noted before, applied sciences advise addressees about how they can better solve problems they face, the question that the welfare economist needs to answer is, who they suppose might care about solving the problem for which they propose solutions. As far as individual citizens as principals are concerned, we can safely assume that they will be interested in proposals for how their own welfare, jointly with that of their fellow citizens, might be improved. They will, however, hardly care for advice on how aggregate social welfare may be enhanced as such, irrespective of whether this increases or decreases their own welfare.

As far as politicians, who act as citizens' agents, are concerned it does not seem to be very plausible either to assume that they have a personal interest in heeding the welfare economist's advice, at least not any more than they expect that by maximizing "social welfare" they can successfully solve problems they personally care about, such as the problem of advancing their political career. If, however, neither citizens nor politicians can be reasonably assumed to be interested in solving the problem of maximizing "social welfare," it is difficult to see, to whom welfare economists think they are talking – other than to themselves.

CONSTITUTIONAL ECONOMICS AND CONTRACTARIANISM

With its gains-from-trade perspective constitutional economics adopts a *procedural* normative standard for judging social matters. By contrast to approaches that, like welfare economics, seek to evaluate social outcomes in terms of attributes of the outcomes *per se*, constitutional economics bases its normative judgment on attributes of the process from which outcomes result. The measuring rod for what can count as "socially preferable" or "welfare enhancing" is located in the subjective preferences or interests of the individuals who are involved in the transaction or social arrangement, preferences or interests that they express with their own *voluntary choices*.

It is not because of attributes that he could read from outcomes per se, but only because of the fact that they result from *voluntary agreement* among the participating individuals that the observing economist may conclude that exchange transactions or collective arrangements are welfare enhancing, as judged by the participants themselves. Accordingly, the analytical focus of the constitutional economist's procedural normative judgment has to be on the issue of whether or not the outcome-generating process can reasonably be assumed to be based on voluntary agreement of the parties involved.

In fact, if examined more closely, the economist's standard assumption that market exchange is mutually beneficial or "efficient" can be shown to ultimately rest on nothing other than the claim that it is based on voluntary agreement of the trading parties. In other words, it is not because of attributes to be found in market outcomes per se, but only because of attributes of the process from which they result that economists can infer their "efficiency." By market exchange economists do not just mean any kind of exchange transaction, no matter what the circumstances are under which the traders make their choices. Instead, by market exchange they mean trades that are carried out under conditions which can be assumed to assure the voluntariness of the transaction.

Even if this is not necessarily reflected in they way they are described in standard text books, in the economist's understanding markets are not just places where demand and supply meet, whatever the conditions may be that prevail in these places. Markets are institutionally secured arenas for voluntary trade and voluntary cooperation, arenas within which rules are enforced that aim at preventing the use of coercion and fraud. It is ultimately only on the assumption that markets are, in this sense, arenas for voluntary exchange that economists can base their efficiency claims for market outcomes.

In effect, constitutional economics simply seeks to generalize to all levels of cooperative arrangements the procedural logic that, even if rarely made explicit, is systematically implied in the economist's standard notion of efficiency in market exchange, by consistently extending it from the level of market transactions to the level of collective-political action and, in particular, to the constitutional level at which the rules for the socio-economic-political game are defined.

The constitutional economist's central tenet is that a consistent normative individualism requires one to regard voluntary agreement among the parties involved as the ultimate criterion on which alone efficiency claims can be based, in the case of collective action and constitutional choice no less than in the case of ordinary market exchange. What is true for market outcomes is, he insists, equally true for political outcomes: Whether or not they are welfare enhancing cannot be judged in terms of attributes of the outcomes per se, but only in terms of attributes of the processes from which they result, namely the extent to which they can reasonably be assumed to result from voluntary agreement among the individuals involved – if not their agreement to the outcomes themselves, at least their agreement to the decision rules that produce them.

As Buchanan has repeatedly noted, there is an apparent affinity between the constitutional economist's approach to politics and the *contract theory of the state* in that both derive the legitimacy of the coercive power of government from the voluntary consent of those who are subject to such power. It is in reference to its emphasis on the legitimizing role of voluntary consent that constitutional economics can be justly described as a "voluntary exchange theory of government." Such label is not meant at all to negate the coercive nature of governmental power.

It is meant to indicate that a government can claim legitimacy for its power of coercion only if, or to the extent that, such power is granted by, and exercised within the limits of a constitution its citizens voluntarily agree to. The reason for individuals to voluntarily submit to such a constitution is that by their joint commitment to the respective set of rules they can expect to realize benefits that otherwise could not be had or, stated differently, to play a "better game" than they would in the absence of such joint commitment. In this sense, the label "voluntary exchange theory of government" is simply supposed to point to the fact that, just as they can realize mutual gains from ordinary market exchange, individuals can realize mutual gains through voluntary exchange of commitments to rules at the constitutional level. And just as efficiency claims for market exchange are contingent on the voluntariness of the traders' choices, efficiency claims for "constitutional exchange" are equally contingent on whether or not the individuals involved voluntarily submit to the rules in question.

The contractarian perspective that constitutional economics shares with the social contract tradition in political philosophy can be given, and has been given, different interpretations, three of which are of particular interest in the present context because they differ markedly in the line of inquiry that they suggest constitutional economics should pursue. A quite common interpretation of the contractarian perspective, prominently exemplified by John Rawls' *Theory of Justice*, centers around the notion of a *hypothetical* contract.

Authors who adopt this version of contractarianism direct their attention to the issue of what kinds of rules a group of self-interested individuals can be expected to agree upon if they were to make their choice among potential alternative rules under 'ideal' conditions, conditions that are presumed to assure that the contractual agreement is reached in a voluntary, informed and fair manner. In the case of Rawls' theory it is the conceptual construct of constitutional choice "behind a veil of ignorance" that is meant to describe ideal conditions under which the contracting parties can readily arrive at a voluntary agreement on mutually advantageous rules because they are, both, informed and uninformed in ways that eliminate potential sources of disagreement. On the one hand, they are assumed to be perfectly knowledgeable about the *general working properties* of potential alternative rules such that, in this regard, disagreement because of differing expectations is ruled out.

On the other hand, they are supposed to be perfectly uninformed about any *particulars* that would allow them to anticipate any specific and differential effects that the chosen rules may have on themselves by contrast to other persons, such that conflicting interests in differentially advantageous rules are excluded as a potential source of disagreement.

Whatever insights the inquiry in what people can be expected to agree upon under 'ideal' conditions – whether what counts as 'ideal' is defined in Rawlsian or in other terms – may generate, it is obvious that they can be of limited value only to constitutional economics as an applied science that seeks to provide advice for how real people may solve their constitutional problems.

As noted earlier, advice that an applied science provides will be of relevance only if it informs the addressees of how they may solve a problem they are *interested in solving*. And the question must be asked of whose problem-solving interest may be served by information about what persons would agree upon under ideal conditions.

The hypothetical contract approach has been criticized for quite some time that the insights it produces are of no consequence. And, surely, if constitutional advice is to be of relevance it needs to inform addressees who know who they are about changes in rules that promise to make them better off, relative to where they are, and not about what would be in their interest if they would not know who they are and were placed under hypothetical conditions.

The hypothetical contract construct can be contrasted to two alternative lines of inquiry that one may pursue from a contractarian perspective, lines of inquiry that, as I suppose, promise to lead an applied constitutional economics onto a more productive research path.

Instead of conjecturing about what might be agreeable under hypothetical conditions the constitutional economist may seek to advance conjectures about potential factual agreement, i.e. conjectures about what changes in rules would promise mutual gains for all parties involved, compared to the status quo, rule-changes that should be agreeable to the parties concerned, given the conditions in which they actually find themselves.

Such conjectures are conjectures about constitutional interests that the individuals involved actually have in common, as opposed to conjectures about constitutional interests that they would share under hypothetical conditions. While conjectures of the latter sort hardly qualify as relevant constitutional advice, by providing conjectures of the first kind constitutional economists inform the addressees about how they may come to "play a better game" among themselves, for the benefit of everybody involved.

Whether the constitutional economist's conjectures about mutually beneficial constitutional changes are in fact true or not depends not only on the correctness of the underlying hypotheses about the factual working properties of rules.

It also depends on the addressees' subjective evaluation of the consequences that the rules under consideration are predicted to have. However correct the constitutional economists hypotheses about the factual working properties of rules may be, if his expectations about what kinds of consequences the addressees themselves regard as beneficial are wrong his conjectures about welfare-enhancing rule-changes will be falsified. In this sense the addressees themselves are the ultimate judges on what can count as 'welfare-enhancing' in matters of constitutional reform, and their agreement to suggested constitutional changes is the ultimate test of the constitutional economist's conjectures about mutually beneficial reform.

The emphasis on "in this regard" is important for two reasons. First, because the addressees can, of course, not be considered to be the ultimate judges on the truth or falsehood of the constitutional economist's conjectures about the factual working properties of rules. And to the extent that their rejection of suggested reforms is based on incorrect expectations about how the reforms will actually work, their rejection of the constitutional economist's advice does, of course, not falsify his conjecture that the suggested reform, if adopted, would work out in ways that the addressees would consider mutually beneficial.

In such cases, lacking agreement would point to the fact, that additional 'constitutional information' may be needed to allow the addressees to make a better educated choice. The second reason why the emphasis on the "in this regard" is important is that a failure to find agreement may not be due to the falseness of the constitutional economist's conjectures but to 'blockages' in the existing decision making procedures that prevent the addressees from reaching an "agreement" on suggested rule-changes that what would in fact be in their common constitutional interest, 'blockages' that may exist because of strategic behavior or for other reasons.

I noted above that there are two alternative lines of inquiry that a contractarian constitutional economy may pursue by contrast to the construct of a hypothetical agreement. The above remarks on 'blockages' in the existing decision making procedures point to the second of these alternative lines of inquiry. Like the first it is concerned with the addressees' *factual* constitutional interests as opposed to constitutional interests that they might have under hypothetical ideal conditions.

Yet, while the first line of inquiry is concerned with the issue of which rules may promise to be mutually beneficial and can, therefore, be predicted to be agreed upon among the relevant parties, the second is concerned with the quite different issue of how well potential alternative rules or procedures for choosing rules are suited to enhance the prospects for those rules to be actually chosen or established that serve, in fact, the common constitutional interests of the parties involved. In other words, the applied constitutional economist who pursues this line of inquiry is interested in identifying potential changes in the rules for choosing rules, or in the procedures for establishing rules, that may enable the individuals concerned to more readily and more reliably select and establish among themselves rules that are in their *common* constitutional interests, whatever these constitutional interests may be in substance.

The distinction between, on the one hand, conjectures about which rules may be in the common constitutional interest of a group of persons and, on the other hand, conjectures about which rules for choosing rules enhance the prospects for common constitutional interests to prevail is an important distinction even if it may appear somewhat subtle. By contrast to the former, the validity of the latter conjectures does not depend on the substantive content of persons' constitutional interests, i.e. on what kind of rule-regime they wish to adopt. They are purely factual conjectures about what procedures for choosing rules make it more likely that rules will be chosen which serve the *common* constitutional interests of the persons concerned, as opposed to constitutional interests that they may harbor individually and separately but that are in conflict with each other. Whether these conjectures are true or not is to be decided on theoretical and empirical grounds.

The persons to whom the constitutional economist addresses his advice may, of course, reject to adopt rules which he supposes favor the choice of mutually beneficial rules. But such rejection does not prove that the constitutional economist's conjectures are wrong, it only indicates that the addressees of his advice prefer, for whatever reason, other procedures for constitutional choice than those which, according to his conjecture, would improve the chances for their common constitutional preferences to prevail.

DEMOCRATIC POLITIES AS CITIZENS COOPERATIVES

In the remainder of this paper the general arguments that have been made above about constitutional economics as an applied science and about the advisory role of constitutional economists will be applied to the case of democratic polities. Before turning to this issue, though, it is useful to briefly discuss in more explicit terms the distinction between different levels of collective-political choice – and, accordingly, between different levels of political advice – that has been implicit in the above analysis.

With his distinction between "the order of rules and the order of actions" Hayek has drawn attention to the systematic interrelation that exists, in terms of the game-metaphor, between the ways in which the rules of a game are defined, i.e. the "order of rules," and the kinds of moves that the players will choose in playing the game, i.e. the "order of actions."

With his distinction between "the constitutional and the sub-constitutional level" Buchanan has pointed to the fact that "the order of rules" may consist of several layers of rules such that in addition to the *rules of the game per se*, i.e. the rules that define what the players may do or not do in playing the game, there are *rules for choosing rules* and even *rules for choosing rules for choosing rules*. The former I propose to call *operating rules*, the latter *constitutional rules*, "constitutional" here understood in the sense of "rules for choosing rules."Applied to the collective choices that the citizens-members of a democratic polity may make the Hayek-Buchanan scheme suggests as distinction between three principal levels of choice.

There are, first, choices at what one may call the *allocational level*, in the sense of policy choices that directly intervene into the "order of actions" or the playing of the game, policy choices that seek to correct directly outcomes of the game by correcting allocational choices the players have made. By and large the attention of traditional welfare economics may be said to mainly focus on this level. Its principal ambition is to provide advice for how "government" may improve social welfare by correcting "inefficient" allocational choices of private economic agents. Constitutional economics, by contrast, focuses attention on the second and third level of political choice. Its principal tenet is that, again in terms of the game metaphor, the more adequate strategy for correcting (systematically and not just incidentally occurring) undesirable outcomes of a game is to seek to improve the *rules* of the game rather than intervening into the playing of the game.

This can be done directly by changes in what I have proposed above to call *operating rules*, i.e. the rules that define how the game is to be played, and it can be done indirectly by changes in the *constitutional rules*, i.e. the *rules for changing rules*. In what follows I shall refer to constitutional choices of the first kind as *constitutional choices type I*, and to those of the second kind as *constitutional choices type II*. The ultimate purpose of political choices at all three levels is, of course, to contribute to a desirable "order of actions," i.e. to make sure that the ways in which the game is played, and the outcomes it produces, serve the interests of the persons involved. Constitutional choices of either type are, in this sense, no less than policy choices at the "allocational level" *ultimately* targeted at improving the resulting "order of actions." They differ with regard to the level at which they "intervene" in order to achieve this ultimate purpose.

As has been said before, advice that an applied science provides must, if it is to be of any practical relevance, be directed at an addressee who has an interest in solving the problem for which the advisor suggests a solution. In case of democratic polities the citizens are, quite obviously, the natural addressees for constitutional advice that seeks to inform about potential mutual gains from trade. Democratic polities can be best described as *citizens' cooperatives* or, in John Rawls' (1971: 84) terms, as "cooperative venture(s) for mutual advantage." Just as the members of co-operative enterprises or voluntary associations are the owners or principals of their joint venture, the citizens of democratic polities are the "owners" or principals of the polity as a territorially based association.

They are the "sovereigns" with whom the ultimate authority to decide on the polity's affairs resides. There are, to be sure, important differences between democratic polities on the one side and "ordinary" co-operative enterprises or voluntary associations on the other, among them, in particular, the fact that a polity is not only a *territorial* but also an *"inter-generational"* organization in the sense that new member are typically "born into the polity" rather then admitted by an express act of voluntary entry. Such differences do, however, not alter the fact that in a democratic polity no less than in any other co-operative enterprise the members-citizens are the sovereigns with whom the ultimate authority to decide upon common affairs rests.

As far as constitutional choices of type I are concerned, i.e. the choice of operating rules, contractarian reflections on what rules of the game citizens would agree upon under hypothetical, ideal conditions can, for reasons discussed above, not be expected to result in constitutional advice of practical relevance. Neither the citizens as members-principals of democratic polities nor politicians as their agents can be plausibly assumed to find such information on hypothetical agreements helpful for solving problems they are interested in solving. If constitutional advice is to be of interest for citizens who know who they are and who can anticipate how they, personally, will be affected by suggested rule changes, it has to provide information on how mutual gains may be realized by all parties involved compared to the status quo and given their actual (not their hypothetical) constitutional interest.

In other words, if he wants his advice to be of practical relevance the constitutional economist must suggest changes in the rules of the game that, as he conjectures, promise mutual gains for all parties involved, in terms of their own judgment, given their actual interests. Or, stated in yet another way, he has to suggest rule-changes that he conjectures to serve the common constitutional interests of the members-citizens of the polity.

The constitutional economist's task as advisor is to examine the existing operating rules for potential "defects" that prevent citizens from realizing mutual gains that could be had, and to suggest constitutional reforms that may correct for such "defects." The ultimate judges on whether or not the rule-changes that the constitutional economist suggests do in fact allow for mutual gains are the citizens themselves. Their voluntary and informed agreement is the *ultimate* test of whether his conjectures about what is in citizens' common constitutional interest are correct or not.

Failure to find such agreement proves the constitutional economist's conjectures wrong, if not his conjectures about the working properties of the suggested rules at least his conjectures about what kind of constitutional environment the citizens themselves consider desirable.

That the citizens' voluntary and informed agreement is the *ultimate* test for what is in their common constitutional interest must be emphasized for two reasons. First, even where the relevant decisions are made under unanimity rule *factual, observed* agreement, or *factual, observed* failure to reach agreement, need not be perfectly reliable indicators of what is and what is not in citizens' common constitutional interest but may be due, instead, to insufficient information, strategic behavior and other reasons. Second, collective choices in democratic polities are typically not all made by unanimity rule. As J.M Buchanan and G. Tullock have argued in their foundational contribution to constitutional economics, *The Calculus of Consent* (1962), there are prudential reasons why citizens-members of a democratic polity – as, in fact, members of any cooperative enterprise – may voluntarily choose to give up the veto power that a unanimity rule grants and to agree to decide, instead, their common affairs by majority rule, or even to delegate decisions to representatives or agents whom they authorize to make political choices on behalf of the polity, at either of the three noted levels.

In this sense a careful distinction must be made between unanimity as the *ultimate legitimizing principle* in democratic polities and unanimity as a *decision rule* for ongoing policy choices. Or, in other words, one must distinguish between the *source of legitimacy* of a democratic polity's constitutional rules and the *content* of these rules. While the constitutional rules of a democratic polity can ultimately derive their legitimacy from no other source than the voluntary agreement among its members-citizens, in terms of their content they may very well allow for non-unanimous decision or the delegation of decision making authority.

The test of whether or not the constitutional economist's suggestions for constitutional reform find acceptance by the actual decision making procedures that the citizens of a democratic polity have established among themselves can only be a *proximate* but not the *ultimate* test of their validity. Such procedures may well allow for the rejection of rules that are, in fact, in citizens' common constitutional interest, and they may allow for the acceptance of rules that are not. Accordingly, if the constitutional economist's proposals for reform fail to find acceptance by the existing decision making procedures this must not be taken as the final verdict on the validity of his conjectures on what serves the common constitutional interests of a polity's citizens.

It may also be due to shortcomings of, or 'defects' in, the decision making procedures, i.e. in the rules for choosing rules, that prevent reform proposals from being accepted even though their acceptance would be in citizens' common interest. There are reasons, therefore, for the constitutional economist to examine whether their might be such shortcomings or defects in a polity's rules for choosing rules, i.e. its *constitutional rules*, and to look for ways in which they may be corrected. This points to the second level of constitutional choice, namely of constitutional choice type II, at which the constitutional economist may play a role as advisor.

CONSTITUTIONAL RULES AND CITIZEN SOVEREIGNTY

In terms of the distinction between *operating rules* and *constitutional rules* the institutions of democracy must be classified under the latter category. Democracy as a system of government is characterized by *particular procedures* for making policy choices and for choosing the operating rules of a polity, namely procedures that are supposed to promote the common interests of the citizens and that derive their legitimacy from citizens' voluntary consent. This is what the characterization of democratic polities as "citizens' cooperatives" or as "cooperative ventures for mutual advantage" is meant to express. Democratic institutions may, therefore, be examined, in particular, with regard to their capacity to actually enhance the prospects for a "citizens' cooperative" to come to adopt mutually beneficial operating rules.

And, how well democratic institutions perform as procedures for choosing rules may, accordingly, be measured in terms of their capacity to promote citizens' common constitutional interest. This criterion for judging the performance of democratic institutions can be called, as I suggest, *citizen sovereignty*. To "improve" democratic institutions means, in terms of this criterion, to make them better instruments for citizen sovereignty, i.e. to change them in ways that better enable citizens to realize mutual gains from joint commitment to rules that are in their common constitutional interest, whatever these common interests may be in substance.

The criterion of *citizen sovereignty* is central to the second capacity in which constitutional economists may serve as advisors in democratic polities, namely in providing information on potential changes in a polity's *constitutional rules*, i.e. in the rules for choosing rules, that enhance the prospects for citizens' common constitutional interests to prevail and, thus, increase the chances for the polity to actually operate as a "cooperative venture for mutual advantage." Proposals for reform that the constitutional economists may submit in this regard are, to be sure, subject to the "test" of whether or not they will be accepted by the citizens to whom they are addressed, or, more precisely, of whether or not they pass the existing decision making procedure by which a citizens' cooperative changes its constitutional rules.

But this test is an "acceptance-test" only, not a test of the validity of the constitutional economist's conjectural advice. Whether or not the constitutional reforms that he suggests are in fact suitable to further citizen sovereignty is to be judged on empirical and theoretical grounds. As the polity's sovereigns citizens are, of course, entitled to opt for other constitutional rules than those which, according to the constitutional economist's conjecture, would allow for more citizen sovereignty. But their refusal to follow the constitutional economist's advice does not prove his conjecture wrong. It only proves that, for whatever reason, the citizens prefer not to follow his advice.

The constitutional economist's advice for how to "improve" democratic institutions in terms of *citizen sovereignty* can actually come in two versions, a "weaker" and a "stronger" version. As the "weaker" version I consider advice about potential changes in the procedures for choosing rules that – by comparison to the existing procedures –promise to improve the chances for choosing rules that serve individuals' common constitutional interests, relative to the status quo. Such advice takes the *existing* constitutional rules as the benchmark against which "improvement" is measured. By "stronger" version I mean advice on how the existing procedures for choosing or establishing rules ought to be changed if the aim is to create more conducive conditions for *voluntary and informed consent* in constitutional choice. As subtle as it may appear, the distinction between the two kinds of constitutional advice is of significance. As noted, in the first case the *constitutional status quo* is taken as the benchmark against which it is to be judged whether or not suggested constitutional changes promise to allow for more citizen sovereignty. In the second case the constitutional status quo is itself judged against a normative criterion, namely in terms of the extent to which it can be reasonably assumed to be based on voluntary and informed consent of the persons concerned. And constitutional advice of the "stronger" version is advice for how the procedures by which rules are chosen and established may be changed in ways that facilitate not just the reaching of *factual* agreement on mutually beneficial rules, but that promote *voluntary and informed* agreement in constitutional choice.

The relevant analogy here is with the notion of voluntary market exchange discussed above. As noted there, the normative quality or 'efficiency' that economists attribute to market exchange is based on their, explicit or implicit, assumption that markets are institutionally secured arenas for *voluntary* cooperation. It is because – or, more precisely, to the extent that – the institutional framework within which they take place assures (as far as this can be assured under real-world constraints) their voluntary and informed nature that market transactions can be assigned the normative qualities that the gains-from-trade paradigm emphasizes.

Analogously, 'efficiency' may be attributed to constitutional agreements or agreements on rules if – or, more precisely, to the extent that – the conditions under which they have been reached justify the presumption that they are based on voluntary and informed consent of the contracting parties. And just as the constitutional economist can inquire into how the institutional framework of markets may be 'improved' by creating more suitable conditions for voluntary and informed exchange, he may likewise inquire into how at the level of constitutional choice more favorable institutional conditions for voluntary and informed agreement may be created.

The "weaker" and the "stronger" version of the constitutional economist's advice for how to promote citizen sovereignty differ in terms of the reasons why the addressees to whom the advice is given, i.e the citizens of a democratic polity, may want to listen. Advice of the "weaker" version directly appeals to citizens' constitutional interests, given the constitutional status quo. It informs citizens about potential changes in the existing procedures for choosing rules that will improve the prospects for mutually beneficial rules to be chosen. Citizens who believe such advice to be correct have prudential reasons to agree to the suggested constitutional changes because they promise to make them better off, jointly with their fellow-citizens. In this sense the "weaker" version of the constitutional economist's advice can surely be expected to be of practical relevance. It informs about possibilities for solving a problem that its addressees, the citizens, presumably have an interest in solving. Apparently, the same cannot be said about advice of the "stronger" version. Advice of this kind does not appeal to citizens' given constitutional interests but refers, instead, to the normative standard against which the constitution of a citizens' cooperative should be measured, namely that it is legitimized by the voluntary consent of the citizens-members of the polity.

It suggests changes in the procedures for choosing rules that one should adopt if one wants to create more suitable conditions for voluntary and informed constitutional choice and, thus, conditions that can lend more credence to the claim that a democratic polity's constitution is based on voluntary and informed acceptance on part of its citizens.

Since advice of the "stronger" version does not appeal to *interests* of its addressees but to a *normative principle*, namely the legitimizing force of voluntary and informed agreement, it may perhaps seem as if advice of this kind is subject to a similar charge as the welfare economist's advice, namely not to be tuned to the interests of real persons but to be directed to an imaginary, benevolent dictator who is interested in the normative principle as such. I do not consider this charge to be justified, nor would it be justified, in my view, to charge the inquiry into suitable conditions for voluntary and informed constitutional choice with committing the same mistake as the "hypothetical contract"-approach, namely to speculate about what hypothetical people would agree upon under hypothetical conditions instead of conjecturing what may be mutually beneficial for real people, given the situation they are actually in. To start with the latter charge, there is a fundamental difference between speculating about the content of hypothetical contracts and seeking to identify institutional provisions that may, under real-world constraints, create more conducive conditions for voluntary and informed constitutional choice. While information on the content of hypothetical agreements is, presumably, of little interest to people who know who they are, information on what may enhance voluntariness in constitutional choice may well be of interest to real citizens, to the extent, at least, that they are interested in living in a polity that can claim to be based on voluntary and informed consent of its citizens. And, this brings me to my answer to the first charge, for citizens of democratic polities there are indeed, as I suppose, good reasons for having an interest of this kind.

With advice of the "stronger" version the constitutional economist reminds citizens of democratic polities of the normative foundation on which their polity as a citizens' cooperative is based. He informs them about possibilities for constitutional reform that, as a matter of normative consistency, they should consider if they want to secure better pre-conditions for their polity to actually operate as a cooperative venture for mutual advantage. Such advice is not at all directed at an imaginary benevolent dictator but at the citizens themselves. It tells them what provisions they may jointly adopt if they wish to enhance voluntariness in matters of constitutional choice, provisions that – in terms of A. O. Hirschman's (1970) classification – may strengthen their voice-options or their exit-options. Apart from reasons of normative consistency, a prudential reason for citizens to follow such advice is that a democratic polity can be expected to be more stable and robust against changing circumstances the more its constitutional foundations can be assumed to be based on the voluntary and informed consent of its citizens.

CONCLUSION

As an applied science constitutional economics inquires into how people may realize mutual gains from joint commitments or, in other terms, how they may come to play "better games" among themselves by "exchanging" commitments to suitable common rules. The citizens of democratic polities as "cooperative ventures for mutual advantage" are the natural addressees for the kind of advice that such an applied constitutional economics may be able to provide. The focus of the above analysis has been to draw a distinction between two different levels at which constitutional economists may provide advice to citizens of democratic polities in matters of institutional-constitutional choice. The first level concerns, as I have called them, the *operating* rules and the second level the *constitutional* rules, i.e. rules for choosing rules.

Advice on operating rules is based on conjectures about which among alternative rules are better suited, in terms of their working properties, to result in mutual advantages for the members-citizens of a polity. Such conjectures have two kinds of components, namely hypotheses about the factual working properties of rules on the one hand and, on the other hand, assumptions about what, in terms of final outcomes, the citizens concerned will find preferable. While the citizens to whom advice for reforms in operating rules is addressed are, to be sure, the ultimate judges on the latter, they cannot be considered the competent judges on the validity of the constitutional economist's conjectures on the factual working properties of rules. Advice on constitutional rules is based on conjectures about which among potential alternative procedures for choosing rules provide better chances for citizens' common constitutional interests to prevail. The validity of such conjectures is to be judged in terms of empirical and theoretical arguments, not in terms of citizens' preferences, even though, of course, it is up to citizens as the sovereigns of democratic polities to decide upon whether or not they wish to follow the constitutional economist's advice in such matters.

THE POLITICAL ECONOMY OF THE U.S. CONSTITUTION

During the bicentennial of the U.S. Constitution it is appropriate to reflect on the political wisdom of our Founding Fathers. No written constitution in history has established a more durable or successful democracy than has the U.S. Constitution. A full appreciation of the Founding Fathers, however, requires an understanding of the economic as well as the political consequences of our Constitution. Every economy is a political economy and the enormous success of the U.S. economy has been as dependent on our political system as on our economic system.

Indeed, many of the problems that currently plague the U.S. economy are the result of our failure to hold on to the political wisdom that guided our Founding Fathers. Economic knowledge is obviously important in the effort to promote economic growth and development. But no matter how sound our economic understanding, economic performance will continue to suffer until we once again recognize that political power is a force for progress only when tightly constrained and directed toward limited objectives.

The genesis of the political and economic wisdom of our Founding Fathers is found in the fact that they distrusted government while fully recognizing the necessity of government for a beneficent social order. The cautious embrace the Founders gave government is reflected in their view of democracy as necessary but not sufficient for the proper control of government.

The concerns that led to the colonists' break with Great Britain were very much in the public mind when the Constitutional Convention met in Philadelphia during the summer of 1787. The well known prerevolution rallying cry, "No taxation without representation," reflected a clear understanding of the dangers that accompanied any exercise of government power not answerable to those who are governed. That the government established by the Constitution would be democratic in form was not in doubt. Unchecked democratic rule, however, was anathema to the most thoughtful of the Founding Fathers.

A grievance against English rule rivaling that of "taxation without representation" concerned the sovereign authority assumed by the English Parliament in 1767. In that year Parliament decreed that, through its democratically elected members, it had the power to pass or strike down any law it desired. The colonists had brought with them the English political tradition, which dated back at least to the Magna Carta of 1215: the people have certain rights that should be immune to political trespass regardless of momentary desires of a democratic majority. The concern was not only that the colonists were unrepresented in Parliament but, more fundamentally, that Parliament assumed unlimited power to meddle in the private lives of individuals whether represented or not:

Although the Founding Fathers were determined to establish a government that was democratic in the limited sense that political decisions could not ignore citizen input, they had no intention of creating a government that was fully responsive to majority interests. In many ways the Constitution is designed to frustrate the desire of political majorities to work their will through the exercise of government power. The most obvious example of this is the first ten amendments to the Constitution, or the Bill of Rights. These amendments guarantee certain individual freedoms against political infringement regardless of majority will. If, for example, freedom of speech and the press was dependent on majority vote many unpopular but potentially important ideas would never be disseminated. How effectively would a university education expose students to new and controversial ideas if professors had to submit their lectures for majority approval?

Other examples exist of the undemocratic nature of the government set up by the Constitution. There is very little that can be considered democratic about the Supreme Court. Its nine members are appointed for life, and their decision can nullify a law passed by the Congress and supported by the overwhelming majority of the American public. In a five to four decision one member of the court, insulated from the democratic process, can frustrate the political will of a nearly unanimous public.

The arrangement whereby the President can reverse the will of the Congress through his veto power is certainly not a very democratic one. Neither is the Senate where the vote cast by a senator from Wyoming carries weight equal to the vote by the senator from California, even though the California senator represents a population fifty times larger than does the Wyoming senator. The senators from the twenty-six least populated states can prevent a bill from clearing Congress, even though it has incontestable popular support in the country at large. Congress is actually less democratic than just indicated once it is recognized that popular bills can be prevented from ever being considered in the full House of Representatives or Senate by a few representatives who serve on key congressional committees.

It is safe to say that the chief concern of the framers of the Constitution was not that of in suring a fully democratic political structure. Instead they were concerned with limiting government power in order to minimize the abuse of majority rule. In the words of R. A. Humphreys, "they [the Founding Fathers] were concerned not to make America safe for democracy, but to make democracy safe for America."

PRELUDE TO THE CONSTITUTIONAL CONVENTION

Fear of the arbitrary power that could be exercised by a strong central government, democratically controlled or otherwise, was evident from the Articles of Confederation. The Articles of Confederation established the "national government" of the thirteen colonies after they declared their independence from England. There is some exaggeration in this use of the term national government, since the Articles did little more than formalize an association (or confederation) of thirteen independent and sovereign states. While the congress created by the Articles of Confederation was free to deliberate on important issues and pass laws, it had no means of enforcing them. The Articles did not even establish an executive branch of government, and congressional resolutions were nothing more than recommendations that the states could honor if they saw fit. The taxes that states were assessed to support the Revolutionary War effort were often ignored, and raising money to outfit and pay the American army was a frustrating business.

Because of the weakness of the national government, the state governments under the Article of Confederation were strong and often misused their power. Majority coalitions motivated by special interests found it relatively easy to control state legislatures and tramp on the interests of minorities. Questionable banking schemes were promoted by debtors, with legislative assistance, in order to reduce the real value of their debt obligations. States often resorted to the simple expedient of printing money to satisfy their debts. Trade restrictions between the states were commonplace as legislators responded to the interests of organized producers while ignoring the concerns of the general consumers.

There was a 1786 meeting in Annapolis, Maryland of the five middle states to discuss ways to reduce trade barriers between the states. At this meeting the call was made for a larger meeting in Philadelphia in the following year to discuss more general problems with the Articles of Confederation. This meeting became the Constitutional Convention.

ACHIEVING WEAKNESS THROUGH STRENGTH

It was the desire of Madison, Hamilton, and other leaders at the Constitutional Convention to replace the government established by the Articles of Confederation with a central government that was more than an association of sovereign states. The new government would have to be strong enough to impose some uniformity to financial, commercial, and foreign policy and to establish some general protections for citizens against the power of state governments if the new nation was to be viable and prosperous. In the words of James Madison, we needed a "general government" sufficiently strong to protect "the rights of the minority," which are in jeopardy "in all cases where a majority are united by a common interest or passion." But this position was not an easy one to defend.

Many opponents to a genuine national government saw little merit in the desire to strengthen government power at one level in order to prevent the abuse of government power at another level. Was there any genuine way around this apparent conflict? Many thought not, short of giving up on the hope of a union of all the states. There were those who argued that the expanse and diversity of the thirteen states, much less that of the larger continent, were simply too great to be united under one government without sacrificing the liberty that they had just fought to achieve.

Madison, however, saw no conflict in strengthening the national government in order to control the abuses of government in general. In his view the best protection against arbitrary government authority was through centers of government power that were in effective com petition with one another. The control that one interest group, or faction, could realize through a state government would be largely nullified when political decisions resulted from the interaction of opposing factions within many states. Again quoting Madison,

The influence of factious leaders may kindle a flame within their particular States but will be unable to spread a general conflagration through the other States. . . . A rage for paper money, for an abolition of debts, for an equal division of property, or for any other improper or wicked project, will be less apt to pervade the whole body of the Union than a particular member of it. A central government strong enough to unite a large and diverse set of states would weaken, rather than strengthen, the control that government in general could exercise.

To the framers of the Constitution weakening government in the sense just discussed meant making sure that government was unable to extend itself beyond a relatively limited role in the affairs of individuals. This does not imply, however, impotent government.

The referees in a football game, for example, certainly are not the strongest participants on the field and have limited control over specific outcomes in the game. Yet in enforcing the general rules of the game the decisions of the referees are potent indeed. Government, in its role as referee, obviously cannot lack the authority to back up its decisions. In addition to performing its refer-eeing function, it is also desirable for government to provide certain public goods; goods such as national defense that will not be adequately provided by the private market. Again this is a duty which requires a measure of authority; in this case the authority to impose taxes up to the limit required to provide those public goods which are worth more than they cost.

How to Impose Control?

In granting government the power to do those things government should do, the Founding Fathers knew they were creating a power that had to be carefully controlled.

But how could this control be imposed? It could not be imposed by specifying a particular list of government do's and don't's. Such a list would be impossibly detailed and even if it could be drafted it would need to be revised constantly in response to changes in such considerations as population size, age distribution, wealth, and the state of technology. Instead, government has to be controlled by a general set of constitutional rules within which governmental decisions are made, with specific government outcomes determined through the resulting political process. It was the hope of those at the Constitutional Convention to establish a political process, through constitutional reform, that brought government power into action only when needed to serve the broad interests of the public.

This hope was not based on the naive, though tempting, notion that somehow individuals would ignore their personal advantages and concentrate on the general advantage when making political decisions. While noble motives are seldom completely absent in guiding individual behavior, whether private or public, the Founding Fathers took as a given that most people, most of the time, maintain a healthy regard for their private concerns. The only way to prevent self- seeking people from abusing government power was to structure the rules of the political game in such a way that it would be costly for them to do so.

The objective of the framers was to create a government that was powerful enough to do those things that received political approval, but to establish a political process that made it exceedingly difficult to obtain political approval for any action that lacked broad public support.

There were, of course, some powers that the national government was not constitutionally permitted to exercise. The national government was created by the states, and until the Constitution all governmental power resided in the states. Through the Constitution the states re linquished some of their powers to the national government, e.g., the power to impose taxes on the citizens, establish uniform rules of naturalization, raise an army and navy, and declare war.

In addition the states agreed to refrain from exercising certain powers; e.g., the power to coin money, pass laws impairing the obligation of contracts, and pass retroactive laws. Important government powers remained in the states, however, with some of them located in the local governments. Thus the powers that could be exercised by government were limited, and the powers that did exist were diffused over three levels of government. The Constitution further diffused power at the national level by spreading it horizontally over three branches of government, the power of each acting as a check and balance on the power of the others.

The intent of the Founding Fathers was to so fragment government power that it would be extremely difficult for any narrowly motivated faction to gain sufficient control to work its political will. Only those objectives widely shared and consistent with Constitutional limits would be realized through the use of government power.

The beauty of the political process established by the Constitution is that it is cumbersome and inefficient. According to Forrest McDonald the process is "So cumbersome and inefficient . . . that the people, however virtuous or wicked, could not activate it. It could be activated through deals and deceit, through bargains and bribery, through logrolling and lobbying and trickery and trading, the tactics that go with man's baser attributes, most notably his greed and his love of power.

And yet, in the broad range and on the average, these private tactics and motivations could operate effectively only when they were compatible with the public good, for they were braked by the massive inertia of society as a whole." Or, as Clinton Rossiter has said of the Founding Fathers' motives in creating the system of checks and balances, "Liberty rather than authority, protection rather than power, delay rather than efficiency were the concern of these constitution-makers."

6

Theories of Political Economy

The origin of the term "Political Economy" dates back to the period when it was used to study the way production was carried out in countries born out of the new capitalist system. More specifically, it was the relation between the production system and law, customs and the government. Theories of political economy were used to study the production, distribution and consumption of goods and services and their effective management in a country or a government system.

In the 18th century, the term underwent a major change when the "Labour Theory of Value" came into being, brushing aside theories of the Physiocrats who claimed.

"Land" to be the source of all wealth. Thus, the theory of profits on land which was up till now only a pattern of distributing wealth accrued from land in a capitalist system framework and collecting rents on land, changed, giving way to the theory of political economy.

The word Political Economy is the coming together of two Greek words "polis"(city or state) and "oikonomos"(one who manages the household). This explains the modern definition that political economy is the relationship between economics and politics in nation states or across different nation states.

The theory of political economy now draws heavily on the subject of economics, political science, law, history and sociology or different closely related branches of economics to explain the politico-economic behaviour of a country.

By the 19th century, economics took over the field of political economy in which axiomatic methods and fundamental techniques of mathematics were used to understand the functioning of the economy. But as mentioned earlier, the social science of political economy has not lost its weight in today's world where international trade and finance, and bilateral trade agreements can be analyzed using the logic of International Political Economy. This branch mainly draws on Marxian liberalism and realism from the theory of Political Science and Rational Choice assumption and also Game Theory from the field of advanced economics.

For example, free trade between countries or among many countries in a particular region is the result of economic and political considerations. Countries may undertake free trade agreements to promote sale of goods between them which will result in increased export earnings. It may also lead to specialization on the lines of "comparative advantage" and large scale production with falling costs. The benefits of the economies of scale can also be reaped through this process.

In this situation, the theory of "Positive Political Economy" investigates how observed differences in institutions affect economic and political outcomes in various economic, social and political systems. These institutional differences might arise in the polity of a respective economy or any other structural differences in the system. Political Economy which formerly rested on:

- Adam Smith- An Inquiry into Nature and Causes of the Wealth of Nations (1776)
- David Ricardo-On the Principles of Political Economy and Taxation (1817)
- John Stuart Mill- Principles of Political Economy with some of their Applications to Social Philosophy (1848)
- William Stanley Jevons-The Theory of Political Economy (1871) has come a long way from the "invisible hand" of Adam Smith as a discourse on Capitalism, the theory of "rent" of David Ricardo, the "social philosophy" aspect of J.S. Mill and the "utility as the origin of value" put forward by W.S Jevons.

Top of Form

Bottom of Form

The theory of political economy now encompasses a wide range of subjects from anthropology to history from psychology to human geography and from law to ecology. The theories of International Political Economy, if applied properly, can lead to the solution of issues such as immigration, environmental degradation, AIDS control and other developmental issues pushing Third World Countries into the low level equilibrium trap. The theory can also effectively and efficiently handle the issues of Intellectual Property Rights and trade liberalization in this globalised world.

The political economy theory is one of the most comprehensive theories in the world which can become a successful tool in combating the complex and serious issues threatening to nullify the bounties of liberalization and globalization.

MARXIST THEORY OF POLITICAL ECONOMY

What is political economy? Students of economics are usually taught their subject in isolation from politics and history, but for Marxists the economic can only be analysed in a political way, here is why.

Economics has taken a battering over the last few years. Economists failed to predict the economic crisis that hit Asia in 1997. The Global Credit Crunch seemed to appear out of nowhere, with most economists predicting the constant expansion of capitalism for many more years to come.

The Economist magazine wrongly predicted in January 1998 that the year ahead would see record world growth as it shrugged off the "Asian contagion". The Nobel Prize winners for economics on the board of hedge fund lost billions of dollars in 1999 by following their own theories.

Economics is more and more about mathematical modelling that abstracts from human relations and behaviour and reduces it to graphs and charts. It is not used as a scientific tool but as propaganda to "talk up" the national or international economy. Most economists' incomes are tied to constant and rapid growth in stock markets – so it is no surprise that their predictions err on the side of optimism. In fact all that economists generally do is look at the last 6 months of statistics and project the same trends forward. The kind of economics they teach in university barely equips people for any kind of critical thinking about the world around us and how it works.

What is economics really about?

Marxist political economy, in contrast, starts from relations between people and classes, and tries to understand the economy not as a perfect clockwork mechanism but as a dynamic system full of contradictions and doomed to be replaced. Political economy is not about the relationship between commodities, prices, supply and demand: it is first and foremost about people and the social relationships between them – about the owners of wealth and how they use it to exploit others; about what is produced and how. In that sense economics is both political and social and historical. Marxists do not agree with these artificial divisions in the academic world which tend to obscure how things are really interconnected together.

CLASSICAL ECONOMICS

Marx did not begin from scratch: he started from the insights of "classical" political economy – a school of thought that the early capitalists gave birth to, as a means of advocating their new system against the defenders of feudalism.

The founders of modern political economy, Adam Smith and David Ricardo, were supporters of the new capitalist industrialists and bankers. They developed a labour theory of value which explained that the labour of the working class was the source of all new value, the profits at the heart of the capitalist system.

They showed that the value of a commodity – which is something produced for sale on the market – was determined by the amount of labour time it took to produce. They showed how all commodities exchanged according to equal amounts of labour within them.Smith insisted that this equal exchange only applied to exchange of goods, not the exchange between a worker and a capitalist (wages for work). Otherwise, how was the existence of profits to be explained? Ricardo disagreed: workers and capitalists did exchange something of equal value. So where did profits come from then?

Ricardo witnessed the enormous strides in industrialisation in the early nineteenth century and with it productivity. He thought that it took less and less time to produce the goods workers needed and so the value of their wages used to buy them was able to decline. So profits grew at the expense of wages.

Early radicals seized on this to suggest that workers were being robbed: they came up with slogans demanding the "full fruits of their labour". So from the 1830s onwards, as the class struggle began to intensify in Britain and Europe, a specialist caste of bourgeois economists arose whose job it was to mystify and obscure the origins of the capitalist's wealth.

These economists rejected the labour theory of value, as it exposed too clearly the exploitation of the working class. And it is from the theories of these "vulgar" economists that modern day capitalist economics originated. Despite the fact that the Thatcherite bosses called their think tank the "Adam Smith Institute", they reject Smith's basic theory as too politically dangerous!

It was left to Marx and Engels in the 1840s to pick up from where Ricardo and Smith left off and develop the labour theory of value.

What Marx Developed?

Marx realised that the answer to the key problem of the political economy of capitalism lay in the two-sided nature of labour. The very concept of what "labour" is needed to be made more concrete.

On the one side, like all commodities, labour has a "use-value". This means that there are many different types of concrete labour: plumbing, computer programming, and a variety of skills and training may be involved. On the other hand all these different types of labour are united at an abstract level by the fact that they can be reduced to a specific amount of social labour – what Marx called "abstract, general human labour".

On the basis of this theory, Marx discovered that the exchange value of a commodity is determined by the abstract, average amount of labour contained within it. It is not decided by the level of skill of the craftsman or how much care someone took over its creation.

Unlike Smith and Ricardo, Marx realised that the distinction between use value and exchange value applied to labour itself. In fact it is not "labour" that is a commodity being bought in the wage transaction: more accurately it was the ability to work: what he called labour power.

Labour power is what the capitalist buys with wages. The use-value of this is labour, which is unique. By setting the worker to work the expenditure of this labour produced more value than it itself contained. So the capitalist pays wages equal to the value of the goods and services the worker needs to survive and reproduce the next generation of workers. The cost of labour power is socially determined. But for this the boss receives a commodity with a special power. The worker is contracted to labour for a certain duration and to a certain quality for the capitalist. Typically, a worker is employed for eight hours a day.

This creates eight hours worth of value, which is spread across the commodities the worker produces; it adds eight hours worth of value to the commodities. For example, if the worker produced one chair an hour then that chair would have one hour of value in it. If the worker produced a tin can every minute the tin can would contain one minute of value.

However, the cost of the worker's reproduction is less than the value of the labour they add to production. During the eight hour day it may take only four hours to create the amount of value equivalent to the worker's wage. But the worker does not go home after four hours. To receive their wage, equal to four hours worth of labour, they must stay at work for the duration of the eight hour working day.

In addition to the four hours worth of labour which pays their wages they create a new surplus value equal to four hours which belongs to the capitalist. This surplus value is the source of all profits under the capitalist system. This was Marx's solution to the problems set by Ricardo's labour theory of value. It is the cornerstone of Marx's theory of capitalist economy. It unlocks the mystery of capitalist production.

Capitalist exploitation is not an unjust or unfair part of the capitalist system. The capitalists do not "steal" their profits from the working class. Exploitation is an inherent and essential part of the system. It is the source of both the class struggle and economic crises, which are just as integral to this system.

The workers have no choice but to work, to be exploited, because we are deprived of owning the means of production. it is only the capitalists own the means of production, we are forced to work for them. Occasionally workers set up co-operatives or try and escape their exploitation by becoming small business people, but this option is only available to a tiny number. Most small business owners fail in the face of the stronger capitalists, and are forced back into the ranks of the working class.

Capital is not just machines, factories, money, stocks and shares: it is a social relation between people. Capital – to the people that own it – appears as a kind of self-expanding money. Under normal conditions, short of burying money in the ground, you cannot stop it making more money: put it in the bank and it makes 5 per cent; in a PEP it makes 7 or 8 per cent; in shares you can double your money. To the capitalist, it seems that it is money itself that "makes money". Hence the fat cat's refrain, "I let my money work for me".

In fact it is only the labour of the working class that creates new value that translates into profit. To own capital is to be part of the process of exploiting the working class. To live off your capital is to be part of a class whose material interest lies in screwing as much profit as possible out of the workers. Likewise the workers have no choice but to resist since the intensification of work, more job flexibility and holding down wages are among the most common methods the bosses use to raise efficiency and increase the rate of exploitation.

The class struggle is an intrinsic and permanent feature of the political economy of capitalism, as is the use of the police and judiciary to enforce this system against resistance from the exploited.

Once we understand the source of profits as the surplus value created by the working class the basic contradiction of capitalism – one that points to its ultimate doom – is opened up. In pursuit of profits the capitalists are forced into competitive innovation – replacing human labour by machinery and technique.

A firm that introduces a technological change that cheapens production gains an advantage over its rivals – in the short-term. But, to compete, the other companies will make the same if not better innovation.

Therefore, in the long-run the capitalists continually make innovations while putting workers – the source of value – on the dole. Marx called this the replacement of living labour by dead labour. But since only the living labour of the workers produces surplus value, the process of mechanisation and automation increasingly undermines the source of profit.

Hence Marx, like Smith and Ricardo, identified the tendency of the rate of profit to fall as a basic "law" of economics – one that could be offset by various factors, such as longer hours or new technology, but which, when unleashed, was the ultimate cause of crisis.

MARXIST CRISIS THEORY

Unlike the failed theories of the capitalists – all of which have to pretend there is nothing fundamentally wrong with their profit system, and which therefore cannot explain why the system regularly goes into crisis – the Marxist theory predicts and explains regular crises and breakdowns of the system. Before capitalism, every economic crisis in history was a result of underproduction (for instance the crops would fail). But under capitalism there is already enough produced to meet the needs of every human being on the planet many times over.

Under capitalism, crises are caused by *overproduction* – and this means the overproduction not just of useful things like food and fuel, but of every form of value – of money, of property, of financial instruments. Crises are caused by the overaccumulation of capital. Through the course of the boom phase of a cycle, the rate of profit received by a capitalist – his or her return on every pound invested – gradually begins to fall. Marx explained how this was caused by the fact that capitalists compete with one another by raising productivity through introducing new technology, but that ultimately this reduces the proportion of their capital that is based on living human labour – and this living labour is the real source of their profit.

The resulting tendency of the rate of profit to fall drives capitalists to direct their money out of manufacturing in the more advanced countries and into speculation on the stock exchange, into property deals, or abroad into developing low wage economies. It also forces them to try to cut wages at home and employ migrant labour on terrible pay and conditions.

Eventually this pressure on the rate of profit causes the actual overall mass of profit to fall. Then the only way the capitalists can get back to turning a big enough profit is to devalue a mass of "overvalued" capital. This is what economic crises are. That is why today banks are losing billions; why house and property prices plummet; why people are thrown out of their homes; why factories and shops will close in the years ahead; why inflation reduces the real value of wages. It is why the bosses will try to get us all to work harder for less and compete among each other for fewer jobs.

It is also why the bosses of different countries will start fighting – first at the negotiating table, but one day on the battlefield – over who will bear the brunt of the devaluation. The main problem is that in every country of the world the leaders of the official labour movement are unable to explain the crisis, unprepared to warn the workers, unwilling to organise the struggles. We must create a new leadership, able to wrest control of the working class movement out of the hands of these misleaders. One hundred and fifty years ago, Karl Marx wrote: "These contradictions, of course, lead to explosions, crises... these regularly recurring catastrophes lead to their repetition on a higher scale, and finally to its violent overthrow." Speed the day.

GROWTH THEORY

The part of economic theory that seeks to explain (and hopes to predict) the rate at which a country's economy will grow over time. Economic growth is usually measured as the annual percentage rate of growth in one or another of the country's major national income accounting aggregates, such as Gross National Product or Gross Domestic Product (almost always with appropriate statistical adjustments to discount the potentially misleading effects of price inflation).

Just about any country's economy will show sizable year-to-year and quarter-to-quarter fluctuations in its economic growth rate, but economic growth theorists tend to concentrate their efforts on analyzing and explaining the smaller variations in the longer-term trend or average rate of economic growth over periods of a decade or more. They leave explanation of the shorter-term fluctuations around the longer-term trend to specialists in business cycle theory because investigation has shown that the predominant influences on short-term growth rates seem to differ in important ways from the determinants of an economy's long term average growth performance. It might also be added that the political effects of variations in long range economic growth rates tend to be substantially different from the political effects of the booms and busts of the business cycle.

The short term ups and downs of the business cycle have dramatic effects on popular perceptions of the country's economic well-being. In a recession, hundreds of thousands or even millions of people may become unemployed and suffer dramatic declines in their incomes for the duration of the crisis — usually for a period of somewhere between six months and one-and-a-half years before more normal economic conditions return again.

Yet over the long haul, even rather small increases or decreases in the trend rate of economic growth will have much more profound and enduring effects on economic production and hence on the material living standards of the population. As an illustration, consider the following: During the period since the end of World War II (1946 to 1999-I), the growth rate of GDP for the United States (corrected for inflation) has averaged about 3.3% per year. Assuming that the typical undergraduate student reading this text was born in 1979, the growth rate of the US economy over his or her lifetime has averaged a slightly lower 2.7% per year - a difference of "only" 0.6 percentage points per year. But if the US had been able to maintain the same average growth rate from 1979 to 1999 that it had enjoyed during 1946 to 1978 (about 3.6%), 1998 GDP would have reached 9.152 trillion 1992 dollars worth of goods and services instead of the 7.552 trillion dollars of production actually achieved.

That means that the income of the average American household in 1998 (and every single year thereafter) could have been more than 20% higher than it actually turned out to be if only a way could have been found to prevent this seemingly slight decline in the trend rate of economic growth. And if the US economy had somehow managed to average the slightly higher growth rate of an even 4% for the whole postwar period, the income of the average American household from 1998 on could have been about half again as much over what was (and will later be) at their disposal.

Explaining differences between countries in their long term economic growth rates is a complex matter, and the scientific literature on the subject is filled with controversies both technical and ideological in nature. Many of the theoretical determinants of long term growth rates are difficult to measure very adequately and many of the least imperfect measurements available for testing the various theories have been systematically collected in much of the world only for a relatively recent historical period — roughly the last 20 to 30 years. Nevertheless one eminent scholar's recent survey of the published professional literature came up with over sixty different variables that have been put forward by theorists as enhancing or retarding long term economic growth and that also actually showed significant evidence of real explanatory power in one or more systematic statistical tests using a broad range of 20th century historical data. There is broad support in virtually all empirical studies for a strong positive impact on economic growth by the investment rate (especially the rate of investment in plant and equipment) and by various measures of human capital (such as the literacy rate, school enrollment ratios, and average life expectancy). Although it is difficult to measure separately from investment and improvement of human capital, there is also substantial support for the positive contribution of continuing technological innovation and improvement in sustaining the process of economic growth by improving productivity.

A majority of the other variables that have been brought into economic growth theory are conceived of as influencing growth rates mainly in an indirect fashion by affecting either the volume or the efficiency in utilization of investment and/or of human capital and/or technological progress. There is also substantial and robust support in the empirical literature for the hypothesis of "conditional convergence" - that is, because of diminishing returns to capital, the lower a country's level of real GDP per capital at the beginning of a given historical period, the faster the country's subsequent growth rate tends to be (an initial advantage of less developed countries that in practice has been all too often offset by counterproductive governmental policies and by disruptive conditions such as frequent coups, lawlessness, warfare and civil strife that tend to retard savings and investment rates and to destroy or drive out a lot of human capital).

Various kinds of public policy variables also seem to make a difference in growth rates. Countries with relatively "open" economies (that is, those which allow relatively free movement of goods and capital in and out of the country without high tariffs, protectionist import quotas, foreign exchange controls or major restrictions on foreign investment) have tended to maintain higher growth rates than countries with more restrictive policies.

Countries that allow extremely rapid expansion of their money stocksand thus bring on high rates of inflation (about 20% per year seems to be a critical threshold) have tended to experience sharply lower economic growth rates than countries with low or moderate rates of inflation. Countries whose legal systems provide relatively reliable enforcement of private contracts and relatively secure protection for private property rights have tended to grow more rapidly than countries whose legal systems are bogged down by corruption, arbitrary judicial decision-making, frequent radical changes in basic legal principles, ex post facto legislation and/or just plain lack of prompt and effective enforcement of the law.

Some of the most emotion-laden and ideologically-tinged debates on economic growth theory deal with two questions on which no broad consensus seems likely in the near future: What sort of mixture of government planning and control versus the free market is most conducive to economic growth?

And what are the effects of different cultures (especially differences in religious and ethical values) on promoting or retarding economic growth?

Taking the second question first, it should be noted that many of the earliest theories about what causes economic growth were largely cultural in nature. Adam Smith, David Ricardo, Thomas Malthus and many others (even Karl Marx) laid great stress on the importance to economic growth of such culturally conditioned values or attitudes as thrift, the value of diligence and hard work, ambition for a better material standard of living, respect for other people's property rights, the sense of obligation to honor agreements and contracts, inventiveness, willingness to adopt new ways of doing things and so on. Many of these values are fostered and reinforced (or possibly denigrated and condemned) in different measure within different cultural traditions, and an especially important role in this is played by organized religion.

It is not surprising then that nowadays we still see a lot of more or less informed speculation about the role of this religion or that in fostering or inhibiting economic growth, especially in less developed regions of the world. (Max Weber's classic essay on "The Protestant Ethic and the Spirit of Capitalism" is one of the best known and most closely reasoned classic examples of this tradition in the social sciences.)

Two or three decades ago, the prevalence of Roman Catholicism in southern Europe and Latin America and its alleged anti-commercial social and economic values were often invoked as a part of the explanation for the relative economic backwardness of these regions compared to mainly Protestant northern Europe and North America.

In much more recent times, the influence of Islam in fostering fatalistic attitudes and anti-commercial or anti-materialist values (such as the condemnation of all lending at interest) is often invoked as part of the explanation for the relative economic backwardness of the Moslem countries, despite the huge advantages many of them enjoy in the form of rich endowments of natural resources like petroleum.

The conservative anti-materialist and fatalistic elements of Hinduism are often put forward as an explanation for India's backwardness. Weber believed that Confucianism greatly hindered China's economic development over the centuries, but ironically the same Confucian heritage is today more often invoked as an explanation for the rapid commercial development of such places as Hong Kong, Taiwan, and Singapore.

The problem with such explanations is that all major religious traditions contain some elements that can encourage economic activity along with other elements that inhibit it, and determining which influences will predominate in any particular place and time is a game that tends to be played with far too many wild cards, with the theorist opportunistically seizing upon whichever elements of the local religious tradition best seem to fit with what he already knows has been happening lately. It is hard to deny that cultural values matter for economic development and that religion plays an important role in fostering the people's values, but correlating*changes* in people's values with *changes* in economic growth performance requires much better measurement than is possible by simplistic references to which particular religious faith has predominated in the particular country for centuries.

A more promising approach is for researchers to go out periodically and directly sample the distributions of particular "pro-growth" and "anti-growth "attitudes among the populations of various countries (perhaps by survey research polling methods) rather than simply assuming the presence of these values and attitudes on the basis of formal religious doctrines. Only then does it make sense to begin gingerly pronouncing upon how the prevalence or lack of particular values correlate with actual long-term economic growth performance in subsequent years.

As to the first question, socialist and communist economists used to argue that a totally government controlled and planned economy would enjoy more rapid economic growth than a capitalist economy, primarily basing their case on the idea that a planned economy would maintain a steadier and higher rate of investment, free of the periodic slowdowns of investment caused by periodic financial crises in the capitalist business cycle. It was also assumed that a morc egalitarian socialist educational policy would be much more successful in promoting widespread education for the masses, greatly enhancing the supply of what we would today call human capital.

Economists more favorably inclined toward the free market system acknowledged that the total amount of investment in both non-human and human capital was indeed very important to rapid economic growth but cautioned that the efficiency with which these resources were allocated was also of extreme importance.

A capitalist economy , they argued, has a much better system of incentives for encouraging the most efficient allocation of economic resources, whereas the socialist economy would tend to get bogged down in bureaucratic waste and misallocation of resources that would lead to even more waste than the "anarchy of the market."

It is now reasonably clear from the historical record of the last thirty years or so that the closer to capitalist the economy has been, other things being equal, the more successful it has been in achieving higher long term rates of economic growth.

During that same period, countries at the extreme socialist end of the scale, especially the countries of the Communist bloc and their third world client states, have seen their initially fairly high rates of economic growth dwindle away gradually to zero and then plunged rapidly into full-scale economic collapse in the late 1980s. Since then, only those relatively few former Communist countries that moved most rapidly and radically to adopt capitalistic institutions and practices have resumed respectable rates of economic growth (such as Poland, Hungary, the Czech Republic, Estonia), while the vast majority of them have stagnated for about a decade in a kind of Never-never land where government bureaucrats have largely lost their power to plan, finance and administer state-owned enterprises but most of the legislation necessary to legalize and unleash private business still remain on hold.

Many of the non-Communist countries of the world that formerly had relatively large public sectors and extensive government controls over the economy have enacted reforms to privatize some of their state-owned enterprises and to open up their economies to more foreign trade and outside investment - and most (but not all) of them have since experienced at least modest improvements in their economic growth rates (although it is still too soon to tell whether these improvements represent changes in the long term trend or only temporary cyclical upswings).

Clearly the advocates of the free market have been scoring a lot of points in the debates over the past decade or two and have won over some of the skeptics, but their remaining opponents have by no means lost all of their intellectual ammunition. Die-hard advocates of full-scale socialism can (and do) still argue that socialism has not failed economically because "true" socialism has never been fully implemented (the Soviets and their former comrades in Eastern Europe and the Far East went ideologically wrong somewhere in the beginning) - and if it were really to be tried in the future , surely it would painlessly combine social justice, perfect democracy and the most rapid possible economic progress.

Less fanciful socialists can argue that there have actually been at least a few relatively successful growth stories in countries that retain many of the trappings of old fashioned state socialism (mainland China being the most telling example, since about one-third of the human species lives and works there). Some elements of the political left (including the economists among them) reluctantly accept the idea that more government control of the economy might lead to somewhat slower economic growth but then go on to say that low (or no) growth in GDP would be worth it if it was required in order to promote greater social justice.

Still others on the left, especially the "Greens," believe that an end to economic growth would be a positive good because people should reject excessively materialistic consumerist values and because it seems to them to be necessary in order to save the planet from environmental catastrophe. More conventional moderate socialists and social democrats more often take the line that they now accept the importance of retaining many elements of the market economy but still insist that a "middle way" with considerably larger amounts of government ownership, regulation and control than now exist in the United

States or much of Western Europe could maintain or even improve upon present economic growth rates if done carefully and in the right way. Only a few of these arguments are susceptible to proof or disproof by reference to numbers in the historical record since they contain value judgments as well as empirical assumptions.

And it must be acknowledged that the limited amount of data we have amassed over just the past few decades is still a very long way from what one would like to have for decisively resolving even the more tractable empirical disputes over just how economic growth rates get determined.

7

International Political Economy

International political economy (IPE), also known as global political economy (GPE), is an academic discipline within political science that analyzes economics andinternational relations. As an interdisciplinary field, it draws on many distinct academic schools, most notably political science and economics, also sociology, history, and cultural studies.

The academic boundaries of IPE are flexible, and along with acceptable epistemologies are the subject of robust debate. This debate is essentially framed by the discipline's status as a new and interdisciplinary field of study. Despite such disagreements, most scholars can concur that IPE ultimately is concerned with the ways in which political forces (states, institutions, individual actors, etc.) shape the systems through which economic interactions are expressed, and conversely the effect that economic interactions (including the power of collective markets and individuals acting both within and outside them) have upon political structures and outcomes.

IPE scholars are at the center of the debate and research surrounding globalization, both in the popular and academic spheres. Other topics that command substantial attention among IPE scholars are international trade (with particular attention to the politics surrounding trade deals, but also significant work examining the results of trade deals),international development (poverty and the role of institutions in development), international finance, global markets, political risk, multi-state cooperation in solving trans-border economic problems, and the structural balance of power between and among states and institutions. Unlike the broader field international relations, power is understood to be both economic and political, which are interrelated in a complex manner.

HISTORY OF INTERNATIONAL POLITICAL ECONOMY

International political economy studies problems that arise from or are affected by the interaction of international politics, international economics, and different social systems (e.g.,capitalism and socialism) and societal groups (e.g., farmers at the local level, different ethnic groups in a country, immigrants in a region such as the European Union, and the poor who exist transnationally in all countries). It explores a set of related questions ("problematique") that arise from issues such as international trade, international finance, relations between wealthier and poorer countries, the role of multinational corporations, and the problems of hegemony (the dominance, either physical or cultural, of one country over part or all of the world), along with the consequences of economic globalization.

Analytic approaches to international political economy tend to vary with the problem being examined. Issues can be viewed from several different theoretical perspectives, including the mercantilist, liberal, and structuralist (Marxist or neo-Marxist) perspectives. Mercantilists are closely related to realists, focusing on competing interests and capabilities of nation-states in a competitive struggle to achieve power and security.

Liberals are optimistic about the ability of humans and states to construct peaceful relations and world order. Economic liberals, in particular, would limit the role of the state in the economy in order to let market forces decide political and social outcomes. Structuralist ideas are rooted in Marxist analysis and focus on how the dominant economic structures of society affect (i.e., exploit) class interests and relations. Each of these perspectives is often applied to problems at several different levels of analysis that point to complex root causes of conflict traced to human nature (the individual level), national interests (the national level), and the structure of the international system (which lacks a single sovereign to prevent war).

For example, analysis of U.S. policy regarding migrants from Mexico must take into consideration patterns of trade and investment between the two countries and the domestic interests on both sides of the border. Similarly, domestic and international interests are linked by trade, finance, and other factors in the case of financial crises in developing countries such as Thailand and Argentina. The distinction between foreign and domestic becomes as uncertain as the distinction between economics and politics in a world where foreign economic crises affect domestic political and economic interests through trade and financial linkages or through changes in security arrangements or migrant flows.

Contemporary international political economy appeared as a subfield of the study of international relations during the era of Cold War rivalry between the Soviet Union and the United States (1945–91). Analyses initially focused largely on international security but later came to include economic security and the role of market actors—including multinational corporations, international banks, cartels (e.g., OPEC), and international organizations (e.g., the IMF)—in national and international security strategies. International political economy grew in importance as a result of various dramatic international economic events, such as the collapse of the Bretton Woods international monetary system in 1971 and the oil crisis of 1973–74.

During the early period of the Cold War, political scientists emphasized the realist, or power politics, dimension of U.S.–Soviet relations, while economists tended to focus on the Bretton Woods system of the international economy—that is, the institutions and rules that beginning in 1945 governed much of the international economy. During the Vietnam War, however, a growing decrease in the value of the U.S. dollar and large deficits for the United States in its balance of trade and payments weakened the ability of the United States to conduct and pay for the war, which thereby undermined its relationship to its North Atlantic Treaty Organization allies.

During the OPEC oil crisis, the realist-oriented U.S. Secretary of State Henry A. Kissinger found himself unable to understand the issues without the assistance of an economist. These events led to a search for a multidisciplinary approach or outlook that borrowed different theories, concepts, and ideas from political science and international relations—as well as from economics and sociology—to explain a variety of complicated international problems and issues. It did not so much result in the development of a new school of political economy as emphasize the continued relevance of the older, more-integrated type of analysis, which explicitly sought to trace the connections between political and economic factors.

Following the end of the Cold War, international political economy became focused on issues raised by economic globalization, including the viability of the state in an increasingly globalized international economy, the role of multinational corporations in generating conflict as well as growth in the "new global economy," and various problems related to equity, justice, and fairness (e.g., low wage rates in developing countries and the dependency of these countries on markets in wealthier countries).

In the 1950s and '60s, American economist W.W. Rostow and other experts on Western economic development made popular the argument that after a period of tension, disorder, and even chaos within a developing country that had been exposed to the West, that country would eventually "take off," and development would occur. In the late 1960s and continuing into the 1990s, many development experts from a structuralist point of view (including many Marxists and neo-Marxists) posited a variety of explanations as to why many developing countries did not seem to develop or change much. For example, the German-born economist Andre Gunder Frank made popular the idea that, when developing countries connect to the West, they become underdeveloped. Social theorist and economist Immanuel Wallerstein, whose works have made a lasting impact on the study of the historical development of the world capitalist system, argued that development does occur but only for a small number of semiperipheral states and not for those peripheral states that remain the providers of natural resources and raw materials to the developed industrial core states.

Such themes were evident in the 1990s and the early 21st century when a number of politically and economically powerful (and mostly Western) multinational corporations were accused of exploiting women and children in unsanitary and unsafe working conditions in their factories in developing countries. These cases and others like them were seen by some structuralists as evidence of a "race to the bottom" in which, in order to attract investment by international businesses, many developing countries relaxed or eliminated worker-protection laws and environmental standards.

ORIGIN

It has been predominantly considered by authors such as Benjamin Cohen (2008) that IPE emerged as a heterodox approach to international studies during the 1970s as the1973 world oil crisis and the breakdown of the Bretton Woods system alerted academics, particularly in the U.S., of the importance, contingency, and weakness of the economic foundations of the world order. IPE scholars such as Susan Strange asserted that earlier studies of international relations had placed excessive emphasis on law, politics, anddiplomatic history. Similarly, neoclassical economics was accused of abstraction and being ahistorical. Drawing heavily on historical sociology and economic history, IPE proposed a fusion of economic and political analysis. In this sense, both Marxist and liberal IPE scholars protested against the reliance of Western social science on the territorialstate as a unit of analysis, and stressed the international system.

TRADITIONAL APPROACHES

Academic courses, journals, and text books generally cover the various view points from which policy recommendations originate and will endeavour to provide an ideologically neutral presentation of the field of study. Following a precedent set by one of the founding text books of the discipline, individuals and organisations engaged in promoting particular policies, as well as many scholars active in this field, are commonly grouped into one of three worlds views, all of which have existed long before IPE emerged as a distinct academic discipline. These categories are liberal, realist, and Marxist. Constructivism may be classed as a fourth high level view, although scholars such as Ravenhill have grouped it as a sub-class of the Marxist approach. The liberal category is relatively unified, while the realist and Marxist views capture a vast range of outlooks. Widely shared views are found only at the highest level of abstraction:

The 'liberal' view believes in freedom for private powers at the expense of public power (government). It asserts that markets, free from the distortions caused by government controls and regulation, naturally will harmonise demand and supply of scarce resources resulting in the best possible world for populations at large.

The 'realist' view (formerly commonly labelled "nationalist") accepts the power of free markets to deliver favourable outcomes, but holds that optimum conditions generally are obtained with moderately strong public power exerting some regulatory control. The 'Marxist' view believes that only robust application of strong public power can check innate tendencies for private power to benefit elites at the expense of populations at large.

The 'constructivist' view assumes that the domain of international economic interactions is not value-free, and that economic and political identities, in addition to material interests, are significant determinants of economic action.

The Liberal Approach

In economic terms, Liberalism is an approach associated with classical economics, neoclassical economics, Austrian School economics, and Chicago school economics.

History

The Liberal approach often is wrongly traced to the work of Adam Smith. Economics, as some may claim, has been viewed as dawning with the *Smithian* revolution against Mercantilism.

The liberal view point generally has been strong in Western academia since it was first articulated by Smith in the eighteenth century. Only during the 1940s to early 1970s did an alternative system, Keynesianism, command wide support in universities. Keynes was concerned chiefly with domestic macroeconomic policy, however in IPE terms his mature views fall largely into the Realist camp, in that Keynes called for a middle way between public and private power and favoured a managed system of global finance for which he was one of the two chief architects at Bretton Woods. The Keynesian consensus was challenged successfully with attacks launched byFriedrich Hayek's Austrian School and Milton Friedman's Chicago School as early as the 1950s, which by the 1970s had succeeded in displacing Keynes as the dominant influence.

Keynes's approach to international relations, including his thinking on the economic causes of war and economic means of promoting peace, has received further attention with the onset of the global financial crisis and recession since 2008, especially through the work of Donald Markwell.

In policy making terms Western governments have generally pursued mixed agendas drawing on both the liberal and realist view point. This has been the case from the dawning of modern commerce to the present day, although there have been periods where one or the other school had gained temporary ascendency. Sometimes the period leading up to 1914 is described as a golden age of classical economics, but in practice governments continued to be partially influenced by mercantilist ideology, and following WW1 economic freedom was constricted. After World War II the Bretton Woods system was established, reflecting the political orientation described as Embedded liberalism. This has been described as a compromise between the realist and liberal viewpoints, in that it allowed governments to manage international finance, while still allowing considerable freedom of action for private commerce.

In 1971 President Richard Nixon began the rolling back of the Bretton Woods system and until 2008 the trend has been for increasing liberalization of international trade and finance. Domestically, the Atlantic nations since the 1970s and large Asian states such as China and India since the 1990s also have largely pursued a mixture of realist and liberal policies.

The only close to wholesale implementations of the liberal viewpoint being carried out is by smaller developing nations, often with some degree of coercion by actors such as the U.S. treasury or IMF, who have been able to apply financial pressure when the developing nations faced various crises. During 2008, liberal influences began to wane in the wake of the 2008–2009 Keynesian resurgence which the *Financial Times* described as a "stunning reversal of the orthodoxy of the past several decades". From later 2008 world leaders have also been increasingly calling for a New Bretton Woods System.

The Realist View

Within IPE the Realist approach was commonly labeled nationalism until the first decade of the twenty-first century. Historically the earliest distinct school of thought in this category was mercantilism. Contemporary examples of the realist approaches are statism and developmentalism.

History

The mercantilist view largely characterised policies pursued by state actors from the emergence of the modern economy in the fifteenth century up to the mid-twentieth century. Sovereign states would compete with each other to accumulate bullion either by achieving trade surpluses or by conquest. This wealth could then be used to finance investment in infrastructure and to enhance military capability.

The contemporary realist view generally agrees with liberals in viewing international trade as a win-win phenomenon where firms should be allowed to collaborate or compete depending on market forces. The chief point of contention with liberals is that realists assert national interests can be served best by protecting new industries from foreign competition with high tariffs until they've built up the capability to compete on the world market. One of the earliest formal expressions of this view was found in Alexander Hamilton's 'Report on Manufacturers' which he wrote for the U.S. government in 1791.

After WWII a notable success story for the developmentalist approach was found in South America where high levels of growth and equity were achieved partly as a result of policies originating from Raul Prebisch and economists he trained, who were assigned to governments around the continent. After the liberal view re-established its ascendancy in the 1970s, it has been asserted that high levels of growth resulted from generally favourable international conditions rather than the Realist policies.

A contemporary statement of the Realist view is strategic trade theory, and there has been much debate as to whether the policies it suggests could be effective in solving some of the issues with globalisation, such as persistent north/south inequality divide.

THE MARXIST VIEW

This category has been used to group together an array of different approaches which sometimes have very little in common with Marx's focus on class, but which all believe in a strong role for public power. Labels for approaches within this category include: feminist, radical, structuralist, critical, underdevelopment and 'world systems'. Broadly the Marxist approach is associated with Heterodox economics.

History

Marx's Das Kapital was published in 1867 and an economic system based on his ideas was implemented after the Russian Revolution of 1917. Since the collapse of the Soviet union and the COMECON trading bloc in 1991 no major group of trading partners or even single large economy has been run along Marxist lines. Problems with a Marxist command economy are seen as including the very high informational demands required for the efficient allocation of resources and corruptive tendencies of the very high degree of public power need to govern the process.

Few academics currently promote classical Marxist views, especially in America, but there are a few exceptions in Europe. More popular perspectives include feminist, environmental and radical – developmentalist. The social – constructivist view is an unusual school of thought sometimes grouped into this category. Rather than focus on the tradition factors affecting trade such as distribution of resources, technology, and infrastructure, it emphasises the role of dialogue and debate in determining future developments in international trade and globalisation.

Criticisms of the Traditional Divide into the Liberal, Nationalist, and Marxist Views

Critics have asserted there is now too much variation in the different viewpoints grouped into each category, especially those under the Nationalist and Marxist headings. Also, the names can be considered misleading for the general public. The labels nationalist and Marxist have negative connotations, with many of the perspectives grouped under the Marxist label having very little to do with the classical Marxist position. Many advocates within the nationalist tradition, being themselves strongly opposed to nationalism in the commonly understood fascist or racist sense, and some professors, have replaced the label "nationalist" with "realist" in their most recent books and courses.

The Constructivist View

Constructivism is an emerging field in international political economy. In general, the constructivist view propounds that material interests, which are central to liberal, realist, and Marxist views, are not sufficient to explain patterns of economic interactions or policies, and that economic and political identities are significant determinants of economic action.

American vs. British IPE

Benjamin Cohen provides a detailed intellectual history of IPE identifying American and British camps. The Americans are positivist and attempt to develop intermediate level theories that are supported by some form of quantitative evidence. British IPE is more "interpretivist" and looks for "grand theories". They use very different standards of empirical work. Cohen sees benefits in both approaches. A special edition of *New Political Economy* has been issued on The 'British School' of IPE and a special edition of the *Review of International Political Economy* (RIPE) on American IPE.

One forum for this was the "2008 Warwick RIPE Debate: 'American' versus 'British' IPE" where Cohen, Mark Blyth, Richard Higgott, and Matthew Watson followed up the recent exchange in RIPE. Higgott and Watson in particular, queried the appropriateness of Cohen's categories.

INTERNATIONAL TRADE AND STATE SECURITY

International economic structures range from complete autarky to complete market openness. This structure has undergone numerous changes since the beginning of the nineteenth century. The state-power theory as put into perspective by Stephen Krasner (1976), explains that the structure of international trade is determined by the interests and power of states acting to maximize their aggregate national income, social stability, political power and economic growth. Such state interests can be achieved under free trade.

The relationship between these interests and the level of openness depends upon the economic power of states. Power is dependent upon a states size and level of economic development.

Krasner contends that distributions of potential power may vary from multipolar to hegemonic; and different international trading structures are made of either of these. The key to this argument is that a hegemonic distribution of potential economic power is likely to result in an open trading system. Since states act to maximize their aggregate economic utility, maximum global welfare is achieved under free trade. Neoclassical trade theory posits that the greater the degree of openness in the international trading system, the greater the level of aggregate economic income.

THEORETICAL PERSPECTIVES

Realism

Robert Gilpin and Stephen Krasner are advocates of the realist tradition, which emphasises the hegemonic system. The hegemonic system contends that there are states that are much larger and more developed than their trading partners and therefore, the costs and benefits of openness are not symmetrical for all members of the system. Krasner (1976) contends that the hegemonic state will have a preference for an open structure because it will increase its aggregate national income and power.

Realism emphasizes states' demands for power and security. Military force is therefore, the most important power resource. States must rely ultimately on their own resources and must strive to maintain their power positions in the system, even at high economic costs. For realism, the most important variables are the economic and military strength of hegemonic states; and international hostilities are mainly because of variations in the distribution of political-military capabilities between states.

Hegemonic Stability

The theory of hegemonic stability by the realist school argues that dominance of one country is necessary for the existence of an open and stable international economy. The relationship between hegemony and an open, stable economy has been challenged by some scholars "As US behaviour during the interwar period illustrates, the possession of superior resources by a nation does not translate automatically into great influence or beneficial outcomes for the world."

Development Policy

Realist trade encourages Import substitution industrialization (ISI) replacing imports with domestic production. Realism recognises that trade regulations can be used to correct domestic distortions and to promote new industries. Under realism, states possess a high degree of discretionary power to influence many variables and prices in the economy. The government influences the distribution of investment, thus protecting national industries.

International Institutions

Realists with their focus on power and the struggle for survival in an anarchical world, criticize the role of international institutions that govern the world economy, such as theWorld Bank, World Trade Organization (WTO), EU, and the International Monetary Fund (IMF). Scholars argue that the influence exerted by international institutions is dependent upon the states that form part of them, and therefore international institutions have little independent impact. Accordingly, the realist school emphasises the impact of state power over the strength of the institution per se.

LIBERALISM

The liberal tradition consists of two schools of thought on the causes of peace, one emphasises representative government and international institutions and the other advocates global markets and economic development.

Liberalism traces back to Immanuel Kant. Kantian Liberalism posits that democracy, economic interdependence and international organisations are optimal solutions for reducing the incidence of conflict. It is not individual factors, which lead to a more peaceful world, but rather all three elements working in conjunction, which eliminates conflict.

Oneal and Russett's (2001) research design has become a standard choice of replications in studies assessing the Kantian peace triangle where democracies tend to be interdependent and members of the same International Government Organisations (IGOs). Their research is consistent with the argument that democratic peace advocates economic interdependence and a joint need to attain membership in IGOs in order to prevent the incidence of conflict. However, the empirical findings on the Kantian peace triangle as a joint force to eliminate conflict presents some limitations, as one study found that the three Kantian peace variables are less robust in explaining leaders' conflict behaviour. Keohane and Nye (2000) go further to include the lack of additional components in this theory including environmental and military measurements.

Trade

Liberals emphasise two main aspects of the benefits of trade. First, trade promotes states to work together and cooperatively, reinforcing peaceful relations among trading partners. The second benefit is based on the expected utility model of trade and conflict which emphasises the potential economic consequences of a disruption in trade. Countries are therefore deterred from initiating conflict against a trading partner for fear of losing the welfare gains associated with trade.

Interdependence

Liberals argue that economic interdependence between states reduces conflict because conflict discourages commerce. Recent cost-benefit calculations of trade take into account information as an important component in the explanation of the pacifying aspect of economic interdependence. Through open trade, states reveal their intentions and capabilities and thus "relations become more transparent and reduce uncertainty."

Furthermore, economic interdependence makes costly signals possible. If military action did not entail loss, national leaders would not be able to communicate their capabilities and resolve. This acts as a deterrent and promotes peace between states. "Mechanisms that facilitate the transmission of credible information across international boundaries limit bargaining failure, enhancing interstate peace."

There is some disagreement about the interdependence liberal thesis among some scholars. Kenneth Waltz, for example, argues that since "close interdependence means closeness of contact and raises the prospect of at least occasional conflict . . . the [liberal] myth of interdependence . . . asserts a false belief about the conditions that may promote peace."

Despite the scrutiny, there is a long-held position that economic interdependence has a pacifying effect on interstate relations, evidenced by research conducted by Oneal & Russett 1999 and Xiang et al. 2007.

According to the liberal view, the costly nature of conflict is central to contemporary bargaining theory.

Keohane & Nye (1987) put forth four conditions that make the use of force by large states costly:

1. Risks of nuclear escalation
2. Resistance by people in poor or weak countries
3. Uncertain and possibly negative effects on the achievement of economic goals
4. Domestic opinion opposed to the human costs of the use of force

Development Policy

Liberal trade encourages export led growth (ELG), leaving traders and consumers dependent on foreign markets. Liberals argue that these actors have an incentive to avoid hostilities with their trading partners, since any disruption in commercial relations would be costly.

International Institutions

International institutions are a key feature of the liberal peace, because they represent credible signals of resolve to defend member states in times of crisis, regulate state behaviour, facilitate communication and create common security interests between member states.

THE ARGUMENT ABOUT TRADE AND CONFLICT

The relationship between international trade and conflict has been a source of controversy among international relations scholars. Some scholars argue that trade does not reduce conflict even though conflict reduces trade; while others report that international trade fosters a peaceful disposition among states, which are less likely to resort to armed conflict in times of crisis.

The argument that open trade inhibits conflict dates back to the classical liberal movement of free trade and world peace. This view argues that increasing interaction among traders and consumers (interdependence) promotes peace; free trade fosters a sense of international community that reduce interstate conflict and tensions. Liberals posit that free markets and economic development contribute to a reduction in interstate conflict. The contrasting contemporary view is that open trade dampens political conflict by promoting economic dependence.

Economic dependence has negative consequences for interstate conflict. Albert O. Hirschman (1945) for example, has pointed out that the "gains from trade do not accrue to states proportionately and the distribution of these gains can affect interstate power relations. Moreover, shifts in power relations are widely regarded as a potent source of military conflict."

Economic Interdependence

Economic interdependence and greater openness exposes domestic economies to the exigencies of the world market. Social instability is therefore increased by exposure to international competition. This negative force undermines the Kantian peace and remains a cause for concern in international conflict. Although this concern seems legitimate given the economic disparities between developed and developing countries, studies fail to provide comprehensive empirical evidence.

Another view at odds with liberalism is that technological innovation and industrialization increase the ability of some countries to exercise power. As trade flows and the level of interdependence increases, so do the incentives for states to take military actions to reduce their economic vulnerability.

The adverse effect of trade on state security is difficult to determine, however the more competition, the more aggressive the environment. Openness and competition increases social instability because domestic prices need to adjust to changes in international prices. Consistent with the realists view that states are essentially always in conflict, social instability and resource competition are motives for conflict and states will rely on the use of force to attain their own political goals and interests.

The Role of Military Power

A number of international relations scholars, notably Xiang, Xu & Keteku 2007; Mearsheimer 2001, recognise the role of military power in initiating conflict, as well as the role militarily powerful countries play in international trade. One argument suggests that militarily capable countries are more likely to have the motivation to initiate armed conflict due to their awareness of their capabilities and to their confidence in achieving favourable outcomes. A second argument suggests that power facilitates trade. Third, there are positive benefits from economic interdependence on military power. Finally, the economic stature of a country determines both the military power and level of trade of that country, hinting that economic powerful states trade more. Because powerful countries are better positioned to take advantage of the benefits resulting from international trade and to transform welfare gains into military power, they also are more likely to use force when their positions are threatened. Similarly, Gartzke & Hewitt (2010) argue that the "extension of economic and other interests beyond national borders increases incentives to police relevant regions and exercise influence, sometimes through force."

Unequal Peace

The motives for conflict, which historically were concentrated among the powerful and their ambitious challengers, are today clustered among the poor, and between the poor and the rich. Theory has prompted to inequality as a potential source of internal conflict. "Inequalities within the same countries has increased, not through impoverishment of the masses, but because while wealth is created many people remain left behind in poverty. Thus, we have an unequal peace." Around 60 countries suffer not only from low GDP per capita but also low or negative growth. These countries tend to be caught in armed conflict among other development traps. Some argue that the evidence surrounding inequality and conflict remains inconclusive, calling for further empirical studies.

Studies show that states with the most dissimilar interests possess a motive for conflict but whether they experience conflict (or not) depends on external determinants of bargaining success or failure. These determinants include uncertainty about the balance of power, opponent's resolve as well as policy dissimilarities between competing states. Interests are important determinants of whether conflict occurs. According to Gartzke & Hewitt (2010), promoting democratic interests, or even imposing them for peace, is not likely to reduce conflict "it may even lead to a weakening of the actual determinants of liberal peace", thereby increasing interstate tensions. Contemporary research demonstrates that promoting free markets and economic development helps mitigate conflict and promote peace

CAPITALIST PEACE

The capitalist peace thesis suggests that free markets and economic development contribute to a reduction in interstate conflict. Research on the capitalist peace has chosen to pursue the liberal political economy school, with a particular focus on Kant's Perpetual Peace. The same set of theoretical frameworks that evolved in democratic peace research now asserts itself in the capitalist peace. The capitalist peace sees capitalism as creating conditions to make war more costly and therefore undesirable by trading states. Traditional interpretations of the capital peace contend that development and global markets will eventually eliminate resource competition as a motive for war. This view was eventually deemed outdated, as "it became clear that needed raw materials would continue to make their way to industrial centers through free markets, rather than through mercantilist autarkies.

The capitalist theory contends that as economies become stronger, prosperous capitalist states no longer need to threaten one another over access to inputs to production. Consequently, the security dilemma loses its relevance.

Scholars like Michael Mousseau argue that democracies are only peaceful in pairs. Other research has demonstrated that the democratic peace is even more exclusive than previously imagined, limiting the finding to developed democracies. Gartzke and Hewitt (2010) challenged this by demonstrating that it is economic development and market freedoms, rather than political liberty that result in interstate peace.

Deterrent Effect of Institutional Ties

International Government Organisations (IGOs) are designed to promote cooperation and inhibit political disputes. Institutional ties promote the exchange of information about the economic gains and losses of participating member states, thereby reducing uncertainty about the distribution of benefits.

Regional institutions also present great influence in addressing issues beyond trade. Regional economic institutions help develop trade expectations for the future. "High economic stakes that states have in the continuation and growth of economic activity in the context of economic regionalism lead to a security community in which states develop a genuine interest in not only keeping peace with each other, but also defending their relationship against outside aggressors." In addition to their role in dispute settlement, regional arrangements can deter aggressors from targeting institutionally connected states.

Aydin (2010) makes an important contribution to the extended deterrence literature and economic peace research through his empirical study on the deterrent effect of economic integration. This study shows that trade has a general deterrent effect on attackers when the target is economically integrated with potential defenders through regional trade institutions. When trade is conducted in an institutionalised setting it can have political implications beyond bilateral interdependence.

Research shows that economic integration decreases the opportunities to fight and enhances the opportunities to intervene in crisis. Mansfield & Pevehouse (2000, p. 776) present strong evidence that "the combination of PTA membership (preferential trading arrangements) and a high level of trade is quite likely to discourage belligerence."

Many PTAs have become venues for addressing political disputes between participants and fostering cooperation. Observers have widely acknowledged, for example, thatASEAN has helped to manage tensions in Southeast Asia. Mercado Comun del Sur (MERCOSUR) has done likewise, improving political-military relations throughout the southern cone. (Mansfield & Pevehouse, 2000, p. 781). The reciprocal nature of this system helps guarantee that economic concessions made by one state will be repaid, rather than exploited by its counterpart.

INTERNATIONAL INVESTMENT FLOWS

Another area to add to the existing literature on economic integration is the impact of militarized conflict on foreign investment. Bussman's (2010) contribution to the liberal notion that conflict inhibits foreign investment, complements the liberal peace arguments in conflict studies. Bussman's research shows that international conflict reduces international investment flows considerably. Bussman contends that "as with trade, foreign investment could be an important factor in promoting peace.

States might avoid violent conflict in order not to deter foreign investors." By ensuring political stability, states can thus create an environment that is desirable to foreign investors. It is therefore, in the best interest of states to keep away from belligerent behaviour as they could potentially miss out on the welfare gains associated with foreign investment.

THEORIES OF INTERNATIONAL POLITICAL ECONOMY

WHAT IS IPE?

This is the most basic aspect of the discipline. Those of you who study economics in the business school may be taught that there are no political influences on economics; however, in a Political Science class you will get a different perspective. From this perspective, politics has a great role in economic life and the study of IPE is the study of how politics influences economics relations within nations and between nations. When I say economic relations I mean the buying and selling of goods and services across borders, the flow of investment around the world, the wealth or poverty of regions and nations, and the ways in which economic power influences the political relationships among states (everything from alliances to war).

From the perspective of a political leader (imagine you are President or Prime Minister of a nation), you are concerned with two major issues:

1. What makes a nation wealthy? How can you design policies that make your nation wealthy or wealthier than it is now?
2. How can you design policies that spread that prosperity to your people? In theory you must do that to get reelected if you rule a democracy.

Or if you rule in an authoritarian state you need to spread the wealth to prevent yourself from being overthrown. Then again, you may just be trying to enrich yourself. So you hoard your own nation's wealth, keep your own people poor and eventually face a potential backlash by millions of impoverished people when they discover how you have plundered the nations resources and the people's work to make yourself wealthy.

From the perspective of scholars and political leaders alike, the first step in answering the above question is to answer the following questions:

- What is the proper role of government in economic activity?
- How much of a role should government play?
- Is deep involvement of the government they key to economic growth or is it the one thing that is sure to doom economic growth?
- To make a nation wealthy doe the government lead or get out of the way or lead in some areas while letting others flow naturally?

THE ROLE OF THEORY

Theories of international political economy provide different ways of answering the above questions. Theories show the different ways these questions have been answered by scholars and policy makers and also allows for an assessment of how well these theories work. Below I am going to describe four leading theories. They will provide a framework through which you can analyze everything you are reading.

We'll discuss three main bodies of theory: Economic Liberalism, Economic Nationalism, and Economic Structuralism. Economic Structuralism has two variants: Marxism and Dependency. Liberalism, Nationalism, and Dependency are capitalist theories. They all are based on the idea that creating wealth is the goal of economic activity. They differ on how that should be done. Marxism, however, is not a capitalist theory. Its argument is very different from the others: capitalism — the creation of wealth and accumulation of profit — is evil to Marxists.

One more thing about theory is important. Theories are models of how the world works. They are tools for analysis. You will find contradictions within the theories and aspects that don't make sense to you. That's good. The world is much more complex than any theory could ever illustrate, so be critical of theory and skeptical of theory.

Economic Liberalism

The theories of liberalism were stated best by Adam Smith in *The Wealth of Nations*, 1776. The key to national wealth and therefore national power is economic growth. The key to economic growth is free trade – the free flow of goods and services and investment across borders. Political leaders should allow trade between nations to expand and deepen and keep government intervention in that trade down to a minimum. This means that imports (products from other nations' companies that are sold in your nation) and exports (products from your nations' companies that you try to sell in other countries) should flourish with as little restriction as possible.

Liberals want the marketplace to make the economic decisions, not the government. This may not make sense yet, but it will further down the page. Just hold the thought for a moment.

Here's the problem as liberals see it. Governments have several tools they use to interfere or influence the flow of trade: tariffs, quotas, non-tariff barriers, and bans. Let's talk about tariffs first and explain their purpose. A tariff is a tax imposed by a government on a product as it crosses a border. So for instance a government might use a 10% tariff on all foreign shoes being sold in the US. This means that for the privilege of access to the US marketplace every foreign shoe company must pay the US government a 10% tariff. So if a pair of shoes cost $40, then $4 goes to the US government for every pair of shoes that enters the US. Generally, that means that a shoe that might have cost $40 without the tariff winds up costing you $44 when you try to buy it. Traditionally every government in the world places tariffs on every product that enters its marketplace. A 10% tariff is a low one.

So, let's analyze a fictitious market for chalk. Assume we live in State A. Now there's a company in Richmond (Richmond Chalk) that sells its chalk for $100 per box (great chalk!). There is also the Foreign Chalk Co. from State B – a foreign country) and it makes its chalk, ships it across the Pacific and into Richmond and sells it for $90 per box. The quality of the chalk is the same, but the price is different. Maybe Foreign Chalk Co. pays its workers less or has some new process technologies which make it cheaper to make chalk. Anyway, as a chalk consumer you will go down to Target or Wal-Mart and you will probably buy the $90 chalk from the Foreign Chalk Co. because you want to save $10. But there is a local congressman in Richmond. And he's worried that Richmond Chalk will go out of business because the Foreign Chalk Co. sells the same quality chalk for less money.

He wants to protect that local business from the foreign competition. There are 3,000 Richmond Chalk jobs that will be lost if Richmond Chalk goes out of business. The congressman may be blamed for it. But if he can somehow protect the home company from foreign competition, he gets the credit and gets reelected. So he lobbies the leaders of the House of Representatives and he tries to make some deals.

There's a big vote coming up. The President of the US wants to invade Iran and he asks for a congressional resolution in support of overthrowing the Iranian government. The Richmond congressman thinks it's a bad idea and is inclined to vote against it, but he then proposes a deal. He says: "Mr. President,

I will support the resolution calling for the overthrow of the Iranian government if you impose a 20% tariff on foreign chalk." The President says, "Done!"

Now, when you go to Target or Wal-Mart to buy chalk here are the prices: Richmond Chalk $100 per box and Foreign Chalk Company $108 per box ($90 per box, plus the 20% tariff — $18). Now which one will you buy? You'll buy Richmond Chalk and save $8 per box. Richmond jobs are saved. And they lived happily ever after.

Not according to liberals. Liberals see it differently. No one lives happily every after. Here's how liberals see it:

- You now pay $10 more for each box of chalk. Not only that, but Richmond Chalk may raise its prices to $105 a box and it will still be cheaper than the Foreign Chalk Co. chalk.
- Richmond Chalk has been rewarded for its inefficiency. It could not compete against the Foreign Chalk Co., but it is rewarded for that.
- The Foreign Chalk Co. is punished for being efficient. It was winning the competition, but it winds up getting punished through a political deal.
- Essentially, it's like this: Imagine a fast sprinter who wins every race. Someone decides it's unfair for him to win so many races because it makes the other sprinters sad, so we force that sprinter to wear ankle weights to slow him down. We make Michael Jordan use only one hand; we tell Jerry Rice he's only allowed to score one touchdown per game. We make Roger Clemons pitch from a lower pitcher's mound.

This burns liberals up. Ultimately liberals argue this: Without competition and winners and losers, you will not have economic growth; you will not have innovation; you will not have progress. If Foreign Chalk Co. is punished because it is winning, then why should it or any other company try to win? If Richmond Chalk is rewarded for losing, then why not continue to lose; save the effort and it will still be rewarded.

Here's what liberals want to happen. Richmond Chalk and Foreign Chalk compete. Foreign sells at $90; Richmond sells at $100. So Richmond can do several things. It can quit the chalk business and maybe go into erasers, or it can change the way it does things. Maybe it automates and makes the same amount of chalk with 20% fewer workers and it can sell for $88 per box. Maybe it simply cuts salaries to make it to $88 per box and the employees are happy because a pay cut is better than a layoff. So maybe Foreign Chalk responds by going to $87 a box and then Richmond Chalk goes to $85, then Foreign Chalk goes to $83 and Richmond goes to $82. Then they can't cut prices anymore so they try another tack. Maybe Richmond uses research and development and comes up with dustless chalk and colored chalk and maybe dry erase markers and sells them for over $100 per box.

In this situation you can get innovation and excellence and a cut in prices. Competition creates new ideas and new things for consumers. And here the consumer is king. Getting better products for lower prices is the goal. It doesn't sound like a big deal, but imagine we're talking about building safer cars or developing new medicines or better engines that reduce pollution or save travel time. Then competition starts to benefit people in a big way. Think of it this way: would we have cell phones and computers and new Windows operating systems every few years if the companies in the telecommunications and computer industries didn't feel the need to compete with each other for our business? Probably not.

Quotas do the same thing in a bit different way. Let's say that in the US there are 1 million boxes of chalk sold annually (I'm just making a number up; I have no idea how much chalk is sold in the US). The USgovernment might decide that of those 1million, only 100,000 can be boxes of chalk made outside the US. This saves Richmond Chalk's market share another way. Non-Tariff barriers are ways of keeping out foreign products through other means. For example, the US government could declare that foreign chalk has carcinogens in it or does not meet some new US-government standard imposed just to keep out foreign chalk. There are also outright bans – simply saying that a foreign product cannot be sold in the US.

Nations around the world do all of these things and liberals generally hate them because they impede economic growth; they discourage excellence and innovation; they make consumers pay more for inferior products.

What liberals want is this: all economic decisions should be made by the marketplace – the free market. Get the government out of foreign trade (and the domestic economy) as much as you can. Then winners and losers in the economy are not decided by the government, but by the market – the aggregate decisions of consumers, sometimes called the "invisible hand." What does this mean? People like Coke better than Pepsi. Who knows why, but they do. That's the market decided.

The sum of all the decisions made by consumers is the marketplace, the invisible hand. In this case the marketplace has decided that that it will buy more Coke than Pepsi. In 1985 Coke tried to change its formula – New Coke. The invisible hand slapped the company around. People wanted the old formula. Coke had to choose – go out of business or change back to the old formula. Coke changed back. Consumers won the argument. People don't buy plaid cars; people don't wear hats anymore to work; few people listen to jazz. Why? Who knows? The important thing here is that it is the decision of the consumers when you add up all their choices and that is the market and a free market creates growth and wealth. It creates growth and wealth because it gives the people what they want and forces companies to compete to find new ways of satisfying the needs of the people.

Liberals argue that along with innovation you get a division of labor. Everyone finds a niche to make a living. If you lose one competition, you move on to compete in a new arena. You specialize. So the US, with its huge amount of land and great soil, has the largest food companies in the world. Saudi Arabia has oil, so its companies produce oil. Japanese and South Korean companies go into shipbuilding. Chinese companies make inexpensive, labor intensive products because China has an abundance of people. This is called comparative advantage. You find your niche – what you can excel in — and you do it.

Multi-National Corporations (MNCs, sometimes called Transnational Corporations – TNCs)

The world now has a global marketplace. Much of what you will read is based on that idea. Within this global marketplace are MNCs – large corporations that operate all around the world. They are present everywhere. For example, you can buy a Coke in just about every place in the world. And little slimy McDonald's burgers infest just about every nation in the world. Exxon is everywhere. So are Toyota, Honda, British Petroleum, and General Motors. About 90% of the taxis in Shanghai, China are Volkswagens because VW has a plant there. The majority of taxis in Beijing, China are Hyundai's because Hyundai has a plant there. Hyundai is South Korean; VW is German. Also, this is not new. Shell Oil is not an American company; it's Dutch. Nestlé's is Swiss; Siemens is German. Bayer is German. And these companies have been in the US so long they are as American as French Fries!

More recently, there is something besides MNCs that runs the world economy. Products are losing their nationalities. Something you buy on a shelf or a showroom may have been made by five, ten, fifteen different companies based in five, ten, fifteen different nations. Companies from all over the world work together to produce a product. They don't care about where the company is based; they care about skills, quality, and cost. Look around your house or apartment and see where things were made. Call up Dell customer service and you are likely to be talking to someone in India. Much of the medical transcription business – the business of taking medical records dictated by a doctor and typing them up – is based in the Philippines. The doctor's office e-mails the audio file to the Philippines at the end of the work day. Overnight a Filipino company types them up and they are e-mailed back to the US for the start of the next business day.

Liberals think this is a good thing. MNCs spread wealth and technology and jobs around the world.

CLASSICAL LIBERALISM VS. MODERN LIBERALISM

Classical liberals have a tendency to believe that as long as the government doesn't interfere in the economy, everyone will live happily every after. They look at economic growth and identify something called "the business cycle."

The economy grows then contracts then grows then contracts then grows again in a series of booms and busts. The bottom arrow represents time.

This was the common belief until the Great Depression. The Great Depression was a global depression in which the world economy collapsed. It led to mass starvation and World War II among other things. Two ideas developed in response to the experience of the Depression.

1. Modern Liberalism – the belief that the business cycle is not always self- regulating. Sometimes a bust can be so bad it causes the economy to collapse. The solution is for the government to essentially jump start the economy by creating jobs and creating investment – putting money in people's pockets so they will begin to buy and sell products. This happened all over the world after the depression and in the US is known as the New Deal and was administered under FDR. It changed the way the US government and most nations' governments deal with economic issues. Now it is expected that the government will have some role in economic life to make sure that the economy keeps growing. It's usually tinkering, but it is now an expected part of life in the industrialized world. In the US it is accepted by both parties, no matter what their rhetoric. Republicans have a tendency to talk like Classical Liberals, but they won't get very far if they talk about doing away with Social Security, Medicare, Medicare, Unemployment Insurance, etc.

2. Faith in Free Trade — A belief that free trade and the expansion of free trade is the key to preventing another economic collapse. Before the Depression many nations responded to a slowdown in economic growth by placing restrictions on trade. Most economists believe that these restrictions on trade made a particular deep bust into a world wide economic catastrophe. Since then end of WW II the US has based its foreign policy on expanding free trade – doing away with tariffs, quotas, non-tariff barriers, and bans. This belief in free trade was one of the pillars of US policy in the Cold War. For reasons described below the USSR – a Marxist state – was against free trade. The US has worked very hard to create an international economic order based on liberal beliefs. The International Monetary Fund, the World Bank, the General Agreement on Tariffs and Trade, which gave way to the World Trade Organization, all have as their founding principal a belief in free trade. Globalization is the success of that liberal international economic order. The US has been able to write the rules and since the collapse of the USSR those rules are accepted by more and more of the globe.

Currently, the US is the leading liberal state in the world.

ECONOMIC NATIONALISM (SOMETIMES CALLED NEO-MERCANTILISM)

Economic nationalism developed theoretically as a criticism of liberalism. It is based on three basic ideas:

1. States compete economically. This is very different from liberalism. Liberals believe that companies compete economically, but states do not. Nationalists see companies as elements of a state's power. So Exxon, and Ford, and McDonalds's and Coke contribute to US power. Mitsubishi, and Honda, and Fuji contribute to Japanese power.
2. Free trade only benefits the wealthiest, most advanced nations. In head-to-head competition, which is what you get in free trade, only the advanced or "mature" industries will defeat less advanced or "infant" industries. Therefore free trade helps the rich get richer and the less advanced stay less advanced.
3. For the less advanced nations there needs to be an alternative way of getting rich. Free trade won't lead to riches.

Its main theorists are Alexander Hamilton, the first US Secretary of the Treasury, who wrote the *Report on the Subject of Manufactures* (1791) and Friedrich List, a Prussian economist who wrote *The National System of Political Economy* (1841).

Hamilton was writing at the early stages of US independence and his concern was how the US might structure its economy to make sure the US remained independent. He said this:

Industrial power = national power = independence.

Essentially, he argued that if the US wished to remain independent it had to become an industrial power. At this time Jefferson was arguing that the US would be better off as a nation of farmers. Hamilton felt that a nation of farmers would lose the next war with a European power because it could not produce manufactured goods – housing, clothing, particularly boots, and of course, weapons. So the US needed to end its dependency on the British economy for many of its manufactured items. The US needed to become self-sufficient so if the US and British had another war, the British would not win it by using an economic embargo against the US. Obviously, if the US cannot feed itself or make enough weapons without British help, the British could bully us. So to Hamilton, political independence from Britain required economic independence from Britain.

Hold that thought.

List lived in the US during the early days of US independence and read all of Hamilton's writings. He traveled back to his native Prussia and wrote about how Prussia could get out from under the economic dominance of Britain. Britain was the most economically advanced nation in the world at the time. List felt free trade was essentially a scam. It was a British trick to get everyone to move toward free trade in hopes of creating wealth, but instead only the British would prosper. Here is List's analysis of why the British would win. In a nutshell, the advanced economies would always win the economic competition against the less advanced economies. Imagine you are a consumer and you walk into Target or Wal-Mart or maybe it's an automobile showroom. Here's what you have a choice of:

Characteristic	Advanced Economy	Less Advanced Economy
Type of Industry	Mature industry	Infant industry
Product Cost	Low cost	High cost
Product Quality	High quality	Low quality

So how often do you walk into a store and say give me the most expensive piece of crap you have. In almost all cases, in head-to-head competition, the consumer chooses the product of the industry from the advanced economy, the low cost, high quality product. How does the industry from the less-advanced economy ever gain? To List, it can't, not under free trade.

To Hamilton and List then the answer was this.

1. Protect infant industries from foreign competition. Protectionism consists of using tariffs, quotas, non-tariff barriers, bans, whatever means possible to protect key industries.
2. Importantly, this does not mean ending trade with other nations. It means protecting industries that are identified as being crucial to national power. So Japan, for example, which has had nationalist economic policies since WW II, traded with the US, but has pushed US automobiles, US consumer electronics, and US telecommunications out of its market. This way Japan could build up its own industries in those areas. The US, a liberal nation, allowed Japanese companies to export to the US and the result has been that the US consumer electronics industry essentially died off due to Japan's success and the US has had to restrict sales of Japanese cars in the US in retaliation and to keep US auto makers from collapsing (Chrysler did collapse, but the US government, in a huge exception to its typical policies, bailed it out.). So to nationalists, this is evidence of the wisdom of their policies. It protected its industries from foreign competition and prospered, while the liberal US saw its industries founder. To liberals, you win some, you lose some. US companies should have been better prepared to face Japanese competition.
3. When the less advanced economy catches up to the advanced economy then it can open up to free trade and compete head-to-head as equals.

MNCs in the Nationalist View

MNCs are agents of national power. Foreign MNCs operating in your nation are competitors to your industries. They may weaken your nation and your industries. Keep them out or key sectors of your economy or they will hurt your economic development. The leading nationalist economies in the world are Japan, South Korea, France, and Germany. However, they are reforming their economies and becoming more liberal.

ECONOMIC STRUCTURALISM

The reason why Marxism and dependency are placed together under the heading of structuralism is that both are concerned with the international division of labor created by capitalism. Both theories see that division of labor as unfair, creating categories of rich and poor people and rich and poor nations. The Marxist approach is to reject capitalism completely. The Dependency approach is to reform it.

Marxism

Karl Marx and Friedrich Engels were two German economists who created a huge body of literature outlining a theoretical critique of capitalism. The developed these theories in the mid-19th century. The best place to look for details would be in *The Communist Manifesto* (1848) or *The German Ideology* (1845). There is so much on Marxism that this essay can only scratch the surface. Remember this is an ideology that spawned political movements and revolutions that shook the world for roughly 150 years. So, this will be the short version.

Marx and Engels examined advanced capitalist nations, particularly England and Prussia. These were nations in the midst of the industrial revolution – manufacturing was booming; people were working in factories; rapid urbanization had begun. To Marx and Engels this advanced capitalism divided people into several classes. For our purposes two classes are important: owners and workers, or rich and poor or haves and have-nots. Owners own everything, and have all the power, and all the money. Workers do all the work, and have no power, and no money. Marx and Engels hypothesized that one day the workers would realize that they were being exploited by the owners and rise up to overthrow the owners' control of society. This would include overthrowing the government of the country because the government's main purpose was to enforce owner control of society. Marx and Engels felt that this revolution – workers' revolution or proletarian revolution – was a natural phenomenon, something that would occur naturally in any nation that reached an advanced capitalist stage. So they predicted it would happen first in England or Prussia and would not happen in more agricultural societies such as France or Russia until much later in those nations' histories.

After the revolution, the theory gets a bit uncertain. There would be several phases of evolution until the development of Communism, a society which would have these characteristics:

- A system in which there is no private property; all property is owned by everyone and everyone shares
- There is no exploitation since workers are the owners
- Everyone gets what they need from the society as a whole
- Everyone contributes based on what they can contribute

- Capitalist ideas such as the idea that people work to gain reward are outmoded; people work to contribute and do not care if there is no relationship between what they give to society and what they receive in return. So a young healthy person who works like an ox, but has no family, contributes a great deal to society, but receives very little. The lazy person with a large family receives a great deal even though he/she contributes little.

We'll get to what happened after the revolution in reality in just a minute.

The next big theorist was Lenin, a Russian intellectual. He wrote *Imperialism* in 1917 and in it he developed a theory that applied Marxism to international affairs. Essentially, he said wealthy capitalist nations exploit poor nations. They force people into slave labor; they steal resources; they dominate and impoverish these nations. He was talking about imperialism or colonialism. At this point in world history European nations had control of just about the entire rest of the world. Almost everything but the Western hemisphere was under European control. Lenin said that the poor nations would one day overthrow their colonial masters, reject capitalism because of its linkage to colonialism, and develop Communist societies.

Lenin also said, in other works and through his deeds, that the workers revolution can be created by a clever and committed leadership. Nations don't have to wait for the revolution to happen naturally. A vanguard of the revolution can begin the revolution in any nation. Lenin did just that. In 1917 his Bolshevik movement seized power in Russia and led the first Marxist revolution. In 1949 Mao Zedong led the second big Marxist revolution. Dozens of nations followed their examples from the 1940s to the 1970s. This was the Communist or Soviet Bloc during the Cold War.

Now what were these nations like? What was Marxism like when actually put into practice in the USSR and the People's Republic of China?

- Marx and Engels thought that after the revolution the government would wither away. Once having created the proper economic relationships, a government would not be necessary. However, in every Marxist state, the government became more powerful; power became more centralized; and the nation was ruled by one person or a handful of dictators, who ruled in a totalitarian manner through a Communist Party apparatus that penetrated every aspect of the society. The goal was total control over every individual. Their word was law and you risked your life if you questioned that word – imprisonment, torture, execution of the person who challenged the government his/her friends and family. It was not unusual for a dissident (someone who challenges the totalitarian state) to wind up in prison, his wife may end up being given to a Communist party leader to do with as he pleased, and their children would be given to a Communist Party leader's family that didn't have children.

- In all these nations the revolution was rammed down the peoples' throats. Those who disagreed were considered enemies of the state. In Russia, Lenin killed millions who opposed the revolution. He would have been seen as a huge mass murderer except his successor, Stalin, killed more. Roughly 20 million people were killed by Stalin's regime from the 1920s to the early 1950s because they opposed his government and/or its policies. Mao in China was worse. The number of deaths may be as high as 100 million from 1949 to 1976, many from starvation; many from execution, torture, and the long-term effects of imprisonment.
- Ideological purity was a necessity to the leaders. One party was allowed to exist and any ideas not approved by the Communist Party were treasonous. People were executed for thinking the wrong thing. So in most Marxist states, the government tried to control what people thought.
- Economically these nations closed themselves off to trade with other nations. There were no economic freedoms. Every aspect of economic life was controlled by the government, decided by the government, regulated by the government. These economies are called command economies and every single one, even those that may have prospered for a bit, ran itself into the ground – people became poorer than they were before; the states became technologically backward; and many had severe problems even feeding their people. China, Russia, Viet Nam, North Korea, Ethiopia all had famines.
- Importantly, Marx and Engels never said: Kill everyone who disagrees with you. Marxism as implemented was very different from Marxism the theory. The vagueness and paradoxes of Marxist theory were interpreted by dictators to mean absolute power, death, and destruction. That doesn't necessarily mean that Marxism would have worked if its implementation hadn't been accompanied by dictatorship and slaughter. Marxism does give huge amounts of power to revolutionary leaders and that much power usually leads to corruption at best and carnage at its most typical. Also Marxism considers human nature to be one in which people will be willing to share in ways that are counterintuitive — where the person who works extremely hard is willing to receive less and willing to allow the person who doesn't work hard to receive much more if it is judged that he needs more. Capitalism is based on a less optimistic version of human nature – people will only work hard if they are rewarded. It's not pretty, but as we'll see in the class no communist system has ever sustained economic growth for more than a generation. In fact, all command economies have led to economic collapse. Currently, one of the last

communist command economies is North Korea, a nation where roughly 5 million people starved to death in the 1990s. South Korea has a capitalist economy and has accepted globalization. It has a growing economy and corporations that are building factories in Europe to find cheaper labor.

Dependency

Dependency also argues that the rich nations exploit the poor nations. But this is not because capitalism is evil. It is because capitalism needs to be more regulated so it will be more just. The problem is that poor nations remain dependent on rich nations. Even after colonialism, when the poor nations became free, their economies remained dependent on the economies and the technology of the rich nations.

Dependency theorists see the world divided into two types of nations that have a clear division of labor: Characteristics Economically Developed Countries – EDCs (the Rich) Less Developed Countries – LDCs (the Poor) Who? North America, Western Europe,Northeast Asia (Japan, South Korea, Taiwan) Asia (except North East Asia),Africa, Middle East, Latin America Producing what? High tech goods, industrial products: cars, machine tools, planes, computers, chemicals, electronics Primary products, commodities, things you grow or extract from the ground: bananas, coffee, minerals, rubber, timber What kinds of jobs are created? High skills, high wage jobs creating a middle class society Low skills, low wage jobs, which create a society with a small wealthy elite (who own the land) and huge class of people on the edge of poverty or living in poverty (people who work the land). A small middle class exists.

The problem is this. What the LDCs produce is cheap. Minerals and farm products make landowners rich, but not the people who work the land and not the nations who rely on the land for its source of wealth. Even oil, the best of the primary products, because it can lead to wealth, is often seen as a curse. Nations who produce oil have a tendency to rely on it for their revenue and never develop a manufacturing base and it is a manufacturing base and the high skills and high wages that go along with it that make a nation wealthy. EDCs produce the manufactured goods then the LDCs and the EDCs trade. LDCs buy expensive things from the EDCs and the EDCs buy inexpensive things from the LDCs. The result is that the EDCs make money and the LDCs go into debt because they are paying more for the expensive products (aircraft, computer software, cars, or health care technology) than they are receiving for their coffee and bananas and oil. So the rich get richer, the poor get poorer.

Dependency theorists call for a number of solutions:

- International rules that raise the price of commodities (oil, coffee, bananas, timber, copper) regardless of market forces. EDCs refused to do this.

- Massive amount of aid to poor nations. Most EDCs refused to do this.
- Debt forgiveness. EDCs have agreed, but it doesn't fix the problem because as soon as the old debt is forgiven, new debt accumulates.
- Nationalization. Government seizure of the MNCs of the EDCs that operate in the LDCs. The profit of the home-controlled MNCs is used to enrich the nation. But the EDCs don't like this and often retaliate with trade embargoes and even attempts to overthrow the government that does this. During the Cold War the US would label such governments as communist (some of them were) and tried to overthrow the government.
- Import Substitution: Banning the import of foreign manufactured goods from EDCs (like computers and cars) and forcing the nation to make its own. EDCs might retaliate with trade sanctions.

In the long run, none of these strategies have worked.

MNCS IN STRUCTURAL THOUGHT

As you may have guessed, neither Marxists nor dependency theorists are fond of MNCs. They are seen as the way rich nations exploit or dominate poor nations.

GLOBALIZATION

Globalization needs to be seen in a historical context. When WW II ended in 1945 a new era began. The Cold War was a struggle between the US and its allies vs. the USSR (Soviet Union) and its allies. From an economic standpoint, it was Liberal and Nationalist economies vs. Marxist economies or relatively free traders vs. economies closed off to trade. Countries all over the world chose one or the other, in what people called a bipolar world. Nations were seen as either communists allied with the USSR and using command economies or allies of the US with capitalist economies.

It was never that simple and there were some big exceptions to this from time to time (India was a Democracy with a command economy – no dictators bringing the deaths of thousands, but a really crappy economy; China became an exception after 1972 when its rivalry with the USSR led it to establish ties to the US – the far enemy in this case was less dangerous than the near one and both the US and China had one thing in common; they were both sure that the spread of Soviet power was against their interests).

The economic struggle was one over how best to organize economic life: should nations choose capitalism or communism. The capitalist world, by the 1980s had economic growth and a technological, telecommunications, and information revolution, all the changes and benefits that computers brought – an economic revolution as important as the agricultural and industrial revolutions. The communist world missed the boat. Why would anyone develop computers since there was no reward for innovation and no incentives for research and development except fear that your lack of innovative ideas may lead you to prison? The computer revolution never hit the communist world. Many people think that fact is the best explanation for the end of the Cold War. The economic ideas of the capitalist world proved to be better.

The capitalist world generated wealth and innovation and the communist world just generated shortages of everything and a lack of productive ideas. Nation after nation, beginning with China in 1978, abandoned command economies for some level of capitalism. By 1986 the Soviets began to move toward capitalism. By 1991 the Soviet Union collapsed. The cold war ended and little by little everyone moved toward capitalism and a capitalism that grows more liberal every year.

Along with that development was another one. Ultimately, the only thing that has worked to bring wealth to poor nations has been to open up their economies to foreign investment, to become more liberal, but retain elements of nationalism in certain sectors. It is called globalization and it has led to the greatest wealth creation in world history.

It is the method pursued by the Four Tigers (South Korea, Taiwan, Singapore, and Hong Kong – the only four economies to go from poor to rich since WW II). It is the strategy pursued by China since 1978. China is the world's fastest growing economy. India has been following this since 1991 and it has the best economic performance in its history. It is a strategy used by most nations in the world and has lead to huge wealth and job creation. There are some exceptions:

- Socialist/Communist states that have not reformed: North Korea, Viet Nam, Cuba
- Oil states that still have command economies based on oil production (just about every nation in the Middle East)
- States flirting with Dependency remedies (Venezuela, Bolivia)

But all these economies are doing poorly, much worse than the economies that have embraced globalization. During the cold war, the issue was whether a free market or a command economy was better. The answer to that seems definitive – free markets work much better.

They prospered while the command economies collapsed. That may have answered the first question that this essay posed: How does a nation generate wealth? The second question is still at issue: What is the proper role of government in economic activity? It seems clear that almost all governments in the world have decided that the government should not control the economy. But how much regulation or intervention is the right amount? That question is at issue throughout the world.

Having said all that, however, does not mean that everyone believes that globalization is the greatest thing in world history and the answer to all our problems. Some say yes; some say no. The readings in the class will debate that issue, but here are some questions:

- Does globalization benefit everyone or just the richest?
- Does globalization sacrifice the environment?
- Does globalization prevent or encourage higher wages and enforceable labor standards?
- Globalization may make everyone a little richer, but does it make the rich even more rich than everyone else?
- Does globalization help or hurt the poorest of the poor?
- Can we develop a smarter globalization?
- If you tried to stop globalization, how would you do it and what would be the consequences?
- For all of its flaws is there a better way to spread wealth or feed and clothe people or provide people opportunities to make their lives better or discover and invent new technologies that change the world or guarantee basic freedoms? In other words, what are the alternatives?
- You may find that globalization is like democracy. To paraphrase Churchill, globalization may the worst system imaginable, except for all the others. You may find that globalization is simply reality. It's what happens when people are free. So how do we make it work for everyone?

These are some of the questions this class will address.

8

Political Economic Systems and the State

COMPARATIVE POLITICAL AND ECONOMIC SYSTEMS

Is there such a thing as a perfect government? One "answer" was the utopian society established by the Shakers. In order to make their society perfect, the Shakers adhered to a strict policy of communal living, religious devotion, (pictured above in their distinctively animated form of worship) celibacy, rigorous labor, and equality.

The last two decades of the 20th century were great for democratic governments. The Cold War ended with the collapse of communist dictatorships throughout Eastern Europe, including the Soviet Union itself. South Korea and Taiwan moved out of their authoritarian pasts toward greater democracy. Apartheid was ended in South Africa.

But democracy is still not the only form of government in the world today. Despite differences in form and function, most of the world's governments still try to fulfill similar primary objectives.

PURPOSES OF POLITICAL SYSTEMS

A government can use propaganda to reinforce its image as defender of the nation. This American poster from World War II shows how scare tactics can drum up support (as well as fresh recruits) for the military.

Most governments are designed to provide their inhabitants with two important services: protection from outside invasion and protection of citizens from one another. How many different ways can a government protect from invasions? They can form large armies and navies, build fortified cities, provide border patrols, negotiate with potential enemies, threaten or punish "rogue" states, or join international organizations.

The list goes on and on. It makes sense, then, that every country has its own way of accomplishing these basic needs. Of course, some are more successful than others. But some similarities between governments will surely exist as well. For example, more than one country has thought to build strong armies and navies.

Likewise, try to think of different ways that countries can protect citizens from one another. Some commonalties will surely appear — police forces, crime prevention, putting criminals in jail, passing laws that define what is a crime and what is not. Again, governments have different ways to accomplish this end. Some allow more individual freedoms than others, some will have national police forces, and others will organize protection on the local level. As modern governments have taken on more responsibilities, such as regulating the economy and providing social services, the possibilities for different government structures and functions increase.

PURPOSES OF ECONOMIC SYSTEMS

Economic systems provide needs for citizens by answering several questions:

- What resources does the country have, and what can be produced from them?
- How should goods and services be produced from the available resources?
- How are goods and services distributed among the inhabitants?

Different economic systems around the world answer these questions in different ways.The resources of an economic system are called factors of production because the economy needs them to produce goods and services. They may be grouped into four categories: Governments must consider how their citizens use (and replenish) natural resources. Forests, for example, are being depleted at an alarming rate because of human activities like logging. But which is more important: wildlife, or the thousands of families that depend on the income that the logging industry provides?

- Land. This category includes all natural resources, such as soil, water, air, and minerals.
- Labor. Every economy needs human resources — people who produce goods and services.
- Capital. Capital includes money, factories, heavy machinery — anything used to produce products and goods.
- Management. Managers organize and direct the other three factors of production.

The world at the turn of the 21st century was becoming smaller, as global interconnections made distant places seem close. At the same time, bloody nationalist conflicts turning neighbor against neighbor still raged. Government leaders around the world examined their own systems and each others to chart a course for the new millennium.

COMPARING GOVERNMENTS

However, it is possible to examine the similarities and differences among political and economic systems and categorize different forms of government.

One simple way to categorize governments is to divide them into démocratic and authoritarian political systems.

DEMOCRACIES

Many countries today claim to be democracies, but if the citizens are not involved in government and politics, they are democratic in name only. Some governments are more democratic than others, but systems cannot be considered truly democratic unless the meet certain criteria: Whither democracy? It was not until 1920 — after decades of tireless protest and campaigning — that women were granted suffrage by the ratification of the 19th Amendment.

- Freedom of speech, the press, and religion. Democracies in general respect these basic individual liberties. No government allows absolute freedom, but democracies do not heavily censor newspapers and public expression of opinions.
- Majority rule with minority rights. In democracies, people usually accept decisions made by the majority of voters in a free election. However, democracies try to avoid the "tyranny of the majority" by providing ways for minorities all kinds to have their voices heard as well.
- Varied personal backgrounds of political leaders. Democracies usually leave room for many different types of citizens to compete for leadership positions. In other words, presidents and legislators do not all come from a few elite families, the same part of the country, or the same social class.
- Free, competitive elections. The presence of elections alone is not enough to call a country a democracy. The elections must be fair and competitive, and the government or political leaders cannot control the results. Voters must have real choices among candidates who run for public office.
- Rule by law. Democracies are not controlled by the whims of a leader, but they are governed by laws that apply to leaders and citizens equally.
- Meaningful political participation by citizens. By itself, a citizen's right to vote is not a good measure of democracy. The government must respond in some way to citizen demands. If they vote, the candidate they choose must actually take office. If they contact government in other ways — writing, protesting, phoning — officials must respond.

The degree to which a government fulfills these criteria is the degree to which it can be considered democratic. Examples of such governments include Great Britain, France, Japan, and the United States.

AUTHORITARIAN REGIMES

Mao Zedong's position as authoritarian ruler of the People's Republic of China is glorified in this propaganda poster from the Cultural Revolution. The poster reads: "The light of Mao Zedong Thought illuminates the path of the Great Cultural Revolution of the Proletariat."

One ruler or a small group of leaders have the real power in authoritarian political systems. Authoritarian governments may hold elections and they may have contact with their citizens, but citizens do not have any voice in how they are ruled. Their leaders do not give their subjects free choice. Instead, they decide what the people can or cannot have. Citizens, then, are subjects who must obey, and not participants in government decisions. Kings, military leaders, emperors, a small group of aristocrats, dictators, and even presidents or prime ministers may rule authoritarian governments. The leader's title does not automatically indicate a particular type of government.

Authoritarian systems do not allow freedoms of speech, press, and religion, and they do not follow majority rule nor protect minority rights. Their leaders often come from one small group, such as top military officials, or from a small group of aristocratic families. Examples of such regimes include China, Myanmar, Cuba, and Iran.

No nation falls entirely into either category. It also dangerous to categorize a nation simply by the moment in time during which they were examined. The Russia of 1992 was very different from the Russia of 1990. Both democratic and authoritarian governments change over time, rendering the global mosaic uncertain and complex.

COMPARING ECONOMIC SYSTEMS

Karl Marx and Friedrich Engels turned the world upside down.

Until the publication of their 1848*Communist Manifesto*, much of the western world followed a course where individuals owned private property, business enterprises, and the profits that resulted from wise investments. Marx and Engels pointed out the uneven distribution of wealth in the capitalist world and predicted a worldwide popular uprising to distribute wealth evenly. Ever since, nations have wrestled with which direction to turn their economies.

Capitalism

- Capitalism is based on private ownership of the means of production and on individual economic freedom. Most of the means of production, such as factories and businesses, are owned by private individuals and not by the government. Private owners make decisions about what and when to produce and how much products should cost. Other characteristics of capitalism include the following:
- Free competition. The basic rule of capitalism is that people should compete freely without interference from government or any other outside force. Capitalism assumes that the most deserving person will usually win. In theory, prices will be kept as low as possible because consumers will seek the best product for the least amount of money.

The antitrust lawsuit against Microsoft is one way that the government has tried to promote competition. Supporters of Microsoft say that forcing Microsoft to allow companies to bundle arch-rival Netscape's web browser with Microsoft Windows is not unlike making Coca-Cola include a can of Pepsi in each six-pack it sells.

- Supply and demand. In a capitalist system prices are determined by how many products there are and how many people want them. When supplies increase, prices tend to drop. If prices drop, demand usually increases until supplies run out. Then prices will rise once more, but only as long as demand is high. These laws of supply and demand work in a cycle to control prices and keep them from getting too high or too low.

COMMUNISM

Karl Marx, the 19th century father of communism, was outraged by the growing gap between rich and poor. He saw capitalism as an outmoded economic system that exploited workers, which would eventually rise against the rich because the poor were so unfairly treated. Marx thought that the economic system of communism would replace capitalism. Communism is based on principles meant to correct the problems caused by capitalism. The most important principle of communism is that no private ownership of property should be allowed. Marx believed that private ownership encouraged greed and motivated people to knock out the competition, no matter what the consequences. Property should be shared, and the people should ultimately control the economy. The government should exercise the control in the name of the people, at least in the transition between capitalism and communism. The goals are to eliminate the gap between the rich and poor and bring about economic equality.

SOCIALISM

Socialism, like communism, calls for putting the major means of production in the hands of the people, either directly or through the government. Socialism also believes that wealth and income should be shared more equally among people. Socialists differ from communists in that they do not believe that the workers will overthrow capitalists suddenly and violently. Nor do they believe that all private property should be eliminated. Their main goal is to narrow, not totally eliminate, the gap between the rich and the poor. The government, they say, has a responsibility to redistribute wealth to make society more fair and just. There is no purely capitalist or communist economy in the world today. The capitalist United States has a Social Security system and a government-owned postal service. Communist China now allows its citizens to keep some of the profits they earn. These categories are models designed to shed greater light on differing economic systems.

ECONOMIC SYSTEM

An economic system is a system of production and exchange of goods and services as well as allocation of resources in a society. It includes the combination of the various institutions, agencies, entities (or even sectors as described by some authors) and consumers that comprise the economic structure of a given community. A related concept is the mode of production.

The study of economic systems includes how these various agencies and institutions are linked to one another, how information flows between them, and the social relations within the system (including property rights and the structure of management).

Among existing economic systems, distinctive methods of analysis have developed, such as socialist economics and Islamic economic jurisprudence. Today the dominant form of economic organization at the global level is based on market-oriented mixed economies.

Economic systems is the category in the *Journal of Economic Literature* classification codes that includes the study of such systems. One field that cuts across them is comparative economic systems. Subcategories of different systems there include:

- Planning, coordination, and reform
- Productive enterprises; factor and product markets; prices; population
- Public economics; financial economics
- National income, product, and expenditure; money; inflation
- International trade, finance, investment, and aid
- Consumer economics; welfare and poverty
- Performance and prospects
- Natural resources; energy; environment; regional studies
- Political economy; legal institutions; property rights.

COMPONENTS

There are multiple components to economic systems. Decision-making structures of an economy determine the use of economic inputs (the factors of production), distribution of output, the level of centralization in decision-making, and who makes these decisions. Decisions might be carried out by industrial councils, by a government agency, or by private owners.

In one view, every economic system represents an attempt to solve three fundamental and interdependent problems:

- What goods and services shall be produced, and in what quantities?
- How shall goods and services be produced? That is, by whom and with what resources and technologies?
- For whom shall goods and services be produced? That is, who is to enjoy the benefits of the goods and services and how is the total product to be distributed among individuals and groups in the society?

Thus every economy is a system that allocates resources for exchange, production, distribution and consumption. The system is stabilized through a combination of threat and trust, which are the outcome of institutional arrangements. An economic system possesses the following institutions:

- Methods of control over the factors or means of production: this may include ownership of, or property rights to, the means of production and therefore may give rise to claims to the proceeds from production. The means of production may be owned privately, by the state, by those who use them or be held in common.
- A decision-making system: this determines who is eligible to make decisions over economic activities. Economic agents with decision-making powers can enter into binding contracts with one another.
- A coordination mechanism: this determines how information is obtained and used in decision-making. The two dominant forms of coordination are planning and markets; planning can be either decentralized or centralized, and the two coordination mechanisms are not mutually exclusive and often co-exist.
- An incentive system: this induces and motivates economic agents to engage in productive activities. It can be based on either material reward (compensation or self-interest) or moral suasion (for instance, social prestige or through a democratic decision-making process that binds those involved). The incentive system may encourage specialization and the division of labour.
- Organizational form: there are two basic forms of organization: actors and regulators. Economic actors include households, work gangs and production teams, firms, joint-ventures and cartels. Economically regulative organizations are represented by the state and market authorities; the latter may be private or public entities.
- A distribution system: this allocates the proceeds from productive activity, which is distributed as income among the economic organizations, individuals and groups within society, such as property owners, workers and non-workers, or the state (from taxes).
- A public choice mechanism for law-making, establishing rules, norms and standards and levying taxes. Usually this is the responsibility of the state but other means of collective decision-making are possible, such as chambers of commerce or workers' councils.

TYPES

There are several basic questions that must be answered in order for an economy to run satisfactorily. The scarcity problem, for example, requires answers to basic questions, such as: *what* to produce, *how* to produce it, and *who*gets what is produced. An economic system is a way of answering these basic questions, and different economic systems answer them differently. Many different objectives may be seen as desirable for an economy, like efficiency,growth, liberty, and equality.

In a capitalist economic system (capitalism) production is carried out for private profit, decisions regarding investment and the use of the means of production are determined by individuals, corporations and business owners in the marketplace. The means of production are owned primarily by private enterprises and decisions regarding production and investment determined by private owners in capital markets. Capitalist systems range from laissez-faire, with minimal government regulation and state enterprise, to regulated and social market systems, with the stated aim of ensuring "social justice" and a more equitable distribution of wealth or ameliorating market failures.

In socialist economic system (socialism), production is carried out to fulfill planned-economy objectives; decisions regarding the use of the means of production are adjusted to satisfy state-conceived economic demand, investment is carried out through state-guided mechanisms. The means of production are either publicly owned, or are owned by the workers cooperatively. A socialist economic system that is based on the process of capital accumulation, but seeks to control or direct that process through state ownership or cooperative control to ensure stability, equality or expand decision-making power, are market socialist systems.

The basic and general economic systems are:

- Market economy ("hands off" systems, such as laissez-faire capitalism)
- Mixed economy (a hybrid that blends some aspects of both market and planned economies)
- Planned economy ("hands on" systems, such as state socialism or communism, also known as "command economy")
- Traditional economy (a generic term for older economic systems)
- Participatory economics (a system where the production and distribution of goods is guided by public participation)
- Gift economy (where an exchange is made without any explicit agreement for immediate or future rewards)
- Barter economy (where goods and services are directly exchanged for other goods or services)

Anarchist and libertarian economies

Various strains of anarchism advocate different economy systems, all of which have very small or no government involvement. These include:

- Anarcho-capitalism
- Anarcho-communism

Libertarianism also advocates a minimal role for government, including economic systems like:

- Libertarian communism
- Libertarian socialism
- Syndicalism

Capitalism

Capitalism generally features the private ownership of the means of production (capital), and a market economy for coordination. Corporate capitalism refers to a capitalist nathan characterized by the dominance of hierarchical, bureaucratic corporations.

Mercantilism was the dominant model in Western Europe from the 16th to 18th century. This encouraged imperialism and colonialism until economic and political changes resulted in global decolonization. Modern capitalism has favored free trade to take advantages of increased efficiencies due to national comparative advantage and economies of scale in a larger, more universal market.

Some critics have applied the term neo-colonialism to the power imbalance between multi-national corporations operating in a free market vs. seemingly impoverished people in developing countries.

Mixed Economy

There is no precise definition of a "mixed economy". Theoretically, it may refer to an economic system that combines one of three characteristics: public and private ownership of industry, market-based allocation with economic planning, or free-markets with state interventionism.

In practice, "mixed economy" generally refers to market economies with substantial state interventionism and/or sizable public sector alongside a dominant private sector.

Actual mixed economies gravitate more heavily to one end of the spectrum. Notable economic models and theories that have been described as a "mixed economy" include:

- Georgism - socialized rents on land
- Mixed economy
- American School
- Dirigisme
- Nordic model
- Japanese system
- Social market economy also known as *Soziale Marktwirtschaft*
- Social corporatism
- Socialist market economy
- Progressive utilization theory
- Indicative planning also known as a planned market economy
- State capitalism

Socialism

Socialist economic systems (all of which feature social ownership of the means of production) can be subdivided by their coordinating mechanism (planning and markets) intoplanned socialist and market socialist systems. Additionally, socialism can be divided based on their property structures between those that are based on public ownership, worker or consumer cooperatives and common ownership (i.e., non-ownership). Communism is a hypothetical stage of Socialist development articulated by Marx as "second stage Socialism" in Critique of the Gotha Programme, whereby economic output is distributed based on need and not simply on the basis of labor contribution.

The original conception of socialism involved the substitution of money as a unit of calculation and monetary prices as a whole with calculation in kind (or valuation based on natural units), with business and financial decisions replaced by engineering and technical criteria for managing the economy. Fundamentally, this meant that socialism would operate under different economic dynamics than those of capitalism and the price system. Later models of socialism developed by neoclassical economists (most notablyOskar Lange and Abba Lerner) were based on thc use of notional prices derived from a trial-and-error approach to achieve market clearing prices on the part of a planning agency. These models of socialism were called "market socialism" because they included a role for markets, money and prices.

The primary emphasis of socialist planned economies is to coordinate production is to produce economic output to directly satisfy economic demand as opposed to the indirect mechanism of the profit system where satisfying needs is subordinate to the pursuit of profit; to advance the productive forces of the economy in a more efficient manner while being immune to the perceived systemic inefficiencies (cyclical processes) and crisis of overproduction so that production would be subject to the needs of society as opposed to being ordered around capital accumulation.

In a pure socialist planned economy that involves different processes of resource allocation, production and means of quantifying value, the use of money would be replaced with a different measure of value and accounting tool that would embody more accurate information about an object or resource.

In practice, the economic system of the former Soviet Union and Eastern bloc operated as a command economy, featuring a combination of state owned enterprises and central planning using the material balances method. The extent to which these economic systems achieved socialism or represented a viable alternative to capitalism is subject to debate.

In orthodox Marxism, the mode of production is tantamount to the subject of this article, determining with a superstructure of relations the entirety of a given culture or stage of human development.

Other Aspects

Corporatism refers to economic tripartite involving negotiations between business, labor, and state interest groups to establish economic policy, or more generally to assigning people to political groups based on their occupational affiliation.

Certain subsets of an economy, or the particular goods, services, techniques of production, or moral rules can also be described as an "economy". For example, some terms emphasize specific sectors or externalizes:

- Digital economy
- Green economy
- Information economy
- Internet economy
- Knowledge economy
- Natural economy
- Virtual economy
- Circular economy

Others emphasize a particular religion:

- Arthashastra - Hindu Economics
- Buddhist economics
- Islamic economics
- Distributism - Catholic ideal of a "third way" economy, featuring more distributed ownership in a mixed economy

EVOLUTIONARY ECONOMICS

Karl Marx's theory of economic development was based on the premise of evolving economic systems; specifically, in his view, over the course of history superior economic systems would replace inferior ones. "Inferior" systems were beset by "internal contradictions" and "inefficiencies" that make them "impossible" to survive over the long term.

In Marx's scheme, feudalism was replaced by capitalism, which would eventually be superseded by socialism. Joseph Schumpeter had an evolutionary conception of economic development, but unlike Marx, he de-emphasized the role of class struggle in contributing to qualitative change in the economic mode of production. In subsequent world history,Communist states run according to Marxist-Leninist ideologies have either collapsed or gradually reformed their centrally-planned economies toward market-based economies, for example with perestroika and the dissolution of the Soviet Union, Chinese economic reform, and Vietnam.

Mainstream evolutionary economics continues to study economic change in modern times. There has also been renewed interest in understanding economic systems as evolutionary systems in the emerging field of Complexity economics.

CONTEXT IN SOCIETY

An economic system can be considered a part of the social system and hierarchically equal to the law system, political system, cultural, etc. There is often a strong correlation between certain ideologies, political systems and certain economic systems (for example, consider the meanings of the term "communism"). Many economic systems overlap each other in various areas (for example, the term "mixed economy" can be argued to include elements from various systems). There are also various mutually exclusive hierarchical categorizations.

PREDOMINANT ECONOMIC SYSTEMS

The two predominant economic systems today are capitalism and socialism. Between these two opposite extremes lies a continuum of variations on the models.

CAPITALISM

Three key principles define the economic system of capitalism:

- Private ownership of production and distribution of goods and services
- Competition, or the laws of supply and demand directing the economy
- Profit- seeking, or selling goods and services for more than their cost of production

Laissez- faire (French for "hands off") capitalism represents a pure form of capitalism not practiced by any nation today. The ideology driving today's capitalism says that competition is in the best interest of consumers. Companies in competition for profit will make better products cheaper and faster to gain a larger share of the market. In this system, the market—what people buy and the laws of supply and demand—dictates what companies make, and how much of it they make. Workers are motivated to work harder so they can afford more of the products they want.

Supporters of a capitalist system point to the higher production, greater wealth, and higher standard of living displayed by capitalist countries such as the United States. Critics, however, charge that while the standard of living may be higher, greater social inequity remains. They also denounce greed, exploitation, and high concentration of wealth and power held by a few.

SOCIALISM

Three key principles also define the economic system of socialism:

- State ownership of production and distribution of goods and services
- Centraleconomy
- Production without profit

The ideology of socialism directly rejects the ideology of capitalism. In a socialist economic system, the state determines what to produce and at what price to sell it. Socialism eliminates competition and profit, and focuses upon social equality—supplying people with what they need, whether or not they can pay. The ideals driving socialism come from Karl Marx who saw all profit as money taken away from workers.

He reasoned that the labor used to produce a product determined the value of that product. The only way for a company to arrive at profit is to pay workers less than the value of the product. Thus, wherever profit exists, workers are not receiving the true value of their labor.

Just as nations do not adhere to pure capitalism, neither do nations adhere to pure socialism. In pure socialism, all workers would earn exactly the same wage. Most Socialist countries do pay managers and professionals such as doctors a higher wage. But, because the state employs all members of the society, thereby controlling the wages, far less disparity exists between highest and lowest wage earners.

Supporters of socialism, then, point to its success at achieving social equality and full employment. Critics counter that with central planning's gross inefficiency, the economy cannot produce wealth and all people are poorer. They also object to what they see as unnecessary control of personal lives and limited rights—exploitation.

DEMOCRATIC SOCIALISM AND STATE CAPITALISM

Ironically, critics of both capitalism and socialism accuse each system of exploitation. Consequently, some nations have carved out systems more in the middle of the continuum between the two.

One hybrid is democratic socialism, which is an economic system where the government maintains strict economic controls while maintaining personal freedom. Scandinavian nations, Canada, England, and Italy all practice democratic socialism. Sweden provides the most common example in which high taxation provides extensive social programmes.

State capitalism is another economic hybrid. In this economic system, large corporations work closely with the government, and the government protects their interests with import restrictions, investment capital, and other assistance. This economic system commonly exists in Asian countries such as Japan and South Korea.

FASCISM IS A CURRENT POLITICAL AND ECONOMIC SYSTEM

Lew Rockwell offers us in *Fascism vs. Capitalism* a provocative and insightful diagnosis of the political and economic ills of our time. The situation that we face, he says, is dire; but, fortunately, he does not leave us without remedy. To the contrary, the wisdom of Mises, Rothbard, and their colleagues in the Austrian School offers the means to rescue us, and the inspiring leadership of Ron Paul shows us the way to put their ideas into practice.

As the book's title suggests, Rockwell finds "fascism" to be the key concept needed to analyze the modern American era. He is quick to deflect an objection:

"Fascism" has become a term of general derision and rebuke. It is tossed casually in the direction of anything a critic happens to dislike. ... But fascism is a real concept, not a stick with which to beat opponents arbitrarily. The abuse of this important word undermines its true value as a term referring to a very real phenomenon, and one whose spirit lives on even now.

What, then, is fascism? To Rockwell, it is an aggressive nationalism and imperialism, together with domination of the economy by the state.

The state, for the fascist, is the instrument by which the people's common destiny is realized, and in which the potential for greatness is to be found. Individual rights, and the individual himself, are strictly subordinate to the state's great and glorious goals for the nation. In foreign affairs, the fascist attitude is reflected in a belligerent chauvinism, a contempt for other peoples, and a society-wide reverence for soldiers and the martial virtues.

To what extent does this conception of things apply to contemporary America? Rockwell demonstrates in detail that it applies all-too-well. Following one of his great predecessors, the Old Right stalwart John T. Flynn, he distinguishes eight "marks of fascism," and for each one he illustrates its contemporary relevance.[1] We have space to discuss only a few of these, but the reader is urged to read Rockwell's complete discussion to grasp fully the strength of his analysis.

When the ordinary person thinks of fascism, he probably identifies it with the cult of the Leader, in the style of Hitler and Mussolini.

I [Rockwell] wouldn't say that we truly have a dictatorship of one man in this country, but we do have a form of dictatorship of one sector of government over the entire country. The executive branch has spread so dramatically over the last century that it has become a joke to speak of checks and balances. What the kids learn in civics class has nothing to do with reality. ... As for the leadership principle, there is no greater lie in American public life than the propaganda we hear every four years about how the new president/messiah is going to usher in the great dispensation of peace, equality, liberty, and global human happiness. The idea here is that the whole of society is really shaped and controlled by a single will — a point that requires a leap of faith so vast that you have to disregard everything you know about reality to believe it.

The increased power of the executive branch has been accompanied by a policy of militarism and war.

Ronald Reagan used to claim that his military buildup was essential to keeping the peace. The history of US foreign policy just since the 1980s has shown that this is wrong. We've had one war after another, wars waged by the United States against noncompliant countries, and the creation of even more client states and colonies.

US military strength has led not to peace but the opposite. It has caused most people in the world to regard the United States as a threat, and it has led to unconscionable wars on many countries. Wars of aggression were defined at Nuremberg as crimes against humanity.

At the heart of fascism lies state control of the economy. As Mises long ago pointed out, socialism can come about while the form of capitalism remains. In this type of socialism, the government dictates economic decisions and the ostensible business owners must obey its orders. It was precisely this pattern that Mises found in Nazism, and, unfortunately, it has become increasingly prevalent in America today.[2]

The reality of bureaucratic administration has been with us at least since the New Deal, which was modeled on the planning bureaucracy that lived in World War I. The planned economy — whether in Mussolini's time or ours — requires bureaucracy. Bureaucracy is the heart, lungs, and veins of the planning state. And yet to regulate an economy as thoroughly as this one is today is to kill prosperity with a billion tiny cuts.

Those devoted to freedom will of course reject fascism, with its blind power worship and dangerous economics, but what if one finds the fascist vision appealing? Can it maintain itself in power for the indefinite future? Rockwell does not think so; we have entered the period of "late fascism," and the appeal of the "cult of the colossal" has passed from the scene.

The fascist style emphasized inspiration, magnificence, industrial progress, grandeur, all headed by a valiant leader making smart decisions about all things. This style of American rule lasted from the New Deal through the end of the Cold War. ... Fascism, like socialism, cannot achieve its aims. So there is a way in which it makes sense to speak of a stage of history: We are in the stage of late fascism. The grandeur is gone, and all we are left with is a gun pointed at our heads. The system was created to be great, but it is reduced in our time to being crude. Valor is now violence. Majesty is now malice.

What, then, is the way forward? Rockwell looks to the great Austrians for an answer. By contrast with intellectuals who pander to the powerful, the Austrians must go against the grain. They must say the things that others do not want to hear. They must be willing to be unpopular, socially and politically. I'm thinking here of people like Benjamin Anderson, Garet Garrett, Henry Hazlitt, and, on the Continent, L. Albert Hahn, F.A. Hayek, and, above all, Ludwig von Mises. They gave up career and fame to stick with the truth and say what had to be said.

Rockwell finds particular inspiration in the work of Murray Rothbard. We all do well to emulate this master when we go about our work. When Rothbard would take on a subject, his very first stop was not to sit in an easy chair and think off the top of his head; instead, he went to the literature and sought to master it. He read everything he could from all points of view. He sought to become as much an expert in the topic as the other experts in the field. ... There is another respect in which we can all emulate Murray. He was fearless in speaking the truth. He never let fear of colleagues, fear of the profession, fear of editors or political cultures, stand in the way of his desire to say what was true. This is why he turned to the Austrian tradition even though most economists at the time considered it a dead paradigm. This is why he embraced liberty, and worked to shore up its theoretical and practice rationale at a time when the rest of the academic world was going the other way.

How are the ideas of Mises and Rothbard to be put into practice? How can we enlist a wide public in the cause of liberty? Rockwell points to the career of Ron Paul. He knew that the philosophy of liberty, when explained persuasively and with conviction, had a universal appeal. Every group he spoke to heard a slightly different presentation of that message, as Ron showed how their particular concerns were addressed most effectively by a policy of freedom.

POLITICAL SYSTEM INCAPABLE OF MEETING SOCIAL, ECONOMIC, ENVIRONMENTAL CHALLENGES

It's a commonplace sentiment that politics in America is broken. Each week brings more evidence of deadlock in Washington, of social and economic decay and of disillusionment. The debased nature of politics, however, is only the most superficial symptom of our problems. Beneath the surface-level partisan bickering, much deeper currents have begun to shift.

Recent polls, for instance, show that roughly 80 percent of Americans believe their Congressional representatives to be "more interested in serving the needs of special interests groups" than "the people they represent." Almost four out of five believe a few rich people and corporations have much too much power. And only 37 percent - not much more than a third of the population - have confidence in the most solemn and august of American institutions, the Supreme Court.

It is clear that something different is going on - both with the economy and, more fundamentally, with democracy itself. The data on long-running trends are clear:

Real wages for roughly 80 percent of American workers have not gone up more than a trivial amount for at least three decades. At the same time, income for the top 1 percent has jumped from 10 percent of all income to roughly 20 percent. Put another way: Virtually all the gains of the entire economic system have gone to a tiny, tiny group at the top - for at least three decades.

Another disturbing trend: Almost 50 million Americans live in officially defined poverty. The rate is higher, not lower than in the late 1960s. Moreover, if we use the measuring standard common throughout the advanced world - half of median income - the number would be just below 70 million, and the rate almost 23 percent.

This is to say nothing of an unemployment rate that, if properly measured, is stuck in the range of roughly 14 to 15 percent. At the same time, a record 46.7 million Americans were on food stamps in 2012, up by 51 percent from the depths of recession in October 2008: another milestone on our collective road of decay. And looming over all this, of course, is the mother of all difficulties: the building climate crisis.

The current political system is simply incapable of dealing with such challenges. It focuses on deficits, not answers. But long trends that don't change are a clear signal that it's not simply partisan bickering and Congressional stalemate - or even politics in general - that are the problem.

The trends were moving steadily downward long before the rise of the Tea Party, long before the Citizens United Supreme Court decision allowed corporations and the super-rich to pump big money directly into politics, and long before many other changes that have been heralded as tipping points of one kind or another.

When long, long trends, do not improve - when they grow steadily worse, year in and year out - it is clear that we face systemic problems, not simply political problems in the usual sense of the term. The question is: How do we deal with a systemic crisis - something built in to the political-economic system rather than the usual garden-variety political or economic crisis? How do we really confront that question squarely?

Part of the problem for progressives is that - as historian Lewis Namier once quipped - we all tend to "remember the future." By which he meant that we don't and can't document what will happen in future. Instead, most of us unconsciously project forward assumptions about what is possible from our actual experience of the past. We "remember" forward that which we unconsciously take for granted. This works much of the time, when things are unfolding in roughly the same way they always have. But it works terribly when the game changes, when deep and fundamental systemic challenges are being posed.

It is difficult in the extreme for most people to grasp the possibility - *embrace and understand fully the likelihood* - that we may be entering a many-decades-long period in which the dominant reality is one of erratic growth, stagnation, commodity inflation, substantial political stalemate and decay. But - give or take an occasional political or economic uptick - that is, in fact, the most likely long-term context flowing from the deep and continuing trends.

Progressives need to recalibrate our strategies to the likelihood of such a context if a new era of political-economic change is to be forged in America. The challenge is extraordinary, but the options definable:

OPTION NUMBER ONE: A NEW PROGRESSIVE REALIGNMENT?

Some observers offer what they hope may be a *politically* viable way out of the pain and a way to reverse the long-decaying trends. The respected analyst

Ruy Teixeira, for instance, holds that growing numbers of minorities (especially Hispanics) and pronounced shifts among women and educated professionals are likely to produce increasing Democratic majorities over time. In Teixeira's view: "All this adds up to big change that is reshaping our country in a fundamentally progressive direction." Other observers, more simply, consider the 2008 and 2012 elections to be a political "realignment" and optimistically predict enduring Democratic majorities and electoral successes.

But the question we face is not simply whether Democrats or even progressives can be *elected*. Commonly lost in predictions based on demographic changes is that the question of who is elected (and even the question of whether they can do something useful) is radically different from the question of whether the decaying long trends, and the challenging economic management problems emerging throughout the system, can be dealt with.

Put another way: Given the underlying and ongoing changes in institutional power balances, the deepening economic difficulties, the growing fiscal crisis, and the Supreme Court's Citizens United decision, there is little reason to believe demographic changes, important as they are, will easily be translated into a force sufficiently powerful to alter the long-decaying income, wealth, climate and other trends, even if the balance of party affiliations in Congress (and their relative political views) begins to shift.

OPTION NUMBER TWO: BUILD A MOVEMENT

It is possible, to state the hope of many others, that a massive and far-reaching populist or progressive form of political movement-building, along with new labor-organizing strategies, will produce a renewal of traditional reform capacities in ways that may achieve more than modest gains - in other words, that, again, may actually begin to alter the downward trends. Such movement building is clearly useful no matter what.

The central question, however, is how far down the road traditional reform strategies can take us, and what else, *substantively and institutionally*, a serious movement needs to embrace to create trend change, to say nothing of larger system-wide change. Demonstrations; sit-ins; direct action; civil disobedience where relevant; labor-community alliances and the like are very important, but they are unlikely on their own to achieve trend-altering change in the face of the deepening systemic crisis - especially given the decline of unions, the institutions that have historically given weight and muscle to progressive reform efforts.

In a variation of older "pendulum-swing" and "cycle" theories of history, some progressives all too easily cite populist- and progressive-era gains in the hope that these provide precedents for our own time in history. But many forget that populism, in fact, was largely defeated in its major policy proposals, and that despite important regulatory and other gains, progressive-era achievements were of a radically different order. The federal government was a mere 3.7 percent of GDP (compared with 24.1 percent in 2011) - even after most of the gains traceable to the progressive era and World War I's impact on political-economic change had been incorporated into public policy.

The modest size of the modern American welfare state compared with that of many European nations - even after the unusual gains of the Great Depression era - also reminds us of the weakness of traditional American reform capacities even without considering the modern decline of labor and other fast-growing modern challenges.

Among the factors commonly cited to explain our much weaker state-managing politics are: racial and ethnic divisions, a complex history of immigrant rivalries often exploited by conservative forces, the huge scale of the nation, the absence of feudalism and the fact that the United States did not experience massive war on its own territory during the 20th century - a force (as the late historian Tony Judt in his book, *Postwar*, powerfully demonstrated) that helped pull together the modern welfare state and political-economic capacities of many European states.

None of these considerations suggest that labor organizing, reform efforts, and progressive movement building should be abandoned. Quite the contrary; all are extremely important. The critical challenge is to find a way, as we move ever deeper into a much more profound systemic crisis than many have as yet confronted, to dig much deeper in the quest for a new way forward than we have previously been forced to do. The ultimate challenge is to simultaneously - and as part and parcel of an integrated strategy - begin to deal directly with the core institutional issue of how wealth is owned and controlled at the heart of the system.

OPTION NUMBER THREE: GO LOCAL

It is also possible that in addition to traditional progressive movement-building efforts, new strategies created especially by the young, by environmental activists, by the Occupy Movement, by progressive business groups like the Business Alliance for Living Local Economies (BALLE) and American Sustainable Business Council, along with the many others who are beginning to coalesce in the New Economy Movement, will add new energies and a different kind of developing thrust to a larger movement-building effort. Especially important are localist efforts and building from the bottom both economically and ecologically to achieve greater local resilience.

Again, important as such a direction also is - and important as it is to build wherever possible - the power of such activism to address some of the large-order system-driven trends, and especially those involving climate change, is also all but certain to be severely limited unless and until it becomes possible to fundamentally alter the underlying institutional and systemic power imbalances and the growth-driven corporate institutions that continue to produce the ongoing trends and stand in the way of change. And this, in turn, requires a much deeper approach, side by side with such efforts.

OPTION NUMBER FOUR: FRIENDLY FASCISM

It is also possible, of course, that the growing social and economic decay will lead to one or another form of violence on either left or right (or both), even over time to growing domestic terrorism from one or more directions. Explosions of urban unrest like those of the 1960s may well occur again as the pain deepens. It is also a mistake to forget that even more threatening possibilities may develop elsewhere in the system: The 1995 Oklahoma City bombing of the Alfred P. Murrah Federal Building was committed by an angry white terrorist, Timothy McVeigh.

If there is violence, there will also be repression and - depending upon which party is in power and the precise circumstances - the already deepening trends of ever-declining civil liberties are likely to be intensified. It is possible that this logic may lead to what the late Bertram Gross termed "Friendly Fascism" or to a corporate state in which civil liberties and democratic processes are subverted as politicians exploit fear in the wake of violence.

However, even massive repression almost certainly does not end the challenge - and in fact can provide the impetus for widespread change. The dictators who dominated Latin America for many decades have disappeared in most countries - and progressive groups, once suppressed and tortured, are back in force and building anew. Their determination to continue to build through even very dark times stands as a reminder of what is also possible, and what might become necessary in the challenging historical context we may face.

OPTION NUMBER FIVE: EVOLUTIONARY RECONSTRUCTION

It is also possible that quietly developing "New Economy" wealth-democratizing, institution-building trends such as cooperatives, employee-owned firms, ecologically sustainable small businesses, publicly owned enterprises, land trusts, social enterprises, community development corporations and the like will continue their little-noticed but ongoing growth trajectory and build in scale and power over time, decade by decade, *precisely because of the pain of the emerging historical context*. As a result, such institutions might begin in critical areas to partially displace corporate institutions at the same time they slowly create new political constituencies.

The developing longer-term processes might thereby (minimally) begin to achieve steadily expanding institutional capacities to bolster traditional progressive movements - and in turn such movements might ultimately help enact policies to nurture and expand the developing wealth-democratizing institutional thrust.

If so, although the resulting longer-term, decade-by-decade development path would not serve to replicate the institutional power of the labor union in progressive strategy, it could slowly help create institutional alternatives and new associated constituencies that might help strengthen a revised strategy.

First, it could provide alternatives to the corporation as the only significant choice for local municipal economic development.

Second, it could slowly displace corporate institutions in a number of key areas (for instance, state single-payer health insurance, electric power development, large-scale banking in crisis, possibly national health insurance over time, plausibly other major corporations over time).

And third, it could help create new institution-shifting *ideas* of what must ultimately be done, and how longer-term strategic approaches might be changed so that, when the opportunity arises, developments nurtured at the local and state (and, in part, national) levels might one day be available for further, larger-scale implementation.

This long and slow-developing path might be called "evolutionary reconstruction." It is a path, like that followed in the state and local "laboratories of democracy" in the decades prior to the New Deal, that might offer the basis, too, of longer term political-economic ideas when the moment is right . . . *especially if combined with new movement building strategies.*

An obvious conclusion is that it is important to build forward, positively, on all fronts over time - and in particular to self-consciously advance new wealth-democratizing, institution-building strategies that may add new forms of power, along with new vision, to a politics of reform. Over the long haul, such a direction could help forge - slowly, agonizingly (and in significant part precisely because of the ongoing systemic failures) - new institutional foundations and related political efforts that might become sufficiently powerful to begin to alter the downward-moving direction of the great social, economic, and environmental trends that now define the decaying pattern of our corporate-dominated system. Even possibly to create some elements of a new "mixed" economy more favorable to progressive concerns.

And with all this, too - *and beyond* - we might also begin to see the slow development of a new vision and wealth-democratizing culture and movement capable of beginning to challenge the dominant hegemonic ideology, holding out the prospect of system-altering change much more far-reaching than many currently imagine. This, of course, is the real prize - but one that is likely to be achieved only if sufficient groundwork is laid and genuine knowledge of how to democratize the economy developed in advance.

'THE RENAISSANCE STATE' VS. 'NATURAL HARMONY'.

In 1338 Ambrogio Lorenzetti finished his frescoes *Allegory of Good and Bad Government* in the Town Hall of Sienna. The fresco symbolising *good government* shows thriving shops, fine buildings and dancing citizens enjoying their leisure. *Bad government* is shown as ruin, rape, robbery and murder. The *Allegory of Good and Bad Government* represents the optimistic Renaissance view of Man's untapped potentials to improve his own situation. Theirs was a view of history being a continuous optimisation process where 'Man's wit and will', applied to harnessing the forces of Nature, held enormous potentials for improving his lot: 'the never ending frontier of knowledge.'

The starting point for Renaissance economics, and the birth of the modern State, was an acute awareness of the suboptimality of the present situation of Mankind - steeped in the ignorance and poverty of the Middle Ages. This situation could clearly be improved, and this optimisation was chased as an ever-moving target in the distance. The propellant of this process was learning - the acquisition of new knowledge. This process resembles today's evolutionary economics at its best .

The usefulness of a State in this process arises out of the Renaissance concept of the *common weal* - or the 'common good' - a *systemic dimension* which is lost in the atomistic and static structure of today's mainstream economics. In this paper we use the term 'Renaissance State' for a type of activistic and idealistic State which, we shall attempt to show, has been an 'obligatory passage point' for all presently industrialised nations, bringing the nation into economic activities creating a *common weal* through increasing returns and self-enforcing feedback mechanisms. At a very simple level, a *common weal* arises out of the synergies stemming from the sharing of fixed costs - either resulting from specialised *tools* or from specialised *knowledge*, like the old story of the blind man and the deaf man whose *weal* was improved by acting together.

We shall argue that the growth of complex economies has important similarities to the growth of complex technological systems - and that, in both cases, increasing returns are at the core of positive feedback mechanisms which increase welfare. Such systemic synergies are further based upon *diversity* - just as the both the very existence and the *common weal* of a household fundamentally rests on synergies arising from Man and Woman being different. A *common weal*, then, is systemic and synergy-based - it is a dynamic concept in a process which increases the size of the economic pie - much as the process described by the early Adam Smith at the cover of this paper. Adam Smith here recommends government intervention to promote a certain industry (which operated under increasing returns), neither to help the consumer nor to help the producer, but because it benefited the system as a whole - the *common weal*. At this point it is important to point out that the actions emanating from an understanding of a *systemic common weal* are very different from the idea of distributive *collective action* - in a setting of static rent-seeking and zero-sum games - in modern Anglo-Saxon economics.

The economics of State involvement in the Renaissance was both immensely activistic and idealistic. Albert Hirschman, in his 1991 book, discusses the arguments which, since the late 18th century, have been used against this type of activistic and idealistic interference with the 'natural harmony' created by the market mechanism. Hirschman in his book gives us the history of ideas listing the arguments why Ambrogio Lorenzetti's optimistic frescoes expressing Man's ability to improve his own destiny were, at best, naive and futile.

Hirschman has collected the arguments in favour of *passivity as a strategy* - a natural corollary to Ricardo's 'dismal science'. In this paper we shall discuss the role of the State in economic growth and in the history of economic thought as being torn between two fundamentally different economic outlooks: a *production-centered* and *activistic-idealistic* Renaissance tradition and a *barter-centered* and *passivistic-materialistic* tradition of Adam Smith, David Ricardo and neo-classical economics.

Hirschman divides the arguments against any active strategy on the part of the State in three categories, and finds to his surprise that both the traditional 'right' and the traditional 'left' gradually started to make the same kind of arguments:

1. Perversity. Any attempt at improving the economic or social order will have the opposite effect of that intended. This argument is clearly present already in Adam Smith's late works.
2. Futility. Any attempt at changing the social or economic order is doomed to fail.
3. Jeopardy. Any attempt at changing the social or economic order will carry with it costs that are so high as to jeopardise what has previously been achieved.

The *zeitgeist* of the late 1990's is clearly closer to that described by Hirschman than to the optimism of Lorenzetti and his times. But, the fall of the Berlin wall now gives us an opportunity to re-examine the role of the State in economic development under less ideological pressure than, not only since the start of the Cold War, but since the *Ghost of Communism* entered the stage 150 years ago. However, we are seriously hampered by the fact that at the core of present-day mainstream economics - as a result of the standard assumptions of neoclassical theory - still lies a 'natural harmony', in a world void of any systemic effects, of Samuelson's *factor price equalisation*: The natural harmony which will make all wage earners of the planet equally rich - if we can only 'get the prices right' and 'provide a level playing field'.

Out of these philosophies of 'natural harmony' rises the rejection of the State as such, like in the 'Civil Disobedience' of Henry David Thoreau (1849) and its present-day manifestations, as in the 1995 bombing of the US Federal Building in Oklahoma City. We live in a society caught between, on the one hand, the wish for the simple individualistic life of Thoreau, with its roots in the late 18th century, whose ideal is living outside any society ('Why are people so worried', says Thoreau, 'the one who does not eat, does not have to work.') On the other hand, we are addicted to a standard of living which can only be kept up in the network of a fine grained specialization, the synergies and scale of which are essential to the production of *systemic* effects, to the *common good* of Renaissance economists.

These economists observed the wealth of populous and economically diversified cities - like Venice - in stark contrast to the poverty of the undiversified economic base in the countryside and in agricultural/administrative cities like Naples. Even the often pessimistic Machiavelli, who 'wants to present us with Mankind in its most negative and depressing aspects' , says it this way: 'Il bene commune è quello che fa grandi le città' - 'The *common good* is what makes the cities great'.

However, today considerable tension is created by the fact that any systemic effects in the economy - and consequently any role of the State - are external to the core of the ruling economic theory. This fact is all the more harmful because, as we shall attempt to show in this paper, the experiences of the presently industrialised countries indicate that the need for State interventions is stronger the poorer the country. Those who produce economic theory all live in nations where a strong State is taken for granted - where the 'obligatory passage point' of a Renaissance-type state is long history.

The assumptions of neo-classical theory correspond to a world which fits Henry Thoreau's ideal: *no human institutions* and *no systemic effects*. Reading Thoreau is the key to understanding the dissatisfaction of the average American with Governments of any kind. Thoreau shares with Adam Smith a strong aversion to any type of human institutions and collective action, a view - clearly inspired by Rousseau - that the institutions of civilised society have corrupted Mankind. To Adam Smith all human institutions - private and public - 'so invariably produce 'absurd' results that they have no presumptive legitimacy' .

Neo-classical economics has kept Thoreau's and Adam Smith's myth alive by failing to internalise the systemic synergies of societies, among multitudes of professions, each with a minimum efficient size of operation, which, in turn, also cause societies themselves to have a *minimum efficient size.* This *minimum efficient size of societies* grows as more knowledge is added and more professions are formed - increasing the standards of living - and forming the fundamental connection between geography and economics. These same factors led to the creation - in succession - first of the Mediaeval city economies, then of national economies, and finally of 'globalisation'. The needs for a State essentially arise from the same synergies and interdependencies, and from the differing abilities of economic activities to provide the increasing returns which are at the core of this system.

One of the problems of today's mainstream is then, that - through its assumptions of a complete absence of increasing returns to scale and of perfect information - it has produced a theory which is as individualistic as Henry David Thoreau's visions: there are no systemic external effects present at the core of the theory.

Economic theory today fails to tell us why we cannot have our cake (atomistic individualism) and eat it too (a high standard of material living). This is essentially the reason why theories of the State, of the Firm, or of any other human institutions are external to the core of economic theory. Renaissance economists tell us that the State exists because of the systemic effects in an economy, effects which also the early Adam Smith glorifies. Today's practice of labeling - in a rather *ad-hoc* manner - all unexpected economic effects either as 'externalities' or 'market failures' contributes little to the understanding of economic systems.

Ad-hoc exceptions are more easily seen, and acted upon, close to home, in the industrialised countries, rather than far away in the Third World. For this reason, the fundamental argument for the single market in the European Union is the existence of increasing returns observed in practice (The Cecchini Report), but without any ties to trade theory. On the other hand, the theoretical foundation for the EU policy against the Third World is that such increasing returns *do not* exist (conventional trade theory which does not allow for asymmetrical trade between increasing and diminishing return activities). In other words, the theory behind the European Single Market is based on exactly opposite assumptions from that of the EU policy towards the Third World. A consistent use of assumptions would have lead to the EU recommending protection of increasing return activities - industry - in resource-based Third World countries (which has been shown to work under sometimes extreme Diminishing Returns).

This frequent and inconsistent 'assumption-juggling' in economic theory was denounced already by Joan Robinson. From the point of view of the Third World this may be seen as an alternative version of 'The Golden Rule' - the one who has the gold makes the rules. We see it as an important task ahead for economic theory to *internalise the externalities* which produce welfare: the systemic synergies of scale and scope which have their origin in the creation and implementation of new knowledge in those production processes which are subject to increasing returns.

The World Bank 1997 World Development Report - to be entitled 'The State in a Changing World' - will focus on the role of state in economic development. Predictably it will continue the discussion on the role of the State which was started with the publication of *The East Asian Miracle* . This paper discusses the historical role of the State in a different framework of assumptions than that of the World Bank. These assumptions. In our view, the successful

East Asian nations essentially follow very similar strategies to those followed first by England (starting in the 1480's) and later by all other presently industrial nations in the early stages of development. World Bank studies do not go back more than 50 years, so these similarities are unlikely to be uncovered in their normal process. Likewise, the history of economic thought having today largely been reduced to a genealogy of neo-classical economics, the record of the past economic policies of the presently industrialised countries has to a large extent been 'unlearned'.

There is no such thing as an academic sub-discipline called 'History of Economic Policy', and the industrial powers of Europe and North America seem to be unified in a common misconception about their own past, about the role of the State in bringing them out of poverty.

MECHANISMS CAUSING AND DIFFUSING ECONOMIC GROWTH AND WELFARE

A paper purporting to trace the influence of the State on economic growth must - implicitly or explicitly - be based on a model of the mechanisms which cause economic growth. Below we shall attempt to clarify how our assumptions differ from those of Adam Smith and of the neo-classical system. Partly using the terminology of Werner Sombart, we base our analysis on a *production-centered, activistic-idealistic* set of assumptions, in contrast with today's mainstream, which in this context can be labeled *barter-centered and passivistic-materialistic.*

Our set of assumptions differs from that of today's mainstream economic theory, and therefore also concludes with a different view of the role of the state in economic growth. To clarify: If the conditions of 'real world' did correspond to the assumptions of neo-classical theory, we would have shared the view that any attempt to influence income growth and distribution would be futile. However, as we shall argue, the factors causing uneven economic development - where State intervention may play a role - are the very factors which neo-classical theory assumes away. When neo-classical theory is 'right', it is, on key points, 'right for the wrong reason'.

We would for example argue that the benefits from international trade are mainly caused by what Schumpeter called *historical increasing returns* - a blend of increasing returns and technical change - rather than on the static gains in the Ricardian theory. The need for 'governing the market' arises from such factors which are left out of mainstream theory.

There seem to be three important aspects to this question, *one*: how economic growth is *created, two*, the alternative mechanisms through which growth and welfare are *diffused* between and within the nation-states, and to the individual, and *three,* how this alternative understanding is based on a different philosophical basis. These three aspects are briefly discussed in the next three sub-sections.

THE THREE ROLES OF THE STATE.

For the purpose of the paper we find it useful to divide the roles of the State into three broad categories:

1. The State as a provider of Institutions - in the widest possible sense, including order and security. ('Establishing the rules of the game'/ 'providing an even playing field')
2. The State as a provider of Income Distribution and as an 'insurance company.' (Preventing evil/'Sharing the pie')
3. The State as a promoter of Economic Growth (Promoting happiness/ 'Increasing the size of the pie').

There are, of course, other alternative classifications of the roles of the State. Wilhelm von Humboldt says: 'A State then, has one of two ends in view; it designs either to promote happiness, or simply to prevent evil.' Another German economist, Adolph Wagner, divides the role of the State into two different categories of objectives: Law and Power (Rechts- und Machtzweck) and Culture and Welfare (Kultur- und Wohlfahrtszweck).. However, for our purpose it is important to divide the welfare aspect expressed in the other classification into *two very different categories*: the *creation* vs. the *distribution* of income.

This paper essentially deals with point 3 - the role of the State in the Creation - rather than the Distribution - of Income, but a few remarks on points 1 and 2 are necessary to draw lines of delimitation, and to clarify where and how the categories overlap.

'The State as a *Provider of Institutions*'. These institutions may, on the one hand, be seen as preconditions required by the invisible hand in order to get on with its job of creating economic growth. On the other hand they may be seen as part of a wider and more active strategy as that under point 3, the State as actively 'increasing the size of the pie'. However, we choose to put these fundamental institutions - which hardly come under the attack of the thesis of futility, jeopardy and perversity - in this separate category.

These basic institutions include private property and the well-worn German concept of a *Rechtsstaat* (Civil- or Legal- State). As standards of living grow, secondary demands are created and the State is extended into a *Kulturstaat* (a Culture State), providing institutions for education, science, charity, sanitation, etc. Summing up, one German author says: 'Food, drink, clothing, shelter, amusement, social intercourse, - these are the primary wants with the covering of which private economy is mainly occupied; peace, order, security, culture, relief - these are the higher needs which are mainly served by the public economy.'

'Sharing of the Pie and Distributing Risk': The thought of distributing the inevitable risks of life is a very old one - the participants of the camel caravans of the Near East 2.200 b. C. had a risk sharing system. Modern insurance traces its root to the middle of the 14th Century. The same ideas of risk sharing are present during the beginnings of the welfare state, already in Byzantine Empire, where the idea of sharing the risks of life gradually develops into a role of income distribution. Thoughts around welfare are found very clearly in the writings of German philosophers Gottfried Wilhelm Leibniz (1646-1716) and Christian Wolff (1697-1754).

Leibniz suggested that a national health system should be established. The health system should be the basis for a welfare guaran-teed by the State. Wolff specifies clearly that he wants a State which secures welfare for the individual, but not one which automatically provides for him ('Ein Wohl-fahrtsstaat, aber kein Versorgungsstaat') - a most difficult balance to this very day.

Clearly 'sharing the pie' is not a wholly independent exercise from that of 'increasing the size of the pie'. Economic arguments for income redistribution include the argument that a certain income distribution is required to create and maintain a mass market. This argument seems to be one used to defend the enormous transfer payments within the European Community; i.e. 'Poverty is bad for business'. One can further argue that an unequal income distribution threatens the social fabric of society, and therefore the nation itself and its economy. A most important argument - similar to that used by 19th century US economists - is that a continuous increase in the price of labour relative to the price of capital is a key factor in the virtuous circle created by State intervention: the increasing relative price of labour is a strong incentive for further mechanisation, which again allows for even higher wages and higher profits, and so on.

By making labour more skilled, it is made more valuable. This was also an important argument of 19th century US economists against the dismal pauperisation theories in English classical economics, and formed the basis for the dual policy of 'The High Wage Strategy' and 'The American System of Manufactures' giving protection to increasing return activities. We would see this argument for income distribution as part of the virtuous circles which are created by State intervention under the next point.

'The role of the State in Increasing National Wealth (Increasing the size of the pie)'. Clearly the institutions in point 1 and 2 are necessary, but in our view not sufficient, conditions for economic growth.

The objective of this paper is to look at the more active role of the state in economic development - 'the developmental State'. We most look behind the State as a provider for institutions for which there is a 'natural demand' into another role of *creating demand* for things which are necessary, but for which there is no articulated demand. If people do not want to educate their children - because they are themselves not educated, and because they need their daily labour - the State plays a new role: The State uses 'its power of coercion in order to create a general demand for the institutions which it has established', says Cohn. Here enters a more visible hand - the role of *The State as a Factor of Production* to use Luigi Einaudi's term, originally from Adam Müller (1809). It is the role of this visible hand which forms the core of this paper. The role played by the State is contained in the felicitous term coined by Robert Wade in 1990: 'Governing the Market'. It is clearly particularly to this role of the state that the message of futility, perversity, and jeopardy is directed.

Historically the roles of the State as a promoter of economic growth can be listed under the following headings:

(a) Getting the nation into 'the right business', i.e. recognising, as a historical starting point, the *activity-specific* nature of economic growth. The importance of this neglected point in today's economic theory cannot be overestimated. We are tempted to quote John Stuart Mill, who, when talking about *diminishing returns*, makes the following statement: 'I apprehend (the elimination of this factor) to be not only an er-ror, but the most serious one, to be found in the whole field of political economy. The question is more important and fundamental than any other; it involves the whole subject of the causes of pov-erty;...and unless this one mat-ter be thoroughly understood, it is to no purpose proceeding any further in our inquiry' . We all intuitively understand that stockbrokers make more money than people washing dishes. But in economic theory, and accordingly in our economic policy towards the Third World, the profession does insist - making a hypothetical case - that a *nation* of stockbrokers would achieve *factor price equalisation* (the same wage level) with a *nation* of people washing dishes. We intuitively understand that Japan could not have reached her present position by making inexpensive shirts, rather than inexpensive cars or electronics, and that Pavarotti could not have made the same fortune picking lettuce as singing, but this intuitive knowledge is not compatible with today's barter-centered economic theory .

At any point in time, different economic activities present different *windows of opportunity* for adding new knowledge under dynamic imperfect competition, and thus for creating positive feedback systems. As long as there is a demand both for *low* and *high* skill activities, the world market may produce *lock-in effects* trapping nations in a comparative advantage of being poor and unskilled. The State plays an important role in the opening of such *windows of opportunity*. Historically all presently industrialised nations - for the right or for the wrong reasons - have passed through an initial stage with a policy based on the understanding that *not all economic activities are equally feasible as starting points* for the self-enforcing positive feedback system which we call development. Appendix 1 and 2 of this paper outline economic systems in the *presence* and *absence* of such positive feedback mechanisms - of *development* and *underdevelopment.* The benefits from dynamic increasing returns which spread as higher wages - not only as lower prices - is *activity specific.*

This argument - so crucial to the understanding of the wealth and poverty of nations - is closely related to the debate on the residual which was started by Moses Abramowitz in 1956. Abramowitz showed that capital *per se* can only explain 10- 20 per cent of growth in the United States - the rest, 80-90 per cent, is the 'residual' which Abramowitz called 'a measure of our ignorance' about the causes of economic growth. We find it of utmost importance to our argument that Abramowitz today sees this residual as being activity-specific' - that it varies between different economic activities. In a letter to this author, dated August 16, 1996, Abramowitz comments on my previous publications on this issue: 'I agree with much of what you say.

I agree in particular that the "residual" and growth in general are industry-specific.' A recognition of the activity-specific nature of economic growth in our opinion not only completely undermines the assumptions on which today's world economic order rest, but it also explains the why an unintended by-product of the World Bank 'Adjustment Policies' in poor Third World and former communist countries sometimes has been to reinforce a negative *lock-in effect* producing a fall in GNP per capita. In other words, the activity-specific nature of economic welfare explains why a notoriously inefficient planned industrial economy produced *a higher standard of living* in the former Soviet Union than a largely deindustrialised and more 'efficient' market economy now does in Russia. These are fundamental issues which the world community and the World Bank now must face - they can no longer be hidden under the veil of 'transitology', of being temporary effects of a transition from one system to another.

(b) Creating a comparative advantage in 'the right business'. A common element of all successful strategies for catching up with richer nations is conviction that free trade is not wanted until the nation has *created* a comparative advantage in the 'right' eco-nomic activities (which, among other things, means skill-based, not resource-based). There is an important underlying perception in this that a world economic system, if there is world demand *both for skilled* (well paid) *and for unskilled* (poorly paid) *labour,* a nation may end up *locked into* a permanent comparative advantage in being poor and un-skilled.

c) A very strong emphasis on the role of the State as a supplier of infrastructure. This is a unifying element of most 'enemies' of classical and neo-classical economists, from Colbert (canals, turnpikes, ports, merchant marine, navy) to Friedrich List (known in Germany as 'the father of the German railway system') and to Al Gore/Robert Reich (the electronic super-highway). Infrastructure is, as all other *systemic* elements of the economy, conspicuously absent from today's economic theory (e.g. not to be found in *The New Palgrave*). Infrastructures are key factors in *extending markets* and are 'highways' which the positive feed-back mechanisms need in order to displace themselves geographically.

(d) Setting standards has been a very important task of the State, from the neo-classical point of view to lower transaction costs, from the evolutionary point of view to form a basis for standardised mass production. A visitor to the Renaissance towns of Italy can to this very day observe the iron bars fastened to the church wall on the main square, establishing the standard units of measurement valid in the city. Each city had different measurements, which made information and conversion tables on these issues an important task for early economic books.Today the *setting of standards* is important to hi-tech products like mobile telephony. Clearly the state also has an important role in setting legal standards and providing a social virtue which is crucial to prosperity. This was a point much emphasized by Renaissance philosophers, and is rediscovered today in Fukuyama's book *Trust*. .

(e) A responsibility of the State to provide skilled labour and entrepreneurship if in short supply. Early policy measures - often helped by religious wars - were aimed at bringing in skilled labour and entrepreneurs from abroad by granting exclusive rights (patents) for a limited time, or through bounties, tax relief, etc. The State is also an entrepreneur of last resort.

(f) Unless one firmly believes in Say's Law - that supply creates its own demand - the State clearly has an important role in creating demand in general. Out of the Victorian slums with only subsistence demand, a better income distribution of a growing economic pie paved the way for the mass markets. This development made industrial production and 'Fordism' possible, e.g. through the establishment of minimum wages. 19th Century US economists saw particularly well the role of raising labour skills to increase their market value - the policy which was called 'The High Wage Strategy'. There is reason to believe that the sharp fall in economic welfare experienced by weakly industrialized nations in the wake of 'structural adjustment', in part was due to the elimination of demand created by the State. In this context it is important to keep in mind that what we call 'economic development' is little more than a collective 'industry rent', the national distribution of which - in spite of our laissez-faire mythology - is the result of decades of 'artificial' redistribution, partly due to the activities of labour unions. Our understanding today of the connection between the key variables *growth of demand, income redistribution* and *higher wages pushing mechanisation* is very limited. In several nations today - like e.g. in Peru - there is evidently a break in the positive circuit created by these factors.

(g) The State has played a very strong role pushing the technological frontier by being a supplier of high-quality demand for national production, of demand for goods at the borderline of what, at any time, was technically feasible. Key mechanisms here have been infrastructure projects and warfare. Werner Sombart, in 1913, describes the destructions of war as being the starting point both for the creative spirit of Man - for searches for synthetic substitutes for raw materials in short supply, but also for the *organizational capabilities* of the State. This is a most important argument in the spirit of Chandler and Lazonick. Not only was State demand crucial for purposes of war and infrastructure, but the personification of the State - royalty and nobility - served as Porterian *demanding customers* for luxuries, and provided the basis for future technological expansion into lower-cost mass production. Historically the demand for luxury has played a role similar to that played by people who, 10 years ago, paid 4.000 dollars for a cellular phone, enabling later mass production to deliver better phones for 80 dollars today. Again, the function of State demand for luxury is brilliantly described by Werner Sombart.

(h) An emphasis on the value of knowledge and education per se. See the list of policy measures collected as *Schumpeterian Mercantilism*. (Scientific academies, education, patent laws and copyright protection, tariffs protecting the few activities where the production of new knowledge was focused, etc.).

(i) A long term goal similar to what in the 19th Century United States was called 'The High Wage Strategy' - i.e. seeing high wages *per se* as a goal. At the core of this economic thinking was Man and his Needs ('Der Mensch und seine Bedürfnisse'), rather than a 'dead equilibrium' which reduces Man to one of several factors of production, the high or low reward of which has no place in the system. The importance of the wage level in explaining GNP is illustrated by the fact that today wages are typically 70 % of GNP: i.e. maximising wealth essentially means maximising national wages.

(j) An understanding of the importance of a legal system built to strengthen the above structures. To Christian Wolff - the 18th Century German economist and philosopher of law - a system of property rights assisting the dynamic symbiosis between 'persons who collected knowledge and people who collected money' was seen as the core of a system creating - like Francis Bacon's system before him - a never-ending frontier of development.

(k) The State as an entrepreneur and capitalist of last resort. There is no reason to assume a 'sufficient' supply of entrepreneurship at any point in time and in any culture - the poorer the nation the less so. As we shall discuss in the short chapter on State-owned enterprises, moving the State into a role of capitalist of entrepreneur resulted from 'reverse salients' in the system, rather than from any ideological preference.

We would argue that - as economic agents - States exist for fundamentally the same reasons that firms exist, both of them for reasons not well captured by today's economic theory, which focuses on barter and atomism. We suggest that the absence of a *theory of the firm* in modern economic theory is caused by the same reasons which cause the absence of the *theory of the State* in the same body of theory. Both firms and states are institutions which are brought to life by the kind of *systemic synergies* which are excluded in neo-classical theory through the assumptions of full divisibility of resources, of perfect information, perfect competition, and of the absence of increasing returns.

To continue this analogy between *the State* and *the Firm,* we would argue that the size and strength of a firm to a large extent is determined by the sum of the countervailing forces of *economies of scale* and *diseconomies of scale*. Large chemical firms are the product of huge economies of scale in production, advertising and finance; coupled with the opposite effect - the diseconomies of bureaucratisation - in administration and coordination.

Similarly the strength and size of the State is also torn between two opposite effects, well captured by von Humboldt: *'The highest good'* which arises from associations, like the State, *'is the very variety* arising from the union of numbers of individuals'. This *variety* is a core part of the synergies creating the common weal, and in my view also the underlying principle why, as in Adam Smith's argument, 'the division of labour' is so important. However 'this variety is undoubtedly merged into uniformity in proportion to the measure of State interference'. Thus, the existence of a State tends to produce *'uniformity and inertness'*, which is the very reverse of what caused State intervention in the economy in the first place, which was the need for *'variety and activity'* - i.e. the establishment of a large number of professions ('division of labour') through entrepreneurship.

The extent and size of a firm is a result of competitive powers - which are industry- and product-specific - on the underlying trade-off of increasing and decreasing returns to scale. Similarly, the extent and activity of the State (what we could call 'The Optimal State') should, at any point in time, reflect the paradox that having united in order to exploit the synergies and economies of scope which result from the *variety and activity* of Mankind, the potentially perverse effect of producing *uniformity and inertness* is likely to occur. This *uniformity and inertness* threatens the variety and activity, the synergies of which the State was established to foment and exploit in the first place. Both in the case of the firm and the State, one important answer to the diseconomies of scale produced by size and growing complexities, lies in the concept of *organizational capabilities*. The Managerial Revolution was, in the world of business, the reply to these challenges.

The Role of the state in industrialised countries is often seen as one of protecting 'civil liberties', or the form of freedom which we would call *freedoms to*. However, the role of the State in the early stages of economic development is one of jump-starting the systemic effects which were to secure the *freedoms from* - freedom from hunger, freedom from injustices, freedom from ignorance. With time, however, another aspect of the dynamic balancing creating an 'optimal state' appears when the actions of the State to provide *freedoms from* are gradually seen as encroaching upon Man's *freedoms to*.

The Smithian revolt against Renaissance economic policy can be seen as such a conflict, as seen in Turgot's arguing against the excesses of Colbertism. In England at the time, the policies of the 'developmental state' had entered into an area of diminishing returns of static and individual rent-seeking rather than the synergetic collective rent-seeking. Clearly a big dose of 'markets' was needed. However, as German, US, and Japanese economists in the 19th Century were so eager to point out, this did not mean that nations which had not reached the level of England could use the same policies there and then. The role of the State - like the particular balance of emphasis on freedoms *to* and freedoms *from* - is highly context-specific.

9

Modern Capitalist Conception Of Money

Money is only a means of exchange. It is quite possible to have communities use barter instead, such as "I give you a cow for (whatever)". In a society that uses money care should be taken, if at all possible (unfortunately very often it is NOT possible), to ensure that the total of the spending of money per year is always less than the total income per year of the individual, or community, concerned.

Money loses its value continually; this is called inflation, because prices increase as the value of the currency decreases. This could be thought of as being a tax on all savings and also at the same time as a reduction of all debts.

Many people borrow money and later repay that amount - unfortunately borrowing can be very expensive, because interest usually has to be paid in addition to the amount borrowed (called "The Principal"). Sometimes the economic conditions are so very bad that no repayment of the principal is possible for a very long time, if at all; even to get enough money for paying the interest on the debt may be quite difficult. If interest is not paid at the time it is due, then the loan is said to be "in default", and considerable trouble can be the result.

MONEY MONEY

Money is any object or record that is generally accepted as payment for goods and services and repayment of debts in a given socio-economic context or country. The main functions of money are distinguished as: a medium of exchange; a unit of account; a store of value; and, occasionally in the past, a standard of deferred payment. Any kind of object or secure verifiable record that fulfills these functions can be considered money.

Money is historically an emergent market phenomenon establishing a commodity money, but nearly all contemporary money systems are based on fiat money. Fiat money, like any check or note of debt, is without intrinsic use value as a physical commodity. It derives its value by being declared by a government to be legal tender; that is, it must be accepted as a form of payment within the boundaries of the country, for "all debts, public and private". Such laws in practice cause fiat money to acquire the value of any of the goods and services that it may be traded for within the nation that issues it.

The money supply of a country consists of currency (banknotes and coins) and bank money (the balance held in checking accounts and savings accounts). Bank money, which consists only of records (mostly computerised in modern banking), forms by far the largest part of the money supply in developed nations.

HISTORY HISTORY

The use of barter-like methods may date back to at least 100,000 years ago, though there is no evidence of a society or economy that relied primarily on barter. Instead, non-monetary societies operated largely along the principles of gift economics and debt. When barter did in fact occur, it was usually between either complete strangers or potential enemies. Many cultures around the world eventually developed the use of commodity money.

The shekel was originally a unit of weight, and referred to a specific weight of barley, which was used as currency. The first usage of the term came from Mesopotamia circa 3000 BC. Societies in the Americas, Asia, Africa and Australia used shell money – often, the shells of the cowry. According to Herodotus, the Lydians were the first people to introduce the use of gold and silver coins. It is thought by modern scholars that these first stamped coins were minted around 650–600 BC.

The system of commodity money eventually evolved into a system of representative money. This occurred because gold and silver merchants or banks would issue receipts to their depositors – redeemable for the commodity money deposited. Eventually, these receipts became generally accepted as a means of payment and were used as money. Paper money or banknotes were first used in China during the Song Dynasty.

These banknotes, known as "jiaozi", evolved from promissory notes that had been used since the 7th century. However, they did not displace commodity money, and were used alongside coins. In the 13th century, paper money became known in Europe through the accounts of travellers. Banknotes were first issued in Europe by Stockholms Banco in 1661, and were again also used alongside coins. The gold standard, a monetary system where the medium of exchange are paper notes that are convertible into pre-set, fixed quantities of gold, replaced the use of gold coins as currency in the 17th-19th centuries in Europe. These gold standard notes were made legal tender, and redemption into gold coins was discouraged. By the beginning of the 20th century almost all countries had adopted the gold standard, backing their legal tender notes with fixed amounts of gold.

After World War II, at the Bretton Woods Conference, most countries adopted fiat currencies that were fixed to the US dollar. The US dollar was in turn fixed to gold. In 1971 the US government suspended the convertibility of the US dollar to gold. After this many countries de-pegged their currencies from the US dollar, and most of the world's currencies became unbacked by anything except the governments' fiat of legal tender and the ability to convert the money into goods via payment.

CONFUSIONS AS TO MONEY

There is no social idea or instrument with which civilized men are more generally and personally familiar than money. From early infancy to latest age we all use it in thought and speech and daily transactions, without practical difficulty in distinguishing what is money from what is not money. Yet as to what it really is and what it really does, there are both in common thought on economic subjects and in the writings of professed economists the widest divergences. This is particularly obvious in the United States at the time I write. For twenty years the money question has been under wide discussion, and before that, has had similar periods of wide discussion from the very foundation of the American colonies, to say nothing of the discussion that has gone on in Europe. Yet the attitude of Congress, of the State legislatures, of the political parties, and the press, shows that nothing like any clear conclusion as to first principles has yet been arrived at.

As for the vast literature of the subject which has been put into print within recent years any attempt to extract from it a consensus of opinion as to the office and laws of money is likely to result in the feeling expressed by an intelligent man who recently made this attempt, that "The more one reads the more he feels that any sure knowledge on the question is beyond his comprehension."

The very latest American cyclopedia (Johnson's, 1896) gives this definition: "Money is that kind of currency which has an intrinsic value, and which thus if not used as currency would still be wealth." Thus, there are some who say that money really consists of the precious metals, and that whatever may be locally or temporarily or partially used as money can be so used only as a representative of these metals. They hold that the paper money which now constitutes so large a part of the currency of the civilized world derives its value from the promise, expressed or implied, to redeem it in one or another of these metals, and by way of assuring such redemption vast quantities of these precious metals are kept idly in store by governments and banks.

Of those who take this view, some hold that gold is the only true and natural money, in the present stage of civilization at least; while others hold that silver is as much or even more entitled to that place, and that the gravest evils result from its demonetization.

On the other hand there are those who say that what makes a thing money is the edict or fiat of government that it shall be treated and received as money. And again, there are others still who contend that whatever can be used in exchange to the avoidance of barter is money, thus including in the meaning of the term, notes, checks, drafts, etc., issued by private parties, as fully as the coins or notes issued by governments or banks.

Much of the contradiction and confusion which exists in popular thought proceeds from the pressure of personal interests brought into the question by the relation of debtor and creditor. But the confusions which prevail among professed economists have a deeper source. They evidently result from the confusions which prevail in economic thought and teaching as to the nature of wealth and the cause of value. Money is the common measure of value, the common representative and exchanger of wealth. Unless we have clear ideas of the meaning of value and the nature of wealth, it is manifest therefore that we cannot form clear ideas as to the nature and functions of money. But since we have cleared up in the preceding chapters the meaning of the terms value and wealth, we are now in a position to proceed with an inquiry into the nature, functions and laws of money.

It is unnecessary to waste time with any attempt to disentangle the maze of contradictory statements of fact and confusions of opinion with which the current literature of the subject is embarrassed. The true course of all economic investigation is to observe and trace the relation of those social phenomena that are obvious now and to us. For economic laws must be as invariable as physical laws, and as the chemist or astronomer can safely proceed only from relations which he sees do here and now exist to infer what has existed or will exist in another time and place, so it is with the political economist.

Yet we find, if we consider them, that these divergences in the definition of money spring rather from differences of opinion as to what ought to be considered and treated as money, than from differences as to what, as a matter of fact, money actually is. The men who differ most widely in defining money find no difficulty in agreeing as to what is meant by money in daily transactions. Since we cannot find a consensus of opinion among economists, our best plan is to seek it among ordinary people. To see what usually is meant by money we have only to note the essential characteristics of that which we all agree in treating as money in our practical affairs.

After we have seen what money really is, and what are the functions it performs, we shall then be in a position to determine what are the best forms of money.

FUNCTIONS OF MONEY FUNCTIONS OF MONEY

Try to imagine an economy without money. Without money, it would be almost impossible to carry out the usual day to day business of life. For instance, if you wanted to buy a hamburger without cash, you would have to give the restaurant something else in return. Perhaps you could wash the dishes, or sweep the floor. Either way, the ability to pay for goods and services with money greatly simplifies consumer life and eliminates the necessity of bartering goods and services for other goods and services. What exactly does money do? Sure, you can buy things with it and save it, but how does it function within the economy?

There are four basic functions of money:

- The first is as a medium of exchange.
- The second is as a unit of account.
- The third is as a store of value.
- The fourth is as liquidity.

By understanding each of these functions, it is possible to see how important money is to the economy. The most obvious function of money is as a medium of exchange. When you hand the waiter a five-dollar bill in exchange for your hamburger, you are using money as a medium of exchange. You might have a hard time paying for your hamburger with five dollars worth of apples, but if you did, the apples would serve as a medium of exchange as well. To simplify, a medium of exchange is something that buyers give to sellers in exchange for goods and services.

Perhaps money's most compelling advantage is that it is a commonly recognised and universally accepted medium of exchange. This allows anyone with money to walk into any restaurant with the confidence that the waiter or clerk will take your cash in exchange for goods or services. This would likely not be the case with a basket full of apples.

The second function of money, as a unit of account, is rather obvious, but you may never have considered it before. When you walk into a restaurant, the menu tells you that a hamburger costs $5 and a steak costs $15. You know what this means and are able to compare these prices.

If, on the other hand, apples and oranges were used as units of account, comparison between the costs of goods and services would be much more difficult. Imagine trying to determine what costs more, a hamburger costing 25 apples or a steak costing 30 oranges. As a unit of account, money serves as the common base of comparison that people use to present prices and record debts. Without a common unit of account, these tasks would be much more difficult.

The third function of money, as a store of value, is one that we all know well. When you work, you are paid a wage. The portion of that wage that you do not spend gets saved. By saving money, you are able to spend some now and some later. In this way, money serves as a store of value, allowing you to trade current consumption for future consumption. Imagine if you were paid in bananas. Any bananas that you did not eat or trade immediately would rot, rendering you unable to enjoy the fruits of your labour at a later time.

The fourth and final function of money, as a means of liquidity, is important for an economy to move beyond a simple system of bartering. Imagine that you have 30 apples, and you really want a steak. You walk to the local restaurant and ask the waiter if you can trade 30 apples for a steak. He informs you that they have plenty of apples, but could use some oranges. Frustrated and hungry, you walk out of the restaurant. In this example, apples lacked liquidity since they could not easily be traded for what you wanted. Liquidity describes the ease with which an item can be traded for something that you want, or into the common currency within an economy. Money is the most liquid asset because it is universally recognised and accepted as the common currency. In this way, money gives consumers the freedom to trade goods and services easily without having to barter.

MONEY SUPPLY MONEY SUPPLY

In economics, money is a broad term that refers to any financial instrument that can fulfill the functions of money. These financial instruments together are collectively referred to as the money supply of an economy. In other words, the money supply is the amount of financial instruments within a specific economy available for purchasing goods or services. Since the money supply consists of various financial instruments (usually currency, demand deposits and various other types of deposits), the amount of money in an economy is measured by adding together these financial instruments creating a *monetary aggregate*.

Modern monetary theory distinguishes among different ways to measure the money supply, reflected in different types of monetary aggregates, using a categorization system that focuses on the liquidity of the financial instrument used as money. The most commonly used monetary aggregates (or types of money) are conventionally designated M1, M2 and M3. These are successively larger aggregate categories: M1 is currency (coins and bills) plus demand deposits (such as checking accounts); M2 is M1 plus savings accounts and time deposits under $100,000; and M3 is M2 plus larger time deposits and similar institutional accounts. M1 includes only the most liquid financial instruments, and M3 relatively illiquid instruments.

Another measure of money, M0, is also used; unlike the other measures, it does not represent actual purchasing power by firms and households in the economy. M0 is base money, or the amount of money actually issued by the central bank of a country. It is measured as currency plus deposits of banks and other institutions at the central bank. M0 is also the only money that can satisfy the reserve requirements of commercial banks.

MARKET LIQUIDITY

Market liquidity describes how easily an item can be traded for another item, or into the common currency within an economy. Money is the most liquid asset because it is universally recognised and accepted as the common currency. In this way, money gives consumers the freedom to trade goods and services easily without having to barter. Liquid financial instruments are easily tradable and have low transaction costs. There should be no (or minimal) spread between the prices to buy and sell the instrument being used as money.

MONEY AND INFLATION

WHAT IS INFLATION?

Inflation can be defined as the increase in the overall level of prices. Whilst the price of individual goods or services may vary due to changes in supply and demand, production costs or technological progress, inflation refers to the increase in the price level as a whole or for a selection of goods and services (commonly referred to in economics as abasket of goods). The result of inflation is that the nominal amount of goods and services that a unit of currency can purchase (its purchasing power) declines over time.

Of course, there is, in theory, nothing which make inflation an inherent feature of our economies. In historical times there have been prolonged periods of deflation (where the overall level of prices falls) as well as hyperinflation and disinflation.

Examples 1) ..... The average price of a specific "basket" of goods and services today is 100. If one year later the average price of a "basket" containing the SAME goods and services will cost you 300, then the currency of your country is worth only 1/3 as much as a year ago as a result of inflation. As a result of inflation all the prices of the SAME goods and services have increased.

..... Inflation is stated as a percentage. Assume, for example, that inflation is steady, every year the same, at 2% per year. Then an item that costs now 100 would cost after 1 year 102, then in future years: 104.04 106.12 108.24 110.41 112.62 114.87 117.17 119.51 121.90 and so on. 2) ..... Labor or labour unions always want more and more money to "make ends meet", and so do most other people. The price of goods and services must cover all costs, including all involved salaries and wages. If the currency is worth less as a result of inflation, then all costs go up, and therefore all prices go up. But because prices go up, everybody wants a raise in wages/salary. Therefore the costs go up again, the prices go up some more, and so on and so on. THAT is the unfortunate result of the inflation "spiral".

THE COMMON UNDERSTANDING OF MONEY

When we are confused as to the true meaning of an economic term, our best plan is to endeavor to obtain a consensus of opinion as to what the thing really is; what function it really performs.

If we have agreed to pay money to another the common understanding of what money is will not hold my agreement fulfilled if I offer him wood, or bricks, or services, or gold or silver bullion, even though, as closely as can be estimated, these may be of equal value to the money promised. My creditor might take such things in lieu of what I had agreed to pay. But he would be more likely to object, and his objection if fully expressed would amount to this: "What you agreed to pay me was money. With money I can buy anything that any one has to sell, and pay any debt I owe. But what you offer me is not money. It is something I would be willing to take if I happened to have any personal use for it. But I have no personal use for it, and to get any one to give me for it what I may want I must find some one who wants this particular thing and make a trade with him. What you propose would therefore put on me trouble, risk and loss not contemplated in our agreement." And the justice of this objection would be recognized by all fair men.

In this — in the ease with which it may be passed from hand to hand in canceling obligations or transferring ownership — lies the peculiar characteristic of money. It is not the intrinsic nature of the thing, but the use to which it is applied that gives its essential character to money, and constitutes the distinction between it and other things. Even children recognize this. I make friends with a little one of four or five, and, showing it a stick of candy, ask what that is for? it will say, "That is to eat." If I show a hat or a pair of shoes, it will say, "That is to wear." If I show a toy, it will say, "That is to play with." But if I show a piece of money, it will say, even though to it as yet all money may be pennies, "That is to buy things with."

Now, in this, the little child will give a definition of money that, whatever may be our monetary theories, we all practically recognize. The peculiar use of money — what as money "it is for" — is that of buying other things. What by virtue of this use is money, may or may not have capability for any other use. That is not material. For so long as a thing is reserved to the use of buying things any use inconsistent with this use is excluded.

We might, for instance, apply sticks of candy to the use of buying things. But the moment a stick of candy was applied to the use of being eaten its use in buying things would end. So, if a greenback be used to light a cigar, or a gold coin converted to the use of filling teeth, or of being beaten into gold-leaf, its use as money is destroyed. Even where coins are used as ornaments, their use as money is during that time prevented.

The use of money, no matter of what it be composed, is not directly to satisfy desire, but indirectly to satisfy desire through exchange for other things. We do not eat money nor drink money nor wear money. We pass it. That is to say, we buy other things with it. We esteem money and seek it, not for itself, but for what we may obtain by parting with it, and for the purpose of thus parting with it. This is true even where money is hoarded, for the gratification which hoarding gives is the consciousness of holding at command that with which we may readily buy anything we may wish to have.

The little child we have supposed would probably not know the meaning of the word exchange, which is that of the voluntary transfer of desired things for desired things. But it would know the thing, having become familiar with it in the little exchanges that go on between children — in the giving of marbles for tops, of candy for toys, or in transactions based on "I will do this for you, if you will do that for me." But such exchanges it would probably speak of as trades or swaps or promises, reserving the words buying or selling to exchanges in which money is used.

In this use of words the child would conform to a practice that has become common among careful writers. In the wider sense, buying and selling merely distinguish between the giver and receiver in exchange; and it is in this wider sense that Adam Smith uses the words, and as in poetry or poetical expression we continue to use them.

But both in ordinary usage and in political economy we now more generally confine the words buying and selling to exchanges in which money is given or promised, speaking of an exchange in which money is not involved, as a barter or trade, or simply an exchange. It is where money is one of the things exchanged that the transaction is called a purchase and sale; the party who gives money for another thing being termed the buyer, and the party who gives the other thing for the money being termed the seller.

In this usage, we habitually treat money as though it were the more notable or more important side of exchanges in which things not money are given for money — that side of exchange from which or towards which the initiative impulse proceeds. And there is another usage which points in the same direction. Among the masses of our people at least, and I presume the same usage obtains in all countries, good manners is held to require that where money passes in a transaction of exchange, the receiver of the money should by some such phrase as "Thank you," indicate a sense of benefit or obligation.

The reason of both these usages is, I think, to be found in the fact that money is the thing in which gain or profit is usually estimated; the thing which can usually be most readily and certainly exchanged for any other thing. Thus whatever difficulty there may be in exchanging particular commodities or services for other commodities or services is generally most felt in exchanging them for money. That exchange once made, any subsequent exchange of the money for the things that are the ultimate objects of desire is comparatively easy. It is this that makes it seem to those who do not look closely, that what is sought in exchange is money, and that he who gets money in return for other things, is in a better position than he who gets other things in return for money.

To see in what money really differs from other things having exchangeable or purchasing power let us imagine a number of men to undertake a journey through a country where they have no personal acquaintance. Let them for instance start from New York, in pleasant weather, to make a leisurely trip by the highroads for one to two hundred miles. Let them for the defrayal of the expenses of the journey provide themselves with exchangeable things of different kinds. Imagine one to have a valuable horse; another some staple commodity, such as tobacco or tea; another gold and silver bullion; another a check or bill of exchange, or a check-book; and a fifth to have current money. These things might have value to the same amount, but at the first stop for rest and refreshment the great difference between them as to readiness of convertibility would be seen.

The only way the man with the horse could pay for the slightest entertainment for man or beast, without selling his horse for money, or bartering for things that might be very inconvenient to carry, would be by trading him for a less valuable horse. It is clear that he could not go far in this way, for, to say nothing of the delays incident to horse trades, he would, if he persisted in them under pressure of his desire to go on, soon find himself reduced to an animal that could hardly carry himself.

Though of all staple commodities, tobacco and tea are probably those most readily divisible and easily carried, the tourist who tried to pay his way with them would find much difficulty. If not driven to sell his stock outright for what money he could get, he would virtually have to convert his pleasure excursion into a peddling trip; and, to say nothing of the danger he would run of being arrested for infringement of Federal or local license laws, would be put to much delay, loss and annoyance in finding those willing to give the particular things he needed for the particular things he had.

And while gold and silver are of all commodities those which have the most uniform and staple value, yet the man who had started with bullion would, after he had left the city, hardly find any one who could tell their real value or was willing to take them in return for commodities or service. To exchange them at all at anything like a reasonable rate he would have to hunt up some village jeweler who could test and weigh them, and who, though he might offer to give him a clock or a trinket, or to repair his watch in exchange, would hardly have the commodities or service our traveler needed at his disposal. To get what he wanted for what he had to give without recourse to money he would be driven to all sorts of intermediate exchanges.

As for the man with the check-book, or check or bill of exchange, he would find himself the worst off of all. He could make no more use of them where he was not known than of so much blank paper, unless he found some one who could testify to his good credit or who would go to the expense of telegraphing to learn it. To repeat this at every stopping-place, as would be necessary if his trip were to be carried through as it had been begun, would be too much for the patience and endurance of an ordinary man.

But the man with the money would find no difficulty from first to last. Every one who had any commodity to exchange or service to render would take his money gladly and probably say "Thank you" on receiving it. He alone could make the journey he set out to make, without delay or annoyance or loss on the score of exchanges.

What we may conclude from this little imaginative experiment is not that of all things money is the most valuable thing. That, though many people have in a vague way accepted it, would involve a fallacy of the same kind that is involved in the assumption that a pound of lead is heavier than a pound of feathers. What we may safely conclude from our experiment is, that of all exchangeable things money is the most readily exchangeable, and indeed that this ready exchangeability is the essential characteristic of money.

Yet we have but to extend our illustration so as to imagine our travelers taking with them beyond this country that same money they had found so easily exchangeable here, to see that money is not one substance, nor in all times and places the same substance.

What is money in the United States is not money in England. What is money in England is not money on the Continent. What is money in one of the Continental states may not be money in another, and so on. Although in places in each country much resorted to by travelers from another country, the money of the two countries may circulate together, as American money with English money in Bermuda; or Canadian money with American money at Niagara Falls; or Indian money, English money, French money and Egyptian money at Port Said; yet the traveler who wishes to pass beyond such monetary borders with what will readily exchange for the things he may need must provide himself with the money of the country. The money that has served him in the country he has left becomes in a country using a different money a mere commodity the moment he leaves the monetary border, which he will find it advantageous to exchange with some dealer in such commodities for money of the country.

Is money therefore a matter of mere governmental regulation? That is to say, can governmental statute or fiat, as is today contended by many, prescribe what money shall be used and at what rate it shall pass?

It is unnecessary for those of us who lived in or visited California between the years 1862 and 1879, to look further than our own country and time to see that it cannot. During those years, while the money of the rest of the Union was a more or less depreciated paper, the money of that State, and of the Pacific coast generally, was gold and silver. The paper money of the general government was used for the purchase of postage stamps, the payment of internal revenue dues, the satisfaction of judgments of the Federal courts, and of those of the State courts where there was no specific contract, and for remittances to the East. But between man and man, and in ordinary transactions, it passed only as a commodity.

If it be said that governmental power was not fully exerted in this case; that the United States government dishonored its own currency in making bonds payable and Custom-House dues receivable only in gold, and that the California specific contract law virtually gave the recognition of the State courts only to gold and silver, we may turn to such examples as that of the Confederate currency; as that of the Continental currency; as that afforded by Colonial currencies prior to the Revolution; as that of the French assignats; or to that comical episode in which the caustic pen of Dean Swift, writing under an assumed name, balked the whole power of the British government in its effort to induce the Irish people to accept what was really a better copper money than that they were using.

Government may largely affect the use of money, as it may largely affect the use of language. It may enact what money shall be paid out and received by government officials, or recognized in the courts, as it may prescribe in what language government documents shall be printed or legislative or legal proceedings held, or scholars in the public schools be taught. But it can no more prescribe what shall be used as the common medium of exchange between man and man in transactions that depend on mutual consent than it can prescribe in what tongue mothers shall teach their babes to lisp. In all the many efforts that governments, limited or absolute, have made to do this, the power of government has signally failed.

Shall we say then, as do many who point out this impotency of mere government fiat, that the exchange value of any money depends ultimately upon its intrinsic value; that the real money in the world, the only true and natural money, is gold and silver, one or both — for the metal-moneyists differ as to this, being divided into two opposing camps — the monometallists and the bimetallists?

This notion is even more widely opposed to facts than is that of the fiatists. Gold and silver have for the longest time and over the widest area served, and yet do serve, as material for money, and sometimes have served, and in some places yet do serve, as money. This was the case, to some extent, in the early days of the California diggings, when every merchant or hotel-keeper or gambler or bartender was provided with a bottle of acid and a pair of scales, and men paid for goods or food or lodging or drinks or losses out of buckskin bags in which they carried gold dust or nuggets. This is to some extent still the case in some parts of Asia, where, as was once the case in parts of Europe, even gold and silver coin passes by weight. But gold and silver are not the money of the world. The traveler who should attempt to go round the world paying his expenses with gold and silver bullion would meet the same difficulty or something like the same difficulty that he would meet in the country around New York. Nor would he obviate that difficulty by taking instead of bullion, gold and silver coin. Except in a few places, such as Bermuda or the Hawaiian Islands, they too would become commodities not easily exchangeable when he left the United States.

The truth is that there is no universal money and never yet has been, any more than there is or has been in times of which we have knowledge a universal language. As for intrinsic value, it is clear that our paper money, which has no intrinsic value, performs every office of money — is in every sense as truly money as our coins, which have intrinsic value; and that even of our coins, their circulating or money value has for the most part no more relation to intrinsic value than it has in the case of our paper money. And this is the case today all over the civilized world.

The fact is that neither the fiat of government nor the action of individuals nor the character or intrinsic value of the material used, nor anything else, can make money or mar money, raise or lessen its circulating value, except as it affects the disposition to receive it as a medium of exchange.

In different times and places all sorts of things capable of more or less easy transfer have been used as money. Thus in San Francisco in the early days, when the sudden outflow of gold from the mines brought a sudden demand for money which there was no ready means of supplying, bogus coins, known to be bogus, passed from hand to hand as money; and in New York at the beginning of the Civil War, when there was a great scarcity of circulating medium, owing to the withdrawal of gold and silver from circulation, postage stamps, car tickets, bread tickets, and even counterfeit notes, known to be counterfeit, passed from hand to hand as money. Shall we say then that they are right who contend that a true definition of money must include everything that can be used in exchange to the avoidance of barter?

Clearly, we cannot say this, without ignoring a real and very important distinction — the distinction between money and credit. For a little consideration will show that the checks, drafts, negotiable notes and other transferable orders and obligations which so largely economize the use of money in the commercial world today, do so only when accompanied by something else, which money itself does not require. That something else is trust or credit. This is the essential element of all devices and instruments for dispensing with the mediumship of money without resort to barter. It is only by virtue of it that they can take the place of the money which in form they are promises to pay.

When I give money for what I have bought, I pay my debt. The transaction is complete. But I do not pay my debt when I give a check for the amount. The transaction is not complete. I merely give an order on some one else to pay in my place. If he does not, I am still responsible in morals and in law. As a matter of fact no one will take a check of mine unless he trusts or credits me. And though an honest face, good clothes and a manifest exigency might enable me to pass a small check upon one who did not know me, without the guarantee of some one he did know, I could as readily, and perhaps more readily, get him to trust me outright. So, I cannot, except to one who knows me or to whom I am identified as a man of good credit, pass the check of another or his note or draft or bill of exchange in my favor and without guaranteeing it by endorsement. Even then I do not make a payment; I merely turn over with my own guarantee an order for payment.

Thus there is a quality attaching to money, in common apprehension, which clearly distinguishes it from all forms of credit. It is, so far as the giver of the money is concerned, a final closing of the transaction. The man who gives a check or bill of exchange must guarantee its payment, and is liable if it be not paid; while the drawer on the other hand retains the power at any time of stopping payment before that has been actually made. Even the man who gives a horse or other commodity in exchange must, save as to certain things and with the observance of certain requirements, guarantee title, and that it shall possess certain qualities expressed or implied. But in the passing of money the transaction is closed and finished, and there can be no further question or recourse. For money is properly recognized by municipal law as the common medium of exchange.

All such things as checks, drafts, notes, etc., though they largely dispense with and greatly economize the use of money, do so by utilizing credit. Credit as a facilitator of exchange is older than money and perhaps is even now more important than money, though it may be made into money, as gold may be made into money. But though it may be made into money, it is not in itself money, any more than gold of itself is money, and cannot, without confusion as to the nature and functions of money, be included as money.

What then Shall we Say that Money is?

Evidently the essential quality of money is not in its form or substance, but in its use. Its use being not that of being consumed, but of being continually exchanged, it participates in and facilitates other exchanges as a medium or flux, serving upon a larger scale the same purpose of keeping tally and facilitating transfers as is served by the chips or counters often used in games of chance.

This use comes from a common or usual consent or disposition to take it in exchange, not as representing or promising anything else, but as completing the exchange. The only question any one asks himself in taking money in exchange is whether he can, in the same way, pass it on in exchange. If there is no doubt of that, he will take it; for the only use he has for money is to pass it on in exchange. If he has doubt of that, he will take it only at a discount proportioned to the doubt, or not take it at all.

What then makes anything money is the common consent or disposition to accept it as the common medium of exchange. If a thing has this essential quality in any place and time, it is money in that place and time, no matter what other quality it may lack. If a thing lacks this essential quality in any place and time, it is not money in that place and time, no matter what other quality it may have.

To define money: Whatever in any time and place is used as the common medium of exchange is money in that time and place.

There is no universal money. While the use of money is almost as universal as the use of languages, and it everywhere follows general laws as does the use of languages, yet as we find language differing in time and place, so do we find money differing. In fact, as we shall see, money is in one of its functions a kind of language — the language of value.

TYPES OF MONEY TYPES OF MONEY

Money comes in a number of different forms. We saw apples and oranges used as money. When something with intrinsic value, like precious metals, is used as money, it is called commodity money. It is interesting to think about the enormous variety of goods that can serve as commodity money. Basically, anything that can fulfill the four functions of money, to so some degree, can be used as commodity money. Barter economies depend on commodity money. When something lacking intrinsic value is used as money, it is called fiat money. This system only works if a government backs the fiat money and regulates its production. In most countries, the cash or currency is a form of fiat money. The advent of fiat money is a great convenience in many ways— imagine trying to carry a week's pay in apples and oranges.

THE TWO KINDS OF MONEY

While value is always one and the same power, that of commanding labor in exchange, there are as we have seen, with reference to its sources, two different kinds of value — that which proceeds from production and that which proceeds from obligation. Now money is peculiarly the representative of value — the common medium or flux through which things are exchanged with reference to their value, and the common measure of value. And corresponding to and proceeding from this distinction between the two kinds of value, there are, we find, two kinds of money in use in the more highly civilized world today — the one, which we may call commodity money, originating in the value proceeding from production; and the other, which we may call credit money, originating in the value proceeding from obligation.

This distinction has of course no relation to differences of denomination, such as those between English pounds, French francs and American dollars. These are but differences of nomenclature. Nor yet does it coincide with differences in the material used as money, as for instance that between metal money and paper money. For while all paper money is credit money, all metal money is not commodity money. What I understand by commodity money is money which exchanges at its value as a commodity, that is to say, which passes current at no more than its "intrinsic value," or value of the material of which it is composed. Credit money is money which exchanges at a greater value than that of the material of which it is composed. In the one case the whole value for which the money exchanges is the value it would have as a commodity. In the other case the value for which the money exchanges is greater than its commodity value, and hence some part at least of its exchange value as money is given to it by credit or trust.

For instance, a man who exchanges ten dollars' worth of wheat for a coin containing ten dollars' worth of gold makes in reality a barter. He exchanges one commodity for an equal value of another commodity, crediting or trusting nobody, but having in the coin he has received a commodity which, irrespective of its use as money, has an equal value to that he gave. But the man who exchanges ten dollars' worth of wheat for a ten-dollar note receives for a commodity worth ten dollars what, as a commodity, has only the value of a bit of paper, a value practically infinitesimal.

What renders him willing to take it as an equivalent of the wheat is the faith or credit or trust that he can in turn exchange it as money at the same valuation. If he drops the coin into the sea, he loses value to the extent of ten dollars, and the sum of wealth is lessened by that amount. If he burns the paper note, he suffers loss to the value of ten dollars, but he alone; the sum of wealth is only infinitesimally lessened. Paper money is in truth of the same nature as the check or order of an individual or corporation except (and in this lies the difference that makes it money) that it has a wider and readier credit. The value of the coin of full intrinsic value, like the value of the wheat, is a value that comes from production. But the value of the paper money is, like the value of the check or order, a value from obligation.

The first money in use was doubtless a commodity money, and there are some countries where it is still the principal money, and places perhaps where it is the only money. But in the more highly civilized countries it has been very largely superseded by credit money. In the United States, for instance, the only commodity or intrinsic value money now in circulation is the gold coinage of the United States. Our silver dollars have an intrinsic or commodity value of only some fifty cents, and the value of our subsidiary coinage is still less. That they circulate in the United States at the same value as gold shows that their exchange value has no reference to their intrinsic value.

They are in reality as much credit money as is the greenback or treasury note, the difference being that the stamp, which evidences their credit and thus secures their circulation, is impressed not on paper, but on a metallic material. The substitution of what is now the cheapest of metals, steel, or the utter elimination of intrinsic value, would not in the slightest lessen their circulating value. What is true of the United States in this respect is also true of England, of France, of Germany, and of all the nations that have adopted gold as the common measure of value. Their only commodity money is certain gold coins; their other coins being token or credit money. In the countries that have retained silver as the common measure of value the standard coin is generally commodity money, but the subsidiary coins, having less intrinsic value, are in reality credit money.

QUANTITY THEORY OF MONEY QUANTITY THEORY OF MONEY

VALUE OF MONEY

What gives money value? We know that intrinsically, a dollar bill is just worthless paper and ink. However, the purchasing power of a dollar bill is much greater than that of another piece of paper of similar size. From where does this power originate? Like most things in economics, there is a market for money. The supply of money in the money market comes from the Fed. The Fed has the power to adjust the money supply by increasing or decreasing the number of bills in circulation. Nobody else can make this policy decision. The demand for money in the money market comes from consumers. The determinants of money demand are infinite.

In general, consumers need money to purchase goods and services. If there is an ATM nearby or if credit cards are plentiful, consumers may demand less money at a given time than they would if cash were difficult to obtain. The most important variable in determining money demand is the average price level within the economy. If the average price level is high and goods and services tend to cost a significant amount of money, consumers will demand more money. If, on the other hand, the average price level is low and goods and services tend to cost little money, consumers will demand less money.

The value of money is ultimately determined by the intersection of the money supply, as controlled by the Fed, and money demand, as created by consumers. The money market in a sample economy. The money supply curve is vertical because the Fed sets the amount of money available without consideration for the value of money.

The money demand curve slopes downward because as the value of money decreases, consumers are forced to carry more money to make purchases because goods and services cost more money. Similarly, when the value of money is high, consumers demand little money because goods and services can be purchased for low prices. The intersection of the money supply curve and the money demand curve shows both the equilibrium value of money as well as the equilibrium price level.

The value of money, as revealed by the money market, is variable. A change in money demand or a change in the money supply will yield a change in the value of money and in the price level. Notice that the change in the value of money and the change in the price level are of the same magnitude but in opposite directions. Notice that the new intersection of the money supply curve and the money demand curve is at a lower value of money but a higher price level. This happens because more money is in circulation, so each bill becomes worth less. It takes more bills to purchase goods and services, and thus the price level increases accordingly.

The quantity theory of money is based directly on the changes brought about by an increase in the money supply. The quantity theory of money states that the value of money is based on the amount of money in the economy. Thus, according to the quantity theory of money, when the Fed increases the money supply, the value of money falls and the price level increases. In the SparkNote on inflation we learned that inflation is defined as an increase in the price level. Based on this definition, the quantity theory of money also states that growth in the money supply is the primary cause of inflation.

VELOCITY

While the relationship between money supply, money demand, the price level, and the value of money presented is accurate, it is a bit simplistic. In the real world economy, these factors are not connected as neatly as the quantity theory of money and the basic money market diagram present. Rather, a number of variables mediate the effects of changes in the money supply and money demand on the value of money and the price level.

The most important variable that mediates the effects of changes in the money supply is the velocity of money. Imagine that you purchase a hamburger. The waiter then takes the money that you spent and uses it to pay for his dry cleaning. The dry cleaner then takes that money and pays to have his car washed. This process continues until the bill is eventually taken out of circulation. In many cases, bills are not removed from circulation until many decades of service. In the end, a single bill will have facilitated many times its face value in purchases.

Velocity of money is defined simply as the rate at which money changes hands. If velocity is high, money is changing hands quickly, and a relatively small money supply can fund a relatively large amount of purchases. On the other hand, if velocity is low, then money is changing hands slowly, and it takes a much larger money supply to fund the same number of purchases.

As you might expect, the velocity of money is not constant. Instead, velocity changes as consumers' preferences change. It also changes as the value of money and the price level change. If the value of money is low, then the price level is high, and a larger number of bills must be used to fund purchases. Given a constant money supply, the velocity of money must increase to fund all of these purchases. Similarly, when the money supply shifts due to Fed policy, velocity can change. This change makes the value of money and the price level remain constant. The relationship between velocity, the money supply, the price level, and output is represented by the equation $M * V = P * Y$ where M is the money supply, V is the velocity, P is the price level, and Y is the quantity of output. P * Y, the price level multiplied by the quantity of output, gives the nominal GDP. This equation can thus be rearranged as V = (nominal GDP)/M. Conceptually, this equation means that for a given level of nominal GDP, a smaller money supply will result in money needing to change hands more quickly to facilitate the total purchases, which causes increased velocity.

The equation for the velocity of money, while useful in its original form, can be converted to a percentage change formula for easier calculations. In this case, the equation becomes (per cent change in the money supply) + (per cent change in velocity) = (per cent change in the price level) + (per cent change in output). The percentage change formula aids calculations that involve this equation by ensuring that all variables are in common units. The velocity equation can be used to find the effects that changes in velocity, price level, or money supply have on each other. When making these calculations, remember that in the short run, output (Y), is fixed, as time is required for the quantity of output to change.

Let's try an example. What is the effect of a 3 per cent increase in the money supply on the price level, given that output and velocity remain relatively constant? The equation used to solve this problem is (per cent change in the money supply) + (per cent change in velocity) = (per cent change in the price level) + (per cent change in output). Substituting in the values from the problem we get 3 per cent + 0 per cent = x per cent + 0 per cent. In this case, a 3 per cent increase in the money supple results in a 3 per cent increase in the price level. Remember that a 3 per cent increase in the price level means that inflation was 3 per cent.

In the long run, the equation for velocity becomes even more useful. In fact, the equation shows that increases in the money supply by the Fed tend to cause increases in the price level and therefore inflation, even though the effects of the Fed's policy is slightly dampened by changes in velocity. This results a number of factors. First, in the long run, velocity, V, is relatively constant because people's spending habits are not quick to change. Similarly, the quantity of output, Y, is not affected by the actions of the Fed since it is based on the amount of production, not the value of the stuff produced. This means that the per cent change in the money supply equals the per cent change in the price level since the per cent change in velocity and per cent change in output are both equal to zero. Thus, we see how an increase in the money supply by the Fed causes inflation.

Let's try another example. What is the effect of a 5 per cent increase in the money supply on inflation? Again, we being by using the equation (per cent change in the money supply) + (per cent change in velocity) = (per cent change in the price level) + (per cent change in output). Remember that in the long run, output not affected by the Fed's actions and velocity remains relatively constant. Thus, the equation becomes 5% + 0% = x% + 0%. In this case, a 5 per cent increase in the money supply results in a 5 per cent increase in inflation. The velocity of money equation represents the heart of the quantity theory of money. By understanding how velocity mitigates the actions of the Fed in the long run and in the short run, we can gain a thorough understanding of the value of money and inflation.

MONETARY POLICY MONETARY POLICY

When gold and silver are used as money, the money supply can grow only if the supply of these metals is increased by mining. This rate of increase will accelerate during periods of gold rushes and discoveries, such as when Columbus discovered the New World and brought back gold and silver to Spain, or when gold was discovered in California in 1848. This causes inflation, as the value of gold goes down. However, if the rate of gold mining cannot keep up with the growth of the economy, gold becomes relatively more valuable, and prices (denominated in gold) will drop, causing deflation. Deflation was the more typical situation for over a century when gold and paper money backed by gold were used as money in the 18th and 19th centuries. Modern day monetary systems are based on fiat money and are no longer tied to the value of gold. The control of the amount of money in the economy is known as monetary policy. Monetary policy is the process by which a government, central bank, or monetary authority manages the money supply to achieve specific goals. Usually the goal of monetary policy is to accommodate economic growth in an environment of stable prices. For example, it is clearly stated in the Federal Reserve Act that the Board of Governors and the Federal Open Market Committee should seek "to promote effectively the goals of maximum employment, stable prices, and moderate long-term interest rates."

A failed monetary policy can have significant detrimental effects on an economy and the society that depends on it. These include hyperinflation, stagflation, recession, high unemployment, shortages of imported goods, inability to export goods, and even total monetary collapse and the adoption of a much less efficient barter economy. This happened in Russia, for instance, after the fall of the Soviet Union.Governments and central banks have taken both regulatory and free market approaches to monetary policy.

Some of the tools used to control the money supply include:

- Changing the interest rate at which the central bank loans money to (or borrows money from) the commercial banks
- Currency purchases or sales
- Increasing or lowering government borrowing
- Increasing or lowering government spending
- Manipulation of exchange rates
- Raising or lowering bank reserve requirements

- Regulation or prohibition of private currencies
- Taxation or tax breaks on imports or exports of capital into a country

In the US, the Federal Reserve is responsible for controlling the money supply, while in the Euro area the respective institution is the European Central Bank. Other central banks with significant impact on global finances are the Bank of Japan, People's Bank of China and the Bank of England.

For many years much of monetary policy was influenced by an economic theory known as monetarism. Monetarism is an economic theory which argues that management of the money supply should be the primary means of regulating economic activity.

The stability of the demand for money prior to the 1980s was a key finding of Milton Friedman and Anna Schwartz supported by the work of David Laidler, and many others. The nature of the demand for money changed during the 1980s owing to technical, institutional, and legal factors and the influence of monetarism has since decreased. However, since the emergence of new dynamic models (such as New Keynesian DSGE models), some authors show that money has a role on the economy and business cycles depending on the households' risk aversion level.

WORLD CURRENCY WORLD CURRENCY

In the foreign exchange market and international finance, a world currency, supranational currency, or global currency refers to a currency that is transacted internationally, with no set borders.

HISTORICAL AND CURRENT WORLD CURRENCIES

Spanish Dollar (17th – 19th Centuries)

In the 17th and 18th century, the use of silver Spanish dollars or "pieces of eight" spread from the Spanish territories in the Americas westwards to Asia and eastwards to Europe forming the first ever worldwide currency. Spain's political supremacy on the world stage, the importance of Spanish commercial routes across the Atlantic and the Pacific, and the coin's quality and purity of silver helped it become internationally accepted for over two centuries.

It was legal tender in Spain's Pacific territories of the Philippines, Micronesia, Guam and the Caroline Islands and later in China and other Southeast Asian countries until the mid-19th century. In the Americas it was legal tender in all of South and Central America (except Brazil) as well as in the US and Canada until the mid-19th century. In Europe the Spanish dollar was legal tender in the Iberian Peninsula, in most of Italy including: Milan, the Kingdom of Naples, Sicily, Sardinia, the Franche-Comté (France), and in the Spanish Netherlands. It was also used in other European states including the Austrian Habsburg territories.

Gold Standard (19th – 20th Centuries)

Prior to and during most of the 19th century, international trade was denominated in terms of currencies that represented weights of gold. Most national currencies at the time were in essence merely different ways of measuring gold weights (much as the yard and the meter both measure length and are related by a constant conversion factor). Hence some assert that gold was the world's first global currency. The emerging collapse of the international gold standard around the time of World War I had significant implications for global trade.

Pound Sterling

Before 1944, the world reference currency was the United Kingdom's pound sterling. The transition between pound sterling and United States dollar and its impact for central banks was described recently.

U.S. Dollar

In the period following the Bretton Woods Conference of 1944, exchange rates around the world were pegged against the United States dollar, which could be exchanged for a fixed amount of gold. This reinforced the dominance of the US dollar as a global currency. Since the collapse of the fixed exchange rate regime and the gold standard and the institution of floating exchange rates following the Smithsonian Agreement in 1971, most currencies around the world have no longer been pegged against the United States dollar. However, as the United States remained the world's pre-eminent economic superpower, most international transactions continued to be conducted with the United States dollar, and it has remained the *de facto* world currency.

Only two serious challengers to the status of the United States dollar as a world currency have arisen. During the 1980s, the Japanese yen became increasingly used as an international currency, but that usage diminished with the Japanese recession in the 1990s. More recently, the euro has increasingly competed with the United States dollar in international finance.

Since the mid-20th century, the *de facto* world currency has been the United States dollar. According to Robert Gilpin in *Global Political Economy: Understanding the International Economic Order*:

- "Somewhere between 40 and 60 per cent of international financial transactions are denominated in dollars. For decades the dollar has also been the world's principal reserve currency; in 1996, the dollar accounted for approximately two-thirds of the world's foreign exchange reserves".

Many of the world's currencies are pegged against the dollar. Some countries, such as Ecuador, El Salvador, and Panama, have gone even further and eliminated their own currency in favour of the United States dollar. The

U.S., dollar continues to dominate global currency reserves, with 63.9 per cent held in dollars, as compared to 26.5 per cent held in euros.

Euro

The euro inherited its status as a major reserve currency from the German mark (DM) and its contribution to official reserves has increased as banks seek to diversify their reserves and trade in the eurozone expands. As with the dollar, some of the world's currencies are pegged against the euro. They are usually Eastern European currencies like the Bulgarian lev, plus several west African currencies like the Cape Verdean escudo and the CFA franc. Other European countries, while not being EU members, have adopted the euro due to currency unions with member states, or by unilaterally superseding their own currencies: Andorra, Monaco, Kosovo, Montenegro, San Marino, and Vatican City.

As of December 2006, the euro surpassed the dollar in the combined value of cash in circulation. The value of euro notes in circulation has risen to more than □610 billion, equivalent to US$800 billion at the exchange rates at the time (today equivalent to circa US$968 billion).

RECENT PROPOSALS (21ST CENTURY)

Governmental

On 16 March 2009, in connection with the April 2009 G20 summit, the Kremlin called for a supranational reserve currency as part of a reform of the global financial system. In a document containing proposals for the G20 meeting, it suggested that the International Monetary Fund (IMF) (or an *Ad Hoc* Working Group of G20) should be instructed to carry out specific studies to review the following options:

- Enlargement (diversification) of the list of currencies used as reserve ones, based on agreed measures to promote the development of major regional financial centers. In this context, we should consider possible establishment of specific regional mechanisms which would contribute to reducing volatility of exchange rates of such reserve currencies.
- Introduction of a supra-national reserve currency to be issued by international financial institutions. It seems appropriate to consider the role of IMF in this process and to review the feasibility of and the need for measures to ensure the recognition of SDRs as a "supra-reserve" currency by the whole world community."

On 24 March 2009, Zhou Xiaochuan, President of the People's Bank of China, called for "creative reform of the existing international monetary system towards an international reserve currency," believing it would "significantly reduce the risks of a future crisis and enhance crisis management capability." Zhou suggested that the IMF's special drawing rights (a currency basket comprising dollars, euros, yen, and sterling) could serve as a super-sovereign reserve currency, not easily influenced by the policies of individual countries. US President Obama, however, rejected the suggestion stating that "the dollar is extraordinarily strong right now." At the G8 summit in July 2009, the Russian president expressed Russia's desire for a new supranational reserve currency by showing off a coin minted with the words "unity in diversity". The coin, an example of a future world currency, emphasized his call for creating a mix of regional currencies as a way to address the global financial crisis.

On 30 March 2009, at the Second South America-Arab League Summit in Qatar, Venezuelan President Hugo Chavez proposed the creation of a petro-currency. It would be backed by the huge oil reserves of the oil producing countries.

SINGLE WORLD CURRENCY

An alternative definition of a world or global currency refers to a hypothetical single global currency or *supercurrency*, as the proposed terra or the DEY (acronym for Dollar Euro Yen), produced and supported by a central bank which is used for *all* transactions around the world, regardless of the nationality of the entities (individuals, corporations, governments, or other organizations) involved in the transaction. No such official currency currently exists. Advocates, notably Keynes, of a global currency often argue that such a currency would not suffer from inflation, which, in extreme cases, has had disastrous effects for economies. In addition, many argue that a single global currency would make conducting international business more efficient and would encourage foreign direct investment (FDI).

There are many different variations of the idea, including a possibility that it would be administered by a global central bank that would define its own monetary standard or that it would be on the gold standard. Supporters often point to the euro as an example of a supranational currency successfully implemented by a union of nations with disparate languages, cultures, and economies. Alternatively, digital gold currency can be viewed as an example of how global currency can be implemented without achieving national government consensus.

A limited alternative would be a world reserve currency issued by the International Monetary Fund, as an evolution of the existing special drawing rights and used as reserve assets by all national and regional central banks. On 26 March 2009, a UN panel of expert economists called for a new global currency reserve scheme to replace the current US dollar-based system. The panel's report pointed out that the "greatly expanded SDR (special drawing rights), with regular or cyclically adjusted emissions calibrated to the size of reserve accumulations, could contribute to global stability, economic strength and global equity."

In addition to the idea of a single world currency, some evidence suggests the world may evolve multiple global currencies that exchange on a singular market system. The rise of digital global currencies owned by privately held companies or groups such as Ven suggest that multiple global currencies may offer wider formats for trade as they gain strength and wider acceptance.

DIFFICULTIES

Limited Additional Benefit with Extra Cost

Some economists argue that a single world currency is unnecessary, because the U.S., dollar is providing many of the benefits of a world currency while avoiding some of the costs. If the world does not form an optimum currency area, then it would be economically inefficient for the world to share one currency.

Economically Incompatible Nations

In the present world, nations are not able to work together closely enough to be able to produce and support a common currency. There has to be a high level of trust between different countries before a true world currency could be created. A world currency might even undermine national sovereignty of smaller states.

Wealth Redistribution

The interest rate set by the central bank indirectly determines the interest rate customers must pay on their bank loans. This interest rate affects the rate of interest among individuals, investments, and countries. Lending to the poor involves more risk than lending to the rich. As a result of the larger differences in wealth in different areas of the world, a central bank's ability to set interest rate to make the area prosper will be increasingly compromised, since it places wealthiest regions in conflict with the poorest regions in debt.

Usury

Usury – the accumulation of interest on loan principal – is prohibited by the texts of some major religions. In Christianity and Judaism, adherents are forbidden to charge interest to other adherents or to the poor. Islam forbids usury, called riba. Some religious adherents who oppose the paying of interest are currently able to use banking facilities in their countries which regulate interest. An example of this is the Islamic banking system, which is characterised by a nation's central bank setting interest rates for most other transactions.

Bibliography

Baran, Paul A. (1957). *The Political Economy of Growth.* Monthly Review Press, New York.

C. Sakrey et al., "Karl Marx and the Contradictions of Capitalism," *Introduction to Political Economy*, (Boston: Economic Affairs Bureau, 2005)

C. Sakrey et al., *"Social Class: An Impediment to the Good Life?" in Introduction to Political Economy*, (Boston: Economic Affairs Bureau, 2005)

C. Sakrey et al., "U.S. Monopoly Capitalism: An Irrational System?" in *Introduction to Political Economy*, (Boston: Economic Affairs Bureau, 2005)

C. Sakrey et al: *Introduction to Political Economy*, (Boston: Economic Affairs Bureau, 2005)

C. Sakrey: *Introduction to Political Economy*, (Boston: Economic Affairs Bureau, 2005)

Commons, John R: *Institutional Economics: Its Place in Political Economy*, Macmillan. Description and preview.

Georgescu-Roegen, Nicholas 1971: *The Entropy Law and the Economic Process*, Cambridge, Mass., und London, England: Harvard University Press.

Hirschman, Albert O. 1970: *Exit, Voice and Loyalty – Responses to Decline in Firms, Organizations, and States*, Cambridge: Harvard University Press.

John Maynard Keynes and the Turbulent Birth of Macroeconomics," in *Introduction to Political Economy*, 4th ed., 105—30 (Boston: Economic Affairs Bureau, 2005)

Jump up Higgott, Richard and Payne, Anthony: *The New Political Economy of Globalisation*, Two Volumes, Aldershot: Edward Elgar(2000).

Jump up Krugman, Paul: *The Return of Depression Economics*, London: Allen Lane(1999).

Jump up Robert E. Goodin, Philip Pettit, Thomas W. Pogge, *A Companion to Contemporary Political Philosophy*, John Wiley & Sons, 2012.

Jump up Stiglitz, Joseph: *Globalization and Its Discontents*, London: Penguin (2002).

Jump up Charles S. Mayer *"In search of Stability: Explorations in Historical Political*

Economy", Cambridge University Press, Cambridge, 1987.

Jump up David Baker, "The Political Economy of Fascism: Myth or reality, or myth and reality?" *New Political Economy, Volume 11*,Cambridge University Press, Cambridge 2 June 2006.

Jump up Rodrik, Dani: *Has Globalization Gone Too Far?*, Washington, DC: Institute for International Economics(1998).

Jump up Watson, Matthew *The Political Economy of International Capital Mobility, Basingstoke,* Palgrave Macmillan (2007).

Jump up Watson, Matthew: *Foundations of International Political Economy*, Basingstoke: Palgrave Macmillan(2005) .

Jump up, Gamble, Andrew, *"The New Political Economy", Political Studies*, (1996)

Leroux, Robert: *Political Economy and Liberalism in France : The Contributions of Frédéric Bastiat*, London, Routledge.

Maggi, Giovanni, and Andrés Rodríguez-Clare: *"A Political-Economy Theory of Trade Agreements," American Economic Review*,London, Routledge.

O'Hara, Phillip Anthony, ed. *Encyclopedia of Political Economy*, 2 v. Routledge. 2003 review links.

P. Kenway: *Keynes's Economics and the Theory of Value and Distribution*, (New York: Oxford University Press, 1983)

Pressman, Steven, *Interactions in Political Economy: Malvern After Ten Years* Routledge, 1996

Rausser, Gordon, Swinnen, Johan, and Zusman, Pinhas: *Political Power and Economic Policy.* Cambridge: Cambridge U.P.

Rawls, John 1971: *A Theory of Justice*, Cambridge, Mass.: Harvard University Press.

Rawls, John 1999: "The Idea of Public Reason Revisited," in J. Ralws, *Collected Papers*, Cambridge, Mass., and London: Harvard University Press.

Vanberg, Viktor J. 2001: *The Constitution of Markets. Essays in political economy*, London and New York: Routledge.

Vanberg, Viktor: *Ordnungstheorie' as Constitutional Economics*. The German Conception 1988.

Walras, Léon : *Elements of Pure Economics – Or the Theory of Social Wealth*, Orion Editions, Philadelphia.

Winch, Donald: "The Emergence of Economics as a Science, 1750–1870." In: *The Fontana Economic History of Europe, Vol. 3*. London: Collins/Fontana.

Winch, Donald: *Riches and Poverty : An Intellectual History of Political Economy in Britain, 1750–1834* Cambridge: Cambridge U.P.

Index